THE STARKER

THE STARKER

BIG JACK ZELIG, THE BECKER-ROSENTHAL CASE, AND THE ADVENT OF THE JEWISH GANGSTER

ROSE KEEFE

CUMBERLAND HOUSE
NASHVILLE, TENNESSEE

THE STARKER
PUBLISHED BY CUMBERLAND HOUSE PUBLISHING INC.
431 Harding Industrial Drive
Nashville, TN 37211

Cover design: Gore Studio Inc.
Text design: John Mitchell

Library of Congress Cataloging-in-Publication Data
Keefe, Rose.
The Starker : Big Jack Zelig, the Becker-Rosenthal case, and the advent of the Jewish gangster / Rose Keefe.
p. cm.
Includes bibliographical references and index.
ISBN-13: 978-1-58182-602-9 (hardcover : alk. paper)
ISBN-10: 1-58182-602-8 (hardcover : alk. paper)
1. Zelig, Jack, 1888-1912. 2. Gangsters—United States—Biography. 3. Jewish criminals—United States—Biography. 4. Becker, Charles, 1870-1915—Trials, litigation, etc. I. Title.

HV6248.Z38K44 2008
364.1092—dc22
[B]

2008027007

Printed in the United States of America

1 2 3 4 5 6 7—14 13 12 11 10 09 08

Sheenie Mike sleeps in a bronzed casket
A kingdom of twelve blocks weeps for him
And so do his mother's wig and his father's old beard.
His orphaned cronies stand on the street corners
Rolling cigarettes with thin nervous fingers.
Terror and guardian, king and commander
From around and around twelve whole blocks
He lies there, all dandied up, asleep.

— Jacob Glatstein, "Sheenie Mike"

DEDICATED TO THE MEMORY OF RICHARD SHOENFELD

CONTENTS

FOREWORD I

Just as World War I has been overshadowed by the Second World War, so too have the pre-Prohibition Era gangsters been eclipsed by their liquor-dealing, machine-gun-toting brethren of the Roaring Twenties and early 1930s. Like the world wars, to better understand the latter, it helps to know about the former. Unfortunately the majority of authors who have discussed this era spent little time actively researching it, instead choosing simply to rehash stories out of Herbert Ashbury's *The Gangs of New York*.

As a result, there is a gaping hole in studies of pre-1920s organized crime, and Jack Zelig has been largely dismissed as simply one of the gang leaders to follow in the wake of Monk Eastman. What attention he does receive is that of a supporting player in the Becker-Rosenthal saga. Thanks to Rose Keefe, however, Zelig has now been brought out of the wings and given his rightful place on the stage. As you read this book, you will see that there is much more to Zelig than simply being the gang leader after Kid Twist and before Dopey Benny Fein.

In Zelig's day there was hardly a neighborhood that wasn't under the influence of a gang. Chinatown had the Tongs; the West Side had the Hudson Dusters, the Marginals, and the Gophers; the Mafia terrorized the Italian communities; and the Lower East Side had the Jewish hoodlums.

If you had lived in early twentieth-century New York City, chances are that you would have known the gangsters in your neighborhood, if not by name, then by sight. If you passed them on the street, you would have avoided eye contact. If you were a business owner, your heart would have skipped a beat every time they walked into your establishment. If they "asked" you to buy tickets to their racket, you bought and were happy to do so lest you insult one of them. If they killed someone in front of you, as was the case for numerous pedestrians, you didn't talk to the police because chances are they knew who you were, too.

An example of this lifestyle can be seen in the murder of one Salvatore "Big Curly" Guargadatti. Though unknown today, Big Curly was a big shot in his neighborhood, and on July 19, 1913, in front of dozens of witnesses, another hoodlum walked up and fired two bullets into his heart. Of course none of those present were able to tell the police anything about the shooting. Everyone happened to be looking elsewhere when the shots were fired. The only man who talked was a bootblack who operated his stand near the spot where Big Curly drew his last breath. He didn't say anything about the killer, mind you, only that he knew the dead man, as he had often polished his shoes for free. When asked why he didn't charge the young gangster, the bootblack told police that there were certain young men on the Lower East Side whom you never considered charging to help keep up their sleek appearance. For a time, Jack Zelig was king of these men.

Though Zelig was a thug, he was also a bit of an anomaly. Whereas most gangsters sought underworld greatness, Zelig had it thrust upon him. Prior to 1910, he was simply a pickpocket trying to make his way, albeit crooked, in the world. As you will read, all of that changed after a fateful brawl with a couple of rival hoodlums. Thereafter, the Jewish community was Zelig's oyster, happy (at least less offended) to pay tribute to one of their own instead of the hated Italians.

One can't talk about Zelig without discussing the Becker-Rosenthal murder case. At this writing we are creeping up on the centennial of the killing, and its magnitude at that time can't be overstated. The notoriety of the trial can be illustrated by revisiting the murder of another gangster, Harlem Mafioso Fortunato Lo Monte, who on May 23, 1914, was strolling down the street, perusing a newspaper, when a man came up from behind and fired three bullets into his back. Lo Monte was rushed to the hospital where he was questioned by cops. "I was walking along reading about Becker when I was shot," he told them a short time before expiring.

Although almost two years had passed since the killing of Rosenthal, nobody had to guess what or whom the gangster was referring to when he said the name Becker. Hardly a day had passed without mention of NYPD Lt. Charles Becker in the newspapers. The murder of Rosenthal and the subsequent trials and executions of those involved was to pre-World War I America what the O. J. Simpson saga would be to the country at the close of the century. While the murder and its aftermath have been the subject of at least a half-dozen books, little has been said about Jack Zelig and what he knew about the case. That changes here. Once and for all, the question of whether Becker was guilty or innocent is answered.

Had Herbert Asbury never written *The Gangs of New York,* chances are that Jack Zelig wouldn't be remembered at all. In the decades since, a few authors have added to the narrative, but now, finally, through interviews of Zelig's descendents and his contemporaries, and long-buried information mined from national and international archives, we know not only the story of Zelig's short and violent life (and an abundance of new information on the early gangsters of New York), but what he would have said had he lived to take the stand at Becker's trial.

So sit back, turn the page and return to old New York where a 911 call meant sticking your head out the window and yelling for help, where the cobblestone streets held more hansom cabs than automobiles, and where sleek young men with names like Gyp the Blood, Spanish Louis, and Big Jack Zelig got their shoes shined for free.

— Patrick Downey

Author, *Gangster City: The History of the*

New York Underworld, 1900–1935

FOREWORD II

Big Jack Zelig.

Although he was the protégé of Monk Eastman, America's earliest celebrity gangster; a contemporary of Arnold Rothstein, the criminal mastermind who allegedly fixed the 1919 World Series; and the forerunner of Bugsy Siegel, Lepke Buchalter, and the vicious Murder Inc. thugs; his name is largely forgotten today. He makes the odd cameo appearance in the books and articles that continue to be published about the Becker-Rosenthal case, but always in the context of being a short-lived player. The fear, awe, and respect he inspired during his heyday as "the terror" of New York's Lower East Side is mentioned rarely, and delved into even less. This is surprising, given the fact that his name once generated headlines all over the United States. He was known to cops and his Five Points enemies alike as "the Starker," an Anglicization of *Yiddisher Shtarker,* a moniker reserved for the toughest, most eminent Jewish gunmen. He earned it in spades, something to which devoted underlings, battered challengers, harried cops, and grateful politicians would attest.

Zelig, whom Professor Arthur A. Goren described as "the 'terror" and "commander" of downtown's Jewish underworld, and who was, for some, the quarter's guardian as well,"[1] is best remembered for his connection to the Becker-Rosenthal case, which created an international sensation in 1912. Police Lt. Charles Becker, head of one of the NYPD's anti-vice "strong-arm squads," and who had a reputation for greed and brutality, was accused of engaging, through intermediaries, four Zelig gangsters to murder gambler Herman Rosenthal, who had been bombarding the newspapers and the district attorney's office with complaints about Becker's corruption. Rosenthal was gunned down outside a seedy hotel on a sweltering July night, and Lieutenant Becker himself lived only another three years, having been found guilty of the gambler's murder after two trials. He died in Sing Sing's electric chair on July 30, 1915, and to this date is the only police officer ever put to death by the State of New York.

It is a tragic event that might never have occurred if Zelig had lived. Although not involved with the Rosenthal murder plot, he knew who its real masterminds were. He had refused them when they approached him weeks before, offering first money and then rescue from a gun-carrying charge he was facing, in exchange for ensuring Rosenthal's demise. After four of his friends were sucked into the scheme's black vortex and their lives subsequently imperiled by arrest for a capital crime, Zelig was boiling with rage—and planned to retaliate by naming the guilty parties in court. But he never had the chance: days before the Becker trial commenced, Jack Zelig was murdered under mysterious circumstances on a Second Avenue streetcar.

Before his death, however, he relayed his intended testimony to friends and relatives, who were too frightened to repeat it publicly in 1912 and for years afterward. Their reticence was not groundless. During Lieutenant Becker's two trials, defense witnesses and those whose knowledge could potentially exculpate the policeman often found themselves on the receiving end of indictment threats; one, a reporter named Hawley, testified that he'd declined to submit his defense evidence to the D.A.'s office for that very reason. When Hawley was fired from his paper, some said that he got off lucky.

Those privy to Zelig's information, therefore, stayed silent out of fear while Becker was alive and on trial, and after his execution, a sense of futility kept them mute. But some of their descendants, reassured by the passage of time, have shared their knowledge for this book.

♕ ♕ ♕

I first became aware of the Jack Zelig story while researching a possible New York City angle to the murder of my first biography subject, Prohibition-era gang leader Dean O'Banion. One of the many dusty volumes to land on my desk was a first edition of Herbert Asbury's classic *The Gangs of New York*. Although the book contained nothing that found its way into the O'Banion manuscript, Asbury's dramatic summary of Big Jack Zelig's life and crimes introduced me to a forgotten personage who took the Lower East Side by storm upon his ascension in 1910, and was still rising when he was suddenly murdered on October 5, 1912.

Even so, I didn't immediately see biography material in Zelig. The twenty-four-year-old gangster had not remained in power—or for that matter, *lived*—long enough to merit more than inclusion in the more comprehensive crime almanacs. Books about the Rosenthal murder case, such as Jonathan Root's *One Night in July* and Andy Logan's *Against the Evidence,* mentioned

Zelig because four of his followers were executed after a jury declared them guilty of shooting down Herman Rosenthal in cold blood on a hot night. But even Root and Logan dealt with Zelig only peripherally, because his role in the Rosenthal killing—if indeed he had one in the first place—was unclear. Only Herbert Asbury went into any detail about the young gangster's antecedents and exploits. His account was sanguinary and floridly written, portraying Zelig as a shrewd if not exactly intelligent character, who was so proficient in robbery, assault, and murder that he became the natural leader of a band of like-minded hoods. There were dozens like him in the New York City of his day . . . or so I thought.

Ten years later, I came across another version of Zelig's career that diverged so sharply from Asbury's account that I took immediate notice. Arthur A. Goren's *Saints and Sinners: the Underside of American Jewish History* acknowledged that Jack Zelig had headed one of the most feared gangs in turn-of-the-century New York, and, as Goren put it, "protected illicit businesses against competitors' thugs or the threat of using his own, supplied toughs at election time to intimidate the rival party's followers, and hired out his 'gorillas' to commit murder or mayhem as enforcers and labor racketeers."[2] But Goren also cited the reports of Abe Shoenfeld, a private detective who had been engaged by a powerful collective of Jewish business leaders, to report on crime conditions in the Lower East Side. Shoenfeld, who was vitriolic where Jewish outlaws were concerned, agreed that Zelig "was not an angel—he was nearer the devil than to the angel—but give the man his due."

Due? What could the urban savage from *The Gangs of New York* possibly be due except life in prison or a cell on Sing Sing's death row?

"The city [New York]," Shoenfeld continued, "has been stirred by means of copies of newspapers containing his name and pictures and his awful record, but I wish to state that if ever a man has done real good work for the East Side unknowingly, it was he. . . . Outlaw he may be classed, but he has done a good thing and that is, he has rid the East Side of Italian pimps and thieves." The detective had been incensed at the number of young Jewish girls recruited into prostitution by Five Points gangsters, whom he classed as "Italians" because their successive leaders—Paul Kelly, Jack Sirocco, Chick Tricker—were all of Italian descent. Shoenfeld applauded the fact that Zelig and his men would attack these "talent scouts" on sight and described Zelig himself as "above all a man of principle, which readily understood is a quality seldom found amongst thieves. You may find honor but never principle."

Goren also quoted Judge Jonah Goldstein, who recalled that during his youth, Zelig's gang had taken streetcar rides all over Manhattan with the sole intention of making sure that Jewish passengers were not harassed. If they saw an obnoxious character pull an old man's beard or knock a dark hat to the floor, they hurled the offender off the car and dispensed justice on the spot. Goldstein said, "These fellows [Zelig's gang] made it possible for the Jews to not get tossed around."[3]

Now I was really intrigued. In 1912, the American gangster had little use for community approval—Al Capone's sponsoring of soup kitchens to bolster his public image during his tax evasion trial was twenty years in the future. Yet Zelig had protected his co-religionists with an uncalculated fervor that could not be totally attributed to territorial aggression, and it had earned him the lifelong admiration of an accomplished jurist like Goldstein, who was instrumental in the creation of the Family Court. The judge, whom one writer described as "an honest man who devoted himself to the public good,"[4] would not have praised a nihilistic thug. Nor would Abe Shoenfeld, who, according to his nephew, spent his entire life investigating crime, condemning criminals, and advocating social justice.[5]

In 2003, I began to research Jack Zelig in earnest, intrigued by the paradox he represented. Because he had been dead for ninety-one years at that point, separating truth from legend was difficult: there was no one still alive to personally dispute what Asbury or anyone else had written about him. But a few New Yorkers who knew or had come into contact with Zelig left vividly composed records of their impressions and judgments, and I was fortunate enough to obtain access to these written memories. Archival holdings in the United States and Israel yielded a gold mine of primary material in the form of contemporary news accounts, police and court records, and "secret reports" compiled by Abe Shoenfeld and his investigative team. I also made contact with Zelig's relatives, as well as people whose grandfathers, great-uncles, etc. had been members of his gang. These descendants collectively presented me with another example of how he had deviated from the norm: prior to his murder, Zelig had intended to save a police officer's life. That ran contrary to the gangster code, which dictated that the only good cop was a dead one. Big Jack Zelig was so atypical that his story, in my opinion, deserved a book-length examination.

♔ ♔ ♔

The lessening of Zelig's celebrity and historical impact can be blamed on liquor, figuratively speaking. When Prohibition turned the American gangster from a local nuisance into a national and semi-romantic public benefactor, pre-Volstead gang leaders like Zelig suffered unflattering comparisons to the suave and successful bootleg bosses. In a 1935 *New York Times* article titled "Portrait of a Racketeer," Meyer Berger wrote, "Most people still fall into the common error of thinking of gangsters and racketeers as loafers with turtle-neck sweaters, cauliflower ears, and protruding maxilla who beat their women and punt their offspring around in the flat. That type passed out of existence during the liquor gold rush."

In other words, any gangster predating Al Capone (with the possible exception of the aforementioned Rothstein) was assumed to have been a mentally challenged, primordial lout, the bane of the pushcart peddlers and fodder for the beat cop's nightstick. Prohibition, and the refinement that bootleg money could provide, supposedly resulted in a superior breed of hoodlum who might have been successful on Wall Street if their childhood circumstances had been different. Anyone who experienced their heyday B.C. (Before Capone) was a criminal curio.

O. O. McIntyre, whose widely syndicated column "New York Day by Day" made him a newspaper legend during the 1920s and '30s, remembered differently in Zelig's case. He recalled in December 1925, "Some years ago I interviewed Big Jack Zelig for a New York paper. He as no other had thrown the gang terror into the hearts of stuss [a faro-like card game] dealers and small-fry merchants on the East Side." Knowing this, the young reporter had approached his assignment with some trepidation, only to be both surprised and intrigued. "He seemed far removed from the gangster I imagined. He was neatly dressed and had the crisp and aggressive manner of the eminent Herbert Bayard Swope."[6]

McIntyre was not alone in his impression. Brows lifted whenever those who knew Jack Zelig only by reputation finally encountered him. He was tall and athletic in build, dressed well, had an ingratiating smile and firm handshake, and could converse on any subject. Only his wary gaze and crooked nose, misshapen by repeated breaking, outwardly advertised his desperate origins. Zelig did not look like what he really was.

At the time of his murder, the gangster, who had been born Zelig Zvi Lefkowitz to respectable Russian-Jewish parents in 1888, oversaw a criminal network that profited from almost every form of crime that paid. He protected gambling dens, stuss houses and brothels, rented *shtarkers* to unions who needed muscle power in their struggle for fair treatment, and sold the services of his rowdier followers to politicians who wanted to give voters special incentive to get them into office. "Rackets"[7] held in his honor netted piles of cash that gangsters, politicians, and small business owners seeking his favor handed over in the guise of ticket sales.

Albert Fried, author of the excellent *Rise and Fall of the Jewish Gangster in America*, noted, "He consorted with politicians and banker-gamblers, uptown as well as on the Lower East Side, his home base. There was no containing Big Jack Zelig." Robert Rockaway wrote in *But He Was Good To His Mother*, ". . . Big Jack carried on his various activities with great success. For several years he did a booming business in slugging, stabbing, shooting and bomb-throwing."[8] His name exemplified the pinnacle of gangland achievement: New York policeman Cornelius Willemse, recalling in his 1934 memoir the murder of an aspiring "bad man," wrote that the ambitious victim "fancied himself to be another Jack Selig [sic]." Dopey Benny Fein, Waxey Gordon, and Jacob "Little Augie" Orgen, Jewish gangsters who became successful bosses in their own right, all served under Zelig.

When Zelig made his debut in 1900 as a teenaged pickpocket, no one would have predicted the levels he'd eventually reach. He was non-violent; instead of packing a gun or razor, he employed flight—or, when caught, tears—as a weapon. He was good at what he did but lacked the drive that took his kind out of the poolrooms and into the upper echelon, where political favor and public fear turned gangsters like Monk Eastman and Paul Kelly into robber barons. Two years in Sing Sing and close association with the great Eastman hardened Zelig, but not to any extent that put him above hundreds of other "tough guys" who thronged the dives and murderers' roosts of the Lower East Side. It took a terrible beating in 1909 that left him dead—for mere seconds, but it was long enough—and a public thrashing of three feared desperados at the cutthroat Chatham Club in 1910 to turn him into Eastman's successor.

Zelig then picked up where incarceration or murder had forced his predecessors—Eastman, Ritchie Fitzpatrick, and Kid Twist Zweifach—to leave off, and serving as his major-domos were "Lefty" Louis Rosenberg, Harry "Gyp the Blood" Horowitz, "Dago" Frank Cirofici, and Jacob "Whitey Lewis" Seidenshner, all of whom went to the electric chair in 1914 as an indirect consequence of disobeying him.

Zelig's death was almost as remarkable as his life. "Red" Phil Davidson, a local pimp and suspected "horse poisoner," shot him from behind on a Second Avenue streetcar. Davidson's reason for the killing varied with his levels of fear and drunkenness, although he finally told Judge John Goff that he'd done the deed while half-crazed from a recent beating Zelig had supposedly inflicted on him. No one really believed him, but there was less contention over the fact that Davidson's gun had neatly prevented some much-anticipated testimony from being heard at the Becker trial. In consequence, one man moved to the governor's mansion while another ended his days on Sing Sing's death row.

The Starker: Big Jack Zelig, the Becker-Rosenthal Case, and the Advent of the Jewish Gangster is more than merely the posthumous testimony of the Rosenthal case's most enigmatic witness. It is also the story of an aggressive yet intelligent young man, the son of Russian-Jewish immigrants, who learned to fight as a newsboy and never stopped fighting, even after he dressed in expensive tailored suits and sponsored Arlington Hall "rackets" where both the underworld and the legitimate business community paid him tribute. He was a blend of the brutal, brass-knuckled Old Guard and the slowly emerging Thinking Man's Gangster. Or, to put it more vividly; if verbal persuasion failed, he didn't mind getting blood on his elegant suits because he could easily afford to replace them afterward.

The Starker also revisits and documents Zelig's world. The 1890s and first decade of the twentieth century was an era when gangsters hung out in saloons and cafés instead of country clubs and high-class restaurants. People feared the Black Hand and knew little about the now universally dreaded Mafia. The snappy fedora that every cinematic gangster wears at a menacing angle was years in the future; derbies and jaunty straw boater hats concealed a multitude of sins ranging from careless haircuts to badly scarred scalps.

The bobbed-haired, gum-cracking gun moll had not yet been liberated by Prohibition and the right to vote; she had her politically mute yet formidable counterpart in the jaded, rouged "gunwoman" who secreted pistols and knives in fur muffs, specially tailored skirt pockets, and even elaborate hairdos. Jack Zelig, Russian by descent but decidedly American in his aggressive opportunism, ruled over this time, place, and citizenry with an iron fist from 1910 until his death.

To this date, there have been no biographies written about any New York City gang lords predating Arnold Rothstein. The activities of the early gangs proliferating throughout the boroughs and their antagonistic relationship with the police, their political masters, and each other have been documented extensively by such noted authors as Herbert Asbury, Pat Downey, and Luc Sante, but as general phenomena and not the experience of one individual. Until now, no single name has woven together the immigrant experience, specifically that of the Russian Jews in post-Civil War New York City, the Rosenthal murder case, and the gradual transformation of the New York gangster from poolroom terror to sinister businessman.

Detective Shoenfeld, who regarded Hebrew hoodlums as an embarrassment to the Jewish race, did not hesitate to make heavy moral judgments in his written reports. Yet for Jack Zelig, gang leader, killer, and unsurpassed in the art of using knife and razor, his observations assumed a different tone. After learning of the murder, he wrote, "Jack Zelig is as dead as a doornail. Men before him—like Kid Twist, Monk Eastman, and others—were as pygmies to a giant. With the passing of Zelig, one of the 'nerviest,' strongest, and best men of his kind left us."

— Rose Keefe

ACKNOWLEDGMENTS

Good luck," was something I heard more than once when I announced to friends and fellow true-crime authors in late 2003 that I was undertaking the biography of a New York gangland figure who died in 1912. Most meant it as encouragement, but I suspect that others were conveying a gentle doubt. I understood why: research-wise, *The Starker* posed serious challenges.

To begin with, New York City police records covering the 1895–1912 period were scanty. In researching his chilling photo book *Evidence: NYPD Crime Scene Photographs 1914–1918,* Luc Sante sadly observed, "It seems that in 1983 or '84, when the city was in the process of cleaning out the old police headquarters on Centre Street as a condition of its sale to private interests, workers removed roomfuls of files from its innards, and those files were dumped into the East River." Another, similar housecleaning had taken place sometime before 1961, consigning thousands of nineteenth-century glass-plate mug shots to the depths of New York Bay. Microfilmed newspapers and court records remained available and complete for the most part, but the former tended to present a biased view of people and events based on the paper's own stance, while the latter was a cool, detached tabulation of proceedings.

Time also was not on my side. So many years had passed between Jack Zelig's death and the commencement of my research that the personal interviews which can rescue a flesh-and-blood human being from his or her media-inspired legend were beyond my reach.

All told, it was an imposing task, but not as impossible as I initially thought. Luc Sante noted in the foreword to another volume, *Low Life,* "The dead . . . are a notoriously perverse and unmanageable lot. They tend not to remain safely buried, and in fact resist all efforts at obliterating their traces." So it was with Big Jack Zelig. During the course of my research, I found ninety-five-year-old undercover reports in an Israel archive; read typewritten, unpublished interviews with those who had been on intimate terms with the "terror" and "commander" of New York's Lower East Side; and even spoke to an elderly ex-New Yorker who, as a wide-eyed six-year-old, watched Jack Zelig die. But a book is rarely the end result of the author's efforts alone, and there are several people whom I'd like to thank for the assistance they rendered in bringing this project first to life and finally to completion.

The first round of kudos goes to Joseph Lefkowitz, who came across one of the myriad posts I made on true-crime mailing lists and message boards, requesting information about Big Jack Zelig. A distant relative of Zelig, he had been researching the gang leader since the 1950s, but purely out of personal interest. He readily placed his collection of magazine articles, court files, and notes at my disposal. Joe interviewed elderly New Yorkers who had known Zelig personally, and thanks to their neatly typed recollections, I was made privy to the workings of his Lower East Side empire and what he knew about the sensational murder of Herman Rosenthal.

Sincere thanks are extended to Mark and Karen Lefkowitz of New York, who contacted me in August 2007 after finding *The Starker*'s companion Web site at www.jackzelig.com. Mark is the grandson of Zelig's oldest brother, Hyman (Herman). Both he and Karen graciously answered any and all questions I had about the Lefkowitz family and provided the early family photos that appear in this book. Through them, I met Zelig's niece Charlotte Weingarten, a lovely person who shared her memories of Zelig's long-suffering mother, Sarah, and filled in the details about what happened to his eight siblings.

Pat Downey, author of *Gangster City* and *Bad Seeds in the Big Apple,* read the entire manuscript from start to finish, offering corrections when necessary and giving me the benefit of his unparalleled knowledge about turn-of-the-century New York City and its gangsters. When conducting research for his own books, Pat compiled huge dossiers on Jack Zelig, Monk Eastman, Paul Kelly, Dopey Benny Fein, and other pre-Prohibition Manhattan gang leaders, and he placed these at my disposal. Whenever my energy and enthusiasm flagged, he'd tell me to go to the local coffee shop where I normally write, have a "Lefty Latte" or a cup of "Gyp the Brewed" and keep plugging away. Because I made the request on a good day, he agreed to write the foreword for *The Starker*—or so he says.

Thanks to the following parties who obliged me with interviews: Geoff Fein, grandson of Zelig friend and successor Dopey Benny Fein; John Christie, who never forgot the day he saw Red Phil Davidson fire the fatal bullet into Zelig's brain; Miriam Goldberg, whose grandfather Jacob had a final, significant conversation with Zelig less than a month before the latter was killed; the late

Richard Shoenfeld, nephew of undercover investigator Abe Shoenfeld; Jean Gold, whose grandmother Adele Kaufman was rescued from white slavery by Zelig; and Edward Riley, whose great-grandfather Dominick Riley was one of the policemen who arrested Lefty Louie and Gyp the Blood.

Others who deserve special mention are retired NYPD Det. James Muirhead and Doug Walker, formerly of the Metro Toronto Police Department, both of whom obliged me by examining the Rosenthal murder case from a twenty-first-century police perspective and rendering their opinions; Rabbi Meyer Schiller, who translated the Hebrew text on Zelig's tombstone and provided enlightenment whenever I had a question about the Jewish faith; Kenneth Cobb of the New York Municipal Archives, for digging up and copying early case files (1899–1901) involving Jack Zelig and Max "Kid Twist" Zweifach; *Chicago Outfit* author John Binder, for hunting down many of the rare photos that appear in the gallery section; and author Ellen Poulsen, who ran to the library whenever I needed a news article, fast. Bill Helmer is fondly acknowledged for the odd Zelig-related photocopy he threw my way, as well as for "being there" all these years. Same with true-crime author Rich Lindberg and Rick Mattix, co-author of *The Complete Public Enemy Almanac* and editor of *On The Spot Journal,* both of whom are my heroes as well as my friends.

Thanks as well to Mary Becker, Jenny Sirocco, Pat Hickey, Jenny Floro-Khalaf, Daniel J. Kelley (for the introduction to Rabbi Schiller), Jennifer Manuel from the American Jewish Archives, Hadassah Assouline from the Central Archives for the History of the Jewish People in Israel, David Pietrusza, author of *Rothstein,* and Marvin H. Cohen of the Historical Society of Middletown, N.Y.

And a special thank you to Mario Gomes . . . for being you. *Te amo.*

INTRODUCTION

September 1912

A s Jacob Goldberg rounded the corner of Forty-ninth Street and Madison Avenue, the last person he expected to encounter on the bustling sidewalk was his old partner in crime, Harry Smith. Jacob considered himself to be a hard-working, law-abiding citizen these days, but his teenage years had included some wilder moments, and Harry had been an instigator of most of them. Seeing him now aroused equal portions of nostalgia and uneasiness.

Eleven years had passed since that riotous day in July 1901 when they accosted an unsuspecting pedestrian, Mary Sheehan, on Scammel Street and snatched her purse. The escapade had started like any one of the dozens of "snatches" they had carried off throughout the summer: Harry and Jacob closed in on their target like a pair of eager young sharks, then one of them jostled her so forcefully that she stumbled while the other seized her purse. But this time, before they could make their escape, passers-by attracted by the woman's hollering closed in, seized the boys, and held them until a policeman arrived.

While the sixteen-year-old Goldberg emulated his idol, Monk Eastman, and masked his anxiety behind a "tough-egg" composure, Harry commenced a performance worthy of the celebrated Richard Mansfield. Claiming to be only sixteen, he let one fat tear after another soak his youthful face and pleaded poverty and forgiveness in choked, beseeching tones. Mary Sheehan, however, was a paragon of indignation, and instead of dropping her complaint and giving the boys some money to allay Harry's dramatically proclaimed hunger pangs, she pressed charges. The boys could scarcely contain their shock, for up until then the ploy had worked without fail. Now their luck, along with their freedom, was temporarily coming to an end.

Harry Smith and Jacob Goldberg appeared before Judge L. M. McMahon on July 26, 1901. McMahon had a reputation for being a tough judge; earlier that week, he had sentenced panderer Arthur Miller to four years and five months in the state prison, plus a $400 fine, for placing a fifteen-year-old girl in a brothel.[1] He showed more leniency to the young men, releasing Goldberg on his own recognizance after Harry denied that his friend had anything to do with the theft. Harry, whose guilt was made clear by the police and eyewitness testimony, was convicted of larceny in the second degree. McMahon, taking into account his age and lack of a prior record, sentenced him to the House of Refuge, that venerable institution that ostensibly acted as a stern surrogate parent to New York's incorrigible youth.

The two friends were thus separated, but only for a matter of weeks. Goldberg was caught picking pockets again, and this second offense following so quickly on the heels of the first sent him to the House of Refuge. The schooling, scolding, and youthful terrorism practiced within the somber stone walls shook Goldberg out of his tough-guy ambitions quickly. When he was finally paroled to his parents a year later, he eagerly settled for a less exciting life, first in the Rivington Street tailoring shop where his father also worked, then in another, similar establishment in Newark, New Jersey, upon his family's relocation there. He had gotten married that spring and was planning on returning to New York City to live.

Harry was still an inmate when Jacob was released from the House of Refuge, and the two had not crossed paths since. Goldberg often wondered what had become of him. He'd heard rumors that Harry had adopted an alias and was now a big shot in the old Monk Eastman-Kid Twist gang, but he never bothered to investigate. His current life had no place for reunions with old friends who could laugh off the House of Refuge and smirk at the threat of Sing Sing.

Harry would never go straight, Goldberg had always figured. It wasn't due to lack of opportunity to make a decent living legitimately, given his brains and his father's situation in a thriving tailoring business. Jacob sensed that, for Harry, it was not about the money and never would be. The contents of Mary Sheehan's pocketbook ($6.83) could have kept the young men busy at Coney Island or in the Bowery amusement halls for a day or two at least, but Harry would have been prowling the streets before the loot was even halfway spent, alert for another snatch-run-and-spend opportunity. It was a common joke between them that he'd really been born a Vanderbilt, so he stole for fun, not riches. When it was not about the cash, it was about something else that could never be satisfied, and pursuit of such an ongoing and unreachable goal struck Jacob as reckless. For him, the stealing, gambling, and riotous nightlife had served as an escape from a boring existence, but for Harry, they were a lifeline. And that addiction, if what Goldberg had heard was true, made him into a gangster.

By 1912, the two-fisted brawlers whom Jacob and Harry had idolized—men like Monk Eastman, Razor Riley, the dandified but deadly Biff Ellison, and mayhem virtuoso "Eat Em Up" Jack McManus—had gradually been eliminated or replaced in favor of gang bosses who, while still cold-blooded murderers, retained a more subtle public image. Men like Paul Kelly, who spoke more languages than a Yale linguist and mixed as fluidly with society ladies as he did with the ladies of the night, or Max "Kid Twist" Zweifach, erstwhile Eastman successor, whose propensity for dressing like a prosperous young banker did not lessen his ability to terrify his enemies and even his own men.[2] These men were not lone wolves defending a small territory and leading their ragtag packs into battle. They organized, gained some immunity from the law by playing on their value to politicians as vote-getters, and instead of blindly robbing and thieving like their parasitic predecessors, they turned extortion, gambling, and vice into big business.

The new breed of gangster might have learned to dress and talk like those from the dollar side of Broadway, but newspaper "morgue" files and records retained by the coroner's office proved that they were still killing each other in the old, violent style. After Monk Eastman had been sent to prison in 1904, Kid Twist settled the question of succession by inviting his chief rival for the leadership position, Ritchie Fitzpatrick, to a saloon for a drink and negotiation session. Fitzpatrick never got the drink, thanks to the bullet that a Twist minion fired through his heart, tearing open his chest and spraying blood over the sidewalk outside the saloon that had been the proposed meeting site. John "Spanish Louis" Lewis, a hot-blooded gunman who claimed to be of South American descent, spent ten years as a killer for hire, but his career was cut short on April 1, 1910, when he encountered someone with a sneakier technique and faster gun, and perished in a pool of his own gore. No one could dispute that the modern gangster was just as deadly as his predecessors, even if he did fill his time between killing assignments with trips to high-priced tailors and manicurists.

Goldberg was well aware of Harry Smith's dedication to making his living illegally, but he had been perturbed by the rumors that his old associate was now on a par with the likes of Kid Twist and Spanish Louis. Harry may have been a streetwise graduate of the old Crazy Butch gang, with no use for an honest dollar, but violent? Capable of razoring a man's face to bloody ribbons or even murdering him?

If Harry was now one of *them,* what had happened to change him?

Although nine years had gone by since the boyhood comrades had laid eyes on each other, Jacob recognized Harry right away. He was snappily attired in a light gray summer suit and straw boater hat that were notches above his old dress code, but otherwise he looked the same. As he drew closer, however, Goldberg noticed a few unsettling changes. Harry was still in his twenties, but his features were hard in the manner of an older, seasoned man. The dancing brown eyes that could shine with summoned tears and soften the hearts of most "snatch" victims were expressionless to the point of being deadpan. His mouth, which had always looked abnormally small compared to his hawkish nose, was rendered even more minuscule by a preoccupied frown. Even his walk was brisk and aggressive.

Jacob felt uneasy and for a brief moment decided not to hail him. Something, though—nostalgia or curiosity or a combination of both—did not want to let him see Harry pass by without saying something, anything, the dark rumors notwithstanding. "My great-grandfather was standing under a store awning," Goldberg's great-granddaughter Miriam says, "and when [Harry] was just about to go on past, he called out to him."

Harry Smith stopped short, spun abruptly on his heel, and faced Goldberg. At the same instant, two shifty-looking East Side types, who had been walking several yards behind the dapper figure, came in close. For a brief moment Goldberg wished that he had not said anything. Then recognition washed over Harry's grim features, and he darted forward, smiling, in that quick, sprightly style that Jacob remembered.

"Well, if it isn't old Jake Goldberg!"

"That's right—how you been, Harry?"

When the two men pumped each other's hands with genuine pleasure, the bodyguard types halted briefly. Then they slid sideways, coming to rest in a lounging position against a nearby stoop. Hands stuffed in their pockets and cigarettes dangling precariously low on their lips, they alternated their stares between Goldberg and the fashionably attired young women strolling by.

Coaxed by relentless and enthusiastic questions, Jacob summarized his life of the past nine years. When he asked his old comrade for the same information, Harry's reanimated face registered first surprise, then confusion, and lastly a wariness that made Jacob nervous. Equally alarming was how Harry's companions, noticing a change in his expression and body language, stood at attention. They looked like a pair of guard dogs, waiting for the signal to attack.

Minutes, or maybe seconds that just felt longer, passed. Then Harry shook his head and said, "Thought news traveled to Jersey much better than that." He nodded in the direction of the Forty-ninth Street and Seventh Avenue intersection. "Got time for a walk, or are you going someplace, Jake?"

"My great-grandfather was actually on his way somewhere but didn't want to make things tenser by saying so," Miriam Goldberg says. "So he went walking with [Harry Smith]. And half of what he told him, he wished he had not heard. It was information that could have gotten him arrested, or worse."

Speaking rapidly, Harry began to talk about himself, and at the same time give his old friend an inner glimpse into Manhattan's former and current sins and scandals. He detailed his long-standing association with the underworld of the Lower East Side, his apprenticeship under Monk Eastman and Kid Twist

Zweifach, and some of the misdeeds that had vaulted him to his current position in the gangland hierarchy. He also talked about his own vicarious involvement in a murder that had succeeded in shocking a city long accustomed to bloodshed. It had taken place the previous July, at the height of a vicious heat wave, and a police lieutenant had been arrested as the perpetrator. Goldberg had heard about that and had to admit that he was awaiting the policeman's October trial with more eagerness than might be deemed proper. But what Harry told him gave rise to fear instead of fascination. One man had died already, another stood a real chance of being executed in Sing Sing's electric chair, and if Harry had his way, more could be added to the body count. Not that he directly threatened murder, but enough hints were dropped ("That lying bald-headed son of a bitch is going to have me to deal with the moment he hits the streets!") to make Goldberg fear that he was being made an unwilling accessory before the fact.

Harry talked tough, but his own agitation where this murder case was concerned was discernible. He was speaking to Goldberg, but his eyes were everywhere else, scanning the storefronts, doorways, and oncoming pedestrians. He also would suddenly stop and stand for a few minutes, cross his arms, and rock back and forth on the heels of his immaculately shined shoes. "I'm in pretty deep, but I'll come out of it," he said, more to himself than to his old friend. "And when I do, a few sons of bitches are going to be straightened out."

At the corner of Broadway and Forty-ninth, Harry paused yet again, and said, "You better go on your business now, Jake. Too many people know me in this area [Broadway], and if you're seen with me it might not be so good for you." Goldberg, in wholehearted agreement by this point, halted too and shook his hand.

With that, the man Jacob Goldberg had known as Harry Smith, but whom all of New York's Lower East Side knew and feared as Big Jack Zelig, made an abrupt, nervous turn and rounded the corner. The bodyguards followed, one of them giving Goldberg a final once-over before disappearing after his boss. Jacob remained standing near the busy intersection, oblivious to the murmur of the passing crowds and slightly sickened by that realization that he knew too much about the case that had all of New York (and beyond) abuzz. Many of the pedestrians bustling past had newspapers tucked under their arms, which Jacob did not have to read to know that they carried that day's updates about the Herman Rosenthal murder case and Lt. Charles Becker's upcoming trial. The latter event was scheduled for next month, and Jack Zelig, who headed the gang that had furnished the shooters for the Rosenthal hit, was one of the most anticipated witnesses.

Few if any of those newspaper readers knew what Jacob Goldberg, standing dazed and blinking in the midday sun, now knew—namely how Herman Rosenthal's death had really come about, who had actually shot him, and why. It was a version of events that contrasted so sharply with that given by the state's star witness, Bald Jack Rose, that were the victim and the principal players not the same, Goldberg would not have recognized it as the same murder case.

Jack Zelig never lived to tell his story in a courtroom. Weeks later he was dead, thanks to a bullet in his skull fired by a self-proclaimed beating victim whom the gangster's friends suspected, correctly, of being a stooge for powerful gangland and political forces.

His testimony comes ninety years too late, but now, in the pages of this book, Big Jack Zelig finally takes the stand.

CHAPTER ONE

From Eastern Europe
to the East Side

S ometime during the early 1900s, a pioneer investigative journalist who sailed into New York Harbor along with hordes of ragged, exhausted, yet hopeful would-be Americans wrote, "The day of the emigrants' arrival in New York was the nearest earthly likeness to the final day of judgment, when we have to prove our fitness to enter Heaven."[1] It was debatable whether heaven had stricter admission standards than Castle Garden.

When twenty-four-year-old Ephraim Lefkowitz arrived on July 4, 1884, on the *State of Georgia*, a 2,490-ton State Line steamship that began its journey in Glasgow (and stopped over in Larne, Ireland, before continuing to New York), the categorization process began even before he had left the vessel. Just before disembarkation, he and his fellow steerage passengers were lettered and numbered according to the location of their entries on the ship's manifest. Then they all trudged down the rickety gangplank, an anxious, silent human caravan keeping one eye on their worldly possessions and the other on the skyline of the city that promised—or maybe threatened—so much. The Statue of Liberty, which would offer a mute but majestic welcome to millions of immigrants from its perch on the former Bedloe's Island in the harbor, was not yet in place, having just been completed in Paris the previous month. Coincidentally, the statue was formally presented to America by the French people on July 4, the day that Ephraim Lefkowitz stepped onto American soil.

As the entire group was shepherded through the lightly falling summer rain into the teeming immigrant processing facility that was Castle Garden, optimism surely pierced the fatigue they all must have felt. They were finally in America, which had become the equivalent of freedom, opportunity, and hope to them and thousands like them. That impression, however, was severely dampened the moment they entered the hubbub.

Government investigations conducted during the 1880s indicated that Castle Garden was a disorienting and, for many, distressing experience. The aging site, which had been constructed in 1808 to complement Fort Williams on Governor's Island and enjoyed a brief vogue as a restaurant, theater, and opera house,[2] was packed wall to wall with tired, bewildered steerage passengers and the uniformed staff who sorted them roughly into lines so their acceptance or rejection by the medical personnel could be expedited. Those suspected of suffering from a heart condition, having a mental defect, or harboring contagious conditions like scalp vermin, venereal disease, or tuberculosis (sometimes referred to as the "Jewish disease") were marked with chalk and isolated until doctors could make a final judgment on their fitness for admission. This segregation was akin to imprisonment and just as unpleasant. Outraged missionaries later complained of seeing sick people forced to sleep uncovered on hard floors while their cases were being reviewed. Those who passed inspection but had no family or friends waiting for them risked being robbed of their meager funds by roving gangs or the "money changers" who hovered around the Battery like vultures. A New York State commissioner once scorned Castle Garden operations as a "perfect farce."

Ephraim Lefkowitz endured the intimate poking and prodding—and later the series of probing questions posed by a brisk immigration officer—with patience and dignity. He had survived far worse back in his native Russia. The pogroms and the tsar's anti-Semitic decrees had forced him to flee to Great Britain with his wife, Sarah, and one-year-old son, Hyman, in 1882. (Sarah, Hyman, and Alex, a son who had been born in Britain, were back in Glasgow, waiting for him to save enough to bring them over.) Ephraim was a relative latecomer to America's sheltering shores; since 1881, many inches of newspaper column space had been dedicated to covering the mass arrival of Russian Jews and the terrible violence that had brought them here. By 1884, America was the ambivalent host to thousands of Ephraim's countrymen and -women.

⚜ ⚜ ⚜

Russian-born journalist Herman Rosenthal,[3] who headed the Slavonic Department in the New York Public Library and organized, in Louisiana, the first agricultural colony for Russian Jews fleeing the pogroms back home, vividly depicted the hellish conditions experienced by the Lefkowitzes and millions like them in his 1911 article "The Martyrdom of the Russian Jew."[4]

He wrote, "In three decades, one and a half million Jews were forced to leave the Empire. In a series of terrible 'pogroms,' or anti-Jewish riots—outbreaks stimulated and countenanced by subtle government policy—thousands of helpless Jews have been murdered, many more thousands crippled or wounded, and robbery or destruction of the property of the victims has left their widows and children destitute." Historian Shlomo Lambroza elaborated on the motive behind the intolerance: "The official view was that the Jews were a parasitic element in the Russian Empire who lived off the hard-earned wages of the narod [people]."[5]

Those who survived found their daily existence choked by rules and regulations that would have done justice to a prison. Russia's Jewish population was forbidden to buy, lease, or manage real estate in the country districts, and those who had specific skills (e.g., physicians, artisans) that qualified them for special "residency permits" outside the miserable confines of the Pale[6] could find their permits revoked at a moment's notice. They were barred from teaching in the primary, secondary, or high schools (the same institutions denied enrollment to most Jewish children), and only a handful became lecturers at the universities. Jewish men were encouraged to become soldiers (although they were barred from the navy, the frontier or quarantine service, and the gendarmerie), but they could not become officers. Rosenthal noted bitterly, "The Jew may die for 'Holy Russia,' but he need look for no reward."

These demeaning living and working conditions were not merely a pitiless twentieth-century phenomenon. The Russian Jews had never known a time when they stood on equal footing with their Gentile neighbors. It was a case of one regime being more or less severe than the previous.

The reign of Tsar Nicholas I (1825–55), which Sarah[7] Lefkowitz's parents had suffered through, had been especially oppressive. "The purpose in educating Jews," he once wrote, "is to bring about their gradual merging with the Christian nationalities and to uproot those superstitious and harmful prejudices that are instilled by the teachings of the Talmud." Under Nicholas, more than 600 anti-Semitic decrees were enacted that interfered with school curriculums, heavily censored publications, expelled people from villages they had long called home, and, saddest of all, took boys, some as young as eight or nine, away from their parents for a forced conscription that could last up to twenty-five years. Writer Alexander Herzen, later known as the "father of Russian Socialism," recalled a harrowing visit to a village in the province of Vyatka. He saw bewildered Jewish boys facing a future that consisted of either brutal military service or an early grave:

> Pale, exhausted, with frightened faces, they stood in thick, clumsy soldier's overcoats, with stand up collars, fixing helpless, pitiful eyes on the garrison soldiers who were roughly getting them into ranks. . . . And these sick children, without care or kindness, exposed to the icy wind that blows unobstructed from the Arctic Ocean, were going to their graves.[8]

Alexander II's coronation on March 2, 1855, ushered in an era of comparative freedom and privilege. Humane and enlightened by nature, he freed the country's 40 million serfs and made the lives of the Jewish residents more tolerable by reducing military service to five years, opening the universities to them, and allowing businessmen to expand their trade by traveling to parts of the country they previously had been forbidden to enter. Benjamin Disraeli praised him as "the kindliest prince who has ever ruled Russia."[9]

All went well for twenty-six years—until Alexander was assassinated in March 1881. None of the four anarchists who orchestrated the murder plot was Jewish; the party who threw the bomb that fatally wounded the tsar was Polish. But a Jewish seamstress had helped rent the apartment that served as the conspiracy's headquarters, and her participation sparked public denunciations by anti-Semites.

Alexander III ascended the throne. The new tsar viewed the Jewish population with the same visceral hatred that had marked his forebears, thanks to his teacher and adviser Konstantin Pobedonostev, who jumped at the opportunity to turn his fanatical anti-Semitism into political action. The first of many pogroms commenced at the end of April 1881, and their brutality shocked the civilized world. Older Jews saw their pre-1855 memories undergo a terrible resurrection, and the younger people, for whom the horrors of the past had been merely stories, were traumatized by the chaos and violence that now dominated their lives.[10] Irving Howe wrote, "The year 1881 marks a turning point in the history of the Jews as decisive as that of 70 A.D., when Titus's legions burned the Temple at Jerusalem, or 1492, when Ferdinand and Isabella decreed the expulsion from Spain."[11]

Between 1881 and 1883, a total of 226 pogroms took place in the cities and towns of Poland and southern Russia. An estimated 70,000 Jews lost property, and others were killed. Those who survived made frantic arrangements to escape.

The rest of the world greeted the details of the atrocities with revulsion. In Paris, novelist Victor Hugo, whose 1862 work *Les Miserables* riveted the public with its depictions of misery and social injustice, headed a committee to publicly protest the pogroms. On February 1, 1882, the lord mayor of London, England, called a meeting at the Mansion House. The hall was packed to capacity hours before the speeches commenced and included such concerned notables as the Archbishop of Canterbury, Cardinal Manning, the Earl of Shaftesbury, and Sir Alexander T. Galt. Even Alfred Tennyson got involved. While unable to attend the meeting, an emissary read a letter he had penned for the occasion, in which he wrote, "I am dismayed at the madness of the hatred evidenced against the Jews. If the unspeakable barbarities being committed are not universally denounced, it is only because they are so alien to the spirit of the age as to be almost incredible."[12]

Resolutions were adopted, one of which declared, "While we disclaim the right to interfere in the internal affairs of Russia and desire the preservation of amicable relations with that country, it is our duty to express the opinion that the laws of Russia concerning the Jews tend to degrade her in the eyes of Christians."[13]

News of such support for their plight drew Ephraim and Sarah Lefkowitz to England in 1882. (An estimated 150,000 Jews sought refuge in Britain between 1881 and 1914.) Leaving Russia, they probably took one of the two most likely routes. The first was illegally crossing the Austro-Hungarian border, catching a train to Berlin, and making their way by whatever means available to Hamburg, the German port from which they sailed. A second possibility is that they crossed the German border directly (if they were coming from western or northwestern Russia), proceeded to Berlin, and finally arrived in Hamburg, which was renowned as a safe temporary haven for those on their way to England or America.[14]

That reputation was deserved only to the extent that Hamburg was a reliable departure point for potentially greener pastures. The docks were fraught with dangers of all kinds: slithering through the weary and haggard crowds were ticket swindlers, thieves out to snatch any unattended pieces of pitiful luggage, phony recruitment officers who guaranteed fabulous salaries in exchange for a minor "deposit" on their services, and hoodlums who took the emigrants' money and possessions by brute force.

Ephraim and Sarah opted to sail for England instead of America. Perhaps one or both of them had friends or family already settled there, ready to assist them with the relocation process. It's also possible that they had exhausted their financial resources during the escape from Russia and couldn't afford steerage tickets for a transatlantic voyage. England was not only closer, it was also home to thousands of fellow refugees. Ephraim could find a job, and by adhering to strict standards of economy, they would soon be able to move on to America should they decide to do so.

Once on board ship, the Lefkowitz family and their fellow refugees were treated to an uncomfortable voyage. Below deck, people huddled shoulder to shoulder in dark, poorly ventilated quarters, and combated nausea and fatigue. An *Evening News and Post* reporter replicated their voyage in 1891 and was ready to take his chances with the frigid waters several times before the boat finally docked. "The horrors of the place were increased by the accumulation of filth, which had taken place by the ever-increasing indisposition of the passengers the longer we were at sea," he wrote, no doubt shuddering at the memory.[15]

Once they landed on English soil and recovered from any ill effects of the unsanitary trip, the Lefkowitzes headed for London's East End,[16] where they were to spend the next several months. It was a natural gravitation point for them: Whitechapel, Spitalfields, Mile End, and adjacent districts housed thousands of foreign-born Jews, both refugees and voluntary emigrants. These newcomers had already created a niche in this congested and sometimes desperate region of London whose inhabitants would soon reel in terror over the Jack the Ripper murders and receive a grim literary immortality in Jack London's *People of the Abyss*.

Charles Van Onselen, author of *The Fox and the Flies,* described the area as "more of a cultural construct than a geographical entity, it was the Borough of Hamlets that lay east of the City and north of the river that constituted most of the East End." Viewed on a map, it was a rambling territory that reached as far as Hoxton and Shoreditch to the north, and, at its southern edge, nestled along the bank of the Thames all the way to the West India docks. Seen through the eyes of those who lived there or ventured within its borders, the East End was a congested mass of dirty, aging buildings that provided shelter and sustenance to almost a million people. Roughly cobbled streets bled into alleys and court-yards that existed in a perpetual state of walled-in darkness and clammy filth. In winter, the wet fog that lifted in sinister white clouds off the Thames tor-tured one's respiratory system and transformed dwellings into iceboxes. During the summer, the lodging houses and tenement blocks trapped the heat, turning residents into a stewing mass of misery. The respectable working poor struggled for existence alongside loafers, thieves, prostitutes, and other classes of crimi-nals. Dire as living conditions were, the East End attracted immigrants like the Lefkowitzes because it was cheap to live there—possibly because life was so cheap—and newcomers aroused milder degrees of local resentment than they did in London's more gentrified quarters.

The Lefkowitzes made the best of their situation. Ephraim, having trained as a tailor, may have found work in a sweatshop, offering his services to cloth-ing contractors who operated out of badly ventilated basements or lofts. One major Jewish labor exchange operated on the Whitechapel Road. Candidates would huddle on the pavement in packed, anxious lines while employers looked them over and chose the ones who looked as if they could stand the most gruel-ing work schedule without collapsing. Once the recruiting was complete, the din of hundreds of machines at work literally made the air hum. The British publication the *Lancet* observed in 1884, "At all hours of the day and night, the street resounds with the rattle and whir of the innumerable sewing machines, and the windows shine with the flare of gas."

Ephraim remained in London with his young wife for two years, during which time another son, Alex, was born on March 6, 1884. Soon after the child's birth, Ephraim decided to move his family out of the East End, where congestion, squalor, and anti-Semitic sentiments among the native population made living conditions only slightly more bearable than they had been in Rus-sia. Gangs also posed a danger and held potential future appeal for his sons: by 1888, the year the Ripper murders gave Whitechapel the historic bloodstain it still bears, there were dozens of hoodlum bands roaming the streets, all of them well versed in the art of fleecing drunken sailors, shaking down honest trades-men for protection money, robbing and assaulting lone prostitutes, and murder-ing one another in one pitched battle after another. At least two—the Bessara-bians and the Odessans—were Russian, like the Lefkowitzes, but this hardly rendered them more acceptable to their countrymen than the homegrown gangs such as the Hoxton High Rips (who were initially suspected of committing the Ripper murders), the Green Gate Gang, or the Old Nichol Gang.

As soon as his finances permitted, Lefkowitz moved his family from London to the Scottish port city of Glasgow, where a large Russian-Jewish community already existed. They reached their new home in the spring of 1884. The reasoning behind this particular relocation has been lost to history, but it would be their last move before they finally went to America.

A high percentage of the refugees who had accompanied the Lefkowitzes on the first leg of their flight from their beleaguered homeland had gone to the United States. The size and legendary prosperity of this haven across the ocean had been drawing immigrants for decades. Ephraim and Sarah's neighbors in Glasgow probably showed them letters written by relatives who were hard at work, making their fortunes in America's cities. Judging from these transatlantic missives, the streets were not quite paved with gold, but if you worked hard enough, your future could be.

The prospect of working long hours in exchange for a gilded future did not deter a young couple who had known little but hardship for most of their marriage. At any rate, they were less concerned about their own opportunities than those of their two boys and any additional children who might come along. In June 1884, after promising to send for Sarah, Hyman, and Alex as soon as he could afford to do so, Ephraim boarded the *State of Georgia* and began his journey.

⚓ ⚓ ⚓

Much has been said, orally and in print, about the misery that transatlantic steerage passengers often had to endure. One such traveler later noted with vivid and nauseating detail:

> On board the ship we became utterly dejected. We were all herded together in a dark, filthy compartment in the steerage. . . . Wooden bunks had been put up in two tiers. . . . Seasickness broke out among us. Hundreds of people had vomiting fits, throwing up even their mother's milk. . . . As all were crossing the ocean for the first time, they thought their end had come. The confusion of cries became unbearable. . . . I wanted to escape from the inferno but no sooner had I thrust my head forward from the lower bunk than someone above me vomited straight onto my head. I wiped the vomit away, dragged myself onto the deck, leaned against the sea, and lay down half-dead upon the deck.[17]

Most got through it by envisioning the better life that surely lay ahead. Sometimes one had to pass through hell to escape the devil.

Like their British counterparts, the Americans had universally condemned the pogroms. On February 1, 1882, the same day that London hosted a similar event, New York's leading citizens responded to former President Ulysses S. Grant's call for a mass meeting at Chickering Hall. Mayor William R. Grace presided, and the speakers included ex-Secretary of State Everts. Everyone present expressed sympathy for the plight of the Russian Jewry, and recognized that active assistance to incoming refugees, and not mere protesting of the Russian atrocities, was required to relieve suffering. Philanthropist Jacob H. Schiff got the ball rolling by providing a generous financial donation to the cause.

The welcome that the American people extended via proclamations published in the newspapers was genuine enough; the opening up of the West led to farmers in New England, Connecticut, and other Eastern states deserting their properties to seek more attractive financial prospects on the frontier. The refugees were encouraged to come and restabilize U.S. agricultural resources. Kiev-born Herman Rosenthal, who would condemn the oppression of his people in "The Martyrdom of the Russian Jew," founded the first agricultural colony on Sicily Island, in eastern Louisiana, and assisted sixty families in getting settled. He also helped twenty more stake their claim to farmland in the southeastern tip of what would later become South Dakota. Similar assistance and gifts of land were granted to the first wave of immigrants in other states by organizations and workers whose desire to help was as genuine as Rosenthal's.

Ephraim Lefkowitz never headed for green pastures in Louisiana or South Dakota. After passing the Castle Garden inspection, he traveled into New York City and took accommodations in a Manhattan tenement. For months he worked in a tailoring shop from dawn until dark, and by the spring of 1885 had saved enough to bring his wife and sons over from Britain.

♔ ♔ ♔

Almost three-quarters of the Jews who came to New York City before the First World War congregated and settled in Manhattan's Lower East Side, a vast and eroded territory east of Broadway and below Fourteenth Street. One newly arrived immigrant could not conceal his dismay at the sights that greeted him when he first ventured nervously into its midst, seeking an uncle who had preceded him:

> Orchard Street. . . . The crush and the stench were enough to suffocate one: dirty children were playing in the street, and perspiring Jews were pushing carts and uttering wild shrieks. . . . Division Street, Bayard Street, Canal Street, Allen, Ludlow, and Essex streets with their dark tenements, filthy sidewalks, saloons on every corner, sinister red lights in the vestibules of many small frame houses—all these shattered my illusions of America and made me terribly homesick for the beautiful green hills of my native Vilna . . .[18]

Its more unappealing features aside, the area had long been a magnet for those escaping oppression. Among its earliest refugees were ex-slaves. The Irish, Germans, Italians, and Jews followed in successive waves, settling into districts that soon assumed the character of the inhabitants. In the case of the Jews, a unique universal community was built based on what author Joyce Mendelsohn described as "family and hard work, love of learning, religious commitment, and social justice."[19]

Within this greater whole were smaller Jewish enclaves clustered geographically based on their country of origin. Those from Russia, Poland, Lithuania, and the Ukraine settled along Grand Street south to Monroe, between the East River and the Bowery. Hungarian Jews congregated in an area bordered by Houston and East Tenth streets, between Avenue B and the East River. Galicians were east of Clinton Street and south of the Hungarian district, between Houston and Broome. Romanian Jews resided west of Allen Street, their area stretching as far as Forsyth, bounded on the north and south by Grand and Houston streets.[20] These boundaries would shift, flex, and expand as the years passed and Jews began arriving from countries such as Greece, Turkey, the Balkan states, and Syria.

Like Lefkowitz, the Eastern European newcomers arrived in America with little money but a determination to succeed. Long forbidden to farm in Russia, they had instead developed artisan skills that garnered them employment, however irregular or poorly paid, in the clothing manufacturing trade. New York, which was already the garment capital of the United States, was ready to take what they had to offer in terms of skilled work. Those with more of an entrepreneurial inclination became peddlers, selling all types of merchandise on the street or from door to door, and those who saved enough capital opened their own coffeehouses, stores, and other businesses.

Economic necessity forced the majority of the new arrivals to live in tenement accommodations. Jacob Riis, the famous photographer and author of *How the Other Half Lives*, described the typical building and its inhabitants. He wrote, quoting a public document:

> It is generally a brick building from four to six stories high on the street, frequently with a store on the first floor which, when used for the sale of liquor, has a side opening for the benefit of the inmates and to evade the Sunday law; four families occupy each floor, and a set of rooms consists of one or two dark closets, used as bedrooms, with a living room twelve feet by ten. The staircase is too often a dark well in the centre of the house, and no direct through ventilation is possible, each family being separated from the other by partitions. Frequently the rear of the lot is occupied by another building three stories high with two families on a floor.

The aforementioned building did not represent the lowest common denominator. On the contrary, it was positively palatial compared to some tenement housing Riis had come across. He once visited a Crosby Street building that had recently played grim host to a double suicide. A man and wife, both immigrants, had taken poison because they were "tired." "There was no other explanation," Riis wrote, "and none needed when I stood in the room in which they had lived." It was a dismal attic room with a tiny ceiling window and barely enough space to turn around in. He inspected another apartment in the same building and noted, appalled, "Three short steps either way would have measured its full extent."[21]

Filth was as prevalent as cramping. Once, Riis photographed a group of blind beggars in their grimy room. When the flash from the camera subsided, he saw to his horror that he had accidentally set fire to the rags and papers hanging on the walls. After much struggle and panic, he managed to smother the flames. When he came down to the street, he told a policeman about the near-disaster. To his shock, the officer roared with laughter. "Why," the man chuckled, "don't you know that that house is the Dirty Spoon? It caught fire six times last winter, but it wouldn't burn. The dirt was so thick on the walls, it smothered the fire!"[22]

Prior to the passage of the 1901 Tenement House Act, which forced landlords to make cold water accessible within each apartment, tenants had to get their drinking water from a pump located in the hallway or the backyard, usually next to toilet facilities. People froze in winter if they could not afford a regular coal supply, and during the stifling summer months, the poor air flow forced thousands of tenement dwellers to sleep on fire escapes and roofs. The "rear tenements," decaying wooden structures that leaned against the back walls of larger buildings, were the worst. Accessible from the street only via a damp, dark passage and cut off from direct sunlight or invigorating breezes, they were disease traps especially deadly to children. An 1896 exposé estimated the death rate among children born in these places at 236 per 1,000, or ten times higher than normal.[23]

These hives of poverty, squalor, and vice had concerned reformers and social workers for decades, but serious corrective action was not taken because the influx of immigrants had to be housed somewhere, and space was at a premium—at one point the increased population density rivaled that of Bombay, India.[24] The buildings also tended to be owned by politicians or well-connected business leaders who were all too happy to pack in tenants to the suffocation point if it meant increased rental income. These landlords used whatever political power they could command to prevent serious hits to their cash flow.

However desperate their living conditions were, the Jewish immigrants rarely yielded to despair. They worked hard at whatever jobs were available to them, and took comfort and pleasure in religious and community life. For recreation, those whose philosophies were rendered more secular by youth or Americanization played stuss, went to poolrooms,[25] and frequented theaters and dance halls. Stuss was a variation of faro, and the earliest games were held in tenement rooms, cellars, and storefronts. As the number of players increased, the sessions moved into more lush surroundings that also offered games such as pinochle and twenty-one. These evolving resorts were the forerunners of the modern casino.

For most of the men who sat around tables with drinks at their elbows and cards gripped in their hands, these pursuits were nothing more than a source of recreation and the occasional windfall. But what they also did was empower the growing Jewish underworld.

⚜ ⚜ ⚜

Robert Rockaway, author of *But He Was Good To His Mother,* made the following observation about early Jewish crime in America: "Journalists visiting jails in search of a story frequently noted how they 'rarely saw the face of an Israelite' among the prisoners." Police Inspector Thomas Byrnes published a *Who's Who* of the New York underworld in 1886, with Jewish criminals making up only 4 percent of the entire roster. Four years later, in 1890, Adolph M. Radin visited correctional facilities throughout the state, and his report supported the argument that the Jews were an overwhelmingly law-abiding people. The superintendent of Blackwell's Island told him that there was "no need of a Jewish chaplain in the workhouse. . . . We very seldom have Jews among the prisoners. I do not remember that we have ever had a Jewish female prisoner. You can be proud of your race. You are a good class of citizens."[26]

The University Settlement Society, after studying police and municipal court records for the year 1898, concluded that Jews, when they broke the law, were guilty of "forgery, violation of corporation ordinances, as disorderly persons, both grades of larceny, and of lighter grades of assault."[27] Crimes of fraud, not violence, characterized the typical nineteenth-century Jewish outlaw. That would soon change.

One parodist wrote to a Yiddish-language newspaper in Poland, "Akabiah the son of Charlie said: Consider three things and you will be able to exist in America: forget who you are, wear a mask before those who know you, and do anything you can."[28] He was mocking his new home's fixation on dollar worship, which forced family members to work eighteen-hour days and eroded traditional Jewish community life. But he could have been penning the motto of the rising Jewish gangster. Tough young men, their greed overcoming any fear of community disapproval, began letting their fists and cunning vault them out of poverty.

Ironically, the city's reformers indirectly gave them the means to forgo honest labor and become dedicated criminals. Gambling, billiards, and dancehall attendance were a few of the diversions in which Lower East Side residents indulged to ameliorate a bleak existence. Anti-vice crusaders routinely campaigned against these amusements, tossing those who partook of them outside the bounds of respectability and, when possible, over the barriers of the law itself. In the latter cases, the owners and operators of the illegal establishments became fair prey for shakedown artists and had to rely on gangsters to provide the protection they could no longer expect from the police. Their need was filled by men like Monk Eastman (birth name Edward Eastman), first-generation American Jews who could easily match or even beat the old rough-and-tumble Irish mobs like the Whyos and the Dead Rabbits in the ferocity sweepstakes.

Women also found their underworld niche. Some, like Fredericka "Marm" Mandelbaum, who fenced millions of dollars' worth of stolen goods between 1864 and 1884, enjoyed wealth and political protection. Bessie London, Tillie Gold, and Birdie Pomerantz flourished as "gun-mols," which was nineteenth-century slang for lady pickpockets. Jewish streetwalkers became an increasingly common sight as immigration levels increased. The prostitutes who serviced the first wave of Jewish male arrivals (many of whom, like Ephraim Lefkowitz in 1884, had left their wives and children back in Europe) were mostly of Irish, German, or Negro extraction, but as the years passed, the sisters, daughters, and sometimes widows of these men augmented their numbers. These women charged an average of 50¢ a trick, a considerable amount to pay for sex at a time when the normal take-home pay was $6 to $7 a week. Of this fee, the girls rarely had half left over after the pimps, cops, and local political bosses had taken their cuts. But financially speaking, they were still better off than those who stuck to sweatshop work, scrubbing, and other respectable but poorly paid jobs.

Police Commissioner William McAdoo showed some empathy for the growing number of Jewish women selling themselves. He wrote in 1906, "The horrors of the sweatshop, the awful sordidness of life in the dismal tenement, the biting, grinding poverty, the fierce competition, the pitiful wages for long hours of toil under unwholesome conditions, physical depression, and mental unhappiness are all allied with the temptation to join the better clad, better fed, and apparently happier [people]."[29]

Working behind—but not alongside—the prostitutes were the pimps, or "cadets," flashily dressed men who, through seduction or force and sometimes both, recruited women to work for them. They paid the police to look the other way and politicians for the right to conduct business in the first place, but that was about it—neither cops nor local "bosses" offered them or their women anything in terms of protection from other, stronger, underworld predators. They opted to hire gangsters like Monk Eastman, tying prostitution and gangland together economically as well as socially. Since the flesh trade was worth millions annually, the Jewish gangs grew even stronger.

♧ ♧ ♧

Many nineteenth-century New York politicians viewed immigrants like the Lefkowitzes as political poison and acknowledged them only to the extent of initiating or supporting oppressive legislation. Timothy J. "Big Tim" Sullivan was a noted exception.

An Irish immigrant's son who had been reared in poverty, Sullivan perceived the various waves of newcomers not as nuisances, but as valuable political resources. Muckraking writer George Kibbe Turner might have been quoting Big Tim when he wrote in 1909, "These people—not the little froth of life in gay hotels and theaters and on Broadway—made the real New York—and make it still."[30] Sullivan endeared himself to them by participating in their festivals, religious holidays, and public ceremonies—and by digging deep into his pockets to eliminate such distressing circumstances as empty larders, unpaid rent, and fines imposed by zealous magistrates. They in turn voted as Sullivan directed at election time, making him a Lower East Side powerhouse and even vaulting him into the State Assembly for a brief period. His constituents revered him, and those who owned businesses hung his portrait in places of honor, like monarchists proclaiming devotion and fealty to a reigning sovereign.

The smiling, blue-eyed six-footer, who was also known as "Dry Dollar" and "the Big Feller," surrounded himself with political aides who were mostly family members: his brothers Paddy and Dennis; cousins Christie, Florrie, and Little Tim; and half-brother Larry Mulligan. For years he and his cronies headquartered in one saloon after another, and when a growing public profile necessitated a move to better surroundings, Sullivan took a suite at the Occidental Hotel, where an erotic fresco on its bar ceiling attracted thirsty thrill seekers in droves.[31]

A *Times* reporter once accused him of heading a secret gambling commission consisting of four men who collected the protection money and granted the necessary permissions for a gambling house to operate. Although Sullivan never acknowledged leading such a collective, the paper said that it consisted of "a commissioner who is head of one of the city departments, two state senators, and the dictator of the poolroom syndicate of this city."[32] Those claiming to be in the know identified the group as Sullivan, gambling kingpin Frank Farrell (whose betting palace The House with the Bronze Door was a magnet for the carriage trade), state Senator McLaughlin, and Police Chief Big Bill Devery. They also were said to act as an informal regulatory body, listening to grievances, imposing judgments, and making sure the industry did not become so blatant that reformers zeroed in. Gamblers who defied them or their edicts were warned or sent out of town.

Big Tim looked out for the common people and became a much-loved figure in his district. His annual Christmas dinner fed more than 5,000 Bowery derelicts, and in summertime he sponsored clambakes that tenement dwellers looked forward to for weeks. But no district leader maintained his position without catering to the locale's darker element, and Sullivan was as attentive to the needs of the gangs as he was to the plight of the immigrants, given the value of the former as strike forces at the polls. In April 1889, Inspector Thomas

Byrnes asked the Legislature for a peremptory bill allowing him to arrest on sight all criminals he came across in the city on the day of the Centennial celebration the following month. The Senate unanimously passed the bill, but Big Tim, whose chain of Bowery and Five Points saloons was patronized by said criminals, held it up in the Assembly. Byrnes was livid and pilloried Sullivan in the press as a companion of such vile characters as Peter Barry, one of the bloody Whyos gang leaders, and Dan Driscoll, who had been hanged for murder. Sullivan responded to the inspector's barrage by taking the floor of the Assembly and denying that he associated closely with thieves and gangsters. He claimed to have been too busy working to support his widowed mother since he was seven years old. He succeeded in moving his fellow assemblymen to tears and throwing an emotional smokescreen over the essential truth of Byrnes's accusations.[33]

Big Tim was the Tammany Hall political machine exemplified. This long-running and slyly adaptable organization was founded in 1786 as a politically energetic collective and, after 1839, became the New York affiliate of the Democratic Party. Its original name was the Society of St. Tammany, in honor of a Native American chief of high repute, and its senior officials were dubbed "sachems." One of its earliest "wigwams," or headquarters, was in a building on West Fourteenth Street called Tammany Hall, whose name became synonymous with the group itself.

Any noble intentions that may have accompanied Tammany's inception were buried by ensuing years of unabashed corruption.[34] As early as the 1820s, Grand Sachem Matthew Davis, chief lieutenant of Aaron Burr, was convicted of hatching a gigantic scheme to defraud banks and insurance companies. In 1854, Fernando Wood, a staunch Tammany man, was elected mayor of New York City by a narrow margin. The bulk of Wood's support was concentrated in the "Bloody Old Sixth Ward," where he received 400 more votes than there were registered voters.[35] No one was surprised: sending the same man to vote multiple times was a common stunt that became a Tammany trademark.

William Macy Tweed, Tammany's leader from 1860 until 1872, who preferred to be called "Boss" instead of his actual title of Grand Sachem, took corruption to unprecedented levels. He and his cronies stole an estimated $75 million from New York during the years that he held power, mostly via inflated city contracts. The "Tweed Courthouse," which still stands behind City Hall, was a prime example of their underhanded overpricing: it took ten years to build and cost New Yorkers more than $12 million, which was forty-nine times the original estimate. From 1840 until 1860, the city's debt had risen 80 percent, which was bad enough, but during the Tweed years the amount increased sixfold. Tammany, on the other hand, remained comfortably in the black, thanks to "public services" like the courthouse and the regular cash flow from the vice interests, who regarded payoffs as a necessary operating expense. Gamblers, madams, dive operators, and assorted criminals bought immunity from the law by yielding a portion of their income to Tammany's local police representatives, who kept a percentage and made sure their political masters got the rest.

During the 1871 New York Democratic Convention, a *Times* editor was infuriated when an official, speaking on behalf of the organizers, made a stirring promise to "cleanse the party," while admitting Tammany delegates without protest. "Is it 'cleansing the party' to take thieves by the hand, listen to their soft words, and accept with acclamation their hypocritical and impudent professions of virtuous intention?" the editor complained. "Is it 'cleansing the party' to embrace Mr. Tweed's dummies, with their vile record of plunder, and fraud, and forgery, and to be content with frothy denunciation of crimes, while forming a close alliance, defensive and offensive, with the criminals?"[36]

Tweed was finally driven from his throne into the Ludlow Street Jail thanks to a joint effort by future governor Samuel Tilden, political cartoonist Thomas Nash (who depicted the Tammany machine as an insatiable tiger in his hard-hitting and popular drawings), and the frustrated *Times* editors. He was succeeded by the more subtle Honest John Kelly, who came up with the system of installing district captains in each election ward to oversee local affairs and keep voter sentiment favorable to the machine. At the time that Ephraim and Sarah Lefkowitz were beginning their lives as Americans, the reigning Tammany boss was Richard Croker, whose proclaimed motto was, "I am in politics for what I can get out of it."[37] Croker, who had once been tried for murder, was a malignant, self-absorbed figure who became virtually untouchable when his handpicked candidate, Robert A. Van Wyck, became the first mayor to govern New York after its five boroughs had been amalgamated into a single huge metropolis.

Tammany survived for as long as it did because it altered its ideologies to match popular sentiment or accommodate social change. The machine had at one time been staunchly xenophobic: its earliest constitution dictated that only native-born Americans could become sachems. But political necessity dictated a reversal in attitude. The rising tide of immigration symbolized a flood of new voters, and catering to these foreign, friendless arrivals was not inconsistent with the Jeffersonian policy of championing the poor. When the Irish began crowding into New York during the 1840s, the machine's officials waited at the docks with promises of food, shelter, and employment, and therefore captured their votes the moment they stepped off of the leaky, foul-smelling vessels that had brought them across the Atlantic. When bribery failed, the leaders resorted to violence via the gangs that were beholden to them. Their formula worked, for although the public occasionally revolted against the Tammany politicians, especially in the wake of a scandal, they managed to weather all storms and remain a strong force in city and state politics.

It's reasonable to assume that, either directly or indirectly, the Lefkowitzes benefited at some point from the largesse of Big Tim Sullivan or one of his cronies. More than twenty years later, the charismatic politician would also figure strongly in an event that would directly impact the life of their fourth son.

♔ ♔ ♔

May 13, 1888

A dense fog settled over the Hudson River, accompanied by heavy blasts of wind and rain. Ships dropped anchor to wait out the storm. Capt. Jacob DuBois of the steamship *Dawego* told reporters that he had been navigating the Hudson for thirty-six years and in all that time had never seen such thick fog. The summer schedule had just begun on Coney Island, but when a large number of people arrived at West Brighton on May 12, they found it so enshrouded in fog that they boarded the first train back to New York. No doubt many of them satisfied their desire for spectacle by wandering over to Broadway and Worth Street and watching the old New York Times Building, a city landmark since its construction in 1857, be razed.[38]

Residents of the metropolis also read in that morning's paper about a terrible murder-suicide in Indianapolis that was being attributed to the burgeoning new faith, Christian Science. A housewife named Jordan, a devout practitioner, had administered poison to her young son before slashing her throat with a razor. Her distraught husband proclaimed to a sympathetic public that his wife had never been mentally or emotionally strong, and that her problems were exacerbated by the Christian Science teachings in which she had immersed herself.[39]

That afternoon, dignitaries assembled at the headquarters of the Electric Club on East Twenty-second Street. Thomas Edison was there with a dozen of his phonograph discs containing recorded war memories by Gen. William T. Sherman, Scripture readings by Rev. Robert Collyer and Col. Elliot F. Shepard, and more. When Col. Robert G. Ingersoll said to the phonograph, "You are the most ingenious thing that was ever worked out of the human brain," the compliment was recorded and played back with such clarity that Ingersoll howled with wonder and approval.[40]

Not everyone was an active supporter of progress on that day. An "Old Reader" complained in a letter to the *Times* about the electrical wires that crisscrossed over the city streets and, in his opinion, were disasters waiting to happen. "This very morning," he wrote, "only within a few doors of our place of business, a wire fell, doing more or less damage, and striking upon a truck just between the horse and driver. Both lives were spared, but only by accident. All traffic was delayed, and there lay the wire upon the ground, burning everything it came in contact with and endangering even more lives as the curious and passing public approached. . . . I for one would do something to cause this enemy to be overcome."[41]

It's debatable as to whether Sarah Lefkowitz was aware of any of these events. She could not read or write English, and even if she could, more pressing matters were on her mind, namely the delivery of her fourth child (a third son, Samuel, had been born in 1886). She probably labored with the assistance of a midwife and neighbor women, who also kept an eye on her three boys.

Finally, on May 13, a baby's wail broke the tension at the Lefkowitz flat. Another son had joined the growing household. If tradition was followed, on the eighth day after his birth a *bris,* or ritual circumcision, was held either in the *shul* (synagogue) or at home, and the rabbi or an older family member gave him the name Zelig Zvi.

Zvi means "deer" in Hebrew, and those bearing that name were often nicknamed "Hersh," which was Yiddish for "deer."[42] Family members referred to the boy as *Zelig Hersh* except in the synagogue. He would assume different names for less than honorable reasons once old enough to develop his lifelong contempt for the law.

On that foggy spring day, however, his proud parents and curious brothers had no way of anticipating the baby's criminal future. Perhaps they envisioned him becoming a tailor like his father, or going into another trade like diamond cutting or bookkeeping. The notion that this squalling infant would one day become New York's most feared gangster, known on a first-name basis by policemen, lawyers, politicians, and the American public, would have been too incredible to contemplate.

CHAPTER TWO

BUTCH'S APPRENTICE

Ephraim (who by 1888 was also known outside the home and synagogue as "Frank") and Sarah Lefkowitz would have a total of nine children before their family was complete. Zelig's 1888 birth was followed by those of Anna (1890), Ida (1892), Max (1895), Lena (1897), and Benjamin (1901). All would lead solid, respectable lives. Only Zelig, who was also known as Harry[1] to his non-Jewish and more secular friends, deviated.

He was a slight boy, with huge brown eyes and an appealing smile. He was also short for his age; not until he was in his mid-teens would he experience the growth spurt that took him to his full—and for that era, near-gigantic—height of five feet, eleven inches. He did well in school and could have gone far academically had he chosen to do so, but an innate intelligence and inquisitive mind left him restless and bored with the regimented and colorless lesson plans of the day. He was more drawn to the lively goings-on in the street outside, where the noise and activity levels rivaled any foreign port described in the school texts.[2]

The Lefkowitzes lived at 54 Norfolk Street, occupying four rooms on the third floor. Young Zelig spent most of his time outside, playing with equally spirited boys like Max Zweifach, who was four years older and lived with his parents and siblings a few doors away at 70 Norfolk.[3] Zweifach was another Norfolk Street alumnus who, propelled by ambition and savagery, would become a Monk Eastman gunman and, for a time, the gang's leader.

Norfolk Street during the 1890s was a tenement district like many others, its businesses and institutions catering to the heavily Jewish population. Its daily life was reflective of the routines that the locals had observed back home. Every Friday morning the sidewalks of nearby Hester Street were lined with a long double row of pushcarts offering fish, fruit, vegetables, and other eatables to bewigged housewives who were in a hurry to do all their marketing and cooking before the first three stars appeared in the evening sky, signaling the advent of *Shabbes,* the Jewish Sabbath. Vendors who arrived late set up shop along one of the side streets— Norfolk, Essex, Ludlow, or Suffolk. Sarah Lefkowitz, probably with young Zelig in tow, did her Friday shopping along Hester, her ears assailed by merchants who advertised their wares in a jargon that blended German, Hebrew, Russian, and English: "*Gutes frucht! Metziehs! Drei pennies die whole lot!*" She examined grapes and peaches for freshness, chose potatoes and greens with equal care, and then clustered with other women around the carts offering all types of fish.

Professor Milton Reigenstein, who visited the market in 1897, wrote, "These people love fish, and that dish is generally the pièce de résistance of the Friday evening meal. . . . For fish is good, 'kosher' [clean] food, and a particularly appropriate viand with which to usher in the Sabbath." He was amused at the intensity that accompanied each purchase: "They [the women] know that 'mein mann' is very fond of a fish supper, as well as 'Mosche' and 'Rachele' and little 'Smulche' and all the rest of the multitudinous ghetto household."[4]

Even in 1897, there were clear signs that a boisterous and irreverent new order was replacing the old. On the day of his visit, Reigenstein saw a white bearded, dignified patriarch navigating the crowd, expression serene where others appeared rushed and anxious. "Here is the living semblance of the grand old men of the Old Testament," the professor thought . . . until he saw a local gangster brush by the old man so abruptly that the latter stumbled. The young ruffian not only refused to apologize, he also turned around and grinned mockingly at his victim. The patriarch responded to the flagrant disrespect by raising his staff, lunging at his tormentor, and, as Reigenstein put it, cursing "in a tremendous string of strange oaths—English, German, Hebrew, Russian, and jargon."[5] Such conflicts were not rare; public streets and private homes witnessed daily confrontations between those who lived via traditional values, such as parents and religious figures, and the younger generation that prized materialism and independence over respectable poverty and unquestioning obedience.

Even when marketing day was not in session, the neighborhood crawled with activity. Boarding houses and saloons such as Dennis Kelly's at 165 Norfolk, each with a clientele of local drunks and exotic transients, were sandwiched between groceries, garment stores, and synagogues. Sometimes a local scandal or sensation made the sidewalks and hallways buzz with gossip. In December 1892, a Russian immigrant woman named Leah Lesczynski died at 143 Norfolk, and her 73-year-old daughter informed the astonished authorities that the deceased was 124 years old. If the age claim were true, she was the world's oldest person at the time.[6] A vacation school (a school kept open for half days during the summer months, mostly to keep idle children out of mischief) at 25 Norfolk, which Zelig may have attended, caused a minor uproar in July

1897, when the teacher of the bookkeeping class entertained the students by conducting a mock murder trial instead of the usual scholastic debate. A murderer named Martin Thorn had recently been charged with killing and dismembering one William Guldensuppe, and the teacher, Louis Barankoff, recruited enthusiastic students to assume the roles of the principal players in the tragedy. Guldensuppe's head had never been found, and the children relished discussing its possible fate. The New York Association for Improving the Condition of the Poor, which operated the school, was mortified, but their righteous indignation over the affair came too late.[7]

Zelig would have enjoyed such a show had he witnessed it, as he had no patience with conventions, rules, and restrictions. He was also surprisingly astute for his age. In September 1894, thousands of cloakmakers, tailors, and other clothing trade professionals went on strike to protest their dual yoke of low wages and soul-draining work hours. By December, alarming numbers of them were in desperate circumstances, having been evicted for nonpayment of rent and forced to rely on bread and herring from relief organizations to ward off starvation. Zelig, who was only six at the time, must have been struck by the elevated level of suffering, for he asked his parents why so many of their neighbors were poor. The answer about lack of money made him thoughtful. Learning that dollar bills were created using paper and ink, he made a childish attempt to tackle neighborhood poverty by spending long hours drawing his own money and was genuinely baffled and upset to realize that his creations did not have value as currency.[8] No one had an answer that satisfied him when he demanded to know why those in authority did not just print more money so that doctor bills could be paid and larders and coal bins stocked.

"Zelig was not the type of kid you could satisfy by telling him, 'You just can't' or 'Because that's the way it is,'" says historian Joseph Lefkowitz. "If you couldn't give him answers or reasons that made sense to him, he just went out and made his own rules."

His dissatisfaction with rules and barriers stemmed from the reality that in late-nineteenth-century New York, they were not in his favor. His Russian-Jewish heritage and Lower East Side residency combined to make him an undesirable in the eyes of those outside his own community. Even the Sanitary Aid Society of the Tenth Ward, whose members included such social and political luminaries as Theodore Roosevelt and former Mayor Abram Hewitt, and whose aim was supposedly the overall improvement of health and sanitary conditions on the Lower East Side, referred to immigrants like the Lefkowitzes as "human maggots" who required the society's guidance to avoid collapsing into lives of poverty, immorality, and crime.[9] The long-assimilated German Jews who poured money into charities and integration projects kept them at arm's length, denying them admittance to Sabbath services at their Reform temple on Fifth Avenue and noting in their weekly paper, the *Jewish Messenger,* "The surroundings of the Fiji Islander are more conducive to health than those that environ thousands of Israelites who continue to live in the slums of New York."[10]

In 1892, when Zelig was barely four years old, two epidemics, typhus and cholera, hit the city. The first was traced to the arrival of the immigrant ship *Massilia,* which had unloaded some infected Russian-Jewish passengers, and the second led to President Benjamin Harrison's temporary halt on immigration and the ousting of scores of Eastern European immigrant Jews from their New York homes to nearby "quarantine islands." Because many New Yorkers still subscribed to the "miasma theory" which decreed that disease erupted when decaying organic matter such as rotten food and sewage "infected" the air, those who lived among such environmental factors daily, such as Zelig's family and neighbors, were popularly viewed as the personification of disease, rot, and filth. Less attention was paid to evidence that presented the contrary, such as U.S. Army physician John Shaw Billings's 1890 report stating that the Eastern European Jews had the lowest mortality rates among all immigrant groups and the lowest rates of tuberculosis among the entire New York City population.

Like many American-born children of immigrants, Zelig also experienced an internal conflict brought on by the contrast between the threadbare respectability of the immigrant community and the materialistic, striving American way of life. Not that his father and other immigrants did not try to better their condition. On the contrary, they worked long hours to give their children better opportunities than they had ever known. But minutes away by streetcar was the world of the upper classes, where boys Zelig's age could be seen wearing clothes and playing with toys that were notches above what he had access to. Such spectacles intrigued and frustrated the boy, who tried to move up in the class system, albeit superficially. One day his astonished mother returned from a marketing expedition and found him hard at work, hanging up some richly embroidered but badly soiled curtains. The threadbare yet clean ones that had formerly graced the apartment windows were lying in the middle of the floor. When she demanded to know what was going on, he paused in his task and told her that the new curtains used to belong to "swells" uptown, that he had found them in a refuse heap, and that dirty or not, they gave the Lefkowitz apartment a grandeur it had previously lacked. Sarah's response to this minor attempt at upward mobility can only be surmised.[11]

Contrary to what such behavior implied, the family's lot had improved over the years. Frank Lefkowitz, now well established in the tailoring business, was even in a position to participate in the founding of the Free Help Association, whose aim was to "assist the poor of the City of New York, to encourage self-help among them, and to assist the destitute by gratuitous loans of money without interest and without any charges or fees whatsoever."[12] The association was incorporated in Albany in August 1902, and the main office was in New York City. Lefkowitz was one of the nine directors.[13] Such organizations were offshoots of the *Landsmanshaftn,* or mutual benefit societies, that Jews from the same *shtetl,* or town, formed to care for the disabled, look after widows and orphans, provide financial assistance to those rendered destitute, and arrange traditional Jewish burials. Lefkowitz, a pillar in the community who was noted for his kindly disposition, was a natural leader for such a venture.

His altruism manifested itself to some degree in his son. Zelig, who could not only speak but also read and write English, Hebrew, and Russian, would help illiterate neighbors by scribbling letters for them and reading any replies. He showed interest in and concern for the welfare of the community, as evidenced by his question about the reasons behind the prevalent poverty. To those whom he considered friends, he was fiercely protective and unfailingly loyal. But he had a wild streak, and that, coupled with his lack of regard for social convention and his desire for material gain that did not befit his station, took him off the straight and narrow before he had even reached his teens.

He was not the only one from his neighborhood who fell victim to this type of temptation. For years the *New York Times* published a column called "City and Vicinity," which tallied and described arrests, court appearances, accidents, and related dramas or tragedies. Norfolk Street residents made regular appearances; some were Zelig's immediate neighbors.

> For picking pockets in front of a Sixth Avenue store on Saturday afternoon, Abram Finkel, fourteen years old, living at 57 Norfolk Street, was yesterday arraigned at the Jefferson Market Court, and turned over to the Gerry Society to await an examination.
>
> —December 24, 1894

> Twelve-year old Jacob Rosen, a newsboy, living at 55 Norfolk Street, and Louis Schwartz, a tailor, nineteen years old, of 105 Norfolk Street, played craps in a saloon Saturday night. Rosen lost 50 cents, and made such an outcry that a policeman arrested both him and the tailor. In the Essex Market Police Court, yesterday, Justice Burke discharged Rosen and fined Schwartz $2.
>
> —March 4, 1895

Corrupting influences were plentiful in the Lower East Side. Broadway, New York City's oldest street, which ran northward from the Battery and consisted of several miles of retail shops, office buildings, hotels, and theaters, was a favorite stomping ground of Zelig and his friends. Despite its situation as a major commercial center, it was lined with dives, brothels, and gambling houses that were marginally less degraded than those along the waterfront and on the side streets. A popular 1880s quip declared that you could stand at the corner of Broadway and Houston Street and fire a shotgun in any given direction without hitting an honest man. Ten years later things had not appreciably improved: when a theft victim shouted at Broadway and Forty-third, "There's the man who stole my watch!" twelve men ran for cover.[14]

Another thoroughfare that attracted adventurous youngsters was the Bowery. Social historian Luc Sante wrote, ". . . . until fairly recently, the Bowery always possessed the greatest number of groggeries, flophouses, clip joints, brothels, fire sales, rigged auctions, pawnbrokers, dime museums, shooting galleries, dime-a-dance establishments, fortune-telling salons, lottery agencies, thieves markets, and tattoo parlors, as well as theaters of the second, third, fifth, and tenth rank. It is also a fact that the Bowery is the only major thoroughfare in New York never to have a church built on it."[15] Zelig probably became acquainted with its questionable attractions as soon as he was old enough to leave Sarah's sight for extended periods of time, if not before. Dissipated as it was, the Bowery contained the greatest percentage of social clubs, businesses, and amusements aimed at the lower classes, and the Lefkowitzes might have patronized its more respectable stores.

Whether in the commercial hell of Broadway or the degraded depths of the Bowery, Zelig learned from the worst possible examples what New York had to offer an intelligent but greedy and rebellious boy. By the time he was twelve years old, he was supplementing the family income by selling newspapers, and lining his own pockets by picking others'.

♔ ♔ ♔

There was once a time when pickpockets operated in the shadow of the noose, their crime being punishable by death. (No doubt they also made excellent money "working" the crowds who attended the public hanging of one of their number.) By the time Zelig Lefkowitz joined the ranks of the New York "guns," as pickpockets were then called, prison had replaced the gallows as the justice system's method of dealing with them. A hostile public would have preferred that the punishment remained the same. Credit cards were decades in the future, and many did not trust banks, so those anticipating a major purchase, such as a real estate transaction, carried huge sums of cash on their person. In a crowded street, train station, or trolley, one's life savings could be purloined in a matter of seconds. Pickpockets were responsible for relieving citizens of millions of dollars annually.

Unlike the other major urban menace—rowdy, bloodthirsty New York gangs such as the Whyos, Dead Rabbits, and Plug Uglies—pickpockets were rarely violent. A small percentage were "knockdown" artists whose modus operandi was to physically assault the victim; snatch the purse, wallet, or other valuable object; and run. But most pickpockets refrained from such aggressive behavior. They operated by taking advantage of the victim's distraction and ignorance. To allay suspicion and achieve their ends, they dressed fashionably and conducted themselves unobtrusively in public. Children were even more successful than adults, especially if they were neat and appealing, not dirty, ragged street arabs.

Like many legitimate trades and occupations, picking pockets had its divisions, hierarchies, and jargon. A pickpocket in the general sense was a "gun." The streets, trolleys, stores, and other locations where they preyed on the public were "beats." "Gun mobs" were packs of two or more consisting of "stalls," who jostled the target, and "tools," who fleeced the indignant party while the stall apologized profusely. "Carbuzzers" worked the passengers on the public transportation systems, "reader merchants" hovered like slickly dressed vultures around banks, and "kirkbuzzers" and "groaners" fleeced attendees at churches and charity sermons respectively. "Moll buzzers" targeted female victims exclusively. When word arrived of a major public event, such as a county fair, popular dignitary's visit, or funeral of a high-profile public figure, some pickpockets would do a "jump out," or travel to the location and work the crowds.[16]

Being a newsboy, Zelig Lefkowitz likely practiced the "newspaper dodge," the workings of which were recalled with nostalgia by pickpocket Jim Caulfield:

> "I would board a car with a couple of newspapers, would say 'News, boss?' to some man sitting down, would shove the paper in front of his face as a stall, and then pick his 'super' [pocket watch] or even his entire 'front' [watch and chain]. If you can stand for a newspaper under your chin, I can even get your socks."[17]

Boys Zelig's age were eagerly sought by Fagins—adults or older youths who trained them to steal purses, wallets, watches, and other valuables. Caulfield explained, "A boy can get next to a woman in a car or on the street more easily than a man can. He is not so apt to arouse her suspicions; and if he is a handsome, innocent-looking boy, and clever, he can go far in this line of graft." Alfred Henry Lewis, in *The Apaches of New York*, noted, "Children from twelve to fourteen do the best work [picking pockets]. Their hands are small and steady; their confidence has not been shaken by years in prison."

The Fagins trained their apprentices thoroughly. Some rigged a dressmaker's dummy with a coat that had small bells stitched in strategic places. These coats were filled with wallets, watches, and other valuables. Only when pupils could remove every item without ringing a single bell were they deemed ready to go out into the world and begin stealing for their master.

Herbert Asbury, in *The Gangs of New York*, wrote that young Zelig got his start in the pocket-picking racket via a Monk Eastman gangster named Crazy Butch (real name Simon Erenstoft), a well-known Fagin. He came from a disjointed household and had not even reached his teens when he began supporting himself by stealing. In 1896, at the age of thirteen, he stole a young Irish setter dog from its uptown household, named it Rabbi, and taught it to snatch handbags from strolling women. By the time Rabbi's training was complete, all Erenstoft had to do was point out the victim to the dog and retreat to the corner of Willett and Stanton streets. Minutes later, the proud canine would come trotting up with the loot.[18]

It was a simple matter for Butch to progress from training dogs to teaching children. He was frequently arrested over the years for inducing boys to steal. During one court appearance on June 30, 1904, an agent of the Children's Society had one of Butch's pupils, eleven-year-old Izzy Levine, circle him in front of the judge and make a few quick, barely discernible hand movements. When asked to show what he had scored, Levine proudly held up the agent's wallet and handkerchief. After viewing that display and listening to testimony from a Mr. Axman of the Hebrew Educational Alliance, who stated that Erenstoft had actively recruited and trained juvenile thieves, Judge Zeller could barely contain his wrath. "You are the meanest, most despicable thief I ever encountered," he snapped before slapping the twenty-one-year-old Fagin with a $500 fine and one-year prison term, the maximum allowable penalty for that offense. Erenstoft escalated the situation by swearing loudly and grabbing for an inkstand, which he would have thrown at Judge Zeller had an officer not intervened. He was hauled out of the courtroom, red-faced and hurling curses all the way.[19]

Erenstoft could use his hands for more than picking pockets. When riled, he was a berserker, making him someone the warring gangs could use. Butch joined the crew captained by Monk Eastman, who was turn-of-the-century New York's most famous gangster boss. Erenstoft endeared himself to the big man by wreaking mayhem when ordered and by intentionally catering to Eastman's personal passion for bicycling and pigeons.[20] He organized an association called the Squab-Wheelmen and rented a hall on Forsyth Street where Eastman, who was proud godfather of the association, was known to play pool.

Since Zelig Lefkowitz was destined to become an Eastman heir as well as a master pickpocket, he very well may have been one of the Squab-Wheelmen's younger followers. But even if Erenstoft had not groomed him for success as a "gun" and, in all likelihood, introduced him to the great Monk, Zelig would have drifted into the gangs naturally. One of his closest friends from Norfolk Street, Max Zweifach, was running with the Eastmans by 1903.

👑 👑 👑

Zweifach went by the alias of Kid Twist. New York City police officer Cornelius Willemse knew Zweifach personally and remembered the gangster in his memoirs with distaste, referring to him as a "brutal, double-crossing criminal whose own men hated him. He couldn't be trusted even by his friends."[21] It was an overstatement: Zweifach would be noted for sadistic and treacherous behavior, but only to those who actively opposed him or presented an obstacle to his designs. When it came to friends like Zelig, he was loyal without reservation.

Zweifach was born, probably in Austria, on March 14, 1884, to tailor Adolph Zweifach and the former Hanna Reci, who was of Italian heritage.

When Zweifach Senior, who opened his own tailoring business,[22] became a naturalized American citizen on October 23, 1893, nine-year-old Max, his mother, and foreign-born siblings became Americans, too.[23] There were seven children in total born to the parents, although only five survived past infancy.

Max grew to a height of five feet, ten inches, which was unusually tall for that era, and had straight, dark hair that he wore slicked back in the style of the day. George Kibbe Turner referred to him in a 1909 exposé of the underworld as a "hatchet-faced young Jew." It was a harsh description. Zweifach's profile was sharp and angular, but by no means unpleasant. His most unsettling feature was his eyes, which were cold, like a dead mackerel's.

By all accounts, the Zweifach children were bright. Max's sister, Dorothea, received mention in the *New York Times*' June 21, 1903, edition when an essay she submitted as part of a city-wide competition won a silver medal. She became a schoolteacher. A brother, Daniel, became a gang leader in his own right, calling himself Kid Slyfox[24] or Dinny Fox. Dinny was a favored election enforcer for the Tammany Hall mob under Big Tim Sullivan and used Sullivan's backing to acquire a string of poolrooms and stuss houses.

Max Zweifach's first recorded court appearance took place in June 1899, when he was fifteen. On June 10, a gambler named Joseph Kelly parked his bicycle in front of a store near the southeast corner of Thirty-third Street and Third Avenue. He noticed Zweifach loitering nearby but thought little of it. When Kelly emerged from the store five minutes later, the bicycle and the thieving teenager were gone. He reported the theft, and soon received word from Officer John W. England of the bicycle squad that his property had been recovered from a hock shop run by a man named Baker. Baker turned in Zweifach, who had taken the bicycle to a Rivington Street store to be re-enameled and nickel-plated before putting it on the underground market.

Max, accompanied by attorney A. S. Rosenthal, appeared before Judge Crane on June 10 and answered a routine set of questions. He confirmed his name and age, and said he had been born in Austria. When asked his occupation, Zweifach showed a flair for dark humor. "Bicycles," he replied. He pleaded not guilty to the charge of grand larceny. Because he was under sixteen, Crane committed him to the custody of the New York Society for the Prevention of Cruelty to Children until Adolph Tanz, a friend of his father, came forward with the required $500 bail. When he appeared before Judge McMahon in July, Zweifach chose honesty as the best policy, probably for the last time in his criminal career, and pleaded guilty. The record does not show that he served any time for the offense, so Kelly may have dropped the charge upon receiving a compensation offer from Adolph Zweifach, or the punishment may simply have been a fine.

Zelig Lefkowitz was not so lucky when his turn came.

⚓ ⚓ ⚓

It probably wasn't the first time that Zelig had been caught picking pockets. A *New York Times* article published after his death noted that he was an acknowledged master of the "baby game," the slang term for using tears and youthful appeal to dissuade a crime victim from pressing charges. Rather than use his fists or a weapon to free himself when caught, he would weep copiously and melt the heart of most complainants. Sooner or later, however, practitioners of the baby game ran into a victim who proved immune to their wiles.

At around noon on Sunday, July 7, 1901, Zelig and his friend Jacob Goldberg, a fellow newsboy,[25] spotted seventy-one-year-old Mary Sheehan walking along Scammel Street. Although Zelig would later be known for protecting the elderly, on that hot summer afternoon he simply saw an easy mark. After a hurried conference, they moved in on her.

Goldberg blocked Mrs. Sheehan's path on the sidewalk, bumping into her and holding her attention long enough for Zelig to grab her purse, which contained $6.83. Both boys attempted to run, but two male passers-by who had witnessed the incident closed in on them and grabbed them. Zelig dropped the purse on the pavement during the struggle that followed. Two police officers named Hayes and Shea, summoned by witnesses or attracted by the noise, arrived and took Zelig and Jacob into custody. Zelig, who said his name was Harry Smith,[26] wept and pleaded for forgiveness, but Mary Sheehan told Hayes and Shea that she wanted to press charges.

Learning about Zelig's arrest must have been a mortifying experience for Frank and Sarah Lefkowitz. They were respected in the community. Frank was a successful tailor who was in the process of organizing the Free Help Association. Zelig's older brother, Hyman (who had Americanized his name to Herman), augmented the family honor by fighting in the Spanish-American War.[27] He came home a teenage military hero and obtained a job in a printing shop, where he worked long hours to assist Frank in supporting his mother and siblings. Zelig's thievery was a black mark, but the family stood behind him nonetheless. To protect the Lefkowitz name from public embarrassment, Sarah appeared at the station where her son and his friend were being held and identified herself as his mother, but added that she was a widow by the last name of Smith.

Zelig and Jacob appeared before Magistrate Charles Flammer the following day. Zelig told the magistrate that he was sixteen years old,[28] a schoolboy when not selling newspapers, and that he was not guilty of the larceny charge being pressed against him. The boys were released on bail and ordered to appear before Judge L. M. McMahon on July 26. That day brought good news for Jacob: McMahon released him. But Zelig was sentenced to the House of Refuge.[29]

The New York House of Refuge was the country's first reformatory aimed at juveniles. It was the brainchild of the Society for the Prevention of Pauperism, organized in 1816, which had studied American prison conditions for years and offered scathing public criticism of the "spirit of revenge" currently underlying the treatment of prisoners regardless of age or severity of crime. In 1824, the "Managers of the Society for the Reformation of Juvenile Delinquents in the City of New York" was incorporated, and two years later a statute passed authorizing courts all over the state to send juvenile convicts to the new institution.

The state Legislature began providing funds for the proposed reformatory through legislative appropriation and revenue garnered from a "head tax" levied on incoming transatlantic passengers and sailors, as well as the licensing fees paid by New York taverns, playhouses, circuses, and other public entertainments. The Society had always blamed juvenile delinquency on immigration, alcoholism, and morally degrading commercial entertainment, so money for the institution was accepted from these sources with a sense of righteous entitlement.

In July 1824, the Society had collected enough funds to purchase part of an old federal arsenal at the intersection of Broadway and Twenty-third Street, and the reformatory opened in January 1825 with an inmate population of six boys and three girls. Within a decade, more than 1,600 youthful offenders were admitted, and in recognition of a necessary public service, the government granted the Society $125,000 to construct a newer, larger facility on Randalls Island in the East River.

Zelig was escorted to his temporary new surroundings after McMahon pronounced sentence. After an admission interview, the record clerk noted in the record:

> Aged 16 February 3, 1901. Born in New York of Russian parents, Frank and Sarah. The father is dead. The mother lives at 139 Suffolk Street, NY, where an older brother supports the home. There is one younger sister. The mother is temperate and Hebrew.
>
> Harry was a newsboy at City Hall. He has attended school and can read and write. He was never arrested before. He was sent here for picking pockets."[30]

The birth date, home address, and comment about being fatherless were all smokescreens. Zelig or his parents (probably all three in unison) insulated the Lefkowitz family against exposure and shame by twisting most of the facts about his personal history. The New York newspapers of the period published court calendar listings that named plaintiffs, defendants, the judges and prosecutors handling each case, etc., and many criminals resorted to aliases and mock histories to spare their families any repercussions that could arise from name recognition.

In January 1903, after he had been in the House of Refuge for eighteen months, a caseworker with the initials "A.E.A" visited the Lefkowitz home at 54 Norfolk Street to conduct a pre-release visit. The official noted that the building was a three-story tenement housing six families in total, that it did not harbor a liquor saloon, and that the Lefkowitzes occupied four sparsely furnished but clean rooms. Zelig's eight siblings were questioned, the younger ones assuring their visitor that they attended school regularly. The final report was a favorable one and resulted in Zelig being paroled into his mother's custody on March 4.[31]

The final notation on his House of Refuge record is dated August 1904 and states, "Found in police lineup." These four words are proof positive that the first thing he probably did upon release was renew his acquaintance with an old friend who, in 1903, was a rising star in the ranks of the Lower East Side gangs.

CHAPTER THREE

MONK EASTMAN JUNIOR

Max Zweifach had graduated from thieving to murder while Zelig was in the House of Refuge. On August 17, 1903, he and an associate, Thomas "Biff" Comiskey, were lounging about in William Salzman's candy and cigar store at 98 Goerck Street, one of their favorite haunts. Salzman was away on business and had left the store temporarily in Zweifach's charge. John Bayard, alias Mugsy, a thug in the employ of Monk Eastman foe Harry "Big Dave" Bernstein, came in with four or five friends and participated in a card game that ended on ugly terms. Bayard and Zweifach hurled insults at each other, and once sufficiently enraged, went for their guns. When the police arrived, Zweifach was gone and Bayard was lying on the shop floor, arm broken by one bullet and another buried in his abdomen. Asked who shot him, Bayard hissed, "Never mind. I'll get even. I won't tell." He died later that night at Gouverneur Hospital.[1]

To escape the police and his victim's vengeful friends, the young gangster fled to Jersey City, where he hid out overnight at a relative's house. His brother Dinny, who had probably "chatted" with the witnesses to the shooting beforehand, visited and persuaded him to return and give himself up. Zweifach surrendered to Detective Woodle of the Union Market station and was held for the coroner on a charge of murder. It was dropped after Comiskey and other witnesses swore that Bayard had fired the first shot.

The *New York Times* reporter who covered the story noted that Zweifach "was not so much a leader of the Monk Eastman gang as he is a leader of a group of young East Siders on his own account."[2] If true, that changed after the Bayard murder. Zweifach went to work full time for Monk Eastman, who could always use an efficient killer. He was soon joined by his old friend Zelig.

♣ ♣ ♣

Anti-immigration factions liked to think that New York's gang problem had its genesis in the "foreign hordes" that began reaching America's shores during the 1840s. An editorial published in the March 10, 1900, edition of the *New York Times* stated, "Immigration is largely responsible for the great number of habitual criminals among us. Our immigrants are mostly made up of the lower class of Europeans, who bring with them their tendency to crime, and while the elder country is benefited by their leaving its shores, we are injured by their acquisition." The public based such rash judgments on one grain of truth: the criminal element prevailed in the slum districts with a high immigrant population. It's true that the millions who came to America between the mid-1840s (when the Potato Famine brought the Irish in droves) and 1914 had hardened criminals in their ranks, but the street gangs were an American phenomenon brought on by poverty and a sense of alienation. It's also a fact that when the aforementioned editorial was published, a large number of the gangsters were American-born.[3]

Gangs had no shortage of voluntary recruits among the young first-generation Americans who, like Zelig, felt no connection to their parents' Old World traditions but were, as far as the public was concerned, too tainted by foreign parentage to belong anywhere but in the immigrant milieu. Some boys and even girls joined gangs for companionship and recreation, while others were roped into destructive behavior because they simply feared to do otherwise. Lillian Leeban, who later married Zelig gunman Lefty Louis Rosenberg, recalled her own experiences with gang pressure in her 1914 memoir:

> [At my school] there were bands of six or more girls in each class who called themselves "the gang." The leader of this gang was the brightest and boldest of the girls. She would gather us about her in the morning as the last bell was ringing and issue her orders as the captain of a regiment might.
>
> Her plan of campaign was according to her mood. She would say, "We will be good today. Remember, girls, this is a good day. We will treat teacher right." But the next morning the orders would be different. "Let's be bad today. You be bad to teacher, and I will, and all of us." I was in one of the gangs. I was little and timid and dared not stay out. If the leader willed it, I made faces at the teacher when her back was turned or drew pictures of her on the blackboard when she was not looking. . . .
>
> If I told the teacher the truth [about acting up at the behest of the gang] a sound beating awaited me around the corner. The leader would punish me in

this way, and her first assistant would aid in the punishment by pulling my flaxen curls until my head ached. I was afraid to tell my mother, lest she should tell the teacher, and so bring down upon me the wrath of the leader of the gang.[4]

The infamous New York gangs first appeared in recognizable form soon after the Revolution. Smith's Vly Gang, the Bowery Boys, the Broadway Boys, and their like, while rowdy and loving a good brawl, were not full-time criminals like their successors became. Their members maintained regular, legitimate employment as carpenters, dock workers, and in related professions—the turf wars and freelance hooliganism they indulged in were only occasional events in an otherwise run-of-the-mill existence. It wasn't until the 1820s that the first of the truly dangerous criminal collectives appeared, but once established, their presence rotted their surroundings like a social cancer.

They were especially conspicuous in the Five Points slum district (named after a five-street intersection in the Sixth Ward), where they congregated in the grocery stores that doubled as grogshops. Foremost were the Forty Thieves, which was probably the first organized criminal gang in New York City's history. They headquartered in a Centre Street "wet grocery" owned by a woman named Rosanna Peers[5] and made their living by selling the loot they stole from warehouses, stores, and citizens to local fences. At one point they were led by a sadistic brute named Edward Coleman, who pursued and married a beautiful hot-corn girl[6] so that he could live off her earnings. When the money she brought in failed to match his expectations, he beat her to death. He was arrested and convicted of murder and on January 12, 1839, achieved the questionable honor of being the first criminal hanged at the newly constructed Tombs prison.

The "Bloody Old Sixth Ward" also hosted the dives and hangouts of the Kerryonians, the Chichesters, the Roach Guards, the Plug Uglies, and the Shirt Tails, all of whom drew their membership from the burgeoning Irish immigrant community. When the Roach Guards had a factional dispute, a new gang arose from the split ranks—the Dead Rabbits. In the slang of the day, a "dead rabbit" was a tough character, and the group's members fitted the part too well for their enemies' liking. Their activities further connected the name of the Five Points district with lawlessness, vice, and violence.[7]

The Five Points gangs fought one another with gusto but were known to make common cause against the police and the gangs from the Bowery, which included the evolving Bowery Boys, the O'Connell Guards, Atlantic Guards, and the American Guards. When two or more rival bands fought, entire neighborhoods came under siege. It was routine for the war zone to be cordoned off with makeshift barriers of overturned carts and paving stones to prevent police interference. These brawls attracted so many combatants that the police could not do much anyway—the National Guard or the Twenty-seventh Regiment had to be called in. One example that New Yorkers recalled with a shudder for years afterward took place in July 1857, when a dispute between the mayor and the Metropolitan Police Board temporarily left the city without adequate protection.[8] The Dead Rabbits and the Plug Uglies celebrated the Fourth by raiding a clubhouse occupied by the Bowery Boys and the Atlantic Guards at 42 Bowery, triggering a two-day battle that Asbury described as "the most ferocious free-for-all in the history of the city." The *New York Times* of July 6, 1857, published an account of the fight that sounded more like a war correspondent's dispatch than a piece of local, if sanguinary, news:

> Brickbats, stones, and clubs were flying thickly around, and from windows in all directions, and men ran wildly about, brandishing firearms and clubs of almost every sort. Wounded men were lying upon the sidewalks trampled by the crowds that were driven to and fro. Amidst the din and confusion that prevailed, it was almost impossible to tell between whom the fight was raging.

Dozens died in these massive street battles over the years, although the list of reported deaths remained suspiciously low because the fighters carried away as many of their stabbed, battered, and bloody dead as possible before the authorities began tallying.

Gang chieftains like Al Capone, Monk Eastman, Paul Kelly, and Jack Zelig, whose brawling talents were matched if not exceeded by their organizational abilities and business acumen, were years in the future. The bosses of the early New York gangs obtained their bravado through overindulgence in drugs and liquor, and were frequent victims of their own aggression, vices, and stupidity. Brian Boru, who terrorized the Corlears Hook area, passed out drunk one night and was eaten alive by dock rats. Slipsey Ward of the Hook Gang, which preyed on ships moored along the waterfront, tried to take over and rob a large schooner single-handed and suffered greatly for his presumption.[9]

The Whyos, whose name had been generated by their unique and chilling battle cry, appeared after the Civil War and filled the vacuum created by the decline of the Shirt Tails, Plug Uglies, and other early groups, remaining New York City's most powerful gang until death and prison decimated their numbers in the 1890s. Their membership included killers, pickpockets, thieves, dive operators, and brothel keepers. They treated violence as a business instead of a pastime, as evidenced by an eye-opening price list that was taken off a gangster named Piker Ryan:

Punching	$2
Both eyes blacked	$4
Nose and jaw broke	$10
Jacked out	$15
Ear chawed off	$15

Leg or arm broke	$19
Shot in leg	$25
Stab	$25
Doing the big job	$100 and up[10]

The Whyos had their original headquarters in a tough Bowery dive known as The Morgue, because more than a hundred murders had been committed there. They shifted to other hangouts over the years, but their connection to The Morgue's bloody glory stuck. Their earliest leaders were paragons of depravity. "Dandy" John Dolan once used an eye gouger on a businessman who interrupted him during a robbery attempt, and kept the eyes to show off to friends. He was convicted of murder and hanged after a detective who arrested him found the gruesome souvenirs in his possession. Danny Lyons and Dan Driscoll, two more leaders who were also executed for murder, decreed that to even join the gang, one had to have killed at least once. Being a Whyo meant the ongoing commission of burglary, assault, murder, and other mayhem, which led to the gang's leadership keeping a high-priced pair of lawyers, William Howe and Abraham Hummell, on retainer.

Mike McGloin, before following Whyo tradition and going to the gallows for homicide, directed the gang into organized ventures such as extortion, prostitution, and slugging for hire. The aforementioned price list found on Piker Ryan was probably McGloin-inspired. The Whyos' comparative longevity on the New York gang roster can be ascribed to their gaining a controlling interest in almost every type of vice and crime found in the city. They were succeeded in the 1890s by gangs that continued their tradition of mixing business with violence.

The Five Pointers, who at their prime had a membership total of well over 1,000, headquartered at the New Brighton Dance Hall on Great Jones Street and operated in the territory bordered by Broadway and the Bowery, and Fourteenth Street and City Hall Park. Their leader was onetime professional boxer Paolo Vaccarelli, who adopted the alias of Paul Kelly. Author Pat Downey noted in *Gangster City*: "While still a young man, Kelly hung up his gloves, took a job as a foreman for an Italian contractor, and became a padrone."[11] Kelly's crew of thugs and repeaters had helped swing the Second Assembly District primary of September 17, 1901, in favor of Tim Sullivan's man Tom Foley, who was running against Paddy Divver, an old-time Tammany leader. When the final vote awarded a three-to-one victory to Foley, Kelly began a fifty-cent prostitution business in the district, employing an estimated 750 to 1,000 women. He amassed money and power so rapidly that when he assaulted and robbed a man on the street not long after the primary, he received only nine months in jail when the offense—and his previous record—normally dictated a ten- to twenty-year term.[12] When he got out, he opened the New Brighton to serve as his gang's headquarters and began the Paul Kelly Association, of which Big Tim was an honorary member.

Kelly was short, dapper, and prosperous-looking. Rich New Yorkers who got a thrill out of "slumming" in the Five Points saloons and dives would run across him in one of his resorts and assume from his expensive clothing and cultured manner that he was another "slummer." He spoke several languages fluently, kissed a lady's hand upon introduction, and was well-versed in classical literature. Despite the outward show of refinement and reticence, however, Kelly never developed into a silk-gloved pushover. His punch could still break bones, and he could wield a knife or gun in battle as easily as any of his men. But Kelly was as much a businessman as he was a thug, and he ran his undertakings along a business model that future gang bosses, such as his protégé John Torrio (who would be the man responsible for giving Al Capone his start) and another successful Italian crime lord, Frank Costello, would follow and develop to perfection.

The Gophers ranged from Fourteenth to Forty-second streets and from Seventh to Eleventh avenues. They originated in the old Irish Hell's Kitchen neighborhood and formed in the 1890s after a handful of smaller street gangs united to create a collective. Their numbers were small but their reputation gigantic and fearsome. Asbury claimed in *The Gangs of New York,* "Every man was a thug of the first water, and not even Monk Eastman cared to lead his gangsters into Hell's Kitchen unless he outnumbered them at least two to one."[13] Even their women's auxiliary was hyperkinetic. Known formally as the Battle Row Ladies Social and Athletic Club (named after Battle Row, which was Thirty-ninth Street between Tenth and Eleventh avenues), they were led by one Battle Annie, a notorious "lady slugger" who supplied female warriors during labor disputes. Owney Madden, who had been born in England but accepted into the gang's mostly Irish ranks without comment, was a murderer and gang leader who used his apprenticeship in the Gophers as a launch pad to a career of bootlegging and racketeering. In 1931, Madden was number two on the list of New York City's Public Enemies.[14]

The Hudson Dusters prowled south of Thirteenth Street and west of Broadway. They paled in comparison to the Five Pointers, Gophers, and Eastmans when it came to fighting ability, but reporters found good copy in their macabre antics. Asbury estimated that 90 percent of the Dusters were drug addicts.[15]

When they had a grudge against someone, they retaliated in ways that exceeded the original offense. A saloonkeeper who refused to donate half a dozen beer kegs for one of their parties had his store wrecked and his entire booze stock carried away. When a patrolman named Dennis Sullivan arrested several Duster leaders and announced his intention to obliterate the gang completely, a pack of them jumped him on Greenwich Street and beat him with stones and blackjacks. After he lost consciousness, the gangsters rolled him onto his back and ground their heels in his face, trying to inflict permanent injuries.[16]

Thomas P. "Humpty" Jackson led an enterprising gang of ragtags who headquartered in an old graveyard sandwiched between First and Second avenues and Twelfth and Thirteenth streets. Jackson, a hunchback with a passion for classical reading (he counted Voltaire, Darwin, and Huxley among his favorite authors and devoured Greek and Latin texts), would perch like an animated gargoyle on one of the tombstones and plot armed robberies, burglaries, and murder for hire with his followers, who were as quirky in appearance yet innately deadly as he was. His gang included Nigger Ruhl, the Grabber, the Lobster Kid, and Spanish Louie, also known as Indian Louie. The latter hinted at Mexican or Spanish origins and cut an arresting figure on the Lower East Side streets in his solid-black outfit and black sombrero. He also carried two eight-inch dirks to complement his Colt revolvers. When he was finally murdered, an Orthodox Jewish father told the press that his son was not from some remote Latin country but from less exotic Brooklyn.

The Monk Eastman gang controlled everything between Fourteenth and Monroe, and from the Bowery east to the river. Zelig ended up with Eastman, a natural result given his neighborhood location, his association with Crazy Butch and Max Zweifach, and probably his religion. Monk Eastman in 1900 was the poster thug for the New York underworld, famous for being infamous, a personage who drew admirers, imitators, and enemies like flies.

He was born Edward Eastman in December 1876 to Samuel Eastman, a paper hanger, and the former Mary Parks. Eastman Senior, who was a German Jew and whose surname was originally Osterman, left his family for reasons that have been lost to history soon after the birth of daughter Francine in 1878. Mary took the children—Lizzie, Ida, Edward, and Francine—and went to live with her father, George Parks.[17] Eastman's own home life was more stable. He married a woman named Margaret in 1896 and remained with her for almost twenty years. They attempted to start a family of their own, but two children conceived before 1900 died soon after birth, and the Eastmans thereafter remained childless.[18] He operated a pet store on Broome Street as a legitimate front, but popular history alleges that the business folded when he refused to sell any of the animals, being passionately fond of cats and pigeons in particular.[19]

Like many Jewish and Italian gangsters of the era, he adopted an Irish alias, William Delaney, to facilitate business and social transactions with the Irishmen who dominated New York's political scene as well as its police force. But it was as Monk Eastman that he became one of America's earliest celebrity gangsters. The nickname Monk derived from his frequent patronage of the Chinatown opium dives: a common racial slur directed at the Chinese was "monk," short for "monkey."[20]

Little is known about the juvenile record that Edward Eastman surely had. He served his first adult prison sentence in 1898, when he was arrested for attempted burglary and received a three-month term.[21] When he got out, he made a reputation for himself, as well as a number of powerful friends, by working as a bouncer at Charles "Silver Dollar" Smith's resort at 64 Essex Street. He was so good at that particular job that the accident ward at Bellevue Hospital was supposedly nicknamed "the Eastman Pavilion," as many of the patients treated there bore injuries from a recent tangle with the ferocious bouncer.[22]

Silver Dollar Smith's was directly across the street from the Essex Market Courthouse and a major watering hole for local politicians. Smith, who had been born Charles Finkelstone in Germany, had aligned himself with Tammany Hall during the reign of Honest John Kelly, and, according to his December 1899 obituary, "as he was one of the few politicians in the district who understood the Hebrew residents and their language thoroughly, he soon found a large political following among them."[23] He was elected to the state Legislature five times and served three terms as an alderman. Smith became known as "Silver Dollar" after he embedded a thousand trade dollars in the marble floor of his saloon as well as the frame of the huge mirror behind the bar. His Tammany colleagues valued him as a vote magnet, and he in turn depended on Eastman to supply the muscle required to deliver said votes. His protégé's excessive use of violence did not concern him, for Smith himself had been tried in 1889 for gouging out a man's eye and been indicted for attacking rival saloonkeepers.[24]

After Smith died, Tammany Hall politicians, impressed by what Monk could do, employed him and his growing stable of henchmen on a routine basis to terrorize voters into casting ballots for Tammany-endorsed candidates. Eastman also sold his leg-breaking services to pimps, gamblers, trade unionists, and anyone else who needed them and was willing to pay. His fists made him money and, for years, a politically protected species.

Eastman was short and intimidating in appearance. Almost every visible inch of skin was blemished with battle scars, and his squat facial features were rendered even more sinister by a broken nose and ears misshapen by bite marks and badly healed scar tissue. His fashion sense was just as dismaying. Asbury wrote, "He seemed to always need a haircut, and he accentuated his ferocious and unusual appearance by affecting a derby hat several sizes too small, which perched atop his shock of bristly, unruly hair. He could generally be found strutting about his kingdom very indifferently dressed, or lounging at his ease in the Chrystie Street rendezvous[25] without shirt, collar, or coat."[26] When necessary, however, he could put on a good show. During a 1903 court appearance, reporters agreed that he was the best-dressed party in the room.

Unlike archrival Paul Kelly, who dressed and conducted himself like a gentleman, Eastman had no desire to present himself as anything other than what he was: a street fighter who led by example. Although not the mentally challenged, club-swinging urban caveman that popular history has painted him to be, Eastman did believe in doing his own dirty work. He scorned the concept of delegating responsibility and insulating himself with tier after tier of underlings. Whenever a mass brawl or a robbery of serious magnitude was in the works, Eastman was front and center, planning and later present in the trenches.

The great gangster also inspired a junior corps who called themselves the Monk Eastman Juniors.

According to legend (and it may be just that), his favorite weapon was a club that he marked with a notch for every head he bashed in, and when one count yielded forty-nine notches, he took down an unsuspecting saloon patron to make it an even fifty. He supposedly made a concession in the name of delicacy by removing his brass knuckles before disciplining a woman, although this chivalric quirk is probably apocryphal.

Eastman's earliest press mention came on April 14, 1901, when James and "Peggy" Donovan, rival gangsters, entered Silver Dollar Smith's and opened fire on him and pal Samuel Frankel. Frankel's pocket watch deflected a bullet, but Eastman was shot in the abdomen by "Peggy" after a chase that ended on Orchard Street. As he collapsed to the sidewalk, James then ran up and shot him behind the ear. Miraculously, Monk survived, much to the surprise of *New York Times* readers, who read a premature report that he had been killed.[27]

Battles between Eastman's gang and Kelly's Five Pointers (also known as the Five Points Social Club) regularly made the papers. On Monday night, September 29, 1902, more than sixty Eastmans invaded Chinatown, weapons tucked inside their coats and courage pumped by booze and anger. A Five Pointer named Bove had been beaten up on Saturday by two Eastmans at the Chatham Club on Doyers Street, and Bove's comrades retaliated the following night by attacking one Isidore Foster, who was connected to the Eastmans, as he walked along Broome Street. Foster died at Gouverneur Hospital hours later, and the Eastmans vowed revenge.

They went through Chinatown in two heavily armed contingents, breaths and tempers soured by liquor. The Kelly forces, alerted to the invasion, met them at the corner of Walker and White streets. Bullets, bricks, and clubs cleared the area of everyone except the combatants, who fought one another along Walker Street, leaving smashed windows, a gore-splattered sidewalk, and wounded men in their wake. At Broadway, they ran into a swarm of policemen armed with clubs and revolvers, who dispersed them and arrested four gangsters who menaced the cops with weapons. Another clash took place at Centre and White streets, but it was stopped before shots were fired.[28]

Four days later, on October 4, thirty-five armed Kelly gangsters swarmed into William Smith's second-floor poolroom at 96 Suffolk Street, a known Eastman hangout. Eastman, who was on the premises, led his followers in a counterattack. Police officers Rothbach and Cohen, who were on post nearby, came running when they heard gunfire. Noting the number of combatants, they wisely retreated to the Delancey Street station and requested reinforcements. Within minutes more than thirty armed policemen were at the scene, scattering the bloodied brawlers and arresting twenty-nine in all.[29] The Eastman prisoners were arraigned before Magistrate Poole in the Essex Market Court, where ex-Assemblyman Isadore Cohen appeared on their behalf and insisted that his clients were peaceable "boys" who had merely defended themselves from unwarranted Italian aggression. Poole agreed and discharged them. The only casualty of that poolroom scrap was Eastman gangster Samuel Levinson, who died from a fractured skull.[30]

Incredibly, Paul Kelly denied in a 1908 interview that the two gangs were at war for years. He did recall that in or around 1900, an Eastman thug named Hurst had been beaten by a Five Pointer named Fordin, an affront that Hurst's friends reacted to by threatening to kill Fordin on sight. Kelly claimed that he went to Eastman and suggested that the hostility be diffused by letting the two men fight it out in front of both gangs in an organized boxing match. This was done in a barn at College Point, with Kelly acting as referee. (Asbury would write in *The Gangs of New York* that it was the two bosses themselves, and not the underlings, who fought the match.) When Kelly declared Fordin to be the winner after Hurst, trying to hide the fact that he was being beaten, cried foul and refused to continue, the Eastmans began hissing and things got ugly.

"I called on Eastman," Kelly recalled, "and he said I was right. The mob began to get boisterous and I called a lieutenant of mine, 'Crazy' Ernest, to guard the door. Ernest pulled out two big revolvers and kept order. Then the gang left the barn one by one. That was the nearest Eastman's crowd ever came to fighting us, crowd against crowd."[31]

Not quite, but an uneasy peace did prevail between the two sides from time to time. In July 1903, Alderman Tom Foley, fearing a public backlash from all the fighting reported in the press, engineered a truce, and the two gangs celebrated with a party on Staten Island. Returning to the East Side at midnight, the drunken and exhilarated thugs ordered the brass marching band they had hired for the party to accompany them up Broadway, playing at full volume while the Five Pointers and Eastmans cheered and discharged their revolvers. Policemen from the Elizabeth Street station were sent to quell the disturbance. The hoods were defiant, and one even blackjacked an officer. The affair escalated into a free-for-all between the cops and the gangs, with pedestrians being nicked by bullets.[32]

Eastman was arrested regularly, but except for the three-month jail stint in 1898, he never suffered any serious inconvenience for his crimes in the earliest phase of his career. Then, in July 1903, a wealthy Wall Street broker, David Lamar, came to him with a proposal that would backfire for all concerned, and garner for Monk the type of unpopular press that unsettled his Tammany patrons.[33]

Lamar had recently fired his coachman, James McMahon, and the latter had supposedly retaliated with late-night window smashing and other acts of terrorism. The broker first approached an ex-prizefighter whom he knew for assistance, and after being turned down, hired Eastman to guard his summer house in Long Branch, New Jersey. New York summers were infamous for their Hades-level temperatures, so the gang boss cheerfully accepted the offer to break bones in a cooler, greener environment.

Eastman, his second in command Joseph Brown, and three others arrived in New Jersey by ferry on July 4. They had actually boarded the ferry at Rector Street the previous day, but authorities arrested them as suspicious characters and Monk's Tammany protectors had to spring them. After a few days, Eastman and Brown sent the others home, having decided that they could handle the crazy coachman by themselves. On the morning of July 9, McMahon went to court to appear in a civil action against his former employer. The two gangsters and Lamar's new coachman accosted him on the courthouse steps, where he was beaten, kicked, and stabbed in front of shocked witnesses.

A police constable named Van Winkle arrived while the attack was in progress, and although he did not catch the assailants, he did pick their photos out of a rogues' gallery. "They are the fellows, all right!" he declared. "And I saw them make the assault. I can produce other witnesses, too, who saw the scuffle, one of them a woman, who heard Delaney [Eastman] say, 'Give it to him good! Put him out!' I nabbed Delaney, all right, but he got in a quick jab that put me out and then made his escape in the carriage driven by Dunphy, Lamar's coachman."[34]

Eastman and Brown were arrested in New York and spent days locked up in the Tombs prison while their lawyers fought efforts to extradite them to New Jersey. Monk snarled at the police that he was not even in New Jersey on the day McMahon was beaten, as he was attending the funeral of his sister's child. An anxious Lamar phoned Eastman at the prison and assured him, "No harm will come to you." On August 6, after their lawyers finally consented to extradition, the two thugs and their police escorts boarded the train for Freehold, New Jersey, where the trial would be held. After spending eleven days in the county jail, Eastman was bailed out and returned to New York.

He dropped briefly out of sight, but his whereabouts were not a mystery for long. On the night of September 16, 1903, three Eastman gangsters—Lolly Meyers, Isidore Bernstein, and Henry Lewis—encountered a Five Points thug, Anton Bernhauser, in a saloon and opened fire on him. He was taken to Bellevue Hospital with severe facial wounds. After fleeing the premises, the blood-drunk Eastmans held up a civilian, pocketed $46, and went to spend the loot at another saloon, where they traded shots with another Five Pointer, Michael Donovan. Donovan, a bullet lodged in his throat, was also carted off to Bellevue. He was admitted as Bernhauser was being released—the two cronies acknowledged each other. But Donovan, despite assurances that he would handle his assailants himself, died. [35]

Paul Kelly was quick to avenge Donovan, and the Eastmans were just as ready to retaliate. At two o'clock on the morning of September 17, Eastman and Kelly gangsters, an estimated twenty-five combatants in all, clashed beneath the elevated trains at the intersection of Rivington and Allen streets. The fighters ran when the police arrived, so frustrated officials issued an order to pick up known ringleaders. Lolly Meyers's apartment was raided and he, Bernstein, and

Lewis were arrested along with Eastman. Monk was released for lack of evidence, which prompted Inspector Max Schmittberger to complain about the futility of trying to break up the gangs. "We have arrested them time and time again and the magistrates keep letting them go," he said.

Police Commissioner Greene was livid. "I am going to break up this shooting," he told the press. "There will be no more of that kind of lawlessness if I can help it. There is entirely too much of it." Tammany politicians, unbeknownst to Eastman, were in nervous agreement.

Eastman returned to Freehold in mid-October 1903 for his trial. During the proceedings, word reached the court that a huge assembly of his hoodlums had left New York City and were on their way to the trial location, possibly with the intention of springing their leader should the Jersey jury find him guilty. Guards were posted around the courtroom, but the hoods behaved themselves and stated to anyone who asked that they were only there to support their leader. When Lamar, Eastman, and Brown were declared not guilty on October 16, Eastman told the press, "We won't lose any time getting out of this town."

Monk was arrested three more times the following December, once for suspicion of murder and twice for being a "suspicious person." The charges were dropped as usual, but that may have had more to do with lack of evidence than any active string-pulling by Tammany. Their support had slowly but surely been corroded by the headlines and public criticism. Eastman did not appear to notice the shift; he assumed the valuable services he had rendered at the polls in the past would guarantee ongoing protection. When a Monk Eastman Junior was arrested in October 1903, the youth sneered at the cops, "Youse go to entirely too much trouble. The politicians will bail us out. They don't want no one away at registration and election time."

Eastman's point of decline can be traced to the morning of February 2, 1904, when he and a henchman, Chris Wallace, attempted to rob a well-dressed young drunk. Neither gangster knew that two Pinkerton detectives were tailing the man at the request of his concerned, well-to-do father. These bodyguards opened fire on the would-be robbers, and after three police officers joined the chase, Eastman and Wallace were captured.[36] They were indicted for assault in the first degree two days later, but worse trouble than an assault rap lay ahead. A state law had recently been enacted that mandated a twenty-five-year sentence for anyone found guilty of attempted murder, and someone came forward to complain that Eastman had shot at him two weeks previously. Eastman claimed that he was being set up but privately felt sure that a good lawyer would get the charges dropped. He also counted on support from the Tammany quarter, forgetting that public opinion factored in their allegiance just as strongly as past services rendered.

Bailed out, Eastman carried on his activities as usual. On the evening of March 29, 1904, Sergeants Dunn and Stransky arrested a group of men who were seen behaving suspiciously on a Thirty-fourth Street trolley car. The men all claimed during an interrogation at police headquarters that they were on their way to see a boxing match at the West Side Athletic Club, but the policemen noted in their report that the car had contained an after-theater crowd, making it a prime hunting ground for pickpockets.

Those detained were Monk Eastman, Joseph Brown, and four Eastman followers: William Albert, George Wilson, Samuel White, and John Hersch. They were finally released due to lack of evidence, but the arrest itself rated a mention on Page 5 of the March 30 edition of the *New York Times*.

William Albert was Zelig Lefkowitz's newest alias, likely invented to conceal his record from the police. Since his release from the House of Refuge, he had been apprenticed to a diamond cutter and worked weekdays in the man's establishment. He was intrigued by the diamond profession, but not enough to resist the easy money that stealing offered, and the apprenticeship did not last.[37] The *Times* story was his first press mention and a prequel to the media frenzy that would, in eight short years, revolve around him.

In 1904, however, he was no gang leader, nor was he really a gangster. He was a teenaged pickpocket operating on the fringes of the Eastman crowd. Zelig knew how to defend himself as well as anyone who had grown up in the slums and survived the House of Refuge, but any aggression he displayed during those early years was purely reactive. He was no slugger or strong arm, although he counted both among his friends. Private detective Abe Shoenfeld wrote in a 1912 report, "Until about two years ago this widely known character was nothing but a plain ordinary 'gun' [pickpocket]."

He may have been sitting in the courtroom when Monk Eastman's trial for first-degree assault commenced on April 12. Looking quite striking in a new suit, Eastman took the stand on his own behalf and testified that he'd actually been trying to protect the young drunk after noticing two strange-looking men (the Pinkertons) following him. He convinced no one. After deliberating a mere hour and fifteen minutes, the jury found him guilty and he was sentenced to ten years in Sing Sing.

Eastman turned chalk white when the verdict was read, but a week in the Tombs gave him time to resign himself to a long incarceration. When he left the prison on April 23, he was chomping on a stogie and carrying himself with his old, defiant air. He commented to reporters, "Well, I'm going now. This is the last you'll hear of Monk for a while." With those words, he climbed into a van with other prisoners bound for Sing Sing. The slamming of the vehicle doors signaled the end of his tenure as New York's most feared and celebrated gangster boss.[38]

♣ ♣ ♣

Paul Kelly's difficulties did not end with Eastman's imprisonment. Trouble loomed in the shape of two Five Pointers, Frank "Chick" Tricker and John "Jack" Sirocco. Both Tricker and Sirocco ran saloons that they used as bases to attract and maintain splinter groups of their own. They were Italian, like Kelly, and once affiliated with him, but a falling out resulted in a series of ambushes and murders that equaled anything Kelly had ever experienced with Eastman.

Early one morning during the last week of May 1905, Tricker dropped by the New Brighton (now the Little Naples), and made himself unpopular by insulting the dancing ability of one Goldie Cora, a vivacious blonde who was the belle of the ball. "Eat Em Up" Jack McManus, the hall's bouncer as well as Paul Kelly's close friend, ordered him out, and he cockily complied, but none of the hushed onlookers believed that the matter was going to end there. Dance hall insults almost always escalated into street brawls and all their accompanying carnage.

Tricker and a companion, John O'Neil, were ambushed by a seething McManus and an accomplice later that night. Tricker fell with a bullet wound in the thigh, and O'Neil was stabbed six times when he tried to intervene. The latter dragged himself, bleeding, to the Hudson Street Hospital when it became obvious that to avoid medical attention was to invite certain death, while Tricker had his wound treated at St. Vincent's Hospital.[39]

McManus received Tricker's indirect response on May 26. Just before sunrise, he and a companion, Kid Griffo, left the Folly Saloon. They were walking down the Bowery when a man darted silently out of a pitch-black doorway, raised a length of lead pipe wrapped in newspaper, and brought it crashing down on McManus's skull. Griffo had been a few paces in the lead and later told police that by the time he turned around in response to the sickening thud, McManus was face-down on the sidewalk and the assailant was making a speedy getaway. He died hours later without fully regaining consciousness. Griffo's failure to react "appropriately" led to his being held on $5,000 bail by the Coroner's Court, but no further action was taken.[40]

The final straw for Kelly took place six months later. On November 17, he threw a party in honor of himself and another gang member named Harrington. Jack Sirocco showed up, which was akin to tossing a dynamite bundle on a bonfire. Guns came out, and Sirocco was shot in the arm.

Almost a week later, on November 23, Sirocco lieutenant Biff Ellison and a deadly little gangster named Razor Riley took a cab to the Little Naples. Before going in, they checked their weapons and asked the driver to wait.

Inside, they stormed up to a table where Kelly, Harrington, and a third man were relaxing with drinks. Ellison demanded to know who had shot Sirocco the previous week. Kelly said he didn't know. That answer was tantamount to forfeiting his life, so Ellison and Riley began shooting. Kelly managed to duck and escape through a side door, but Harrington fell with a bullet in his lung.

At about half past midnight, Officer Thomas Ryan of the Mercer Street station paused in front of the Little Naples, puzzled by the tomblike silence that pervaded. The place was normally alive with music and laughter at that hour. Trying the front door, he found it open and cautiously peered inside. When he saw no patrons or staff, yet could hear a dog barking frantically, his suspicions were aroused and he called for assistance, which arrived in the form of a policeman named Dillon.

The two officers crossed the saloon, which was lit only by a dim lamp, and entered the dance hall. Finding no one, they were about to leave when Ryan saw a man's legs protruding from a doorway leading into the public washrooms. Venturing closer, they found a young man lying on his back, dead, a fatal wound in his left side. It was Harrington. The gangster's dog, a small spaniel, was cringing and whining beside his master's body.[41]

Revolvers in hand, Ryan and Dillon went upstairs, where the nerve center of the Paul Kelly Association headquartered, and found it ransacked. Bullets had punctured the doors and shattered the windows, tables and chairs were turned over, and at least three emptied revolvers were picked up after the mess of club books and papers were organized.

Kelly had been wounded during the attack, but he recovered after his men got him to a safe location in Harlem to convalesce. He opted to remain uptown afterward, dabbling with businesses both straight and crooked. As far as he was concerned, the new breed of desperados could have his old stomping grounds.

When Eastman was sent to Sing Sing, the *New York Times* suggested that Joseph Brown would be succeeding him. The paper was wrong. Brown was game, but he was a henchman, not a leader. Even if he had ascended to the top spot, his generalship would have lasted just over a year. In May 1905, he tried to rob the bartender of a Third Avenue saloon at gunpoint. When two police officers named Butler and Riordan caught him in the act, he shot at them. It took a jury just fifteen minutes to find him guilty, and on May 16, Recorder Goff sentenced him, as a second offender, to ten to twenty years in Sing Sing.[42]

The question of who would succeed Eastman was an open one for months, but it was finally resolved on November 1, 1904, in a manner that surprised no one.

CHAPTER FOUR

TWIST ON THE RISE

Max Zweifach, now universally referred to as "Kid Twist," was used to getting what he wanted, and ready to meet any obstacles or opposition with violence. When he escaped punishment for the murder of John Bayard he became even more ambitious and daring, satisfied that he had the means and the connections to flout the law and get away with it. His drive and determination won him followers when he proclaimed himself Monk Eastman's successor in the spring of 1904.

Dinny Zweifach, alias Kid Slyfox, was his right hand. Both Dinny and Max were tall at five feet, ten inches and powerfully built. When they advanced on an adversary together, fists clenched and dark faces twisted in fury, they were a terrifying sight. In 1902, the Zweifach brothers, together with Charles Levin, alias Ike the Blood, led a mob of repeaters[1] and guerrillas that backed Sam Koenig, an Eastern European Jew like themselves, in the latter's bid for the Republican leadership in what was then the Sixteenth Assembly District. They got him in, a favor that Max in particular was prepared to use to his advantage when arrested or otherwise annoyed by the police.

Samuel Pristrich was also firmly behind the aspiring boss. Like Zweifach, he was an Austrian Jew, and he had arrived in the United States in 1902 at the age of sixteen.[2] Alfred Henry Lewis wrote that Pristrich, who went by the nickname of Cyclone Louie, was a professional strongman who earned extra cash by wowing Coney Island crowds with feats of strength. If so, it was a seasonal sideline, for Pristrich carried a gun full time in the service of Kid Twist, whom he hero-worshipped. The two young men and their wives eventually shared a residence at 257 Sackman Street in Brownsville.[3]

Another supporter who quickly became devoted to his new leader was nineteen-year-old Harris Stahl. Stahl stood about five feet five inches tall and was stocky. Writing a report about him eight years later, Abe Shoenfeld recalled, "Harry was a lieutenant to Kid Twist. He was never a pimp or a gun. He was, however. . . . a very much feared man on the East Side. He was known as a terror. With Twist behind him he had nerve, and for a song and dance he would crack a man's skull, or break his nose or a rib."[4]

Zweifach's path to the Eastman throne was not without obstacles, however. One, Richard Fitzpatrick, forced him to temporarily restrain his ambition, something that rankled him deeply.

Ritchie "Kid" Fitzpatrick did not adopt an Irish alias like Eastman and Kelly before him. He was the real deal, having been born in New York in February 1872 to an Irish father and American mother.[5] He was a stevedore and labor slugger with a talent for organizing men into battle units. Fitzpatrick spent the 1890s running a dive at 9 Bowery, which made him the nucleus of his own gang as well as a crony of Eastman's. During the same period a gang of arsonists tried to shake him down, torching stables and other property he owned when he defied them.[6] The trouble stopped when gang members began disappearing, and thereafter, Kid Fitzpatrick was given a wide berth. Given his following in the gang and years of experience in the trenches, he saw himself as the natural Eastman heir. As far as Fitzpatrick was concerned, the much-younger Zweifach was an upstart. A shrewd, enterprising, and dangerous one, but an upstart all the same.

Neither could afford to go to war over the leadership spot, however, as mass murder and bloody headlines would result in police crackdowns, withdrawal of the gang's political support, and attacks from rival mobs who would rush to take advantage of the weakened, divided Eastmans. Resigned to the fact that they had to present a united front for the time being, Fitzpatrick and Zweifach agreed to share the top spot.[7] But neither man was satisfied by this makeshift arrangement, and no one believed that the matter would end there.

An uneasy truce prevailed until October 30, 1904, when Fitzpatrick shot a Twist minion, Thomas McCauley, in the hip during a saloon confrontation. McCauley, who had started the fight by being verbally abusive, survived and was taken to hospital. Seeing his long-awaited chance, Zweifach invited Fitzpatrick to meet him in a saloon at 77 Sheriff Street on November 1. He may have allayed any suspicion by warning his co-chief that they had to formulate a damage control plan before McCauley's friends went on the warpath and generated bad press for all concerned. Fitzpatrick may also have seen the meeting request as a natural one given the fact that an election was scheduled for November 8, and united gang muscle was needed by the Tammany Democrats in the Eighth Assembly District.

How far the session progressed before the guns came out is uncertain. Harris Stahl, who was present, disrupted the proceedings by berating Fitzpatrick for shooting McCauley. The hostility that had been simmering when the meeting began now boiled over. Fitzpatrick, sensing that he was being put on the spot, got up and hurried out of the saloon. He was justifiably paranoid: he had been around long enough to know that violent words in one's face were a prelude to bullets in the back. Stahl chased him outside and fired twice. One of the bullets struck their target just over the heart. Fitzpatrick collapsed on the sidewalk, and died before he could be taken to Gouverneur Hospital.

Officer David Meyer of the Delancey Street station, who heard the shots, arrived in time to see Stahl throw away his revolver and flee. The policeman chased the fugitive for a block through the crowded street before overtaking him, placing him under arrest, and hauling him off to the station. When word arrived that Fitzpatrick was dead, Stahl was charged with homicide.[8]

The case went to trial before Judge McMahon in February 1905. That gave the primary witnesses—Meyer and a boy named Jacob Berger, who had actually seen Stahl shoot Fitzpatrick—time to decide that perhaps they weren't so sure after all. When Meyer began waffling on the stand, McMahon—the same tough judge who had sentenced a young Harry Smith to the House of Refuge—snapped, "What's the matter with you?"

"I have considered the case very carefully," was the weak response, "and I am not sure that this [Stahl] is the man who committed the crime. There is a slight doubt in my mind, and my conscience will not permit me to swear his life away."

Young Berger quivered on the stand. "I was afraid before, because a policeman had told me that Stahl was the man who fired. Now I don't know who did."

McMahon turned to the puzzled jury in disgust. "I may have my own idea about the facts in this case, but there is certainly not sufficient evidence. It would be unwise and unsafe to proceed with the case." He then addressed Assistant District Attorney Clark, who was appearing for the prosecution. "I direct the district attorney to make a thorough investigation of this matter. Some facts, I believe, are suspicious and the district attorney should ascertain all facts concerning the case."

He ordered the jury to return a verdict of not guilty, and they complied. Smiling, Stahl swaggered from the courtroom and into a secure position in the Twist gang.[9]

The murder of Ritchie Fitzpatrick and the insulation of his killer against punishment made the twenty-year-old Zweifach, who had orchestrated the entire thing from start to finish, a figure of awe and fear throughout the Lower East Side. He was barely out of his teens, but capable of murdering without hesitation or remorse, and pulling all the necessary strings afterward to escape justice.

Such connections cost money, and Zweifach thought big when it came to making it. He still picked up quick cash by walking into stuss and crap joints and shouting, "I want fifty dollars! What, you're not going to cough up? I'll shoot up your ——— place!" He usually walked out minutes later with the amount demanded, but he was relying less and less on such minuscule undertakings.[10]

During the early winter of 1904, he embarked on a scheme to defraud the New York Central Railroad of thousands of dollars. He, printing shop owner Isadore Hauptmann, Hauptmann's pressman Seymour Singer, and a third man named Albert Neumann printed $4,000 worth of phony passes in Hauptmann's establishment and presented them to scalpers to sell to the public directly. Police investigators later learned that Neumann had fronted the necessary cash to get the operation going and insisted on having a say in every stage of the scam, something that did not sit well with Kid Twist's need to be in complete control. Seymour Singer would confess that Zweifach made repeated overtures to him to help ambush and strangle Neumann so that there was one less party to split the profits with.

Despite precautions taken, the authorities caught wind of the plot. In mid-March 1905, the police, in conjunction with railroad detectives, collected enough evidence to make arrests. Zweifach, Neumann, Hauptmann, and Singer were taken into custody on the morning of March 16 and brought before Magistrate Charles Whitman, who imposed a bail of $2,000 on each defendant and ordered them sent to the Tombs until such bail was posted. Neumann's nerve failed him and he confessed first, even taking the police to the shop so that they could collect the plates and type used to create the forgeries.[11] Zweifach was finally released when Singer retracted his statement about the threat to assassinate Neumann, and the others refused to testify against him. He plunged on, unfazed, into other endeavors.

According to Alfred Henry Lewis, Zweifach invested in the production of a celery tonic, a type of drink favored by his fellow Jews, as a semi-legitimate sideline. After each batch was prepared, he had it bottled, labeled with a colorful sticker bearing his own portrait, and sent around by the caseload to the local shops and saloons. Any proprietor who wasn't inclined to carry his new beverage only had to be reminded of what he did to one Baby Flax (so named supposedly because of a cherubic countenance) after the latter refused to carry it in his grogshop. Zweifach turned into a human cyclone and smashed up the mirror, windows, glasses, and anything else breakable that he could get his hands on. The beat cop, attracted by the noise, raced through the swinging doors and found him puffing a cigar placidly in the midst of a shambles. He told the officer that another party had blown in, demolished the place, and run without saying a word. The petrified Baby Flax quickly confirmed the gangster's version of events and even placed an order for two cases of celery tonic.[12]

Zelig Lefkowitz, who was close to Zweifach because of their boyhood comradeship, was also entrepreneurial, although strangling competitors, breaking bones, and dismantling saloons did not factor in his getting ahead. He prowled the elevated train platforms and worked his way onto packed trolleys, where he divested unsuspecting commuters of their wallets, watches, purses, and stickpins. His reputation as a pickpocket of the first rank was growing daily, and he had no problem finding accomplices who would engage a victim's attention while his nimble fingers plucked small fortunes. This same success also caught the attention of the police. Several officers knew him by sight, and few beat cops passed through a crowd without casting a wary glance about for Zelig's quick, well-dressed figure.

His celebrity backfired on June 11, 1905. Samuel Michaelof, a real estate agent, was boarding the Third Avenue elevated train near Forty-second Street when Zelig, accompanied by two friends, grabbed the diamond pin from the front of his shirt and tried to jump off the train before it started. While his wife, Sophia, screamed for help, Michaelof seized the young thief and held on despite a fierce struggle. Trying to bargain for release, Zelig gave the pin back. When Michaelof took it, Zelig broke free and ran away. Unwilling to end the matter with the forced return of his property, the real estate agent went straight to the police and furnished a thorough enough description for them to determine the identity of the offender and arrest him later that day.

Otto Rosalsky came forward to defend him. Rosalsky, a former assistant district attorney who was also the Republican leader of the Eighth Assembly District, had successfully prosecuted Martin Thorn and Augusta Nack for the 1897 murder and dismemberment of Mrs. Nack's unwanted admirer[13] and emerged from the trial with an augmented reputation. He was now in private practice and found it literally enriching to provide a defense for Monk Eastman's boys. As a defense attorney, he was known for being cagey and overlooking no possible angle when it came to getting his clients off. In 1899, he undertook the defense of Michael Buczny, who had murdered his sweetheart, Regina Klein, and succeeded in convincing the judge that the bright and articulate Buczny was hopelessly insane and needed to be sent to Matteawan State Hospital instead of the electric chair that had claimed Martin Thorn. He represented gamblers and gangsters (usually Eastmans), and defended the policies and practices of the Hebrew Actors' Union whenever the union ended up in court. Now he was Zelig's attorney, probably at Zweifach's request.

Rosalsky and Zelig appeared before Magistrate Peter Barlow on June 12. The eighteen-year-old thief maintained a calm and cool demeanor, answering questions without hesitation, or deference.

Q. What is your name? *William Albert.*

Q. How old are you? *Twenty-two years* [sic].

Q. Where were you born? *U.S.*

Q. Where do you live, and how long have you lived there? *126 and 128 Norfolk Street.*

Q. What is your occupation? *Tailor.*

Q. Give any explanation you may think proper of the circumstances appearing in the testimony against you, and state any facts which you think will tend to your exculpation. *I am not guilty.*[14]

He was indicted anyway for grand larceny in the second degree. On July 25, with the consent of the district attorney, Judge Foster released him on $1,500 bail. Zelig left the courtroom and managed to avoid trouble with the police for the rest of the summer. Then, on October 16, the day before Zelig was due in court, the following telegram appeared on the desk of District Attorney William Travers Jerome:

> NORFOLK, VIR. OCTOBER 16, 1905
> HON WILLIAM TRAVERS JEROME
> DISTRICT ATTORNEY'S OFFICE, CRIMINAL COURT BUILDING, NEW YORK
> HON SIR: MY CASE IS ON FOR TOMORROW, MR. ROSALSKY IS MY ATTORNEY. AM SICK HERE. HAVE WIRED HIM. UNABLE TO BE ON UNTIL NEXT WEEK. HAVE RECEIVED NO ANSWER.
> WILLIAM ALBERTS [sic][15]

Zelig occasionally left New York City to attend county fairs, rallies, and other public events throughout the country, where the dense crowds provided a rich hunting ground. The Michaelof incident proved that he was too well known by the New York police, making it necessary for him to do a "jump out," or become a traveling thief for a while. The telegram he sent Jerome is both amusing and intriguing. What prevented him from returning to New York in time for court? Was he actually sick? Or was he caught stealing a watch or wallet, taken before a Norfolk judge under an assumed name, and released with a warning after he promised to leave the city permanently, at which point he dashed off the telegram? Even his detractors would admit that Zelig was a superb orator and actor, capable of charming a conditional release out of judges not familiar with his criminal history, so the latter scenario is a strong possibility.

Zelig's failure to appear when scheduled didn't hurt attorney Rosalsky in any appreciable manner. On October 17, the day after the perplexing telegram landed on Jerome's desk, Governor Higgins appointed Rosalsky judge of General Sessions. Another judge had resigned suddenly, resulting in a vacancy that needed to be filled right away. Zelig remained on bail while the district attorney's office dealt with other, more pressing cases.

It was a relief for the young pickpocket, whose freedom was crucial to more than just himself by late 1905. The money that he plucked from stolen wallets and received from fences in exchange for the watches and jewelry he turned in was now going toward the support of a wife and child.

⚜ ⚜ ⚜

Zelig Lefkowitz and Henrietta Young were living together as man and wife by 1905, but they may have known each other for a long time before that. In 1903, she bore a son, Harry, whom she declared was Zelig's.

Reporters who interviewed her before and after Zelig's death described her as "plump" but with a pleasing, girlish face and quiet demeanor—except when angered. Then she turned into a lioness. She was originally from Broome Street. The district enumerator for the 1900 census noted her occupation as "office worker" and listed her as living with her mother and five siblings at 284 Broome, next door to 286, where she and Zelig would eventually occupy an apartment. She was also eight years his senior, having been born in November 1880.

In 1913, a ruthless lawyer would grill Henrietta on the stand about her marriage to her boy husband. She would snap that they married in Canada in 1903 (when Zelig was fifteen!) but denied remembering the date or exact place. Since it's highly unusual for anyone, especially a woman, not to remember details about such a major life milestone, she was clearly being evasive for a reason. Were they ever married at all, and if so, was it not until *after* Harry's birth? Was Zelig the father of her child? He was not paroled from the House of Refuge until March 1903, and without access to Harry's birth record (which may not even exist, considering that reporting of vital statistics like births and deaths was sporadic at the time) it's impossible to tell whether Zelig could have been Harry's father.

The details are ultimately irrelevant. Zelig and Henrietta would be officially linked in 1906 (when he noted on a prison admission record that his "mother-in-law," Mrs. Annie Young—Henrietta's mother—was his next of kin) and continue to live together as husband and wife until his death. Regardless of whether or not her son was his, Zelig adored the boy and took an active and concerned role in his upbringing. When Harry was older, they attended sporting events together, spent weekends at Coney Island's beaches and amusement parks, and interrupted homework sessions with playful wrestling matches. Because Zelig's own boyhood was so recent, he interacted with Harry in a carefree, spirited style that the boy reacted to with enthusiasm. Henrietta told a reporter in 1912 that Zelig's "work" took him away from home for days at a time, which she and her son accepted, for he amply made it up to them when he returned. When told that "Dad" was coming home, Harry would tear through the apartment, screaming with delight and hovering around the front door.[16]

The doting youngster soon found himself facing a separation that amounted to years instead of days. At around 7:45 on the morning of April 7, 1906, a stocky, well-dressed builder named William H. Frame was standing on the subway platform near the Grand Central Depot, waiting for a connecting train. Suddenly a newspaper was pushed into his face, blocking his view. Instinctively he reached up, in time to grasp the wrist of a hand that was trying to extricate his scarf pin. It was an attractive piece, with fourteen diamonds lining a cat's-eye stone, and valued at $125. The would-be thief, a tall young man with expressive eyes and a babyish face, struggled to escape, but Frame and another commuter secured him until Officer John McMullen arrived.

Zelig's lucky streak had run out.

Appearing before City Magistrate Henry Steinert later that morning, Zelig sullenly testified that he was twenty-three years old, born in New York, had lived at 11 E. 106th Street for two years, and worked as a tailor. When told, "Give any explanation you may think proper of the circumstances appearing in the testimony against you, and state any facts that you think will tend to your exculpation?" he replied in a firm voice, "I am not guilty."

On April 11, Magistrate D. E. Finn ordered him held on a $500 bail bond. A month later, on May 11, 1906, Recorder Goff sentenced Zelig to a term at Sing Sing.

During sentencing, Henrietta, who was sitting with young Harry in the courtroom, became hysterical. Asbury wrote that one of Zelig's favorite schemes to defeat punishment was to have a girl explode into emotional fireworks in front of a kindly judge, who would melt at her pleas to have her husband, the father of her baby, released. "But at length," he wrote, "Zelig came before Recorder John W. Goff, later a Justice of the Supreme Court and a jurist of exceptional balance. The recorder listened patiently until the girl had finished, then gently ordered her removed from the room and gave Zelig the first of his many jail sentences."[17]

It didn't quite happen like that. Zelig had no stable of teary-eyed actresses at his beck and call; he had a devoted partner who could not control herself when Goff sentenced him to one of the country's toughest prisons. She began to cry. Max Zweifach and his fiancée were also in the courtroom. While the woman tried to comfort Henrietta, Zweifach took Harry from her and carried him out to spare the three-year-old any further drama.[18] Mother and son would live with her mother, Annie Young, at 96 Chrystie Street and receive financial support from Zweifach, so Zelig was more worried for his own welfare than theirs. By 1906, Sing Sing had a reputation as grim as its gray stone walls.

Newgate, built in Greenwich Village in 1797, was the first New York state prison. Seventeen years later Auburn was constructed, but its remoteness from New York City made the transportation of prisoners to and from the facility inconvenient. In 1825, the New York state legislature assigned Auburn warden and former army Capt. Elam Lynds with the task of constructing a new prison. Lynds selected an area near the town of Mount Pleasant, located on the Hudson River about fifty miles north of New York City. Named Sing Sing after the municipality in which it was located, the prison had an oppressive reputation from the moment it officially opened in 1828.

The public considered it a model prison because convict labor made it turn a profit for the state. But the inmates lived in hellish conditions that destroyed the minds and bodies of most of them. Lynds, who became the first warden, imposed a rule of absolute silence, and to break it was to invite flogging, solitary confinement, or worse. Over the ensuing decades, fire and disease ravaged the place. So did riots: the army had to be called in to quell a particularly violent upheaval in 1863.[19]

By the time of Zelig's arrival in May 1906, some improvements had been implemented. In August 1900, the superintendent of prisons abolished the lock-step, that degrading and grotesque "jail chorus line" movement that required inmates to march in tight and perfect unison when they were taken en masse from their cells. Warden Addison Johnson announced the first parole system available to those who behaved, and true to his word, 133 of 288 applicants went free when the new policy took effect in 1902.[20] But living conditions remained harsh for Sing Sing inmates in the form of damp, cramped cells, poor food and sanitation, and intolerant guards.

In December 1906, eight months after Zelig was admitted, Sing Sing was toured by Florence Maybrick, who had spent years in English prisons after being convicted of her husband's murder, and was now on a campaign to reform penitentiaries in her native America. Perhaps he caught a glimpse of the infamous woman as she walked the cold stone corridors, making mental notes of everything she saw and trying not to shudder. Not long after this visit, Mrs. Maybrick spoke before the Young Men's Club of Dr. Charles H. Parkhurst's church in Madison Square.

"I claim for all men," she said, "human rights, the right to sunshine, to ordinary decencies, to labor. Prisoners realize that some things cannot be bettered and put up with them. But at Sing Sing, strong men are shut up in cells, six feet by three, without ventilation, sanitary provisions, or water for thirteen hours a day. I know what it means. In England for nine months, I had solitary confinement in a cell, seven feet by four, with a log for a seat and my food passed through a trap in the door. They do these things for the salvation of souls; they lead to damnation."[21]

When Zelig arrived at the prison, the admissions clerk noted that he stood five feet nine and a half inches tall (more than an inch shorter than his actual height), weighed 160 pounds, had a light complexion, brown hair, and brown eyes. Occupation was "Stealing." Further notes were as follows:

> Small round head, $6\,^5/_8$ hat. $8\,^1/_2$ shoes. Small scar mark at crown. Three small scar marks on back of head. Medium ears. [Hair] full over temples. Neat brows. Large thick crooked nose. Even and good teeth. Small mouth. Small chin. Long neck. Regular features. Scar on back. [Illegible] on shoulder. Curved scar on edge of thumb.

He would remain there until November 1908. Monk Eastman was also a prisoner and would be until 1909, so perhaps Zelig interacted with him during opportune moments. The young thief had no option but to do his time as quietly as possible and wait for the moment when he could be reunited with his family.

CHAPTER FIVE

DEATH ON THE BOARDWALK

While Zelig contemplated the stone walls of his cell, Max Zweifach continued to strengthen and expand his extortion, gambling, and forgery rackets. He hastened their development by destroying or absorbing the competition. When word of a successful undertaking in any of these realms reached him, Zweifach responded as a shark does to blood: he moved in and assessed, and if the target was appealing enough, he claimed it.

If anyone offered serious resistance, two words were usually all it took for their stance to crumble: Charles Greenwich. Known as "the Bottler" because he had once worked in a soda bottling facility, the Russian-born Greenwich was affiliated with the Five Pointers and ran a thriving stuss game at 65 Suffolk Street. His generous nature played no small part in his place's popularity. As a matter of course, stuss players who called it a night had 10 percent of their losings returned to them by the house, a concept and practice called "viggerish." Alfred Henry Lewis wrote, "Stuss licks up as with a tongue of fire a round full fifth of all the East Side earns, and to viggerish should be given the black glory thereof." Greenwich went a step further and made it policy in his place to return 15 percent of all money lost. Each night of the week, the crowd around his tables numbered three to four deep.

Kid Twist was determined to have a part of it, the Five Pointers notwithstanding. Zweifach approached Greenwich and let him know in no uncertain terms that he was going to be splitting the game profits fifty-fifty with the Twist gang by taking on Harris Stahl as a partner. Greenwich was angry but he also wanted to live. He hated the thought of losing half his game, and he could have signaled his Five Pointer allies for assistance, but he was also a realist. To refuse Zweifach's demand would leave him looking over his shoulder for the rest of his probably short life, so he unhappily agreed.[1]

The strained arrangement went on for weeks. Then Zweifach's greed overstepped whatever sense of fairness he may have harbored, and word was sent to the Bottler during the last week of May 1907 that he was out of his own game, that his share was thenceforth going to be enjoyed by another Twist minion known only by the mysterious nickname of The Nailer. Greenwich's response was spurred by resentment and exasperation. He did not want to lose his money or his life, so he forestalled the inevitable by barring the door to his game at 65 Suffolk Street and only admitting trusted parties.

Zweifach's response to the pathetic defiance was not long in coming. On the night of May 31, Central Office Det. Valentine (Val) O'Farrell was passing the Suffolk Street address just as a standoff was commencing. Harris Stahl, pistol drawn, was standing in front of the closed door while Greenwich, also armed, waited inside, trying to prevent himself from trembling. O'Farrell drew his own gun, closed in, and took Stahl into custody. Greenwich also came out when ordered. The would-be combatants were hauled off to jail, with Stahl hissing threats. A judge fined them both $5 plus costs.[2] That ended the matter for the law, but not for Max Zweifach.

The power struggle ended the following night, when Stahl and Greenwich encountered each other at the corner of Suffolk and Broome streets. First voices were raised, then shots fired. Greenwich fell dead on the sidewalk while Stahl hurled his smoking weapon into the darkness and ran away.[3] He was arrested, but released when no one admitted to actually seeing him shoot his enemy. [4]

Greenwich's murder sent rumbles through the Five Pointers camp. He had technically been under their protection, so killing him was a strike at them, too. Zweifach's ruthlessness was making him enemies, increasing the probability that, like warrior kings of old, he himself would one day die by the sword.

♔ ♔ ♔

Coney Island in early May 1908 was not yet inundated with sunbathers and amusement-seekers, but since the area's motto was "It's never too early to catch the holiday penny," some of the resorts and attractions were already open to the public. Although the crowds that wandered up and down the streets, spending money at the shooting galleries, merry-go-rounds, and refreshment stands were sparser than the mobs that would make Coney vibrate during the carefree, "summer fever" months of July and August, the area still had a festive, anticipatory atmosphere. Everyone was talking eagerly about the upcoming grand opening of Dreamland, and the shows and spectacles that it advertised as part of the event. William Ellis's "Hereafter" was the anticipated star attraction, and it was said that the immense tank for the "Deep Blue Sea Divers" performance was almost complete. Luna Park, that brilliantly lighted pleasure jewel, was scheduled to open on May 16, and tourists looked forward to watching Abraham Erlanger, the theater magnate, unlock the gates to the park with a golden key and make accessible the fabulous recreation of "The Battle of the Merrimac and the Monitor" and the "Man Hunt." The latter was later described as "a thrilling and picturesque exhibition, ending in somewhat blood-curdling style with the guilty man burned at the stake for the edification of the couple of hundred more virtuous players."

Max Zweifach had plenty of other amusement options while he waited for the full Coney experience to begin. The gangster had a roving eye when it came to pretty women, and he picked them up wherever he found them: in the dance halls, cellar clubs and, during warm weather, in the Coney Island resorts. Young, arrogant, and brimming with a sense of invincibility, he never entertained the thought that this predilection could one day have deadlier consequences than a failed marriage.

On the night of May 14, he and his faithful lieutenant, Cyclone Louie, were at Coney Island, enjoying the company of two singers, Carroll Terry and Mabel Leon. Kid Twist was not Miss Terry's first gangster admirer.[5] When she left her native St. Catharines, Ontario, to study opera in New York, she had taken up with Paul Kelly adherent Louis Poggi, also known by the unflattering sobriquet of Louis the Lump. It was, from Terry's perspective, an arrangement spawned more out of necessity than romantic feelings. Failing to hit the big time as quickly as she had expected, she ran out of money and had to accept chorus jobs in Manhattan and Coney Island resorts of varying repute. Poggi was a source of protection in the rougher places and also a means of keeping poverty—and prostitution—at bay. They lived together in the Bowery until early 1908, when Terry went away to Rochester to pursue some singing options. Frustrated and broke, she returned to the city on May 7 but refused to reunite with Poggi. When he found her singing in the Imperial Music Hall at the Bowery and Tompkins Walk, he tried to persuade her to come back and became irate when she declined.[6]

Carroll Terry would insist that she had never laid eyes on Max Zweifach before May 14, but circumstances suggest otherwise. By that point, the Eastman boss and her former lover were on murderous terms that could not be accounted for by the usual Eastman-vs.-Five Points enmity. Poggi claimed that Kid Twist had been harassing him for some time; a story made the rounds that prior to meeting Miss Terry and her friend for drinks on May 14, Zweifach and Pristich found Poggi drinking in a Coney Island bar and amused themselves by making him jump out the window at gunpoint.

The two Eastmans attended the Imperial later that afternoon to catch Carroll Terry's show. After inviting her friend Mabel Leon as a companion for Cyclone Louie, Miss Terry accompanied the two gangsters to an Italian café on the Oceanic Walk for dinner. There, the girls would recall, the men "set everything up in first-rate style." The foursome left the restaurant at around 8 p.m., not seeing the seething Poggi until it was too late.

The Italian gangster, who had been crouching in a doorway, struck Terry with his fist, sending her reeling to the ground. He then opened fire on her companions. Kid Twist was hit only once, the bullet embedding in his skull behind the right ear and killing him instantly.[7] Pristrich was savaged by comparison, possibly because he did not drop as quickly as his boss did. Six bullets hit various vital spots, including a fatal location behind his left ear. Terry took a bullet in the shoulder but later recovered. Mabel Leon fled, unhurt.[8]

The gunplay was witnessed by the crowds thronging the Bowery at Coney Island, throwing them into a panic. Dozens gaped at the two bloodied corpses sprawled in the doorway of the new South Brooklyn Hotel, directly beneath a gigantic floral horseshoe that had been presented to the hotel owner in recognition of the place's grand opening the previous day. Reserves from the Coney Island station under the command of Lieutenants Well and Brindley raced to the location. They called Dr. Meeker from the Reception Hospital for Miss Terry and had the bodies of Zweifach and Pristrich taken to the morgue.

While the police searched high and low for the fugitive Poggi, Zweifach's followers took matters into their own hands. On May 18, an audience that had assembled at the Gotham Theatre to see a stock company perform *Anna Karenina* was thrown into a panic when a pack of Jewish gangsters attacked an Italian outside the building and made an anti-Italian demonstration. The hooligans went to a café inside the theater afterward. When Det. Frank Dougherty arrived from the Liberty Avenue station to investigate the disturbance, a gangster named Samuel "English Sam" Koomer told him where he could go and what he could do with himself en route. Dougherty rewarded his behavior with such a heavy beating that Koomer had to be treated by an ambulance surgeon before being tossed into a cell on a disorderly conduct charge.[9]

On May 19, the police got word that Louis Poggi had been spotted in Saybrook, Connecticut. Two detectives from Brooklyn's Italian squad were immediately sent to the town, where they had no problem locating him and taking him into custody. Extra efforts were made to protect him. At the inquest, Coroner Brewer had noticed that almost all available seats and standing room had been taken by stone-faced, cold-eyed young men. It was whispered throughout the Municipal Building that they were Twist gangsters out to avenge their fallen boss at the first opportunity. Brewer ordered seven policeman and six court officers to kick them out.[10]

Poggi appeared before Justice Scudder on June 9. Although he had been indicted on two counts of first-degree murder, his lawyer, John S. Bennett, had advised him to plead guilty to one charge of manslaughter, which, if accepted, would ensure a brief term in Elmira Reformatory. The Italian gangster, through Bennett, intended to back his plea by producing witnesses who could testify that Kid Twist and Cyclone Louie had been tormenting him long before the Coney Island slaughter occurred.

"My client is a lad of nineteen," Bennett told Scudder. Contradicting Terry's statement that she had only met Zweifach on the day of the double homicide, he said that Poggi had incurred the gang boss's wrath via "his attentions to a girl that Twist was attached to. He knew that Twist had been charged with killing several other men who had crossed his path, and the records of the police show that murder was held against Twist but no case was ever proved. The man and his partner, 'Cyclone,' were more desperate in their methods than ever was Jesse James or any Western outlaw."

Bennett also said that the gunplay at Coney Island was not the result of an ambush, but of a two-way gunfight. Poggi claimed that before bullets began flying, Zweifach and Pristrich tried to kill him in the South Brooklyn Hotel and chased him out into the street with their weapons, forcing him to return fire. He said nothing about the girls at all.

Bartender Michael Cleary, who worked in Madden's Saloon at Coney Island, offered intriguing testimony. He said that before the shooting started, he had seen a hack (carriage) parked near the South Brooklyn Hotel. Cleary recalled that after Zweifach and Pristrich fell, the driver jumped away from the vehicle, ran to him in a panic, and asked him to hold his revolver for him in case the police caught him.

Cleary's story about the parked carriage lends credence to the theory that Poggi did not act alone. Alfred Henry Lewis and Herbert Asbury both wrote that the young Five Pointer, enraged by the theft of Carroll Terry's affection and the forced leap from the saloon window, called one of his bosses and declared his intent to kill Kid Twist. Charles Greenwich's 1907 murder and other offenses that never made it into the printed record would have made a chance to assassinate Zweifach irresistible, and reinforcements were supposedly sent to Coney Island in case Twist and Cyclone Louie survived everything Louis Poggi was capable of dishing out.

Poggi, who was described as "slender, alert, and intelligent," also had a clean record, which Judge Scudder took into consideration before deciding to accept his version of events and the manslaughter plea. On October 7, he sentenced Poggi to a term at Elmira, which would only last for eleven months if he were a model prisoner. His was the first case in Kings County where a defendant to two charges of murder was allowed to plead guilty to a charge of manslaughter instead. In retrospect, this turn of events is not surprising, for Scudder despised criminal trials and was a staunch opponent of capital punishment. When capital cases appeared on his docket, he was notorious for trying to pass them off to another judge. Poggi and his lawyers had made his burden much lighter.[11]

Poggi's elderly mother wept for joy when she heard the sentence. She'd been terrified at the possibility that he would leave the courtroom a free man only to be a dead one shortly afterward. Lawyer Bennett was also pleased.

"Poggi killed those two men because he had to save his own life, and we had abundant evidence from the police and others to acquit him of both charges of murder, but we did not dare to let him walk the streets of New York a free man at this time. He would have been killed by the gangs that have lost their leaders by his hand."[12]

Zweifach was not widely mourned. Ritchie Fitzpatrick's killing in the Sheriff Street saloon four years previously and the suggestion that he had been prepared to garrote and rob Albert Neumann, his co-conspirator in the 1905 railroad forgery scheme, had hammered home the fact that Kid Twist could and would execute a former colleague with the same degree of cruelty and nerve that others would normally reserve for a hated enemy. The funeral tributes were more obligatory than heartfelt.

If the press accounts are accurate, the ensuing months witnessed a series of skirmishes intended to settle the question of who would succeed Max Zweifach as boss. On the night of September 20, a particularly nasty battle was fought in and around Brownsville. Not caring less whether they encountered police resistance, the warring factions spent that evening prowling through the district, hunting for their enemies. The terrorized residents stayed behind locked doors, fearing injury or death from stray bullets. Fights broke out like fireworks in saloons and alleys and on street corners. By the time the police got the situation under control, three men were taken to St. Mary's Hospital with life-threatening bullet wounds and three others were treated for knife injuries.[13]

Surprisingly, Dinny Zweifach, who assumed support of his slain brother's wife and child, never tried to become the heir apparent of the Eastman crew. He concentrated on his own private enterprises instead, perhaps feeling that the crown was too hazardous. For a time he owned and managed two fight clubs, the Roman Athletic Club on the northwest corner of Grand and Orchard streets, and the Dry Dock Athletic Club on East Tenth. He also helped to discover the boxer Louis Wallach, alias Leach Cross, who became a fighting legend.[14] Abe Shoenfeld wrote volumes of pages on his other post-1908 endeavors, which included suspected partnerships with known drug dealers and a controlling interest in a string of stuss games.

Harris Stahl, who killed at least twice for his boss, was another likely successor who never attempted to seize the vacated throne. Soon after Zweifach and Pristrich were buried, he met a beautiful, demure blonde named Rosie. Stahl spoke to a friend, whose wife, Bessie London, was a skilled pickpocket, and had her teach Rosie the tricks of the trade. Soon the young woman was making enough money to support both of them in style, and Stahl "retired." The couple married, and he continued to live off of her earnings until she deserted him in 1912. Then he operated a stuss game in Dollar John's place at 284 E. Houston Street.[15]

In the end, a gangster named Abe Lewis assumed the leadership of the Eastmans. The new boss was actually a first cousin to Samuel Pristrich, who sometimes used the surname Lewis as an alias. He was of the same tough breed as his predecessors, being a veteran gunman and political slugger, but he lacked Eastman's allure as a gangland legend and the menace that Zweifach had freely used to keep his less-devoted boys in line. Lewis could have used both at a time when former followers were seeing themselves as leaders and breaking away— as had been the case when Chick Tricker and Jack Sirocco parted ways with Paul Kelly—so his position was initially precarious. Over time he reached firmer ground by spilling blood at the first sign of opposition and protecting the gang's business interests from the encroachers who always moved in when a boss was toppled. But Abe Lewis was nothing extraordinary himself. In hindsight, he was a run-of-the-mill thug who was merely a placeholder until the next great leader emerged.

It was to Lewis that Zelig Lefkowitz came for a job when he was finally released from Sing Sing in late 1908.[16]

⚜ ⚜ ⚜

Manhattan gangland had changed since Zelig had gone inside. Former cronies and mentors were dead, such as Zweifach and Simon "Crazy Butch" Erenstoft. In 1907, Butch, who was prospering as a Fagin, fence, and poolroom operator, stole a beautiful lady pickpocket known as the Darby Kid from her former lover, Harry the Soldier, a Five Points gangster. On the night of November 20, Harry got his revenge. Erenstoft was shot three times in the back as he was walking near Stanton Street and died before he hit the ground. The police went to a poolroom at 131 Suffolk Street, which was run by Erenstoft's brother, Benjamin, and arrested eight witnesses to the shooting.[17] Someone must have talked, for the police later broadcast that they were looking for Harry the Soldier and "Dopey Benny" (not the Dopey Benny Fein who would be Jack Zelig's successor). Both fled the city, Harry taking off to Africa and Dopey Benny going to Canada, where he ended up in prison.[18]

Zelig went to Lewis to reorient himself and get sorely needed cash. His last months in Sing Sing had been spent in the hospital ward, where he'd been slowly and painfully recovering from a bad bout of pneumonia.[19] He had lost weight and hadn't recovered his full strength, making it difficult to resume his pocket-picking livelihood. His fingers would have been as nimble as ever, but should he be detected and seized, his chances of breaking free and making a successful escape would have been poor.

Abe Lewis had a job for him, one that required only the ability to squeeze a trigger:

Kill Chick Tricker.

CHAPTER SIX

BACK FROM THE DEAD

A *New York Times* article published in the wake of Zelig's murder would assert that he had been casual friends with Chick Tricker and Jack Sirocco for years, until greed got the better of him and he cultivated a secret alliance with gangster Jimmy Kelly, an Italian who was crossing swords with the Sirocco-Tricker mob. To further his and Kelly's newly combined interests, the article went on to state, Zelig entered Tricker's Bowery saloon on the pretext of a friendly visit and tried to shoot him in a back room, but failed at the last minute due to sudden loss of nerve.[1]

The *Times* had the general circumstances right (except for an alliance with Jimmy Kelly, which was years in the future) but described the botched assassination as a recent incident and a failed expression of Zelig's own ambition. The truth was that Zelig was an instrument of Abe Lewis when he walked into Tricker's Bowery saloon in December 1908. Although he lacked the killer instinct at the time, he would have been angry about his friend Zweifach's murder, and desperate for the payoff and secure position in the gang that Lewis had promised. Overindulgence in liquor may also have convinced him that he could go through with it. As an Eastman follower, Zelig would have seen many men shot, stabbed, or beaten to death over the years, in both personal and factional disputes. Perhaps he believed that he could rob a man of his life with the same steady nerve that he applied to picking pockets.

Abe Lewis had good reason to want Chick Tricker dead. As a Five Pointers leader, Tricker was, symbolically at least, responsible for the murders of Zweifach and Pristrich. The fact that Lewis targeted him suggests that he may have been the "higher-up" that Louis Poggi supposedly called for reinforcements in case Kid Twist and Cyclone Louie proved to be too much for him to handle alone. Gunning Tricker down would satisfy both battle protocol and Lewis's personal need for revenge.

The new Eastman boss recognized an opportunity in the twenty-year-old ex-convict. Before being sent to Sing Sing in 1906, Zelig had been on mildly friendly terms with Tricker and Jack Sirocco. He and the latter had been playmates during their childhood. Both had also been in the House of Refuge at corresponding times, and associated casually afterward.[2]

Such fraternization between members of opposing gangs was not unusual. When Alfred Henry Lewis was conducting research for *The Apaches of New York,* a police detective friend took him to a hangout on Twenty-eighth Street called the Bal Tabourin, so that he might meet and interview Charles Levin, alias Ike the Blood, a prominent Eastman gangster who had helped the Zweifach brothers vault Republican leader Sam Koenig into power in 1902. Levin was sitting with two Five Pointers of comparable rank, both of whom were unabashed in their admiration of "Ike." Semi-neutral parties like Levin and his admirers were respected instead of reviled for their impartiality and were valued as negotiators for peace agreements. The boyhood connection to Sirocco and his own reputation for nonviolence made Zelig Lefkowitz an ideal candidate to get Tricker in an unguarded position and eliminate him.

It is not known whether he arrived unannounced, using the excuse that he was visiting old acquaintances he hadn't seen since he went to prison, or whether he notified Tricker ahead of time that he was coming as a neutral party authorized to negotiate an end to the Eastman-Five Pointers hostilities. Either way, he and Tricker ended up alone in a hallway that linked the saloon's general area with an office at the back, with Zelig pointing a gun at the older man.[3]

Their eyes met, and what Tricker saw told him right away that he wasn't going to die that night. Zelig looked queasy, and his hand began to shake so badly that a fatal shot might have been questionable even at that close range. Fury at being duped infused the Five Pointer, and he began taunting his pale opponent.[4]

"Go on," Tricker supposedly declared, "you wouldn't shoot anybody who was looking at you. Beat it now before I do you up. Why, you mutt, you haven't got the nerve to touch a soul."[5]

And Zelig didn't. He had been in fights before, but defending oneself took less brass than cold-blooded murder. His reticence was fated to end soon, but at that crucial moment, he didn't have what it took to pull the trigger and kill his man, and both he and his intended victim knew it. As the seconds ticked by, their roles were slowly reversing, with Zelig becoming the marked man and Tricker the future hunter. Gripped now by fear, Zelig backed away until he'd put himself beyond grabbing distance, then fled the saloon.

He probably told Henrietta the truth about what had happened, for he succeeded in convincing her to use the part of their dwindling funds to buy one-way train tickets to Chicago. He couldn't stay in New York after the botched mission, and they both knew it. Even in the event that Chick Tricker was more intent on striking back at Abe Lewis than at the pathetic messenger, there was small chance that Lewis would do anything for them now. And any one of the eager, seething young red-hots seeking to curry favor with Tricker might see the murder of his intended assassin as a good way of doing so.

In January 1909, Zelig, Henrietta, and Harry left her mother's home, where they had been holed up, and boarded a train for Chicago. A former Sing Sing inmate whom he had befriended when both were serving time now lived there and had invited him to look him up should Zelig ever be in town.[6]

He would be lucky to leave the city alive.

♕ ♕ ♕

Chicago's reputation alone was enough to attract an ambitious criminal. With the greater percentage of the aldermen on the City Council ascribing a dollar value to their services, the police willing to overlook almost anything if the bribe was right, and a young, rowdy underworld element that welcomed anyone with a knack for a given crime, Zelig's chances of making a good living outside the boundaries of the law were excellent.

Unlike New York, which could trace some of its gang lineage back eighty years, Chicago was home to a younger breed, with few gangs predating the Great Chicago Fire of 1871. Some organization and structure did exist among the flesh traders and gambling house owners, but overall, it was a city where the criminal entrepreneur had ample opportunity to secure his or her niche. Pickpockets in particular abounded and had ever since the Chicago World's Fair, when scores of them arrived from other cities (after making the proper arrangements with Big Mike MacDonald, head of the underworld at the time) to fleece the thousands of tourists attending the big event. Saloon proprietor Bob Duncan, who ran a popular establishment on State Street, widely advertised his connection with the police and, for a specified fee, guaranteed "dips," as pickpockets were then called, a hunting territory where the local cops suffered from willful blindness.

Ed Klein's cigar store, which Zelig and his ex-con friend frequented, was well known to the Chicago Police Department. Weeks before Zelig and his family arrived, detectives assigned to Assistant Chief of Police Schuettler raided the establishment at 211 Van Buren Street, which was a notorious billiard hall. Thirty-three men, including one of Klein's clerks, were arrested as inmates of a gambling house. The raid was made after the department received complaints about young men flocking to the place and gambling away their wages. Zelig, who became a proficient pinochle player, spent and probably took in enough money there. But however welcome he may have been when he first joined its roster of regulars, he was eventually persona non grata.

What Zelig said or did to offend Klein and/or his habitués is not clear. But one night, the ex-New Yorker arrived to participate in the usual revelry and, as he later put it, was invited to take part in an exclusive private game being held in a part of the store not accessible to the general public. Not considering the request to be unusual, he went down a darkened hallway and entered a room, in which a handful of hard-looking men sat around a table, gripping cards. Zelig's eyes were on the game and the pile of money in the center of the table, rendering him oblivious to the shadowy figure standing to one side of the doorway.

He would later describe what allegedly happened next as a series of fast, violent movements that took place in such rapid succession that his recall was severely disjointed. Hands grabbed him, twisting his arm behind his back with such force that it became dislocated in the struggle. A rag was stuffed into his mouth with equal violence, choking him almost to the point of unconsciousness. In one retelling of this assault, Zelig claimed that his attackers, who included the card players, finally subdued him by clamping a rag soaked in a strong, chemical-smelling agent over his nose and mouth.

When he regained consciousness, he was lying on the floor of a carriage that was moving along at a lively pace. His wrists were bound, and blood and loose teeth left a nauseating sensation in his mouth. He was less concerned with how he was still alive than how to escape.

In a version of events both sensational and questionable, Zelig credited his escape with the shoddy job his captors had made of binding his wrists. Working himself loose with the deft hands that had earned him a decent living as a pickpocket, he lunged for the carriage door, crashed through it, hit the street, and remembered nothing else until he was being examined by doctors in a hospital emergency room.

That was Zelig's accounting of his injuries to his wife and family. It may not have, and probably didn't, happen that way. Did he cheat at cards? Fleece one too many drunks who otherwise could have spent their money at Klein's card tables? Or did he lose more than he'd intended and provoke the other players with accusations of cheating? Did he really jump from a speeding carriage, or was he carried away, bloody and insensible, and dumped somewhere at the request of an anxious Klein, who didn't want anyone dying in his store? However it all actually happened, he was lucky to survive. He was in dire shape: several ribs had been broken, his body was a roadmap of cuts and bruises, and his head, which appeared to have taken the brunt of the punishment, was black and swollen. The skull had even been cracked in places.[7]

While doctors leaned over him, Zelig suddenly lost consciousness a second time, stopped breathing, and went into cardiac arrest.[8] Medical technology in 1909 was ill-equipped to deal with such a sudden onset of injury-induced death, and the few successful revivals can be partly attributed to the patient's own vitality. Such was the case with Zelig, who had been healthy and in good physical shape before the attack. Oxygen application and a strychnine injection[9] succeeded in reviving him, and artificial respiration was applied until he was breathing on his own. But he remained dangerously close to death for days afterward. There was probably an operation performed to ameliorate the head injury's effects, although this is not known for certain.[10]

Zelig remained in the hospital for weeks. At first, he needed staff assistance in performing the most basic functions—eating, brushing his teeth, and even sitting up. Youth and a resilient constitution were on his side, so he made painful but steady progress. When spring percolated into a hot Midwestern summer, he was functioning well enough to leave the hospital. He then made the necessary arrangements to return to New York. He and Henrietta had no family in Chicago, and his inability to work made it necessary that they rely on the generosity of relatives for a time.

Zelig recovered, physically at least. But it was not the same person who returned to the Lower East Side in the summer of 1909. For a long time he was quiet and had a hostile watchfulness in his stare, except around those he trusted. Gradually he reassumed a lot of his old personality and habits, like a Polaroid photo steadily focusing into something recognizable. Strangers and new acquaintances would have been surprised to learn that he'd ever been impaired. He was a fluid, easy conversationalist and, socially, gave a favorable impression. He'd developed a voracious appetite for reading while at Sing Sing, and enjoyed the classics by Dickens, Victor Hugo, and Eugene Sue, all of which contributed to the refined and extensive vocabulary that he became noted for. He maintained his fluency in Russian and Yiddish, and was known to pepper an English conversation with a smattering of phrases from both languages, to the consternation of unilingual listeners. He was physically active, thinking nothing of spending an entire summer's day in the Coney Island surf. He remained devoted and loving to his family. But a dark side now flowed beneath the surface, ready to manifest itself at the first sign of danger by grabbing a weapon or clenching a large fist and lashing out. Never again would Zelig Lefkowitz flee in terror from anyone—Chick Tricker, the police, or a whole army of Five Pointers.

The heightened aggression level and volatile temper were Zelig's souvenirs of the Chicago assault. On the topic of post-head injury behavior, a University of Waterloo dissertation[11] posted on the institution's Web site noted, "The behavioral effects include *agitation and irritability, verbal and physical aggressiveness* [emphasis added], impulsivity, depression and suicidal thoughts, and an egocentric or self-centered orientation in interpersonal relationships."[12] Zelig did not exhibit all of the listed symptoms, but the ones he did experience became the catalyst for his ascent in the Manhattan underworld.

He also hated gamblers with a passion after the attack. They had swarmed him like a pack of jackals and nearly killed him. He saw them as duplicitous human rats, ready to use false flattery and sweet propositions to get their victims into a situation where the only loser was the one who fell for their ploy.

"On the train back to New York," Joseph Lefkowitz says, "Zelig saw a couple of card sharps slowly take a traveling salesman type for almost all he had, and then tell the sucker to come to a private game in one of the compartments. They told him that the bigger money was played for in private games, that he was sure to win his money back. Zelig went over to where they were playing, tells the salesman not to be a damned fool, that these guys were vultures. I think one of them told him to mind his own business, because he suddenly went into a rage, swept the cards everywhere, and went for them. He got a few licks in before the conductor and other rail staff got involved. I didn't hear that anyone was arrested over it, or even put off the train."

He was still known as William Albert, but that wouldn't last too much longer. Big Jack Zelig was in the making.

♛ ♛ ♛

What, if anything, Zelig said to Abe Lewis upon his return to Manhattan has not been preserved for posterity. Lewis probably had more pressing things on his mind than upbraiding or punishing the former underling. In the spring of 1909, the Eastman boss was indicted on two charges, one for shooting a David Krissal in a Brownsville saloon and the other for robbing a grocery store in the Lower East Side. After being freed on $8,000 bail, he disappeared until August 23, when he was spotted and arrested in front of the Brooklyn Post Office on Washington Street. Taking no chances, the police brought Lewis first to the district attorney's office and then before Supreme Justice Crane, who denied bail and committed him to the Raymond Street Jail.[13] Somehow bail was secured once again. Lewis, gleefully confident of his omnipotence, got drunk one night and, with several members of his gang, robbed and wrecked a restaurant at 7 Jamaica Avenue. He was caught, tried before Judge Fawcett, and convicted in November.

Lewis's followers sent threats to the judge. One postcard read, "You are to sentence Abe Lewis Monday morning. If you do sentence him, we will make it hot for you in court." Judge Fawcett shrugged off these and other missives with contempt, but the police implemented precautions. When sentencing took place on November 15, detectives stood ready in the courtroom, their attention focused on what a reporter described as "a group of hard-featured youths, with their hair plastered down over their temples in gang fashion."

Asked if he had anything to say regarding why sentence should not be pronounced upon him, Lewis glowered and replied, "I ain't got nothin' to say."

Judge Fawcett glared back from the bench. "I think that is the best thing for you to do—say nothing. Your record rivals that of the notorious Monk Eastman, Kid Twist, or your equally notorious cousin, Cyclone Lewis [sic].

Several prominent citizens of Brownsville have assured me that your conviction is the greatest benefit that has come to that section in years. You have been a great menace to that community and an enemy to society. It would be a genuine blessing to society at large if you could be kept in prison for the rest of your life. . . . I hope the sentence imposed on you will impress the members of your gang now at liberty that Brooklyn is now unsafe and dangerous for them unless they reform their vicious ways."[14]

With that, he sentenced Lewis to nineteen years and three months in Sing Sing. The gangster's wife and mother both burst into tears, and Lewis himself looked stunned for a brief moment. Then he composed himself, and, like Eastman before him, yielded to the inevitable with a sullen dignity.

While Lewis prepared for prison life, his successor, someone whom he had probably passed off as a high-strung failure, was in the process of coming forward, albeit involuntarily.

♔ ♔ ♔

The year 1910 began fortuitously for Zelig. In a letter dated February 3, Assistant District Attorney Charles G. Nott Jr. wrote to District Attorney Charles Whitman, "Pursuant to your request under date of January 5th, to inquire into the case adjourned to the first Call Calendar in March, I have investigated the case of William Albert, New Calendar No. 19, Indictment No. 51815, and find the following to be the facts." He was referring to the 1905 grand larceny charge that arose from the attempted theft of Sam Michaelof's pin.

Nott outlined Zelig's indictment and the subsequent fixing of bail by Judge Foster. He continued, "On the seventeenth of April 1906, he was indicted on another charge of grand larceny, in another case, indictment No. 55071, and he pled guilty to attempted larceny in the second degree on May 8, 1906, and was sentenced by Recorder Goff to the State Prison for two years and six months. It would appear from the papers that at the time he pled guilty before Recorder Goff and was sentenced, that the Court was cognizant of the presence of the pending indictment [5185]." He summarized Zelig's record, then concluded the letter with, "He is now out on $1,500 bail, given July 21, 1905, by Morris Sigelman, 606 E. Ninth Street, and judging from the second paragraph of your letter, that if the defendant pleaded guilty [to the 1906 charge] and other indictments now pending against him were before the court at the time of sentence, recommendation should be made to discharge him therein. I do so recommend."

In other words, although Zelig had yet to stand trial for the attempted theft of Samuel Michaelof's diamond pin back in 1905, he had been under indictment for it when Recorder Goff accepted his guilty plea in connection with the William Frame incident, and in view of the fact that he'd already served prison time, the district attorney's office had little inclination to prosecute a five-year-old grand larceny case.

When Zelig and his family returned to New York, they stayed temporarily with Annie Young before taking an apartment in Harlem.[15] He associated with old friends who had known him before the unanticipated flight to Chicago, but he did not seek reconnection with the Eastmans, although he sometimes patronized the same saloons and clubs that they did. If anyone taunted him about the Chick Tricker mishap, they rarely did it a second time. It's not a matter of record that he got into altercations over the subject, but given the fact that he worked himself out of a state of disgrace, it's safe to assume that he met all hostility with a level of force and aggression that elicited a grudging respect.

He did not make another attempt at diamond cutting or any other legitimate employment, relying instead on his skills as a pickpocket. His proficiency in the art of stealing, as well as his engaging personality, won him a following among other guns, stalls, and tools. While the Eastmans were dealing with the shock of Abe Lewis's imprisonment, Zelig Lefkowitz, alias William Albert, was the captain of his own small crew of thieves. He used the network of contacts he had made during his years with Eastman and Zweifach to make sure that whatever he or someone connected with him stole disappeared forever with a healthy profit in its wake. Independent pickpockets would approach him to obtain his assistance in getting rid of a troublesome piece of merchandise, such as a monogrammed item or unusual bit of jewelry that would prove easy to identify later, and end up working with him on an ongoing basis.

"I talked to an old guy who worked for Zelig in those days," Joseph Lefkowitz says, "and he said that Zelig was one of those types who showed no fear but wasn't careless either. He knew all the right people and could get you a good price for almost anything you brought him. He apparently never paid off the cops either, which means he *must* have been good, otherwise they'd have nailed him first chance they got."

One of his gang's specialties was "jumping out." Whenever word arrived that a fair or similar public event was being held in one of the towns outside New York City, they would travel to the site and work the distracted crowds. They didn't always enter and escape unnoticed. In August 1910, he and two friends went to Middletown, in Orange County, to fleece the attendees at the annual fair. Unbeknownst to him, two New York City police officers, Lt. John McMullen and Det. James Murphy, were also in town at the behest of the Orange County Fair Association and the Wellkill Transit Company, to assist Chief McCoach in preventing New York thieves from preying on the public.

On the afternoon of August 30, McMullen, Murphy, and Chief McCoach, all dressed in civilian clothes, were riding a streetcar bound for Goshen. At Academy Avenue more passengers got on, three of whom McMullen recognized immediately. It was Zelig and his party.

McMullen nudged McCoach, nodded discreetly in their direction, and whispered, "There are three good ones back there."

At Benton Avenue McMullen got off the car and waited. McCoach and Murphy spoke quietly to the conductor before closing in on the three pickpockets and advising them that they were under arrest. A mad dash for freedom followed. While the two officers subdued his friends, Zelig managed to jump out a side window, right into McMullen's waiting arms.

The bedraggled trio appeared in court and promised the judge that if they were allowed to go, they would return to New York City immediately and warn other pickpockets to stay out of Middletown. It was probably Zelig who did most of the talking, as he had an orator's ability that the best defense lawyers might have envied. The offer was accepted by the impressed judge, who released them with a warning.[16]

When summer cooled into fall and the county fairs tapered off, Zelig confined his activities to New York City, except for the occasional trip across state lines into New Jersey. When the city's workers and shoppers rose to begin their day, he was usually among them, riding the trolley cars and prowling the elevated train platforms, transferring wallets and valuables from the pockets of unsuspecting commuters into his own. Unless he experienced a midday windfall, he kept working until the after-theater crowds had thinned out. Then he would go home to Henrietta and Harry or join associates for an evening of drinks and card playing.

One night at the end of November 1910, he accompanied two friends to the Chatham Club at 8 Doyers Street in Chinatown. For the second time in two years, his life was going to change forever.

CHAPTER SEVEN

NEW KING
ON THE BLOCK

The Chatham Club occupied an odd-looking building that Asbury described as "a curious, many-gabled structure, unbelievably dingy and dirty and tricked out in amazing architectural doodads."[1] It was a popular hangout for Chinatown's "white parasites,"[2] men like Big Mike Abrams, a heartless thug who delighted in brutalizing and even killing every Chinese who crossed his path, and Chuck Connors, the "Bowery Philosopher," whose colorful speech and eccentric behavior made him a press favorite. Connors used to enthrall tourists by sitting in his chair at the Chatham Club and not moving a muscle for hours at a time. The surrounding neighborhood had a violent history. Doyers Street, a jagged alley-thoroughfare that ran between Pell Street and Chatham Square, played host to one gruesome murder after another during the years that the area's Chinese tongs were at war. So many men were stabbed, shot, hacked to death with hatchets, or decapitated in one section of Doyers Street that veered sharply to one side that it became known locally as the "Bloody Angle."

Zelig and two of his old friends from Broome Street, Tim Reardon and Andy Collins, made an after-hours visit to the Chatham Club one night during the last week of November 1910. Reardon was a thief who periodically endeared himself to the reformers by declaring himself rehabilitated, only to return to his trade once the fanfare—and money—ran low. Collins was Irish by birth and a crook by nature. He lived in the Occidental Hotel at the corner of Broome Street and the Bowery, where Big Tim Sullivan regularly held court, and although he made his living as a pickpocket, he occasionally did slugging work at Tammany's behest. Collins moved with a slight limp, the result of being shot in the leg while evading arrest a few years previously.[3]

The place was active despite the lateness of the hour. Gangsters, thieves, pimps, whores, and unusually brave tourists downed whiskey and beer at the crowded bar and packed tables. There was no music, not that any could be heard above the arguing, yelling, and laughter. Zelig and his friends managed to find an unoccupied table and sat down. They placed a drink order with the harried waiter, unaware that three sets of scornful eyes were on them.

Tommy Fitzpatrick, Johnny Ricey, and Jackie (alias Jackeen) Dalton, three local toughs who were always seeking ways to enhance their "bad guy" reputation, were in a fighting mood. Tommy was the younger brother of the same Ritchie Fitzpatrick whom Kid Twist had cut down in the war of Eastman succession six years ago that very month. As Zelig had been close to the now-departed Zweifach, Tommy had ample reason to dislike him, and the crowded Chatham Club was a good enough place to indirectly avenge his brother's death. Fitzpatrick knew that any scores settled there would be the talk of the Lower East Side the next day. Collins and Reardon might interfere, but Tommy could count on help from Dalton and Ricey,[4] who were no strangers to bloodshed. More than a year later they would both be sought for the murder of opium smuggler and unlicensed dentist Eugene Post, who had stolen Dalton's girl from him.

Fitzpatrick, after consuming a few more drinks, pushed his chair back, rose, and approached. He hovered at Zelig's table for a few seconds before nodding down at Tim Reardon, who had been drinking heavily for hours and was now nodding off. He also had personal issues with the "professional reformer" and used them as an impetus for drawing his real target into a confrontation.

"Hey, Zelig," he said in a stage whisper, "I am going to cut that bastard's balls out."[5]

Heads at adjacent tables must have turned, anticipating action. If so, they were disappointed, as neither Zelig nor the sodden and cheery Reardon reacted as hoped. Abe Shoenfeld wrote that Zelig "placated" Tommy; he probably commented that they were there just to drink and didn't want trouble. Fitzpatrick, glowering, finally returned to his seat, where he and his companions continued to guzzle hard liquor and fling dark scowls Zelig's way. They did not stew in their resentment for long. Minutes later, Reardon got up and wobbled across the floor toward the swinging doors that led to the men's room. As he passed Fitzpatrick's table, the latter produced a knife, leaped up, and slashed him in the back.

What happened next shocked a clientele for whom bloodshed was an occupational hazard and frequent entertainment. It wasn't the violence that stunned everyone—it was the perpetrator.

When Reardon cried out and fell, Zelig's expression instantly transformed from annoyed but mellow to a full-blown mask of fury. Red-faced and seething, he leaped out of his seat, crossed the floor at lightning speed, and seized Fitzpatrick. He struck Tommy twice with his huge fist, the second punch sending the other man flying through the swinging doors and down the steps leading to the lavatory.

Jackeen Dalton lunged at him. Dalton was a short man, five feet tall and barely 110 pounds. Opium addiction had left him with hollow cheeks, a pasty complexion, and poor health, but he was a vicious fighter, especially with a gun. He was physically no match for the taller and heavier Zelig, who knocked him out with one blow. Johnny Ricey barely got in one punch before Zelig twisted his fingers in Ricey's hair and pounded his head on one of the tables.

According to a confidential report filed two years later,[6] Zelig then dropped his victim and ran from the Chatham Club up the Bowery, not stopping until he got to Broome Street. He wasn't fleeing from fear this time—he was looking for a gun. He had inflicted a devastating beating on three of Chinatown's worst criminals, and unless he finished them off, he would be hunted until they got another chance at him. This time, with a gun in his hand, he was capable of killing.

Finding someone on Broome Street who was willing to give him a firearm with no questions asked was an easy enough matter. He ran back toward the Chatham Club, intent on hovering in a nearby doorway and shooting his targets the second they emerged. But he made the mistake of taking the weapon out of his pocket as he turned onto Doyers Street. A pedestrian saw him gripping it and shouted, "Police, police, he's got a gun!"

The beat cop, who had been patrolling nearby, grabbed him and confiscated the weapon. Zelig, who was still in the throes of rage and an adrenaline surge, refused to submit to arrest quietly and was beaten about the thighs in consequence. Shouts and curses echoed along Doyers Street, sending some late-night strollers running for cover and attracting others in curious bunches.

Hearing the commotion from inside the Chatham Club, George Browne, who owned the place in partnership with one Joe Stivern, hurried out into the cold night air. He, along with his customers, had witnessed and been stunned by the one-sided brawl. Like all dive owners who kept their businesses open after hours and had a criminal clientele, Browne was beholden to local politicians. He secured their protection not only via payoffs, but also by placing his tougher customers at their disposal during elections. Anyone who could put down his man (or even better, men) like Zelig had incalculable value at the polls. Browne knew a future asset when he saw one—Silver Dollar Smith and his Tammany protectors had seen the same potential in Monk Eastman more than ten years earlier. He intervened and offered the policeman $5 to let his prisoner go. The cop accepted the deal, satisfied that the blows his club had landed would leave Zelig limping for days.

The battle was talked about in the dives and poolrooms and on street corners for days afterward. No one, especially those who knew about the cold feet Zelig had gotten in front of Chick Tricker, could believe that the pickpocket, who had been recognized for his thieving but never his battle ability, had taken out three of the Lower East Side's most violent thugs in the space of mere minutes. He had also intended to end the fight with an act of multiple murder, something that would have been unthinkable for him a year ago. The Chatham Club triple knockout marked the point at which Zelig Lefkowitz became Big Jack Zelig. It transformed his status in the Lower East Side underworld from fringe player to celebrity and made him a figure of intense interest to local politicians and Eastmans who had been feeling the loss of a strong leader.

There were soon repercussions, however, as Tommy Fitzpatrick had no intention of letting the matter end there. Like his brother Ritchie before him, he was a fighter, and he seethed at the battering that his reputation had taken along with his aching body. Fitzpatrick allowed himself a few days to recover and then struck back.

♧ ♧ ♧

The first week of December saw Madison Square Garden crammed with bicycle racing enthusiasts. The celebrated six-day race, which featured both amateur and professional talent, was in town for the eighteenth year in a row. Ten thousand people filtered into the Garden on December 3, and soon the saucer-shaped track was abuzz. At midnight, Big Tim Sullivan fired a pistol to signal the start of an event in which fourteen teams of cyclists from all over the world participated.

There was a minor sensation when New York cyclist Albert Rovere went over the rail during a sharp turn and nearly landed in one of the spectator boxes, spraining his ankle. Another disturbance took place the same night, albeit with fewer witnesses.

Zelig attended the event with George Browne. Tommy Fitzpatrick, still smarting from the previous month's beating, spied him sitting in a box and nudged some companions. When the crowd began cheering loudly, drowning out any lesser noise, they leaped into the box and struck in a maelstrom of fists and heavy winter boots.

Unaware of their approach, Zelig was seized by Fitzpatrick and a gangster named Red Wagner before he could react, thrown to the floor of the box, and stomped. Unable to regain his footing, he took one punch after another to his ribs, back, and stomach. Browne waded in with fists flying, beating them back and preventing worse injury. Attention from the occupants of the surrounding boxes finally forced Fitzpatrick and Wagner to flee, but not before they had thoroughly worked their victim over.

Although badly hurt, Zelig stunned onlookers by springing to his feet, lunging out of the box, and attempting to pursue his attackers. His bulging eyes, the blood that bubbled from his nose and oozed in thick ropes from his mouth, and his disheveled, filthy suit all combined to make him look like an explosion or accident victim come to terrifying life. Repulsed race fans scrambled to get out of his way; spectators from the underworld were as impressed as they were shocked. Browne and others finally caught up with him and took him to a hospital, but not before his intention to finish the battle had been witnessed by dozens.[7]

"By a hair of his head Zelig escaped from the Garden," Abe Shoenfeld remembered. "That, bear in mind, was the death warrant of the Italian gang [sic], and they themselves signed it, with Zelig as the notary of public."

He had the muscle power to accomplish it by the time those words were written. Eastmans and those aspiring to gangland position had started fawning over Zelig hours after the Chatham Club fight became general knowledge, and the Madison Square Garden battle caused the ranks of his admirers to swell. Using one's blood-soured, potentially dying breath to get even with an enemy was the stuff that legends were made from. When Zelig was back in circulation, George Browne sought his company even more frequently and favored him with money, free drinks, and introductions to interested politicians who could always use a popular fighter in their own entourage during primaries and elections. Members of his pickpocket mob found their numbers supplemented by Eastman gangsters who had been rudderless since Abe Lewis was sentenced to Sing Sing. Everywhere he went, Zelig was approached by admirers and well-wishers who relinquished their chairs to him, shook his hand, or asked him to call on them if he needed muscle, money, or favors.

This meteoric rise from fringe operator to Eastman crown prince was not unusual for the era. In 1910, gang bosses were still vaulted into power by their fighting ability. Like the Hollywood ingénue who suddenly receives a lucrative film contract and becomes Tinseltown's overnight sensation, when Zelig Lefkowitz beat Fitzpatrick, Dalton, and Ricey to a pulp in one of Chinatown's toughest dives, he received immediate notice from those whose support could turn him into the next Monk Eastman. The onus was on him to maintain his position through the expected methods—making money for his new followers, being their best friend or worst nightmare as the situation demanded, repelling enemies, and doing a thorough job when hired to protect a vice operation, fight in a labor war or swing votes in favor of the gang's political patron. Two years earlier, it would not have been possible for Zelig Lefkowitz to fulfill those obligations. Now he could—too well.

"It was more than just the fight [with Fitzpatrick, Ricey, and Dalton] that did it for him," Joseph Lefkowitz says. "It was the extent to which he'd changed from the days when he was just a pickpocket. He was good at what he did back then, but harmless, unless you were a sucker not paying attention to your wallet. Then he comes back from Chicago covered with scars and beating up tough guys—that's what got everyone. Zelig was not normal. At the same time you're impressed, you're also scared shitless of him."[8]

The name "Big Jack Zelig" was another byproduct of the Chatham Club and Madison Square Garden brawls. He rarely used it in reference to himself. Abe Shoenfeld's investigators wrote that "[he] is known on the East Side only as Zelig. But the Italians of Chinatown[9] have prefixed to his name 'Jack.'" Nicknames based on origin, occupation, territory, accomplishment, and even appearance were common in pre-Prohibition[10] American gangland, e.g., the Bottler, Kid Dropper, the Lobster Kid, Spanish Louis, Nigger Ruhl. They sprouted up, took hold, and overwhelmed the recipient's previous name and identity. Few knew Zelig Lefkowitz, but before two years passed, everyone would know Big Jack Zelig, "the Starker."

"Starker" was an Anglicized version of the Yiddish word *shtarker*, which meant "strong man" or "strong arm" and was used to denote a hardcore Jewish gangster.[11] Zelig embodied the word, which even sounded harsh when spoken. Arthur Goren wrote in *Saints and Sinners: The Underside of American Jewish History*, "At a critical moment when murders and arrests disrupted the existing hierarchy of gang rule on the Lower East Side, Zelig moved in to fill the vacuum and become the 'terror' and 'commander' of downtown's Jewish underworld. . . ."[12]

That involved seizing control of the protection racket, which was the financial mainstay for gangs not involved in commercialized vice like drug trafficking and prostitution. None of the small business owners and vice figures who paid the gangs protection money in exchange for peace and stability were surprised when his newly assigned henchmen began visiting their resorts to advise that whoever they had formerly been dealing with was now "out" and the Zelig gang was "in." Most paid on the spot because however much they dreaded repercussions from the original extortionists, these businessmen and women now feared Zelig more. Over time, however, any resentment incurred by the forced switch in "service providers" abated, especially after Zelig delivered on his promise to keep marauders away. One madam told the police that the $100 she paid his representative on a monthly basis was the best security investment she'd ever made. An undercover detective who attended a ball thrown in honor of the gang leader reported that he was treated like a benefactor of sorts: "Not alone did crooks, gamblers, and others attend this ball, but [also] East Side businessmen, young and old, came to pay willing tribute to Jack Zelig. There was a large crowd of legitimate businessmen. . . . Jack was very popular."

There was one service, however, that he refused to provide despite a regular need for it. He would not rent his men out as a strike force during the fights that broke out between competing gamblers. Men like Louis "Bridgey" Webber, Dollar John Langer, and Herman Rosenthal, craving one another's clientele and fortunes, were constantly sniping at one another. On the milder end of the harassment scale, they sent anonymous letters to police headquarters advising the vice squads of a competitor's newly opened resort. When really irate, they hired gangsters to ambush the object of their vendetta and do serious physical damage. The problem was, when the victim recovered, his usual response was to send tough guys after the rival gambler who had ordered the beating *and* the thugs who had done the deed.

Abe Meyer was a young waist factory worker who earned extra money as a political slugger. He was an early recruit to the new Zelig gang and recalled to Joseph Lefkowitz more than fifty years later, "Zelig laid down the law about that [acting as soldiers in a gamblers' dispute]. We could protect their houses and give it to anyone who broke in on a game that we were protecting. But we weren't to do their dirty work for them. He said that we'd be the ones who'd end up getting it from the cops and the other gangs. He said that you couldn't trust these guys any further than you could throw them." Chicago had forever darkened the new boss's attitude toward professional gamblers, but in Manhattan it wasn't a misguided outlook to have.

Two of his most devoted new friends/followers were Louis Rosenberg, alias Lefty Louis, and Jacob Seidenshner, alias Whitey Lewis. Although they liked Zelig personally and viewed their connection to him as a means of advancement, the association ultimately led them to the electric chair.

CHAPTER EIGHT

THE BOYS OF
THE AVENUE

"L efty Louis"[1] Rosenberg was, like Zelig, born in New York to respectable and industrious parents. His father, Jacob, was trustee at the local synagogue and had rosy visions of his children's future, never anticipating the thieving and violence that became Louis's downfall. Rosenberg Senior and his wife, Anne, sent Louis and his siblings to Hebrew school and maintained an Orthodox household. The prognosis for a hard-working but honest and religious future seemed excellent.

That began to change when Louis, at the age of six, fell seriously ill. He managed to recover, but the process was slow. The doctors insisted to his parents that he needed fresh air, but their inability to send him to the country as prescribed led to them granting him the next best privilege—large chunks of time spent out of the small, dank tenement and in the streets, where the air quality was marginally better. As had been the case with Zelig, his father was too busy working and mother too occupied with the other children to notice at first when Louis fell in with the boy gangs, whose hijinks appealed to him more than the rituals of Orthodox Judaism.

The Rosenbergs were forced to take heed when Louis and a friend were caught stealing a brother's savings. By that point he was a regular habitué of the poolrooms, where master thief and Fagin Joe English (real surname Feldman) taught him how to pick pockets. He was also arrested twice for disorderly conduct, paying a $5 fine the first time and $10 the second. His worried parents managed to scrape together enough money to send him to a private school in Boston for a year, hoping that that was long enough to break the influence of the gangs. He continued to get in trouble despite the change of scenery. In December 1907, when he was sixteen, he was arrested under the name of Charles Raymond for picking pockets and sentenced to ten months in the House of Correction, which was reduced on appeal to six months. On his release and return to New York, he was put to work, first in the shipping department of a store and finally in his father's office.

In March 1912, at the age of twenty-one, he married seventeen-year-old Lillian Leeban, the beautiful blonde daughter of Russian-Jewish parents. She met him at a dance in August 1911 and married him seven months later, although she was at the time engaged to a wealthy doctor. The five-foot-seven-inch, 140-pound Rosenberg cut such a dashing figure that Lillian instantly forgot the financial advantages of her original engagement. She was smitten, and the devotion persisted despite the glaring signs that her young husband was not earning a legitimate living.

He perfected his ability with a gun at Coney Island shooting galleries and became known as "Lefty" Louis because of his accuracy when using his left hand. Abe Shoenfeld, who knew him, wrote, "A more fitting name would be 'Silent Louie' . . . you cannot get him to talk very much." Louis preferred to speak with his gun. His older brother Sid also became a gangster, but it was Louis who enjoyed the more widespread and dreaded reputation.

When short on money, he collected a few friends and robbed stuss games and brothels. Unlike Zelig, he wasn't discriminating when it came to who he maimed or killed for: Louis sold his services to gamblers when two or more of them feuded, which was often. It was said that he had taken part in the April 1, 1910, murder of gangster John "Spanish Louis" Lewis at the behest of gambler Bridgey Webber, who had been badly beaten by Lewis's goons. He began running with the growing Zelig gang in early 1911 and became a close personal friend of Zelig as well as a prized gunman.

Lillian Rosenberg was introduced to Zelig at a dance when she and Louis were still engaged and recalled being favorably impressed. "He was a big, powerful-looking man, a giant in appearance, with a gentle voice and quiet manner," she wrote in a 1914 article for the *Washington Post*. "He had a pleasant trick of smiling with the eyes as well as the lips. I liked him at once. When Louis introduced him to me he looked at me with considerable interest. . . . He took my hand in his big, brown paw and said, 'Glad to meet you, little girl. Hope we will be friends.'"[2] Her good opinion of him deepened when he gave the newly married Rosenbergs $100 as a wedding present.

If Louis Rosenberg was Zelig's "left-hand" man, Whitey Lewis, who also went by the aliases of Frank Mueller (Miller), Jack Seigel, and Whitey Jack, and whose real name was Jacob Seidenshner, was unquestionably his right. Born in rural Poland and brought to the United States at the age of twelve, Seidenshner worked for a while in a bookbinding shop but quit to try his hand at the tinsmith trade in an uncle's Jersey City shop. Soon he abandoned that job, too, for the excitement of New York's street life killed his enthusiasm for legitimate work. He began hanging around the Chinatown dives and became known throughout the district as a poor shot but a handy man to have around in bare-knuckle fights. Two of his brothers had arrest records for stealing and disorderly conduct, but none as lengthy or varied as his.

Seidenshner, whose friends called him "Whitey" because of his pale complexion and light hair, was arrested for the first time at the age of sixteen and spent a brief term in the New York City Reformatory. He was convicted of grand larceny in December 1904 and sent to Elmira for one year and two months. In September 1907, he was sentenced to Clinton Prison for grand larceny yet again. Fearing that he might receive a more devastating sentence the fourth time around, he joined the army after his release and was shipped to the Philippines. Trouble followed him there, too—another soldier taunted him for being a Jew and was rewarded for the jibe with a knife cut. Whitey was given three months' hard labor for the attack and then dishonorably discharged. When he returned to the United States, he renewed his old underworld acquaintances and met Zelig in early 1911.

Zelig, Lefty Louis, and Whitey Lewis were found most times in Segal's Café at 76 Second Avenue. This choice of headquarters earned their gang the nickname "the Boys of the Avenue." Second Avenue was one of the area's busiest thoroughfares, being densely lined with apartment buildings, shops, restaurants, cafes, and dance halls. It rarely experienced a quiet hour, as the district teemed with shoppers and commuters during the day and a raucous mix of after-theater crowds and underworld types during the evening hours.

Big Alec (real name Aaron Horlig) and his partner "Little" Louis Segal were the café owners. They cheerfully defied the excise laws by selling whiskey and beer to anyone at any time, regardless of age or hour of the day. Gambling went on around the clock. During the daytime, it was confined to a small back room with five tables reserved expressly for that purpose, but at night all but four of the ten tables in the restaurant proper were taken over by those playing stuss, pinochle, stud poker, and other card games.

The nighttime habitués were mostly gangsters, gamblers, pickpockets, pimps, con men of all persuasions, and their women. Anyone who came in after the shadows began darkening the avenue might find themselves rubbing elbows with Zelig's boys, and possibly getting rubbed in return by Jenny Fischer, alias Jenny the Factory, who owned a brothel at 249 Broome Street, or Dinah Hudis, a brassy prostitute with an abrasive attitude. Fights were a nightly occurrence, especially among the women. A Shoenfeld investigator saw Dinah Hudis get into an argument with another lady of the night, and make her point by throwing a sugar bowl into the woman's face, resulting in a black eye. Even if the unwary did not finally leave with a bruised eye or bloody nose, they ran the risk of having their cash and valuables purloined by the pickpockets among the clientele, such as Louis Crueller, alias Little Crueller; Little Natie Lubin, who was related to the Philadelphia Lubins of moving-picture studio fame; or Candy Kid Phil, whose wife, Tillie, was equally adept at stealing.[3]

Once in a while Sam Paul dropped by. Paul, whom Zelig had known casually for years, was of Hungarian-Jewish descent, and described by Abe Shoenfeld as being tall, well-built, and possessing a "military bearing." He lost fortunes as quickly as he made them, due to impulse spending and weakness for pretty women. He was either an owner of or partner in several stuss houses throughout the Lower East Side. He was head of the Sam Paul Association at 31 Seventh Street, where gambling ran unchecked and the membership consisted of all species of crook. Paul, along with the Zweifach brothers and Ike the Blood, was credited with Sam Koenig's acquisition of the Republican leadership in the Sixteenth Assembly District. He never supplied any muscle, only the money that bought votes and paid the gangsters. This gave him political clout, and when he was made graft collector for an Inspector Calhane, he had an "in" with the police, too.[4]

The upstairs floors housed the Manhattan Preparatory School, where young men and women, mostly Jews and recently arrived in the country, took classes to improve their English and learn more about American history and customs. These students, especially the girls, were routinely embarrassed by the Café denizens who lounged outside during warm weather. Abe Shoenfeld passed the place one night with a woman by his side and was infuriated by how a pimp named Harry Goldberg leered at her. He was blunt in his opinion of what should be done to Segal's one busy night: "Plant a fourteen-inch gun and shoot the damn basement and its horde of carrion flesh into perdition."[5]

When not at Segal's, Zelig could sometimes be found in the Russian Casino at 107 Eldridge Street. As the name suggested, the patrons were of Russian-Jewish descent, and Zelig went there both to play cards and to keep his fluency in the Russian language intact.[6] Stud poker and pinochle were played from dusk till dawn, and the music that the management provided to keep the players energized infuriated the neighboring tenements. One of Abe Shoenfeld's investigators lived across the street and became so crazed after two weeks of no sleep that he crawled onto the fire escape at three o'clock one morning and hurled a heavy object at the casino, smashing a window.

There was also a third location that Zelig frequented when not in the mood for riotous café crowds: the New York Harbor, watching Ellis Island discharge the newly arrived immigrants onto American soil.[7] Unlike the pimps and thieves who also prowled the waterfront, Zelig was not there to exploit or steal from the unsuspecting newcomers. Quite the opposite. Snatching fat wallets and jewelry worth hundreds of dollars from anyone who hinted at some prosperity was part of how he made his living, but when it came to robbing exhausted, inoffensive men and women whose worldly possessions could fit in a damp carpet bag or fraying sack, he drew the line, and made sure others stayed behind it. Ephraim Lefkowitz's concern for the welfare of impoverished Jews had passed on to his son, and remained intact despite the desensitization that prison and gang life had caused. Abe Shoenfeld wrote that Zelig "is built so that he cannot bear to see an innocent bystander or unsuspecting person being taken advantage of or wrongfully abused." He was probably referring to the waterfront brawls that broke out during the gangster's vigils.

Jean Gold has a family anecdote to tell about Zelig's protective measures toward his co-religionists. Her great-grandmother, Romanian-born Adele Kaufman, arrived in New York City with her brother in the spring of 1911 and became separated from him in the rush and bustle of the immigrant screening process. She passed inspection first and remained outside the facility, waiting for him.[8]

"A short, ugly man who was dressed to the nines came up to her, because Adele was an attractive girl," Jean says. "He told her that he could take her to a place where she could wait for her brother, because the waterfront was not safe. She believed him. I think she trusted him because he was Jewish like she was and spoke her language."

Miss Kaufman had not gone far with her new benefactor before a second man converged on them so abruptly that she cried out in fright. This man paid no attention to her. He grabbed her escort by the shirtfront, yanked roughly upward until the man was wavering on the tips of his immaculately shined shoes, and spat out angry words in English, which Adele did not understand. Finally the assailant, who looked like a glowering giant to her, looked at her and his expression softened.

"He asked her in Yiddish how she knew this man," Jean says, "and when she could speak, she said she didn't, that he told her he could take her someplace to meet her brother, [and the assailant] became angry again. He shook the man a few more times before dropping him and planting a kick on his rear as [the man] ran away."

Adele Kaufman, terrified, began to cry. Her new escort became gentle as he explained to her that she had almost walked away with a man who made a living by forcing beautiful young women to do ugly things. She knew exactly what he was talking about, having known of soldiers committing similar atrocities on women back home.

"He said his name was William Albert and that he would wait there with her until her brother came out, which he eventually did," Jean says. When the siblings were reunited, Zelig shook hands with the brother, advised him what had nearly befallen his sister and warned both to be more vigilant in the future. Before leaving, he took out a billfold, handed the Kaufmans some money, and wished them good luck. They did not realize who he really was until a year and a half later, when his murder put his picture on the front page of the New York newspapers.

Pimps who abused their women were regular targets of Zelig's wrath. Follower Abe Meyer recalled his boss's reaction to a story that a Polish pimp nicknamed Moishe regularly disciplined poor earners or rebellious girls by holding the offender down and shoving crushed ice or snow into her vagina, which resulted in horrible burning pain at best, severe frostbite at worst. Soon after hearing this ugly tale, Zelig encountered Moishe on Second Avenue near Thirteenth Street. "I hear you like snow, you son of a bitch!" he yelled before battering the vicemonger to a bloody pulp. He tried to finish the job by forcing Moishe's demolished face into a snow bank and smothering him. Meyer, who was watching, said, "A crowd was standing around, yelling, 'Give it to him! Kill him!' and that brought the cops. Zelig and the rest of us gave it up and ran." Meyer added an ominous footnote to the incident: "That was the last time anyone saw Moishe around."

Judge Jonah Goldstein also remembered, "Going to Coney Island, you take the streetcar at the Brooklyn Bridge. Jack Zelig and a couple of his thugs would hire some Jews with berds [beards] to ride on the open trolley cars. Then some good-for-nothing loafers would come along and pull the Jews' beards. [Zelig and his men] would give it to those who pulled the beards. They didn't want a Jew's beard pulled. They had never been educated in Hebrew, didn't go to shul, but they weren't going to have a Jew tossed around because he was a Jew. . . . These fellows made it possible for the Jews not to get tossed around."

Although their livelihoods were at complete odds, Zelig Lefkowitz and Abe Shoenfeld were in perfect agreement when it came to protecting the residents of the Jewish quarter. The son of a militant trade unionist, Shoenfeld was a thorough product of the Lower East Side, having played in its streets, witnessed its dangers, and resisted the same temptations that had ensnared Zelig and the other Boys of the Avenue. He was only twenty-one, but already a seasoned private detective, having investigated New York City's prostitution industry on behalf of a committee financed by John D. Rockefeller Jr. That assignment, which had been performed under the supervision of George J. Kneeland, director of the Department of Investigation of the American Society Hygiene Association, had produced a volume of reports that were remarkable in their frankness and grimy detail. Shoenfeld discussed the workings of the flesh trade and other social vices with a shocking candor that was semi-pornographic in parts, but he believed that only the ugly truth, not preachy euphemisms, could instigate improvements.

In the summer of 1912, New York City's wealthy German-American Jews conceded that yet another study into vice conditions was needed in the wake of the Becker-Rosenthal furor. The worldwide headlines that cried out names like Rosenthal, Horowitz, and Rosenberg were an embarrassment to Judaism that they could not afford to ignore. The Kehillah, a collective of community leaders, elected to finance the selection and activities of a team of private investigators, whose mission would be to infiltrate the Lower East Side's darkest corners and report on the gangsters, killers, and other netherworld characters who flourished there. In August 1912, Rabbi Judah L. Magnes, the Kehillah's chairman, hired young Shoenfeld to serve as the chief investigator for the vigilance committee, whose name was later softened to the Bureau of Social Morals.[9] They intended to use the intelligence gathered to pressure the police and the lawmakers into corrective action.

With such distinguished citizens as bankers Jacob Schiff, Felix Warburg, William Salomon, Adolph Lewisohn, lawyer Louis Marshall, and Judge Samuel Greenbaum expecting results, Shoenfeld went straight to work. He pulled no punches in his flamboyantly worded reports, cursing Italian pimps who lured Jewish girls into prostitution, and railing against the men and women of his own race who sold opium, cocaine, morphine, and other drugs that enslaved the body and mind.

"The mind and body of Jewry is being attacked and poisoned," he warned in one report. "The rats are carrying the plague into the homes of the Jews. Our own kind are accomplishing what a once fanatic, religion-crazed world could not bring about; what anti-Semites cannot do today. Our own are importing and distributing, monthly, in New York, Philadelphia, and other cities principally amongst the Jews, $100,000 worth or more of cocaine and other drugs. Are we to become a drug-crazed people? Are we to perish? Or shall we rise in battle and overcome this Hydra?"

His report on Jack Zelig, which was typed up and filed in August 1912, was written in a strikingly different tone:

> Jack was born and raised on the East Side and is an American. He is known as one of the best "stalls" in a gun mob. Gun in this instance means pickpocket and "stall" means the man who jostles the "sucker." He is also known as a very good "tool," which means the man who sticks his hand into the sucker's pocket. He is also known as a very good stone getter—perhaps one of the best in the world. He is about 26 [sic] years of age, five feet eleven inches; somewhat bandy-legged; raw boned; broken nose; clean shaven; healthful, dark, fearless eyes; splendid disposition and a very good conversationalist. He is known on the East Side only as Zelig. But the Italians of Chinatown have prefixed to his name "Jack."
>
> At all times he has had the reputation amongst his friends and associates as being a good scrapper and above all a man of principle which readily understood is a quality seldom found amongst thieves. You may find honor but never principle.[10]

Shoenfeld later admitted to Professor Arthur Goren that he found much to admire in Zelig, however much he deplored the gangster's villainous deeds. The investigative team rankled at the ongoing infiltration of Five Points gangsters into the Jewish quarter, where they were seen approaching gullible Jewish girls at dance halls and luring them into prostitution. Whenever they witnessed these procurers plying their trade, Zelig and his men sprang into action and sent the offending party out of the district with broken bones. "For a while, there was a big demand for red-haired Jewish girls," Abe Meyer remembered. "Guess it was a fad of some kind among the johns. We were at Coney Island and heard an Italian fellow in front of us—a pimp—say that when he got back to the city he was going to get back to looking for a 'Jew redhead.' Zelig came up behind him and WHACK! Got him in the back of the head and knocked him right to the boards. There was blood everywhere, and Zelig says, 'Think a red-headed dago might do just as well?'"

Shoenfeld asserted, "He cleared the East Side of Italians who were wont to hold up stuss houses and legitimate business places. He cleared the East Side of Italians who could be seen walking through the streets with Jewish girls whom they were working into prostitution. He prevented more holdups and other things of a similar nature during his career than one thousand policemen."[11]

Mingling with the altruism and community concern, however, was the gang chief's instinct to protect his turf. Zelig may have prevented more holdups than Shoenfeld's thousand policemen, but only in the expected process of stopping rivals from threatening a lucrative income. If anyone was going to exploit the madams, lower-level gamblers, and merchants in their district, it was the Zelig gang. Anyone else was put on the run, fast. His harsh treatment of interlopers eclipsed the times when he put his fists to more commendable use.

"One of Zelig's sisters heard about what he was doing—the beatings on the trolleys and the fights in the streets," Joe Lefkowitz says. "I'm not sure whether she only got part of the story, but she was upset with him and asked him why he did those things. Next day, he goes round to the family apartment with an envelope or bag loaded with newspaper clippings. They were stories about the terrible things being done to Jews in the streets—kids throwing stones at them, hooligans beating them up because they looked different. Before turning and leaving, he said just four words to her: 'Because someone has to.'"

Zelig incurred the admiration of another undercover investigator who, like Shoenfeld, was collecting evidence against drug sellers. Florence Clark, only eighteen at the time she embarked on her sleuthing career, worked briefly as a stenographer in a law office before obtaining employment at a detective agency. By 1914, she was the youngest and one of the most successful detectives attached to the district attorney's office.

Miss Clark attended Lower East Side "rackets" and befriended the wives and girlfriends of the gangsters suspected of being ringleaders in the narcotics traffic. When these women began to trust her with information about the drug trade, she reported the details to her superiors, who acted accordingly. It was dangerous work and could have ended fatally early in her career were it not for Zelig.

As she later told the story, she went to one soiree and, possibly overeager to make a useful connection, was less than subtle in her approach to the women present. Blissfully unaware that she was arousing suspicion, she went to the ladies' room, followed by a known prostitute. The woman hovered near the door until Miss Clark was washing her hands, then disappeared . . . seconds before Zelig walked in.

"He asked me immediately if I was a girl detective, and I was frightened," she remembered. "Before I could think of a safe answer, he said, 'I know you are, and if you're not wise, everyone else will, too.'" He spent the next several minutes talking to the bewildered young woman, warning her not to appear overeager. He also gave her the names of a few prominent cocaine sellers who were at the dance.

"I had calmed down because I saw he wasn't going to hurt me, and said, 'If what you say is true, then there is little chance of me getting close to them now,' and he said, 'When you walk out, that won't be a problem.' I said, 'Why?' and he answered, 'Because Kitty [the prostitute who had obviously summoned Zelig] is telling everyone out there that we're in here, sparking.'"[12]

Miss Clark was mortified, but Zelig's prediction was accurate. When she and the gangster emerged from the restroom together and he rejoined his smirking crowd, there was a marked difference in the way the party's other attendees reacted to her. The men looked intrigued, the women, seeing her as "Zelig's girl" of the moment, welcomed her into their confidence. It wasn't until years after his death that she admitted his complicity in her success as an investigator.[13]

In 1914, Florence Clark, who also came to know Lefty Louis, Dopey Benny Fein, and others from their circle, would defend them to reporters. "People have a wrong impression of these gunmen," she said. "I've received the finest treatment at the hands of these men, and if the use of cocaine could be stopped on the East Side, peace and order would undoubtedly be restored."[14]

Zelig must have been aware that his followers included avid users of cocaine, opium, morphine, and other narcotics and opiates that impaired their judgment and rendered their behavior erratic. Although the Smith Anti-Cocaine Bill—which required sellers to label coca products with the word *poison*—had passed in 1907, and the Department of Health was crusading against it and other recreational drugs, their abuse was rampant throughout the Lower East Side. Seventh Avenue between Twenty-eighth and Thirty-third streets was known locally as "Poison Row" because of the ease with which dope fiends could find someone there to satisfy their insidious habit. Zelig neither used nor profited from the sale of drugs, and disapproved of their use among his men, although he doesn't appear to have imposed sanctions on those who indulged. If Florence Clark's story is not an isolated incident, he may have quietly assisted the law in eradicating the traffic, fully playing the role of Shoenfeld's "man of principle."

Opposing attitudes toward the drug trade did cause a break between Zelig and his former mentor, Monk Eastman. Eastman had been paroled from Sing Sing in June 1909 and spent the months between his release on parole and his final discharge in October 1910 (under the law that granted commutation for good behavior) first laboring on a farm in Dutchess County, then working at an undisclosed business in Albany. Although he told Chief Hyatt of the Albany

Police Department that he was moving "out west" to start over, Eastman came back to the Lower East Side intending to resume the life he knew best. But with his gangland prestige irreparably reduced by the years of absence and his body weakened by a string of abdominal surgeries, he was forced to rely on robbery and opium selling to make a living.

"I heard that Eastman came to Zelig wanting to talk partnership in a dope ring," Abe Meyer recalled, "and Zelig turned him down. He wanted nothing to do with the stuff."

Word of his more laudable deeds, as well as his efficiency in battle, reached a Manhattan physician named Dr. Morris Klein in the late summer of 1911. Klein, who had political aspirations, was planning to challenge the Tammany incumbent, ex-coroner Dr. Solomon Goldenkrantz, during the September fight for the Democratic Party leadership of the Tenth Assembly District. He was incessant in his accusations that Goldenkrantz owed his position to voter intimidation at the polls. Determined to have an honest election, Klein sent for Zelig. Big Jack was about to experience his political litmus test.

CHAPTER NINE

TERROR AND GUARDIAN

There had been rumblings well in advance that the Tenth Assembly District would be a battleground during the September 26, 1911, primary. Goldenkrantz's detractors claimed, with some truth, that his past success at the polls was due to the gang muscle the Tammany organization had at its command. Convinced that he would keep using this successful formula, Morris Klein issued public statements to the effect that he intended to fight fire with fire. He wasn't indulging in empty rhetoric—he had secured the services of the Zelig gang.

Klein was not interested in intimidating voters, however—during the meetings that led to Zelig's accepting the assignment, the physician requested that the Boys of the Avenue use their fists and weapons to chase Tammany thugs away from the booths so that the election results could be reasonably reflective of voter sentiment. Word soon filtered throughout the area that Klein had retained gangland's rising star, and just as quickly came the return threats that Zelig's first political slugging assignment would be his last. Additional police officers and deputy sheriffs were dispatched to the district when the day broke on September 26, anticipating the trouble that did arise.

Once the voting began, Zelig gangsters headed to the polling stations throughout the Tenth. They paced the sidewalks and lounged on stoops, remaining inactive until they spotted glowering "Goldenkrantz supporters" menacing voters via threats or physical violence. If no interference was forthcoming from the police, they pulled blackjacks, brass knuckles, and guns from their coat pockets and lunged into battle. Zelig himself headed a floating strike force that made its way from poll to poll, lending assistance whenever his men were getting the worst of it at a given location. Like Eastman and Zweifach before him, he led every charge, taking the same chances that his followers did.

One clash made the papers the next day. At around 6 p.m., a twenty-six-year-old Italian gangster named Dago Frank Cirofici and two henchmen, James Costello and Max Argol, were sitting in an automobile in front of the Tammany Club at 42 Second Avenue, keeping an eye on the Democratic polling station across the street at No. 41.They got out, probably in response to open displays of voter defiance, and started toward the booth. Suddenly Zelig and two others[1] burst through the crowd and opened fire on them. Cirofici fell to the pavement when a bullet lodged in his abdomen. Costello was shot through the left arm, and Argol's right arm was broken by a slug.

Goldenkrantz was inside the Tammany Club with Deputy State Comptroller Julius Harburger, discussing the current voting results, when they heard the gunfire. Coming out onto Second Avenue, they saw the panicked crowd scatter until the shooting stopped. Then hundreds gathered around the three bleeding thugs on the sidewalk. Half a dozen policemen were in the vicinity, and when one of them started to push his way toward the victims, two revolvers sailed over the top of the crowd and the gunmen fled. Both weapons were picked up and turned in to the police.

Cirofici, Costello, and Argol were lifted carefully into their vehicle and hurried to Bellevue Hospital, where surgeons operated on them and confirmed to reporters that they would recover. The wounded trio denied knowing their attackers and went through the usual disclaimers of having no enemies, etc.

Zelig had done more than injure three Tammany-hired thugs. That particular polling station was one of the district's busiest, and the gunplay had sent dozens of voters fleeing, their sense of civic duty overshadowed by terror. Messengers were sent on the run to 207 Bowery, Tim Sullivan's club. In response to the summons, Sullivan's half-brother Larry Mulligan and two associates—Charlie White, alderman of the Third Assembly District, and Johnny White, a fight referee—hurried to the site. Mulligan took one look at the disorder that still prevailed at the station and was incensed.

"Where is that Jew bum?" he bellowed, meaning Zelig. He and his two companions barged along the avenue, Mulligan swearing the entire way. When he shouted again for Zelig's whereabouts, he received an equally loud reply of "Here I am" seconds before he was tackled, punched, and thrown down. Pedestrians stopped and stared, mouths agape, while Zelig Lefkowitz first battered Big Tim Sullivan's half-brother and then put him on the run, placing a kick in the middle of his back for good measure. The Tammany trio fled, with Zelig chasing them for a good half-block.

Abe Shoenfeld could barely conceal his awe when writing about the spectacle more than a year later:

Jack Zelig had defied not only the Sullivan clan by kicking Larry Mulligan but also Tammany Hall. The news spread and when Tim Sullivan heard of it, the feathers on his head commenced to droop and wan.

The East Siders took note of Zelig's defiance hurled at the Sullivan clan, and it showed that Sullivan with his gang of Piggy Donovans, Siroccos, Jimmy Kelleys [sic], and other Italians were full of wind. After Zelig had put to shame and showed up the Sullivans, nominations for district candidates were in order. Goldenkrantz, placed in power by the Sullivan mob, repudiated their candidate Harold Spielberg, who was closely associated with Tim Sullivan. . . . Goldenkrantz figured that there was nothing to fear any longer in the guerilla work of the Sullivan Italians when the East Side possesses such men as Jack Zelig, and he knew just what he was doing, for the Sullivan clan is shorn of all its ancient power.

Hithertofore when a poolroom opened up where races were played or any other gambling house, Sullivan immediately sent jobless men with letters to the new house. They were known as the C.O.D. and received $5 a day for doing nothing. After Zelig showed up Larry Mulligan and the crowd in scorn, the main gamblers of the East Side—Sonny Smith, Jerry Leighton, Sam Levy, Louis Kaufman, and Dollar John—refused to recognize Sullivan's order to place to work these C.O.D. men. This was another blow to the Sullivan clan. Then as he failed to deliver jobs, etc, to his men, his power commenced to go and his men to disburse. With patronage gone, *so went his powers.*[2]

Put less effusively, Big Jack Zelig had beaten Tim Sullivan's half brother in full view of the public and gotten away with it. That inspired dissenters who resented the concessions they had to give the Sullivan clan in exchange for the right to conduct business. Zelig did not quite precipitate the downfall of the Sullivans, but his attack on Mulligan deflated their image for a time and led to temporary acts of rebellion, such as the rejection of the C.O.D. men by gamblers

Goldenkrantz prevailed over Klein at the polls, but Zelig's efforts made it less of a landslide win than anticipated, and everyone knew it. Beating up Larry Mulligan, and therefore opposing the "Tammany Tiger" that had dictated voting policy in the Lower East Side for years, augmented his reputation as a fearless fighter. The election violence even won the fealty of a man whom he had shot and nearly killed: when Dago Frank Cirofici was discharged from Bellevue, he sought Zelig out and ingratiated himself.

Cirofici had been born in Italy and arrived in the United States on March 25, 1889, as a rambunctious two-year-old.[3] When he was sixteen, his family, who had renounced the Catholic faith, introduced him to the Protestant Episcopal Church, which they regularly attended. He had a good singing voice and joined the choir. He left school at the age of fifteen and got a job as a $3-a-week errand boy for a news bureau. His employers would recall that he performed his duties faithfully and gave them no trouble. Soon after he left this job, however, he was arrested for carrying concealed weapons and sent to Elmira for fourteen months. Upon parole he found steady work as a steamfitter's assistant and rated favorably in his employer's esteem.

Cirofici had no qualms about aligning himself with a Jewish gang. He always had been favorably inclined toward Jews. A kindly Jewish neighbor had once helped his mother and his sister Rosa find employment when they needed it, and even assisted the Cirofici family with the rent when times were tough. Cirofici was also a professional freelancer who went where the money was to be found, and in the Lower East Side of late 1911, that meant the Zelig gang. Prior to the September primary, he had been a gunman for a gangster named Decorio, also known as Kid the Second.[4]

Another outsider who joined Zelig in the aftermath of a violent encounter was twenty-three-year-old Harry Horowitz, who went by the vicious-sounding moniker of Gyp the Blood. The source of the nickname was not as savage as assumed: Abe Shoenfeld reported, "He was first called Gypsie on account of his dark complexion and curly hair, and Blood because of his fiery character." Asbury credited him with having superhuman strength and an equally unnatural penchant for cruelty—he supposedly delighted in grabbing inoffensive strangers in saloons and breaking their spines over his knee to win $2 bets. The accuracy of these stories is questionable, but he was definitely one tough customer, although as a regular narcotics user, his fierce behavior may have been artificially induced. He was an expert bomb thrower and experienced dancehall sheriff (bouncer). Like the Lefkowitzes, his family was comparatively well off, and he'd received instruction in the Talmud and the Hebrew language. He was first arrested at the age of seventeen, for petty larceny, but discharged on his own recognizance. A year later, he was charged with a similar offense and got nine months in the city reformatory. One more reformatory stint and a year in the state penitentiary followed. Two of his brothers also had criminal records.[5]

Horowitz rarely hung out on the Lower East Side, his usual haunt being Lenox Avenue and 116th Street, where he captained his own small crew of thieves and gangsters. But when low on funds, he would collect a couple of friends and rob disorderly houses outside their territory, pistol-whipping the operators if money was not immediately forthcoming. One night he went on a rampage in an apartment brothel whose madam was paying the Boys of the Avenue for protection. The woman complained to Zelig, who confronted Horowitz, beat him up, and reclaimed the stolen money. The much-feared Gyp the Blood must have been as impressed as he was bruised, for he approached Zelig in a conciliatory manner afterward and the two young men became friends.[6]

Zelig's forgiving attitude toward former challengers like Cirofici and Horowitz had an ulterior motive: he needed experienced muscle in his war with the Five Pointers, who coveted and made repeated plays for his assets and territory. On September 29, three days after the primary, the Boys of the Avenue launched a counter-strike by converging on a racket being held by a pair of Italian gangsters—Frank Renesi, alias Frankie Neesey, and Julius "Julie" Morrell, both of whom had ties to the Sirocco-Tricker gang. The Jewish thugs burst through the hall doors and fired at every Italian they saw, wounding Renesi and Morrell. Their guests fled in a panic, and those who were standing in front of the box office ran without purchasing tickets, which damaged the revenue.[7]

Although Herbert Asbury dismissed him in *The Gangs of New York* as a clumsy would-be assassin unable to hold his liquor, Julius "Julie" Morrell, aka Thomas Donello, was a vicious and cagey crook with a strong following. The *New York Times* would note, "The Morell [sic] method was one of bravado, making for lifelong feuds, but also for life long friends, and the friends of Morell shielded him whenever he was arrested. They would not come to testify against him because they honored him. His enemies would not come to testify against him because they feared 'Julie' Morell's gun and knife and also his fists." The same article stated that Morrell had been convicted only once, and that for picking pockets. He had done eleven months in the penitentiary, and come out as tough as ever.[8] No one who knew Morrell believed that he would let the demolition of his racket go unpunished.

Two months later, the Boys of the Avenue scheduled their annual ball for Saturday, December 2, at the Stuyvesant Casino at Second Avenue and Ninth Street. These underworld soirees provided a gang's coffers with fresh infusions of cash. Weeks before the grand event, gang members turned-salesmen distributed ticket books to business owners with the not-always-polite demand that all be sold. For additional safety insurance, the same proprietors bought advertising in the ball journal. When guests arrived, the money they submitted at the box office measured the true extent of a gang boss's popularity, something that was explained in colorful slang to Alfred Henry Lewis by a loquacious Five Pointer named Whitey Dutch:

> "Th' tickets is fifty cents," returned Whitey, "but that's got nothin' to do wit' it. A guy t'rows down say a ten-spot at th' box office, like that"—and Whitey made a motion with his hand, which was royal in its generous openness. "'Gimme a paste-board!' he says, an' that ends it; he ain't lookin' for no change back. Every spot does th' same. Some t'rows in five, some ten, some guy even changes in a twenty if he's pulled off a trick and is feelin' flush. It's all right; there's nothin' in bein' a piker. Ike himself sells tickets; an' th' more you planks down th' more he knows you like him."[9]

No sooner had the confirmed ball date become public knowledge than Morrell let it be known that he would make an appearance at the Stuyvesant Casino before the night was through and "smoke the place out." Zelig laughed at the reports that were relayed to him, but he knew that Morrell was angry enough over his own damaged event for retribution to be a real possibility, and precautions were planned.

December second arrived, and within minutes of opening its doors, the Casino was packed with well-dressed men and their gowned female escorts. Zelig navigated the crowds, dispensing greetings and accepting accolades, but Morrell was on his mind constantly. A reception committee consisting of Zelig, Lefty Louis, Whitey Lewis, and three other hoodlums named Ipchkie Livingstone, Lew Fox, and Little Crueller was ready for the Italian gangster. They alternated between mingling with the ball guests and eyeing the hall entrance or going downstairs to spend a few minutes chatting with the ticket takers. When Morrell had failed to put in an appearance by 2 a.m., they relaxed their vigil slightly and stayed upstairs in the main hall, indulging in the liquor and female company.

Not long afterward, three men, all Italians, came in and walked to the box office, where each paid his $1 admission. They then headed upstairs. The ticket taker and the few men lounging in the doorway did not recognize them, but a man named Big Aleck, who was a disorderly house owner and knew Morrell by sight, met them on the stairs and stopped. He extended one hand to the man in the middle and shouted, "Hello, Jules, what are you doing here?"

Morrell and his companions paused to shake hands, giving those who heard Big Aleck's greeting enough time to pass the word around that "Julie" had arrived. To find out whether he was armed, a pickpocket named Benny Weiss was sent to subtly frisk him and report back. Weiss, whom the Italian gangster did not know, pretended to bump into Morrell after the latter came into the main hall. While apologizing profusely and steadying himself, Weiss let his nimble fingers amok and quickly detected a gun tucked into the front of Morrell's trousers. As soon as he could safely do so, he edged away and sent word back to Zelig that Julie was "there" (armed).

According to Shoenfeld, Zelig drew his own weapon and strode through the packed hall until he was face to face with his opponent and would-be assassin. Then he fired twice, both shots burying themselves in Morrell's abdomen. While both of his friends fled for their lives, the Italian fell to his knees, then rose, spun weakly around, and stumbled down the stairs. Zelig followed, stood on the top landing, and shot two more times. With these four bullets in his body, Jules ran to the door leading out to the street, and there dropped in a heap.

Another version of events was that Morrell arrived at the hall alone and drunk, and Zelig's boys, who had been eagerly anticipating his arrival, seized him as soon as he lurched unsteadily through the streamer-festooned door. He fought like a rum-sodden wildcat, and in the scuffle that followed, one of the Zelig hoodlums twisted Morrell's gun arm behind his back. "Julie" squeezed the trigger twice in a reactionary reflex . . . and shot himself.[10]

A police lieutenant named Grabe and other officers were in the hall at the time, supposedly to keep an eye on the revelry. The moment the shooting commenced, Zelig's men began smashing wine bottles to cover the noise and divert the attention of the police from the fray.

A detective named Ransberg found Morrell not long afterward, lying bruised and bleeding on the sidewalk outside the entrance to the Stuyvesant. The diminutive gangster, who looked as if he had been thrown casually down the narrow staircase after being shot, showed spirit when Ransberg asked who had shot him.

"That's my business," he croaked. He refused to talk, even after being examined by doctors at Bellevue Hospital and told that he was dying. His wife, informed of the shooting, left her four children with neighbors and hurried from the family home at 351 E. 167th Street. With the genuine or willful blindness that the police had come to expect from gunmen's wives, she sobbed to reporters, "He [Morrell] never raised his voice, much less his hand, to me. He has always been tender and generous. I know that he has some bad friends, but the police push everything off on him without any excuse for it. Julie is a good man. He is a carpenter by trade. Anyway, his right arm is partly paralyzed, and he couldn't do half the things the police accuse him of."[11]

Zelig was picked up and questioned, but with no one willing to admit to having seen him shoot Morrell, there was no evidence to press a murder charge. Smiling, he left police headquarters with his counsel, ex-Deputy Attorney General Emil Fuchs, whose fees were probably paid from the proceeds of the racket where Morrell had faced Zelig for the last time.

The fighting continued as 1911 turned into 1912. A crowd assembled at the corner of the Bowery and Delancey Street at 11:30 p.m. on New Year's Day bore witness to yet another phase in the battle between Zelig and his rivals. A gray touring car containing five passengers pulled up slowly to the intersection, discharging a man who drew a revolver from his pocket and fired two shots at a younger man standing in front of a brightly lit saloon. When the first bullet hit, the victim cried out and began to run. The second struck him in the back, sending him crashing to his face on the icy pavement. The assassin then threw the smoking revolver into the gutter and stepped back into the idling automobile, which accelerated and went west on Delancey, in the direction of the Williamsburg Bridge.[12] The wounded man, a Tricker associate, was taken to Gouverneur Hospital, where he grudgingly gave his name as Joe Harris of 32 E. Third Street. He refused to give any further information, even when advised that his injuries could prove fatal.[13]

A month later, on February 17, Deputy Police Commissioner George Dougherty was sitting in his headquarters at 8:30 p.m. when a message arrived that a man had been murdered at the northeast corner of Eighth Street and Second Avenue. He dispatched four detectives to investigate.[14] The officers found a large crowd gathered outside N. Rosenberg's drugstore, where a man lay on the sidewalk. Two bullets had blown open the back of his head. While awaiting an ambulance to transport the still-breathing victim to Bellevue, the police made inquiries among the crowd and learned that five young men had been loitering on the corner just before gunfire broke out. Mrs. Rosenberg, wife of the drugstore owner, had been standing outside at the time and told the detectives that she had seen a "little man in dark clothes, with a smooth face" fire a revolver into the victim's head before running north on Second Avenue with a small group of other men. A revolver was later found in the doorway of 136 Second Avenue.[15]

The wounded man eventually died, but not before a tailor's tag sewn into his clothes identified him as Frank Renesi, Julie Morrell's former partner. He had been leaving the stuss house known as Steaks & Chops at 128 Second Avenue, formerly owned by Nathan "Notsy" Paul, brother of Sam Paul, when taken by surprise and fatally shot. A sobbing Mrs. Renesi told the police that her husband had been shot months previously (when the Zelig gang raided his racket) but insisted that he had no enemies that she was aware of. Zelig was questioned by the police, but, as had been the case in the Morrell affair, released for lack of evidence.

Although the law was powerless to punish him, Morrell's and Renesi's friends had better resources and fewer impediments. About one month after Renesi was killed, Zelig walked into a restaurant and gambling joint called the Crystal Palace at 105 Second Avenue. He sat down and ordered food, not noticing that Jonesy, an Italian gangster, was eating at a nearby table.

Charles Rizzo, alias Jonesy the Wop, was a short, overweight hoodlum who made his living selling opium. He owned a cigar store at 129 E. Fourteenth Street, where he sold drug paraphernalia along with tobacco. Although he had a Jewish girlfriend whom he eventually married, he delighted in taunting and even beating Jewish men, especially if they had a tough reputation that he could use to bolster his own.[16] Zelig's disdain for the drug-selling trade was common knowledge, giving Jonesy added incentive to be nasty. He watched Zelig sit down, then remarked in a stage whisper, "Here comes that Jew bastard."

Heads turned. Zelig glared at him. "Who is a Jew bastard?"

"You are," answered Jonesy, who slid one hand into his pocket and prepared to make his reputation.

They both rose from their seats, Jonesy with a knife in his grip. Chairs scraped across the floor as neighboring diners scrambled away. The two men charged at each other. Jonesy was solid, but Zelig was faster and managed to grab the knife from his hand, throw him onto a table on his back, and cut him from ear to ear, disfiguring his features forever. The sight of the Italian thug's butchered, stitched face dampened any ambitions that Renesi's friends harbored about further attempts at vengeance.

These fights and their terrible aftermaths created the false illusion that Big Jack Zelig attained his position and kept it purely through a talent for mutilating the competition. Those not intimately aware of the workings of gangland failed to realize that money was as crucial to a gang's survival as brute force. Dollars, not brawling ability, paid the lawyers and bought some immunity from the law. To keep the cash flow constant, he made further inroads into labor racketeering, and assisting him was Benjamin Feinschneider, alias Dopey Benny Fein, who had been released from Sing Sing in early 1912 and joined Zelig's crew soon after. Fein was a genius when it came to profiting from labor struggles, and the Zelig gang benefited from it.

cb cb cb

"Why I am called Dopey Benny I don't know, as I have never used dope. I got the name as a title years ago," Fein would write in 1915. In one early mug shot, the gangster had a heavy-lidded, drowsy appearance that resulted from adenoidal trouble but made him look suspiciously like a dope fiend. New York City police officers and rival gangsters were willing to believe that Fein was on drugs. He was a shrewd planner but, like Zelig, a wildcat fighter who went crazy in combat.

Benjamin Feinschneider (the family surname would later be shortened to Fein) was born on July 20, 1887, to tailor Jacob Fein. He had four sisters who married well and lived respectably.[17] Benny, the only son, was the black sheep, choosing to pick pockets instead of sew them in a suffocating, poorly lit factory. He also stole packages from unattended delivery wagons and sold the contents to local fences. He was caught at least twice, because he served two brief terms in the workhouse for theft. Upon his release the second time, he joined Monk Eastman's gang and may have become acquainted with Zelig then.

Although an Eastman, Fein did captain a splinter gang of his own, which headquartered near Forsyth and Stanton streets. The members were all young pickpockets whom Fein tutored in exchange for a generous share of what they stole. When six of his boys went to jail in 1905, Fein made his rounds of the local public schools and made his best recruitment pitch to impressionable youngsters whose eyes widened at his fine clothes and fat wallet. Principal H. W. Smith of Public School 20 complained to the police that he frequently saw Fein hanging around the building, striking up conversations with intrigued schoolboys.

"Come with me," he was heard to say on one occasion, "and you won't have to sit in school all day. You'll get into a nice school, where you will be treated right and have plenty of money."[18]

Several boys fell for it, so school authorities breathed a collective sigh of relief when the police arrested Fein on October 3 for holding up one man and assaulting another. Those charges didn't stick, but in January 1906, Fein was convicted of larceny in the second degree and sent to Elmira. After his release, he was arrested four more times, all in 1908, once for disorderly conduct and twice for assault. The fourth arrest had more devastating consequences, as he was convicted in Judge Foster's court of burglary on October 29 and handed a sentence of three years and four months in Sing Sing.[19]

Benny Fein and Zelig Lefkowitz combined their resources to become major players in the labor terrorism that promised big money. Between 1880 and 1920, garment workers ranked behind only their building and mining counterparts in the frequency and intensity of their strikes. Bosses needed muscle to threaten the upstarts back to their needles and machines, and the frustrated unions required protection from such intimidation. (Later, these unions sought gangsters to wreck non-unionized operations.) Both sides were willing to pay well for what Zelig and Fein had to offer, but Zelig was insistent that they accept no contracts from the factory owners. He was firmly on the side of the unions.

Abuse of Manhattan's thousands of garment workers by the unscrupulous and powerful bosses was another concern of Zelig's. Living in the Lower East Side, he had seen firsthand the misery and high mortality rate that went along with unsanitary working conditions and long hours, and applauded those who fought for their rights. He interfered whenever union leaders, who were often as not young women, were assaulted in the street by goons who had been hired by factory management. His sister, Ida, worked in a waist factory, and he probably pictured her being subjected to similar violence.[20]

Although he rarely discussed it unless in a reflective mood, Zelig had been one of the hundreds of New Yorkers who, on the afternoon of March 25, 1911, stood outside the Asch Building,[21] which housed the Triangle Waist Company, and saw one young woman after another (as well as some men) plummet from ninth-story windows to escape the fire that had suddenly and savagely broken out.[22] Some employees were under fifteen years old, and almost all were Italian or Jewish immigrants who warded off starvation by putting in long hours at the cutting tables and sewing machines for sustenance pay. The rickety fire escape had quickly bent under the weight of so many panicked workers, and survivors swore afterward that the ninth-floor doors to the Washington Place stairs had been locked, preventing escape. They told investigators that they were routinely "locked in" during working hours because the company owners feared they would smuggle out property if given the chance. One hundred forty-six of the factory's 500 employees lost their lives, and the outraged public demanded justice. Union organizers pointed out that a strong union presence might have prevented the tragedy by making the Triangle workers more conscious of their rights and insistent on safe working conditions.

Zelig agreed: too many Lower East Side men and women were being sacrificed in the name of industrial greed. Dopey Benny thought so, too. "My heart," he admitted once, "lay with the workers." He turned down $15,000 from a garment manufacturer to silence disgruntled employees through violence. "He put fifteen $1,000 bills in front of me," Fein remembered, "and I said to him, 'No, sir, I won't take it. . . . I won't double cross my friends.'"

The price for a job depended on the size of the operation and the number of gangsters involved. Zelig and Fein charged $150 for small garment factories. Larger businesses cost an average of $600. Shooting a man in the arm or leg or clipping his ear off ranged from $60 to $90, depending on the victim's importance. Invading a factory for the purpose of throwing a foreman or manager down an elevator shaft cost $200.

Years later, Fein would publicly reminisce about his entry into the labor wars:

> "My first job as a gangster for hire was to go to a shop and beat up some workmen there. The man that employed me, a union official, offered to pay me $100 for my work and $10 for each of the men I hired. I planned the job and then told my employer that it would take more men than he figured on, and I would not touch it for under six hundred. He agreed. I got my men together, divided them into squads, and passed out pieces of gas pipe and clubs to them. We met the workmen and beat them up. . . . I was always busy after that."

Fein was injured on the job almost as often as the workers whose rights he claimed to safeguard. Hours after his first assignment, unseen assailants shot Benny in the leg, presumably as payback for wrecking the shop. He was stabbed in the stomach during another confrontation, requiring a ten-day hospital stay. Once, when fighting scabs at a Brooklyn factory, someone smashed an inkwell into his face and broke his nose. For that, he charged the party who hired him an extra $30 to have his nose fixed.[23]

Zelig and Fein paid their sluggers $7.50 a day, a princely wage at a time when a worker's weekly take-home pay rarely exceeded $15. They also hired aggressive women to swarm into female-dominated workplaces and assail troublemakers with glass shards, hatpins, and closed umbrellas that bulged with lead. Recruiting them was probably Fein's idea. He recalled one early job that required him to follow a factory forelady and push her down into a cellar. He insisted afterward, "I didn't want to do the job. . . . I pictured my own sister in that position." Fein only relented after the official who sought his services warned him that refusal could stem the flow of future contracts, but he hated doing it and recruited "lady sluggers" afterward. He once went on the record as saying that Boston women made the best terrorists.

He made it clear that he was not running a democracy where the gang was concerned, but neither was he bluntly dismissive of his people like the business owners he fought against. "My boys," he said, "never asked any questions when I told them to do things. They knew better. My word was law. . . . I was paid well for what they did, and I took good care of those who worked for me."

Elaborating, Fein explained, "When the police got busy . . . the boys concerned in the affrays being investigated were shipped out of town. Some would go as laborers working in railroad gangs, while others would go to a resort in the Catskills, where they were free from surveillance and suspicion. When matters were straightened out they would come back to town. Their expenses would be paid out of the 'sinking fund' that every leader of a well-organized gang sees is provided from the profits made."

Profits abounded by the winter of 1912 from the Zelig gang's business interests and the ball they threw on March 29 at Arlington Hall. It was an event that would be talked about for months afterward. Thanks to Zelig's celebrity, a figure somewhere between $3,000 and $4,000 was realized from ticket sales and ads placed in the ball journal. The hall was jammed with everyone who was someone in the Lower East Side underworld, including Jimmy Kelly, Dollar John Langer, Louis Segal and his partner Big Aleck, and Sam and Notsy Paul.

Zelig spent the entire evening sitting with his wife and closest friends or making his rounds of the hall, shaking hands and exchanging courtesies with the never-ending flow of well-wishers. From time to time he wandered to the box office, where he presented the same cheery demeanor to arrivals. Shoenfeld noticed that if someone placed down more money than their appearance suggested they could afford, Zelig called them back and returned most of their donation.

This level of success and power in the Lower East Side underworld had its price, namely in the form of vultures who saw Zelig as a tool to achieve their ends. One in particular did not anticipate his independent streak, and the resulting conflict made Zelig an unwilling participant in a miscarriage of justice that author Henry Klein would describe in 1927 as "no fouler blot on the fair name of justice in the United States."

CHAPTER TEN

FRAMED

I n April 1912, Zelig received an unexpected visit from one of the Lower East Side's most conspicuous figures.[1] Details as to the time and place have been lost to history, but their conversation, which ended on hostile terms, would figure heavily in the bloody drama destined to unfold three short months later.

Jacob Rosenzweig was more commonly known as Bald Jack Rose or Billiard Ball Jack. Both nicknames originated from the stark baldness that was the aftermath of a childhood bout with typhus. The same affliction had also left Rose without body hair or even eyelashes. His skin was chalk white, his eyes a cool amber, and his facial features narrow and serpentine. He came from a good, Orthodox Jewish family, and his parents and siblings (one of his sisters, Jeannette, was a noted beauty) enjoyed lives of working-class respectability. Personality-wise, he was similar to Zelig in that he was an easy conversationalist and socially adept. Perhaps his disquieting appearance had driven him to compensate by polishing his social graces to perfection.

Rose had been born in Poland and brought to the United States while still a boy. He grew up on the Lower East Side but moved to Connecticut sometime during his teenage years. While there he discovered a passion for professional sports and promoted a few fights and managed a minor-league baseball team that called itself the Rosebuds in his honor. He also perfected his skills as a card player. After almost ten years, he returned to New York City and became a popular figure in gambling circles.

He was, on the surface, happily married to a beautiful woman named Hattie. But like most arrangements that Rose was involved in, there was a sordid underlying element. He'd stolen Hattie away from a stuss dealer named Louis Greene and put her to work as a prostitute. While he slept in one room, she would be with a client in another, earning the steady income that enabled Rose to be a professional gambler and all-around man of leisure. She gave birth to a child who, according to Abe Shoenfeld (who also doubted that she was legally married to Rose), was fathered by one of her wealthier johns. This gallant individual, conscious of his responsibility, paid Mrs. Rose monthly child support in the amount of $200, which supported Jack Rose as much as it did the child.[2]

Another gambler, Herman Rosenthal, helped Rose get a foothold in the Lower East Side's competitive, cutthroat "sporting" business by putting him to work in gambling houses that Rosenthal had an interest in, or recommending him for jobs in others. And, strangely enough, it was Rosenthal whom Jack Rose came to discuss that spring evening. He told Zelig that he wanted his former benefactor killed, and he was willing to pay.[3]

Zelig had no qualms when it came to murder, as Julie Morrell and Frank Renesi would have attested to if the dead could speak. But he had no personal issues with Herman Rosenthal and was suspicious of this soft-voiced gambler with the spectral appearance and treacherous streak. He knew that the man was a graft collector and stool pigeon for Lt. Charles Becker, who headed one of the police department's anti-vice strong-arm squads. The police connection alone made him want to give Rose a wide berth.

"I didn't trust him," Zelig told Jacob Goldberg six months later. "I asked him why he wanted this guy dead, and he said that Rosenthal was busting everything up for him. I told him that wasn't my problem and to find another errand boy."[4]

Zelig's dislike of professional gamblers, which had not abated in the two years that had passed since the attack in Chicago, made him steer clear of their internecine warfare. He had no idea how far gamblers with an ax to grind were prepared to take things.

♣ ♣ ♣

May 12, 1912, was a balmy spring evening. Zelig, Lefty Louis, and Whitey Lewis sat down to dinner at Segal's after spending hours at Coney Island, strolling along the famous Boardwalk and watching the staff finish preparing for the annual return of the summer trade. Zelig's back was to the door, so he did not notice Detectives James White and Charles Steinert until they were at the table, staring down at him with wariness and contempt. A third member of their party, Joseph Shepherd, who was attached to the traffic squad, remained at the café entrance.

Steinert and White were members of one of the NYPD's strong-arm squads. Based at headquarters and reporting directly to Police Commissioner

Rhinelander Waldo, these special squads combated prostitution, raided gambling houses, and collared gangsters, all duties that were normally handled by local cops at precinct level. They were the creation of Mayor William J. Gaynor, a former judge who believed that placing the responsibility for vice-related raids and arrests at headquarters would break up or at least weaken the old system of locally bartered protection. Although the idea was a good one in theory, its success hinged on the appointment of incorruptible men to these new and formidable squads. With more widespread authority, dishonest policemen could apply the paid-protection principle at a city-wide instead of merely precinct level. The strong-arm squads were despised and feared for their heavy-handed methods of maintaining order and dispensing justice: they clubbed defiant prisoners, acted as human wrecking balls when conducting raids, and in general showed more ruthlessness in action than those whom they were supposed to curb.

Sometimes vice figures came to an understanding with squad leaders that bought their resorts a small degree of protection, but it was not an arrangement that they felt safe bragging about, as it usually entailed spying on their fellows and feeding back the detailed information that was required to obtain warrants for raids. Others protected their interests by acting as graft collectors when squad members, with such a wide and rich territory at their disposal, gave in to temptation.

Zelig had never paid off the police at any phase of his career as a pickpocket and gang leader, and he had no friends on the force. Having Steinert and White standing over him at the café table could only mean trouble for him, and he knew it. When told that he was wanted, Zelig stood up and said in a voice loud enough to attract the attention of nearby diners, "What for?"

"For the Annie Sugar case on Sixth Street," White replied.

He was referring to a three-month-old robbery case. On March 11, 1912, three masked men bearing revolvers had entered Annie Sugar's cider saloon at 206 E. Sixth Street. After stealing money from Mrs. Sugar and two customers, the men brandished their weapons in warning and ran outside into a waiting automobile. The investigation was still open; it wasn't until the following November that the perpetrators were correctly identified as two rogue policeman named Gamberdella and Cava, who had enlisted stool pigeons and thieves to help them execute a string of holdups.[5]

Steinert and White reached out to take Zelig by the arms. When he pushed them away, both officers drew their weapons. Facing the curious onlookers, Zelig shouted, "I am not wanted in the Annie Sugar case. They want to frame me up. I want every man and woman to search me before I leave and see that I have no gun on my person."

Zelig's concerns about a frame-up were not exaggerated, especially after butting heads with Jack Rose so recently. He later told friends that he guessed at the time that Rose was behind the officers' arrival.[6] Lower East Side gamblers were notorious for getting cops to do their dirty work—anyone that they had a grudge against was prone to having a concealed weapons charge suddenly leveled against them. For their part, the policemen were only too willing to make such arrests, especially if the gambler in question was a stool pigeon or graft bagman for a ranking officer.

A prime example took place only days after Zelig was approached in Segal's. Jack Rose had clashed with another gambler, Dollar John Langer, and sent gunman Monk Friedman after his rival. Friedman shot and wounded Langer's bodyguard, Little Shea, during a failed murder attempt. Not long afterward he was arrested on a bogus concealed weapons charge by cops who were friendly with Langer. Friedman had completed a term at Elmira a few months previously, and when a jury convicted him as a second offender, he was sentenced to seven years. His lawyer immediately appealed the verdict, and Abe Shoenfeld commented bitterly, "The entire district attorney's office . . . certainly knows today that Monk Friedman was framed up, and at the instigation of Dollar John and Little Shea. They did not raise a finger to obstruct the base designs of that dirty-sneaky little gambler Dollar John. *The district attorney's office has in the past two and a half years demonstrated its capabilities as a railroader of innocent men, sooner than a prosecutor of guilty people.* [It] has today to its credit at least five frame-ups that it has stood for. . . . Aside of these there are other frame-ups of different characters and kinds."[7]

Zelig was not about to be railroaded into anything without a fight. Before Steinert and White could interfere, café patrons moved forward at the gangster's urging and ran their hands over his body, inspecting his pockets. Madam Jenny Fischer, alias Jenny the Factory, a city employee named George H. Greenberg, and actor Harry Gold even pulled Zelig's shirt out of his trousers to show all onlookers that he had no weapon tucked in his waistband. After satisfying the audience that he carried no gun or any other deadly object, he left with his fuming police escort.

Steinert, White, and Shepherd walked with their prisoner up the avenue. Unbeknownst to the three policemen, pickpocket Little Crueller, a friend of Zelig who had also sensed a frame-up in the making, had followed them out of Segal's. When they neared the corner of Fifth Street and Second Avenue, Crueller saw Detective White take a gun out of his own pocket and attempt to insert it in Zelig's. The pickpocket darted forward at lightning speed and grabbed White's hand. The detective cursed and sent Crueller reeling with a savage kick.[8]

Zelig was taken to the Fifteenth Precinct station house, where the officers presented the .38-caliber gun that White had tried to plant in his pocket and claimed that it had been found on the prisoner. It wasn't until then that Steinert realized that they had made a procedural mistake in bringing Zelig to that station. They told the desk sergeant to refer the case to the Twenty-third Precinct. The sergeant obliged and marked the blotter "Error" in red ink. At the

Twenty-third Precinct station house, the fuming gangster was charged with carrying concealed weapons.

After spending an agitated night in a basement cell, he was arraigned in Essex Market Court. Standing before Magistrate P. T. Barlow, Zelig gave his name as William Albert, age as twenty-eight years, and occupation as salesman. He stated that he was not guilty of the charge. Barlow checked the record, then dropped a bombshell by informing Zelig's attorney that his client had been indicted that very morning by the grand jury for carrying concealed weapons. He was indicted as a second offender, and as the potential penalty was more than five years, the magistrate could not fix bail and Zelig's case was scheduled for the Court of General Sessions.

Steinert, White, and Shepherd had worked fast. Abe Shoenfeld wrote, "The officers, seeing what they were 'up against,' went down to the district attorney's office and had Zelig indicted. *Never before had a man held for examination in a police court been indicted by the grand jury.*"

Shoenfeld was sitting in the courtroom when Zelig's case was called, and confirmed its farcical undertones. He wrote in a report to his patrons:

> Zelig appeared with his witnesses and his attorneys. Annie Sugar was there. Steinert and White wanted her to identify Jack Zelig. . . . The attorney in the case demanded that the man [a male witness] and the woman pick Jack out of the crowd in the courtroom. Jack came and took his seat about five seats from the rear and the proceedings commenced. We all sat there, and first the man arose and was led through every row of seats, peering into everyone's face. He could not pick Jack Zelig out. The man had never seen him in all his life. We were all ordered to rise, and again the man was led through the row of seats. When he had positively failed to identify Jack Zelig, the officers told the man, "Go in the back of the courtroom," pointing at the row where Zelig was sitting, "and see if you can't identify him." We all sat down. Everyone laughed at the officers.[9]

Louis Segal, co-owner of 76 Second Avenue, was among the spectators. He made loud and incisive comments about the justice of the entire proceeding and was forcibly removed from the room.

Zelig was ordered lodged in the Tombs prison pending the posting of the $4,000 bail that the judge had levied. While sitting for hours on end in the sweltering cell, he developed a murderous level of rage toward Jack Rose. Word had filtered through the grapevine that the bald gambler had given his strong-arm squad patron, Lieutenant Becker, the malicious tip that Zelig was one of the Annie Sugar holdup men, resulting in Inspector Edward Hughes at headquarters issuing an order to pick him up. The concealed weapons charge had been worked into the scenario in the event that the holdup evidence was deemed too flimsy.

Jack Rose heard the same deadly rumor and was appropriately terrified. He knew that if Zelig's followers didn't kill him while the bond was being raised, the gangster himself would be on the job the moment he stepped out of the Tombs. And, ironically, Rose was actually innocent of the whispered charge. Dollar John Langer, the former colleague with whom he now had a bitter rivalry, had learned of his visit to Zelig and believed that it was Langer's murder, not Rosenthal's, that he'd tried to arrange. Dollar John struck back by sending in the tip that incriminated Zelig and initiating the rumor that Rose was responsible.[10] Rose's other major enemy, Herman Rosenthal, had seized onto the story like it was a delectable steak and repeated it to anyone who would listen, transforming Bald Jack into a dead man walking. Rose turned to two friends, Bridgey Webber and Harry Vallon, for advice.

Louis "Bridgey" Webber, like Rosenthal, was a Second Avenue alumnus. A prominent figure in the gambling world, with houses both uptown and downtown, he was a short man with dark eyes, a long nose, and alert features. He came from a well-to-do family; for years his father had owned a popular grocery at 97 E. Fourth Street but had recently turned away from secular life in order to pore over scriptures at the Talmud on East Seventh Street. Webber's first criminal enterprise had been kidnapping pet dogs and holding them for ransom, but he soon moved on to the flesh trade. His unusual nickname has been attributed to a former working relationship with a prostitute named Bridget, but it's equally possible that it was a dubious tribute to his success as a pimp—in the underworld slang of the day, a woman's pelvic region was referred to as a "bridge."[11] Webber left that business to run an opium den on Pell Street in Chinatown and try his hand at gambling. His fortune was assured when he married a wealthy young woman whose jewelry alone was worth $10,000. The couple lived in the Onyx Court at 193 Second Avenue. Webber was a personal friend of Little Tim Sullivan, Big Tim's cousin, before the latter's death and even partnered with him in a series of gambling enterprises. For years he was a collector for different police inspectors, and because of his easy association with the police, politicians, and gangs simultaneously, often served as a go-between whenever deals between two or all three sides were made.[12]

Gambler Harry Vallon, real surname Vallinsky, was a severe looking individual, with a prominent nose, thick brows, and a stare that bore holes. He had been friends with both Webber and Rose for years, and what little standing he had in the underworld was attributable to that connection. In contrast, his brother Mike Vallinsky was a well-known pickpocket who headquartered at Segal's. Another brother, who was dead by 1912, had been a notorious gangster who terrorized the Ludlow Street area.[13]

Webber and Vallon agreed that Rose was in serious trouble unless Zelig and his men could be convinced that he was not behind the gangster's arrest. The trio went to dinner at the Café Beaux Arts at Sixth Avenue and Fortieth Street. There Webber used the restaurant phone to call around until he located Lefty

Louis Rosenberg, whom he had dealt with when he wanted to even the score with Spanish Louis. Rosenberg, along with Whitey Lewis, came to the Beaux Arts and, for the sake of the old connection with Bridgey Webber, heard Rose out. They appeared to be impressed by his protestation of innocence, which was bolstered by accusations against Langer, and when Webber showed good faith by putting $250 toward the amount required to bail Zelig out, Rose felt the shadow of imminent execution recede.

The following day, the $4,000 bond was furnished by the Empire State Surety Company, a bonding company controlled by a man named Schwartz, who was a son-in-law of Sheriff Julius Harburger, and by ex-Assemblyman Harold Spielberg. The funds required to secure it had been raised collectively by gamblers and other Lower East Side figures who wanted the gang chieftain's goodwill for one reason or another. Bridgey Webber's $250 was also a good-faith bond of sorts for his friend Rose.

Jack Rose met with Zelig after the gang leader was released and pleaded his case. Although he still disliked and distrusted the gambler, Zelig believed his accusation of Dollar John Langer. "I'd also mixed up with one of Dollar John's friends," the gangster told his old pal Jacob Goldberg four months later, "so jobbing me was something I knew he'd do if he thought he could get away with it."[14] Abe Shoenfeld also fingered Langer, whom he described in a report to his superiors as "dirty" and "sneaky," as a co-conspirator in Zelig's dilemma.

Although he knew that his chances of going free on the concealed weapons charge were good, given the number of witnesses who'd searched him at Segal's, Zelig was so infuriated by the frame-up and the ensuing days in the soul-numbing Tombs that he went after Langer with every intention of killing him. He made the rounds of Dollar John's regular haunts and went so far as to lurk in the hallway shadows outside Langer's apartment door for hours one night. The gambler, who anticipated such a move when word came of Zelig's release on bail, stayed out of sight for days. His attempt to take down Rose and Zelig thwarted, he moved only in protected circles until Zelig was taken out of commission, nearly permanently, two weeks later.

♛ ♛ ♛

Sunday, June 2, was a warm and balmy day, and therefore a welcome respite from the severe wet weather that had plagued the city during the latter half of May. Late in the afternoon, Zelig and some other Boys of the Avenue jumped into a rented automobile and motored out to Coney Island for an evening spree. They probably used a vehicle from a Washington Square garage run by Louis Libby and William Shapiro, who enjoyed a brisk business supplying cars to Lower East Siders who could afford them, which in most cases meant gangsters or gamblers.

According to author Pat Downey, their first stop was at a saloon, where they drank freely and created such a disturbance that the proprietor threatened to call the police if they didn't leave. Muttering threats, they retreated to another resort, where a live cabaret held their attention and had a moderating influence on their behavior.[15]

Although Zelig rarely drank to the point of excess, for some reason he made an exception during that excursion. The booze lowered his inhibitions, and when he recognized a male singer as someone who had tried to report friends of his to the police months earlier (for supposedly stealing two diamond rings and $265), he allegedly acted on the old grudge. The singer somehow ended up near their table with a drink in his hand, whereupon Zelig sprang from his chair and punched just as the man was bringing the glass to his lips, shattering it and shredding his face with flying shards. While the injured singer reeled, Zelig pulled a knife from his pocket and carved four criss-cross lines on the already mutilated face, yelling, "Now everyone will know you're a squealer."

Joseph Lefkowitz heard a different version of the same incident. "I heard from some old-timers that it was a waiter, not a singer. Zelig's boys did rob him, and when he saw them in the saloon that night, he made a point of going by their table and telling Zelig that he expected his stuff back. Zelig worked him over pretty badly."[16]

During the chaos that followed, the Boys of the Avenue retreated to their rented car and rode back into Manhattan, where they paid the chauffeur and walked to Segal's for a final round of drinks. As the evening wore on, gang members gradually excused themselves and went home, leaving Zelig, Lefty Louis, and Whitey Lewis to carry on the revelry alone. At about 1:30 a.m., a dark-complected young man came into the café, approached Zelig's table, and told him that Jack Sirocco was at Jack Poggi's Chatham Square Café and wanted to see him.[17]

There are two versions of the prelude to the brawl in Jack Poggi's place.[18] Abe Shoenfeld said that Zelig, Lefty Louis, and Whitey Lewis had gone there to see Sirocco at the latter's request. The reason for the summons and why they agreed to a meeting that wasn't supposed to involve guns and knives was never made clear. The three Jews and the Italian spent about fifteen minutes sitting at a table, drinking and discussing matters that can only be surmised now. Then Chick Tricker, whom Zelig had once feared enough to flee New York, walked in with his lieutenant, James Montello, and Zelig sensed trouble. His alarm rose when the saloon area in the front of the café began to fill slowly with Sirocco-Tricker thugs who muttered in Italian and cast hostile glances their way.

Shoenfeld wrote, "Zelig arose and . . . tried to work his way out of the situation. He faced Sirocco and cried out, 'If anything happens to me or any of my friends, I'll take your life for it.' Sirocco laughed at him, called him a bluffer, and told him to go ahead and do his utmost."

A second version, probably the correct one, states that Zelig and his men sensed a potential trap the moment they received the summons and opted to turn the tables by striking first. The Jewish gangsters entered an alley leading from Doyers Street to Chatham Square and attempted a surprise attack by barging through the rear door to Poggi's. They were met by Tricker, Sirocco, Montello, and other Five Pointers who assailed them with fists and weapons.

There was less contention over the fight itself and the aftermath. Zelig swung his fist and struck Sirocco on the jaw with such force that the Italian collapsed, unconscious. He, Lefty Louis, and Whitey Lewis grabbed heavy bar chairs and swung wildly, flooring the Five Pointers who rushed them. Tricker pulled out a gun and shot Louis in the right foot, but the advantage was only temporary. When the police arrived, only two Five Pointers were still in Poggi's, and not by choice: Zelig, blood streaming from a scalp wound, was sitting astride the supine Tricker, gripping his ears and banging his head against the filthy floor. Whitey Lewis was on top of James Montello, making his face more unrecognizable with each passing second.[19]

The police took all five bruised, bleeding gangsters into custody, along with a nineteen-year-old blonde named Wanda Murphy, who had lunged into the melee and suffered a bruised chest in consequence. The earliest reports of the brawl stated that she had been the cause of the fight, as she had been a hanger-on in the Zelig camp before yielding to a fascination for Chick Tricker. This was later discounted. She was detained after being treated by a surgeon from the Volunteer Hospital, but only as a witness. The others were placed under arrest.

The gangsters were taken to the Elizabeth Street station house and arraigned for disorderly conduct and assault. Zelig growled that his name was John Doe, but his real identity was ascertained quickly enough. Louis, hobbling painfully on his injured foot, said that he was Louis Baker, and Seidenshner got away with calling himself Jacob Siegel. Louis was taken to the Volunteer Hospital to have his wound attended to, while Zelig and Whitey Lewis, along with Tricker and Montello, were herded down to the holding cells pending their appearance before a magistrate later that morning.[20]

When the four gangsters, along with their police escorts, began to descend the stairs leading to the basement cells, Zelig suddenly went berserk. He jumped on Tricker, who was walking ahead of him, and split his scalp open with a few savage punches. The cops jumped into the fray, weakened Zelig with some blows of their own, and dragged him, bleeding and screaming, into a cell.

It was a sorry-looking crew who appeared before Magistrate McAdoo in the Tombs Court hours later. McAdoo fixed the bail for Tricker and Montello at $500 each, as they were only charged with disorderly conduct, but the Zelig gang, having been accused of felonious assault, had their bonds set at $1,000 per man. McAdoo then bound them over for trial in Special Sessions Court. Friends immediately bailed them out.

Zelig, with Rosenberg, Seidenshner, and his lawyer, Louis Spiegel, close behind, descended the steps of the Centre Street exit of the Criminal Courts Building, paused, and then headed across the street, where Spiegel had an office. Zelig had just stepped into the doorway of No. 116 when a roar exploded behind him, milliseconds before a searing pain ripped into his head.

CHAPTER ELEVEN

BULLETS AND BOMBS

He'd been shot. Zelig clapped his hand to the back of his neck and careened through the doorway into the entrance hall's dim interior, with his entourage following. Rosenberg and Seidenshner were unarmed and could not shoot back at his assailant, so they concentrated on hustling him out of the line of fire. They grabbed Zelig, assisted him up the stairs, and laid him on a sofa in Spiegel's office. Blood from an ugly head wound soaked through the wadded-up coat that had been pressed against it to staunch the flow and seeped into the sofa cushions.

"Doc, I guess they got me that time," Zelig whispered to the ambulance attendant who arrived minutes later. "But I don't do no squealing. I don't know who shot me, and I don't care," he added for the benefit of the police officers who also hovered nearby. When one of them pressed him for information, his aggression and agitation mounted. "You bulls make me sick. I don't know who it was, and I wouldn't tell you if I did. You tend to your business now and get a bus [ambulance] for me."[1] He began to fade in and out of consciousness and mutter in both English and Yiddish. One of his escorts, either a policeman or ambulance attendant, attempted to question him in the latter language, but the result was not more favorable. Zelig snarled, *"Freg mir b'acharayim."* ("Ask my behind."[2])

Outside, chaos reigned. Zelig's assailant was a Five Pointer named Charles Torti, an opium addict who preferred to shoot his targets from behind. In July 1911, he had put two bullets into the back of a Chinatown gangster named Frank Smith, alias Peewee, who had allegedly shot one of Torti's associates near the Williamsburg Bridge. Smith survived after passers-by picked him up at the corner of Mulberry Street and Park Row and rushed him to the Hudson Street Hospital. No pistol was found on Torti when a patrolman named Sullivan and two detectives arrested him, but Frank Smith broke gangster code by identifying him, resulting in an attempted murder charge that was still in effect a year later.[3]

According to Shoenfeld, Jack Sirocco, who had been lurking with his followers outside the Criminal Courts Building, placed the gun in Torti's hand the moment he saw Zelig's party emerge and shouted, "There he [Zelig] is, give it to him!" A detective named Oliver saw Torti fire three shots in Zelig's direction and then throw the revolver away. The policeman lunged forward and grabbed him before he could melt into the crowd. When two of Torti's friends, Louis Bull and Victor Merino, tried to prevent his capture by insisting to Oliver that he had the wrong man, they were arrested, too, and hauled to police headquarters for questioning.[4]

Shortly after Torti's arrest and Zelig's removal to the hospital, a large gray automobile drove up and parked directly across from the entrance to the Criminal Courts Building. A small mob of men with pale, hard faces assembled near the same entryway and moved restlessly about, as if waiting for someone or something. Plainclothes detectives who moved among them learned that they were Sirocco men intent on blocking the arraignment of Torti, Bull, and Merino and rescuing them from custody.

The police acted quickly. Twenty-five plainclothes officers surrounded the gray car, while a larger contingent of uniformed cops began patrolling in front of the courthouse. When word arrived that the prisoners were en route from headquarters, court officers closed in on the hovering gangsters, leaving them unable to do anything but watch helplessly as the patrol wagon drove up and discharged Torti, Merino, and Bull. When the handcuffed men and their detective escorts entered the building, the police dispersed the crowd and sent Torti's supporters on their way.

The escape plan now botched, the three Five Pointers appeared before Magistrate Kernochan. After examining the evidence, he ruled that there was no justification for holding Merino and Bull on a felonious assault charge. He directed that it be withdrawn and a disorderly conduct charge substituted. Torti continued to be held without bail and was indicted by the grand jury for attempted murder on June 6. Victor Merino was finally discharged, while Louis Bull got six months in jail for interfering with Torti's arrest.

Zelig's friends wasted no time in striking back at those enemies who weren't safely behind bars. When darkness fell on the day that Zelig was shot, Whitey Lewis, Lefty Louis, and another gang member named Little Nathie came tearing down the Bowery in a taxi-cab, passing Chick Tricker's saloon at 241. Louis fired several rounds at Tricker's head when he saw the latter lounging in the saloon doorway, but the vehicle's speed threw his aim off. One bullet smashed into an adjacent barbershop window, and another buried itself in the leg of one Mike Fagan, who had been chatting with Tricker when the fusillade commenced. The Five Pointer boss escaped with damage done only to his nerves.

Tricker's saloon was not their only stop. Another Five Pointer, Dick Curley, who was a fight promoter of Italian descent, was entering Cushman's Café at 147 Third Avenue at 2 a.m. when he heard the aggressive roar of a speeding vehicle and the whine of bullets. He escaped unhurt, and when the police showed up, would only say that he had seen a "big, dark" automobile that raced past him, turned onto Sixteenth Street, and vanished.

Bombs added to the devastation and terror. The first exploded at around twenty minutes after midnight, shattering the windows of 85 Fourth Avenue. A policeman named Rando was about to pass the building when he heard a noise that sounded like a huge gun going off, followed by a torrent of broken glass and a huge flame that lit up the interior like a lightning flash. Rando and two women who had been strolling nearby were thrown to the pavement. Reserves from the East Fifth Street station hurried to the site but were diverted en route by a second explosion that blew out the front of 103 Fourth Avenue and injured several people. Less than two minutes later, a third bomb went off at 6 St. Mark's Place, which was a gambling joint run by Dollar John Langer.[5] Both 85 and 103 Fourth Avenue were also gambling sites, the latter run by Sam Paul, a longtime friend of Zelig.

On the surface, it appeared that the two fighting gangs were targeting gamblers as well as each other in their escalating war. In all likelihood, however, neither the Boys of the Avenue nor the Five Pointers were behind the bombings. The *Times* suggested that two separate vendettas, one between the gangs and the other between feuding gamblers, were being waged, with the latter hoping that their mayhem would be blamed on the former.

Chick Tricker responded to the attacks by forming a mob that consisted of his faithful lieutenant Montello and a dozen other gangsters. At 4 a.m., bolstered by liquor and armed to the teeth, they marched as a loud, aggressive group into Steckler's Restaurant at 230 E. Fourteenth Street and shouted to some women hanging out there that they were going to kill every Zelig gunman or vassal that they came across. The moment they left, one woman hurried to the telephone, dialed the number for Segal's, and warned the party who answered that Tricker was en route.[6]

Upon receiving the news, three Zelig men named Little Kiever, Mickey Newman, and Charlie Hyman (the latter two of whom were still in their teens but as battle-hardened as their elders) went behind the counter, collected some weapons that had been secreted for just such an emergency, and started up Second Avenue to meet the Five Pointers. A fourth Zelig gunman named Harry Lewis joined them en route. At Ninth Street and Second Avenue, the four Jews met the larger crowd of Tricker gangsters, and guns roared. The skirmish did not last long, as the noise brought two police officers named Pyle and Ryan on the run, but Newman and a Five Pointer named Antonio Angerzio each had a leg shattered by bullets. Little Kiever, James Montello, and a third man were arrested running away from the scene. Hyman and the others escaped. The five prisoners were all charged with felonious assault in Essex Market Police Court but released three days later.[7]

The police had had enough. Deputy Commissioner George Dougherty sent detective squads out with the order to grab all known gangsters on sight, using whatever pretext they could come up with to haul them to the nearest station. Resistance would be dealt with accordingly, as evidenced when a reporter asked Dougherty if liberal use of the nightstick was a proposed medium for cowing the gangs. The commissioner replied grimly, "I wouldn't use a nightstick. If I saw one of those gunmen preparing to draw, I'd use a gun. I don't know whether my men are as good shots as I am, but I hope so."[8]

By the morning of June 8, nineteen young men with known gang connections were in the Tombs and Essex Market police courts, thanks to a thorough sweep of their hangouts by Lt. Charles Becker and his strong-arm squad. Eight were charged with carrying concealed weapons, nine others had been arrested for cocaine possession, and two faced disorderly conduct charges for trying to prevent a friend's arrest. The raiders collected a mini-arsenal of revolvers, clubs, and razors. One place alone, a James Street bar managed by a Fred Lucas, yielded a Chinese dagger, two loaded guns, a black jack and a night stick. When Lucas's lawyer tried to impress upon the magistrate that these items were not found on his client personally, he was curtly told that "such an array of weapons certainly did not show a benevolent spirit."[9]

Special attention was paid to the leaders. Zelig was safely under observation at Bellevue Hospital, so a detective squad consisting of three Italian officers kept Chick Tricker's saloon under surveillance for a day. When he failed to step outside, they entered and found him tending bar. The Five Pointer had a revolver protruding from his waistband, giving the three policemen the perfect excuse to take him into custody on a weapons charge.

"You'll have to come with us," one of the detectives, Gamberdella, said.[10]

"Say, fellows, that ain't square!" Tricker complained. "I guess I've got a right to carry a gun here in my own place. My life is in danger."

His protests got him nowhere, and he ended up at police headquarters along with Jack Sirocco. They were soon joined by Jimmy Kelly, who owned the Mandarin Café on Doyers Street. Kelly was yet another Italian who had adopted an Irish name years ago for survival purposes. He enjoyed the privilege of watching other Chinatown gambling houses be hit by the strong-arm squads while his games went on undisturbed, which suggests that he was a stool pigeon. Kelly and Zelig were casual allies, united by a mutual antagonism toward Tricker and Sirocco. Whatever contempt Zelig may have felt for Kelly's cozy relationship with the police, he admired the gambler's way of dealing with the Five Pointers. A common Kelly stunt was to snatch Sirocco-Tricker thugs, haul them into back rooms or dingy cellars, and toss them into the street hours later with blackened eyes, cracked skulls, and pockets heavy with planted guns or blackjacks. The first police officer who happened along was only too happy to lay a concealed weapons charge on the dazed victim. Louis Poggi, slayer of Kid Twist, had recently been snared in this way, which would have pleased Zelig to no end. Kelly paid a heavy price for his treachery, as he required a constant bodyguard, but his natural pugnacity kept fear at bay. He was not even overly bothered at being included in the mass arrests.

Tricker was not so calm. He appeared before Magistrate Appleton in the Essex Market Police Court, where he pleaded not guilty to a charge of violating the Sullivan Law.[11] Bail was set at $3,000 and quickly furnished by a friend, Peter Hughes, who gave a Second Avenue house as security.

Tricker complained to reporters, "The whole trouble is that the Jews are trying to put the Italians out of business. For myself, I will say I am carrying on a legitimate business. For some of the rest, I cannot vouch. Whenever the slightest occasion arises they begin to pull this gun stuff and expect us to run for cover.

"We regret this as much as the public or the police, but what's to be done? When men fire on you, for no other reason on earth than [that] you were born in some other country, although we are all under the American flag, naturally you would resent that attack. I never have encouraged any man to use firearms, but what's the use of preaching when a war is going on?"[12]

As far as the newsmen were concerned, it was a case of the gang boss protesting too much. Tricker, along with Sirocco, was just as determined to put "the Jews" out of business, and once Zelig recovered, the violence would continue.

Zelig remained at Bellevue for days. The earliest reports about his condition stated that the head wound was too serious and he was not expected to live, but competent medical care and a strong constitution pulled him through remarkably fast. The *Times* even published a rumor that he got into a fight with another hospitalized gangster, but if this "ward battle" actually happened, additional details are unknown.

The police knew that the moment he was back on the streets, violence would be a reality, not a rumor. A concerted effort to take him out of commission via the legal system began. Renewed interest was shown in the murder of Julie Morrell back in December. A lieutenant named Grabe had been at the dance and was asked what he remembered. He responded at first with a written report that matched the one he made at the time of the shooting, but for some reason, changed his mind afterward and submitted an amended version. Grabe claimed that he had heard a pistol shot and someone told him that "a man named Morello" had been wounded, but when he pushed through the crowd, he could see no injured man. When the uniformed police arrived he went home and left them to deal with it. Police Commissioner Waldo promptly suspended

Grabe, a twenty-year veteran of the force, without pay for making the initial false report to his superiors.[13]

After Zelig was discharged from Bellevue, he was taken to the district attorney's office, where Inspector Edward Hughes and Charles Whitman both asked him if he would be a witness against Torti. He replied coolly that he did not know who shot him. Annoyed, Whitman arraigned Zelig before Judge Rosalsky and asked that his bail be raised from $4,000 to $10,000. Shoenfeld claimed that Whitman had demanded a $6,000 raise on Zelig's bond on the advice of Inspector Hughes, who stressed the gang boss's violent record. Rosalsky complied, levying the higher bond on his former client without a pause. Zelig was committed to the Tombs to await either the posting of the new amount or his day in court, and it was not long afterward that he was visited by Jack Rose yet again.

Rose arrived at the prison with Harry Vallon, who had obtained visitor passes for both of them. When they were brought into Zelig's presence, Rose reached into his pocket and laid $100 on the table. Zelig eyed it suspiciously and asked what it was for. Rose replied that the money was a token of respect to purchase some extra favors and privileges in the jail. Then he launched into a vindictive diatribe against Herman Rosenthal, saying that the pudgy gambler had progressed from offending Rose personally to incurring the wrath of both the gambling fraternity and the police department. Zelig was vaguely familiar with Rosenthal's war of wills with the cops, but never interested himself in it, and he couldn't have cared less about what antagonized the Lower East Side's gamblers.

"If he's killed, no one on the force will care," Rose stressed. "If you can persuade your boys to take care of it, I'll talk to Becker. He knows the cops who picked you up. They can be convinced that picking you up was a mistake."[14]

Zelig listened, his mood becoming uglier by the second. For days he had been confined in the Tombs, a solid granite structure whose corridors and cells turned into an oven when warm weather hit. It had been constructed in 1835 on swampy ground that had once been a huge pond known as the Collect. The original design made it resemble a huge mausoleum similar to one that the architect had seen on a visit to Egypt, hence the nickname "the Tombs." "It promises to be one of our finest buildings," one contemporary newspaper predicted, and perhaps it was on the surface. Inside, it was sheer misery, with the lower-level cell floors damp and sometimes ankle deep in filthy water. In 1902, the original structure was torn down and rebuilt in a French chateau style, but the dampness and poor air circulation survived the change in appearance and constantly threatened the health of inmates and staff. Zelig occupied a narrow cell that had no windows to let in light or fresh air, and neither running water nor sanitation facilities except for a tin bucket. The wound inflicted by Torti's bullet had not completely healed, and the restless nights it caused worsened the gangster's demeanor.

Zelig also knew that Jack Rose would never get the concealed weapons charge dropped. "How could he?" he complained to Jacob Goldberg three months later. "I'd already been indicted; the cops who framed me had already sworn in front of the grand jury that they'd found a gun on me. What were they going to do—change their story and perjure themselves?"[15]

Zelig admitted to losing his temper. "I told him that I didn't want his hundred dollars, I was sick of his type and their wars with each other [conveniently forgetting that his battles with the Five Pointers were no less disruptive], and it was down to them that I was in trouble. I could have been looking at fourteen years, easy, as a second offender.

"So I told him that if he had a way of getting me out, he was going to do it, or else he'd have my friends to reckon with. And he was going to do it without me touching Rosenthal. I wanted no part of that anyway. I was in too much trouble to take that kind of chance."[16]

Zelig probably leavened those comments with a hard stare and menacing tones. Rose and Vallon, appropriately scared, withdrew with stammered excuses and left the Tombs. The gang leader had turned the tables in a way that they probably didn't anticipate. Rose had expected him to grab eagerly at any opportunity to get out of the prison and not pause to consider whether the gambler had the pull to get the concealed weapons charge dropped. Not only had Zelig called him on it, but the gangster had also made Rose's future survival hinge on whether or not he went free.

Days later, the National Surety Company came through with Zelig's bail, furnishing as security $5,000 cash and $5,000 in property. The money required to secure the bond had been raised by supporters such as Sam Paul and his brother Notsy, and Harold Spielberg. Bridgey Webber and Bald Jack Rose, who wanted no part of a vendetta from Zelig, had contributed $500.

A Lower East Side figure named Sam Schepps went to the Tombs on July 2 to formally secure Zelig's release. Schepps, an Austrian-born Jew, was known around the underworld as a "lobbygow" (messenger boy) for Jack Rose. Abe Shoenfeld denounced him as "a sneak, egotistical beyond imagination, always 'there' with arguments," and noted in a report that Schepps was an opium smoker who dabbled in gambling and fake jewelry sales.[17]

"I was not in good shape when I got out," Zelig recalled to Jacob Goldberg. "I was having headaches from being shot. When they [the gamblers] bonded me out, they also gave me a ticket to Hot Springs [Arkansas] and some money to keep me going while I was there. I didn't stop to think about it too much, as I wasn't well and I didn't want the cops or the gang to get another shot at me."[18]

Not long after Zelig, Henrietta, and Harry left for Hot Springs, New York was devastated by a hot spell that smothered and stupefied everyone, even in a city that routinely became an oven during the summer. People slept on roofs and fire escapes, flocked to corner drugstores and soda fountains for hot weather bromides, and crowded the beaches if they were fortunate enough to get the time off of work. Wealthy lawyer Daniel Blumenthal, who owned four blocks of vacant land at College Point, Long Island, offered to let tenement poor use the land free of charge to pitch tents and attempt to keep cool. Some Italian boys scorned convention and propriety by stripping naked and romping in the huge fountain at Washington Park. A police officer came along and insisted on collaring them for juvenile delinquency. One of the boys ran for home without bothering to dress first, much to the amusement of the crowd, but he didn't get far before being caught and marched with his friends to the Mercer Street station.

The heat wave officially began on July 7, and by July 11, twenty-one people were dead and dozens more were in the throes of or recovering from heat prostration. One of the more prominent casualties was former state Sen. William F. Mackey, who came to New York on business, collapsed almost immediately from the heat, and was found dead in his room at the Hotel Bristol on July 10. Flags flapped briskly on high buildings, but somehow the breezes did not reach street level. People attempted suicide. A weaver named Morris Cohen jumped into the Harlem Mere, a body of water in Central Park, and would have drowned if a policeman had not jumped in after him and hauled him out. A laborer, Gerasinono Lasenates, became so distraught on his job site that he tried to slit his own throat with a straight razor. Both he and Cohen were taken to Bellevue Hospital for observation. Barber John Anandi actually succeeded in injuring himself with scissors and had to be treated at Fordham Hospital. Even those not actively suicidal died by violence. A sixty-eight-year-old widow, her fan no longer sufficient to keep her cool, learned so far out of her third floor window to catch a stray breeze that she lost her balance, fell to the sidewalk below, and was killed.

Early on the morning of July 16, another death occurred, but this one was not a heat-related statistic. It had its inception in a personal dislike between two competing factions, which grew until several parties were snared in its tangled web of lies, accusations, threats, and duplicity.

CHAPTER TWELVE

HELLO, HERMAN

History has tended to paint Herman Rosenthal as a whining, pathetic figure whose career was a study in failure and bad luck. The truth was that up until the last three years of his life, he was notably successful, thanks to his connection with Big Tim Sullivan. Physically, he was short and stout, but presentable, dressing fashionably and grooming himself well. He had a weakness for flashy jewelry such as gold cuff links and tie clasps, diamond rings and stickpins, and his signature piece, a gold belt buckle bearing his initials. The accessory levels varied with his fortunes—by July 1912, he was reduced to the belt buckle and a few minor pieces. His determination to fight when negotiation might have stood him in better stead had gradually compromised his fortunes and brought him beyond the point where even Big Tim could protect him.

Rosenthal had emigrated to the United States from the Bessarabia region of Russia with his parents and siblings when he was around five years old. He ran with a boy gang, earned a reputation as a good fighter, and caught Sullivan's eye when he was a bright, enterprising fourteen-year-old newsboy. Big Tim, acknowledging that Jewish residents represented a huge voting bloc in the Lower East Side, had a weakness for "smart young Jew boys" like Rosenthal, and showed it by giving them money and job recommendations. Another Sullivan protégé was gambler and racketeer Arnold Rothstein, whose career would eclipse Rosenthal's in money and prestige, although Rothstein, too, would die from assassins' bullets.

With Tim's help, Herman got a job as a runner for a local poolroom. When he married in 1897, he suddenly had his own business: his bride, a petite brunette named Dora Gilbert, was a prostitute who saw no need to let her marital status shut off the money tap. Herman agreed. Whenever johns came to the Rosenthals' West Fortieth Street apartment to call on Dora or one of her girls, he took their money and hovered in the background, ready to protect his female investments.[1] He would have been an adequate bouncer, as prosperity had not yet softened him, and he was but a few years removed from his street fighting days. "He was mighty fast on his feet as a young fellow and could hit hard," a friend recalled.[2]

When the Rosenthals divorced after only a few loveless but lucrative years of marriage, Tim Sullivan got Herman a position as manager of a small but busy crap game. From there he went on to become an off-track bookmaker in Far Rockaway. His assets expanded over the years to include a chain of Second Avenue poolrooms and betting stalls at the Belmont and Jerome Park racetracks. He also took over the gambling concession at the Hesper Club, a popular Second Avenue clubhouse that contained a small casino and was famous for its lively poker parties. Run by Big Tim's brother Patrick, it evolved from small social club to an important meeting place for Tammany politicians, leading gamblers, and office holders of all types. Its membership even included magistrates, assistant district attorneys, and at one point the city treasurer. A framed letter from Big Tim that expressed his pride in being a member and promised ready support to his "brother Hespers" hung inside the front door.[3]

Rosenthal's management of its gambling concession, as well as his close ties with Tim Sullivan, made him a rich man. He maintained a palatial suite of rooms at the Broadway Hotel, which cost him more than $25,000 a year, and indulged in the best fashions and finest dining. He married again; his second wife was an obese, hennaed redhead named Lillian, who had formerly been married to theater personality Sam Harris. As his bank account inflated, so did Herman's ego. One detractor dismissed him as a "flashy, greedy, loudmouthed braggart."[4]

Despite his sometimes repellant personality, Rosenthal could be surprisingly generous. In June 1904, he and others from the Hesper crowd collected money to assist those who survived and/or lost loved ones in the *General Slocum* disaster.[5] On Christmas Day 1905, he and Sam Paul, both of them former newsboys, went to the new clubhouse of the Newsboys' Athletic Club at 74 E. Fourth Street, where Randolph Guggenheimer was giving his eleventh annual Christmas dinner. More than 700 newsboys attended, and Rosenthal was so touched by their obvious enjoyment that he promised to hold a New Year's Day feast of similar magnitude for them.[6] When a desperate and broke actor friend was locked out of his hotel room for nonpayment of the bill, the man located Rosenthal at a race track and appealed for help. Although he was momentarily out of funds, Herman took up a collection among the more flush attendees and presented his grateful friend with more than $400 to make a fresh start. The actor, recounting the story to his young daughter, said, "No matter what anybody ever tells you, Baby, Herman is a great person."[7]

Herman was not so benevolent when it came to the police. He and the NYPD had a long history of mutual antagonism. An inflated sense of superiority, combined with the Sullivan connection, convinced him that splitting his profits with the cops to avoid investigations and raids was beneath him. Instead, he invested his money in reinforced doors, discriminating doormen, and other precautions intended to keep out unfriendly parties, such as undercover policemen collecting evidence for a warrant. In consequence, he became a favored target.

In 1903, Capt. Charles Kemp spent weeks collecting evidence of gambling activity at 123 Second Avenue, a poolroom doing a brisk business under Rosenthal's management. Kemp's undercover man gained access to the tightly guarded establishment by presenting a letter that read:

Herman Rosenthal, Esq,
This introduces my friend, Mr. Ketcham. He's all right.
H. Morgan

Who "H. Morgan" was and why Rosenthal should have been impressed with his endorsement is not known, but the detective succeeded in playing the races. Kemp secured a warrant and, on August 15, headed down to the poolroom with five detectives and twenty policemen in tow. When the doorman barred the entrance, they blocked all doors into and out of the four-story brick building before tackling the front door with axes. Bursting inside, they found Herman tossing the day's racing sheets and slips into the hastily stoked fire. He and three other men were taken into custody, and Rosenthal was charged with keeping and maintaining a poolroom.[8]

Herman remained defiant. On February 3, 1909, he was summoned to the offices of District Attorney Jerome after officers from the Fifth Street station charged that he was refusing to open a string of his gambling houses to police inspection. When Jerome threatened him with a grand jury examination, Rosenthal relaxed his combative stance long enough to state that his places had not been open for gambling purposes for a long time. He objected, he said, to being hounded by the police. Pressured by Jerome, he grudgingly offered to admit the police and men from the district attorney's office any time they wished to inspect the alleged betting parlors.[9] Not surprisingly, he later changed his mind and refused to give Jerome a key to any of them.

When the Red Raven Club at 123 Second Avenue, where Captain Kemp's men had "persecuted" him in 1903, was raided yet again on December 23, 1910, the furious Rosenthal brazenly attempted, and failed, to get a court injunction preventing the police from interfering with the place. He reopened, but three months later, on March 19, 1911, Inspector Russell and Captain Herlihy of the Fifth Street station launched a midnight raid on two of his holdings: the Red Raven and a place at 38 E. Seventh Street. District Attorney Jerome personally oversaw the Red Raven operation, which netted seven prisoners. Although

Rosenthal was not caught in either sweep, he was arrested hours later at the Hesper Club and taken to Night Court, where his bail was set at $10,000.

He also butted heads with his fellow gamblers and sporting men. In 1909, a vote in the Republican legislature made it illegal to quote odds or bet on the horses, forcing the major players in the betting industry to shift their operations to Kentucky or Canada. Unable to do the same, Rosenthal's holdings were reduced to some Second Avenue stuss games and his Hesper Club concession. When he declared himself unable to pay off a $5,000 bet made by one Charles Kohler of piano manufacturing fame, the disgruntled party took him to court in February 1909.[10] For once, the law was on Rosenthal's side, for the Court of Appeals agreed with his bold assertion that he was not legally required to honor an illegal debt. Worried that Herman's refusal to pay would reflect badly on the other New York gamblers and discourage further play, Hesper Club members loaned him the money to pay Kohler off. Rosenthal welshed on that debt as well when the time came.[11]

Anonymous letters, penned by hostile competitors as well as gamblers disgusted by Rosenthal's antics, were sent to the mayor's office. Packed with details about his operation, they furnished both the evidence and the incentive for police raids. Herman struck back at the perceived culprits with his usual vindictiveness. In the fall of 1909, a gangster named Spanish Louis, who was described by the *New York Tribune* as "big bodied and muscular and could deliver more knockouts with his right [arm] than any man his size or double it for that matter,"[12] charged into a gambling den run by Bridgey Webber and stole $400. Rosenthal, who had hired Louis and his gang in the past to guard his houses, would deny that he ordered the robbery, but the fuming Webber suspected otherwise. Bridgey was sufficiently outraged by the incident to take his troubles to the police. He laid off only when influential friends intervened and arranged for him to get his original $400 back, as well as $300 for the inconvenience. He probably spent a lot of that money getting his jaw fixed after Spanish Louis's goons waylaid him outside his home one night and beat him with blackjacks. Webber's revenge was complete on the night of April 1, 1910, when Louis was lured into a vulnerable situation and shot twice in the head.

Tim Sullivan, yielding yet again to Rosenthal's pleas for rescue, helped him set up operations in Far Rockaway, Queens, in late 1910, but the resentful local gamblers used their pull with the police to shut him down. He rallied by partnering with one Beansey Rosenfeld in a gaming house on West 116th Street in southern Harlem. That didn't work out either. Herman and his new partner fell out, and Rosenfeld was savagely beaten by one Tough Tony Ferraci, a Spanish Louis thug whom Rosenthal kept on retainer. In response, Police Commissioner William Baker ordered the Harlem club raided and closed. Rosenthal waited until Baker was out of office (an event that he, Herman, proudly claimed to have brought about via friends in high places) and then reopened. Beansey Rosenfeld's friends promptly bombed the place.[13]

Herman's legal troubles mounted. He was indicted in April 1911 by the grand jury for bribing an officer in the performance of his duty. Emil Klinge, a process server employed by Jerome's office to inspect gambling houses, testified that he'd been offered $15 on two occasions for letting Rosenthal know when raids were scheduled. Klinge said that the gambler, who was notorious for seeking useful connections and then exaggerating them for his benefit, had introduced him around as "my good friend from the district attorney's office." Herman was tried on a bribery charge, but the jury disagreed and he was released.

It was a weak victory, as by this point Herman Rosenthal's fortunes were in serious decline. The ban on race betting had killed a good chunk of his formerly lush income, and his quarrels with Rosenfeld and Webber made those in more lucrative circumstances unwilling to partner with him. Another blow came in the form of the Hesper Club's deteriorated status. When he refused to honor the debt to Charles Kohler or repay the gamblers who did, many Hesper members withdrew their support and went to a new gaming club that had recently been opened by the Sam Paul Association. Those who remained were so low-grade, and in some cases mere hoodlums, that even Tim Sullivan resigned his membership. By the time a police raid closed the place in April 1911, the once-illustrious Hesper Club was just one more penny-ante Lower East Side gambling joint.

Rosenthal was desperate and turned yet again to Big Tim, his perennial breakwater in times of misfortune. Backed by Sullivan, whose excessive fondness for Herman was unbelievable, he set up shop in the high-rolling Tenderloin area of the city, which had previously been off-limits to Lower East Side types. This move made Bridgey Webber furious. In early 1911, he and his partner, Jew Brown, had opened a faro house at 117 W. Forty-fifth Street, making him the first of the Hesper Club crowd to invade the lush territory formerly dominated by Richard Canfield, Lou Busteed, and other affluent gamblers whose houses were practically private clubs for rich men. Rosenthal followed and thumbed his nose at Webber by leasing a three-story brownstone at 104 W. Forty-fifth, just across the street from Bridgey's place.

After spending close to $35,000 to fit the place out with elegant furnishings and deluxe gaming equipment, Herman opened for business on November 17, 1911. He later swore that soon afterward, Police Inspector Cornelius Hayes, who had command of the district, summoned him to a private conference and demanded graft payments totaling $1,000 a week. Rosenthal refused, and the inevitable followed: a police squad battered down the door and smashed the equipment, which had been in use for only four days.

Despite his dismal reputation and worse credit, Herman managed to borrow enough money to reopen on March 20, 1912. The club survived for just under a month. Then, on April 15, 1912, Lt. Charles Becker's squad raided the place while he was out. They smashed up the custom-made gaming tables that he had purchased at Grote's on Second Avenue, and among the prisoners taken was his wife's nephew. The Rosenthals would insist angrily that the young man had been there merely on a social visit and not gambling, but he was charged nonetheless.

After Becker's raid, Big Tim supposedly tried to bribe Police Commissioner Waldo to let Rosenthal reopen. Waldo, outraged, ordered Inspector Hayes to post a police guard in Rosenthal's place to keep it closed. Thereafter a police officer was stationed in the shuttered club around the clock, effectively preventing reopening and driving the already harried gambler to distraction.[14]

Rosenthal hurried to the district attorney's office, now occupied by Charles Whitman, and complained about the constant police guard without success. He even sought audiences with Waldo and Mayor Gaynor, who as a magistrate had raked police officers over the coals for intrusive tactics, but was stonewalled. Frustrated beyond endurance, he lashed out at his persecutors in petty, spiteful ways. On July 11, he locked the day-shift police guard, an officer named Beatty, in the building and didn't release him until Beatty's replacement arrived at midnight, discovered the stunt, and sent for a bevy of reinforcements bearing axes and a hydraulic jack. Rosenthal then announced that he would fire up the coal furnace to make the internal temperatures unbearable and send the cop into the street, sweating and gasping. It might have worked, for the law stated that once out of the house, the police could not break back in again without obtaining enough new evidence for another warrant. But for some reason he changed his mind and resorted to legal avenues.

On July 12, Rosenthal and his lawyer, Jacob Rosenbach, went to the West Fifty-fourth Street Police Court and lodged a complaint of oppression against Inspector Hayes and Capt. William Day, precinct head. The magistrate heard him out but declined to issue the requested warrants, saying there wasn't sufficient evidence to support the charge. He advised the gambler to prepare an affidavit that proved malicious intent on the part of the police. A furious Rosenthal promised to renew his application at the first opportunity and turned to the press, which always had a receptive ear when it came to police scandal.[15] A young reporter at the *New York World,* Herbert Bayard Swope, gave his complaints and accusations the public forum that he had been seeking.

Born in St. Louis, Missouri in 1882, Swope got his start as a reporter with his hometown paper, the *Post-Dispatch,* and joined the staff of the *World* when he moved to New York. A brash-voiced live wire in human form, he held his own against veteran newsmen, landing plum assignments such as the March 1911 coverage of the Triangle Shirtwaist Fire. A year later, in April 1912, he was the first American newsman to arrive in Halifax, where ships bearing the corpses of *Titanic* victims were docking.[16] Always on the alert for stories that would spawn shocking headlines and enthrall New Yorkers like real life soap operas, he had the enviable ability to detect a promising news item and make it flare up into a sensation by playing people and words like chess pieces.

Swope, who stood six foot one and dressed like a dandy, was a regular at Manhattan's gambling houses and a personal friend to many gamblers: he had been Arnold Rothstein's best man at the latter's wedding. Rosenthal, knowing how much he craved notoriety, had been after Swope for a while to print his tale of police harassment. The reporter finally agreed to risk it, appreciating the furor that the story would generate, even if Rosenthal's charges could not be substantiated. On Friday, July 12, the two of them got together and prepared a long, sensational affidavit, scheduled for publication in the *World*'s Sunday edition. This time a new bugbear was the focus of Herman's endless supply of venom: Lt. Charles Becker.

LIBRARY OF CONGRESS PHOTO

- *Between 1855 and 1890, Castle Garden (above) was New York City's landing center for immigrants. Zelig's father, Ephraim, arrived there in 1884.*

- *Sarah and Ephraim Lefkowitz (below), parents of the future Big Jack Zelig.*

- *The Jewish Quarter (below right) in Manhattan's Lower East Side, circa 1907.*

THE EARLY YEARS

COURTESY OF KAREN LEFKOWITZ

LIBRARY OF CONGRESS PHOTO

• A bustling street scene (above) in the Jewish Quarter in Manhattan's Lower East Side, circa 1907.

• Monk Eastman (below left) was a slugger, gang leader, and killer who had more than a thousand gangsters at his command. He facilitated Zelig's entry into the criminal underworld.

• Paul Kelly (below right) was a leader of the Five Points gangsters. He and Eastman were at war for years.

- *Max "Kid Twist" Zweifach (left), a boyhood friend of Zelig's, was a ferocious killer who led the Eastman gang from 1904 until his murder at Coney Island in 1908.*

- *Otto Rosalsky (center) was Zelig's attorney until he was appointed a judge. Zelig would later appear before him as a defendant.*

- *Harris Stahl (right) killed Ritchie Fitzpatrick in 1904 and cleared Kid Twist's way to the head of the Eastman gang.*

- *In October 1905, Zelig sent the telegram below to avoid a penalty for failing to appear in court on a larceny charge.*

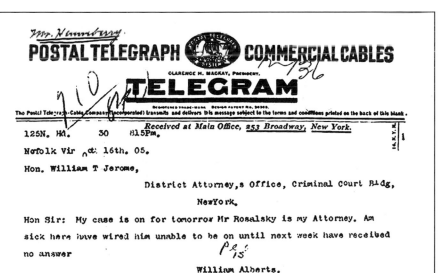

THE WILD YEARS: 1910-1912

• *The photo above includes Harry "Gyp the Blood" Horowitz (standing, second from left), Lefty Louis Rosenberg (standing, middle), Dago Frank Cirofici (standing, right), and Jacob "Whitey Lewis" Seidenshner (seated, right), four of Zelig's most devoted followers.*

• *At right is a a wanted poster for a young Gyp the Blood.*

WANTED FOR MURDER

NO. 3   **HARRY HOROWITZ**

Alias "Gyp The Blood," alias Levy, alias Jones

THE PHOTOGRAPH TAKEN JUNE 7 1909

BERTILLON MEASUREMENTS

Height - - - 1.64.8	Right Ear Length 6.7
Outer Arms - 1.71.0	Left Foot - - 26.5
Trunk - - - - 82.2	Middle Finger - 11.6+
Head Length - - 18.6	Little Finger - 9.2
Head Width - - 15.1+	Forearm - - - 45.5

DESCRIPTION

American Hebrew, clerk, age 25 years, height 5 ft. 5¾ in., weight 140 to 145 lbs., slender build, dark complexion, chestnut black hair, parts his hair on side; smooth shaven, brown eyes; stoop shouldered; served terms of imprisonment for burglary and robbery, New York. Is a stick-up and gun man, uses automobiles in committing crimes, associate of professional thieves, house burglar; opium habit; dresses fairly neat.

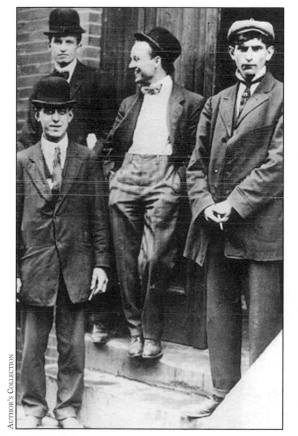

• *Benjamin Feinschneider (above right), alias Dopey Benny Fein, was a close friend of Zelig's and would succeed him as gang leader.*

• *Zelig and Fein employed men like those pictured at left in the labor wars that shook Manhattan during the 1910s.*

• *Dago Frank Cirofici (above left) was shot by Zelig during the September 26, 1911, primary in the Tenth District, but he was so impressed by the gangster's fearless bashing of Tammany-hired thugs that, upon his release from Bellevue, he sought out Zelig and ingratiated himself.*

• *Zelig kicked and beat Larry Mulligan (above, at left), half brother of political boss Big Tim Sullivan (right), in full view of the public during the September 1911 primary, greatly enhancing his reputation.*

• *At right is a sinister depiction of Zelig terrorizing a delivery boy. In reality, he never snatched packages in this manner.*

• *The photo of Zelig below appeared in New York newspapers after he was arrested for instigating the "battle of Chinatown" in June 1912.*

• *This photo of Zelig was taken in June 1912, likely after the brawl at Jack Poggi's.*

• *Curious New Yorkers line the streets (above) to watch Herman Rosenthal's funeral procession.*

• *Louis Libby (below left) was the owner of the "murder car" and an early suspect in Rosenthal's killing.*

• *In the photo at right below, Gyp the Blood (seated, at left) and Lefty Louis are shown with their police captors after a lengthy manhunt.*

- *Jacob "Whitey Lewis" Seidenshner (above right) is taken to the Criminal Courts Building after arriving in New York City. He had just been arrested in a resort community where he had been hiding.*

- *Whitey Lewis (above left) was the first of the Rosenthal gunmen to publicly blame Jack Rose for the murder.*

- *Dago Frank Cirofici (below, hiding face) is shown with several police escorts.*

LIBRARY OF CONGRESS PHOTO

AUTHOR'S COLLECTION

• *Sam Schepps (above, second from right) under police guard.*

• *The mug shot of Zelig at right was taken by the Providence Police Department after he was arrested there for picking pockets in August 1912.*

• *Lillian Rosenberg (bottom right, at left) and Lillian Horowitz visiting their husbands at Sing Sing.*

AUTHOR'S COLLECTION

• *This photo of a dapper Zelig was taken before his August 1912 grand jury appearance.*

• *Lt. Charles Becker and his wife, Helen, are surrounded by well-wishers and police.*

AFTERMATH

- *Philip "Red Phil" Davidson (above) murdered Zelig at the direction of combined gang and political interests.*

- *Below: A newspaper depiction of Davidson shooting Zelig.*

Photograph of street car on which Zelig was slain, with figures in white showing how crime was committed.

- *Above left: Dopey Frank's coffin is loaded into the hearse. His wake attracted crowds of curious onlookers to the Cirofici home.*

- *Above right: Dopey Benny Fein with his youngest son, Paul. Fein assumed leadership of the gang after Zelig's murder.*

- *Below: Benny Fein with his wife, Gertrude, and sons Paul (left) and Morton. Fein's career in the Manhattan underworld would span almost fifty years.*

under indictment for various offenses, and it was rumored that McAuliffe was going to give evidence at their trials as well. Confronted with such powerful motives for police-directed murder, reporters dug deeper and unearthed details about the victim's last hours that stunned New Yorkers and led to sweeping condemnation of the NYPD as an autonomous and sinister society that followed its own laws while sworn to enforce those on the books.[1]

The night before he died, McAuliffe was arrested for public intoxication and locked in a cell at the West Forty-seventh Street station. He appeared before Magistrate Mayo at the Fifty-fourth Street Court at 9:10 a.m. the following morning and seemed sober enough to be discharged. Half an hour later, two patrolmen found him lying unconscious and bleeding in the trampled snow outside 863 Sixth Avenue. The mystery intensified when Magistrate Mayo said that while he could not remember exactly what the prisoner had looked like, having dealt with so many cases that morning, he did recall that the man who appeared before him was perfectly sober, enough so to be discharged. When found a mere half hour later, James McAuliffe stank of liquor, and no plausible explanation was offered for how he could travel two cross-town blocks and then six downtown blocks, become blind drunk, and suffer terrible injuries all within the space of half an hour.

One explanation that had an explosive effect was that the man in Mayo's court was merely a stand-in, providing a human smokescreen while the real James McAuliffe was being force-fed liquor and savagely beaten in a police cell. It gained credence when, on February 27, the coroner's jury returned a verdict of murder "caused by violence at the hands of some person or persons unknown to the jury." Their finding spawned an investigation, during which Assistant District Attorney Lord learned that a police officer had been heard making threats against McAuliffe in a Sixth Avenue saloon.[2]

Asked by reporters why the police at the West Forty-seventh Street station took more than two days to admit that the dead man had even been in their custody, a Sergeant Shibles there offered the weak explanation that they had not wanted to bring disgrace on McAuliffe's family. It also did not bode well that one Detective Sergeant Kiernan, who was attached to that particular station, was a personal friend of Edward Glennon. Later in the investigation, a woman witness stated that on the morning of February 16, she had been passing the station and saw Kiernan and another officer hauling a staggering man into a cab. H. S. Stark, a noted athlete, came forward to say that he had seen a man pushed roughly out of a cab into the street shortly before McAuliffe was found in the same general vicinity.

In an editorial published the following day, the *Times* noted: "It might appear that McAuliffe was killed to silence his testimony against other indicted officers and to discourage citizens who value life from manifesting any readiness to tell what they know of blackmail for the protection of vice."

District Attorney William Travers Jerome investigated the case for months,

but reluctantly conceded in the spring of 1902 that he found nothing sufficiently convincing to warrant a murder indictment against any particular individual. Legally, at least, the ball stopped there. But public condemnation of the
police rose above legal technicalities. An editorial in the *New York Sun* stated
boldly, "Brute resentment against him [McAuliffe] as an element in the case
against the system flamed into a deathly fury of which he became the victim.
Such things have happened in station houses before. . . . When McAuliffe was
found dying, his arrest and imprisonment were matters which it was hoped
would soon be forgotten. . . ." Trying to give McAuliffe's family hope and to
reassure the public that such a covert assassination could not happen again, the
writer concluded with, "In all, the gathering and shifting of such evidence as is
not controlled by the System, something definite may be collected and fused
together into a convincing arraignment of one or more of the guilty men. If not,
then at any rate we know that the thing will not soon again be tried in this city.
The System knows that it is watched."[3]

The "System" referred to was not a secret society of rogue policemen who
rubbed shoulders with vice figures, banked fortunes for turning a blind eye to
crime in their districts, and murdered those who threatened to expose them.
The System, which shifted its components and practices as the political climate
demanded, was present in the NYPD hierarchy and all levels of city and even
state government. Graft money from those seeking favors or immunity from the
law was its lifeblood, reformers its crippling illness. Its members included police
officers, politicians, lawyers, judges, and other public officials, who carried out
their duties as the System dictated. McAuliffe threatened it, and ten years later,
Herman Rosenthal did, too, with identical results.

⚜ ⚜ ⚜

By 1912, the New York City Police Department had a sixty-seven year history that aroused mingled feelings of pride and shame. It was established in
1845 to replace an archaic law enforcement body consisting of one night watch,
one hundred city marshals, thirty-one constables, and fifty-one police officers.[4]
Closely modeled after London's Metropolitan Police Force in its military-style
organizational structure and emphasis on order and rank, the nascent NYPD
was an improvement over the old system but still primitive compared to its
European counterparts. The earliest recruits underwent no aptitude testing
except for physical ability, no formal training in the law was given, and uniforms weren't donned until the 1850s. For years, officers were identifiable only
by the shiny copper eight-point stars that they pinned to their coats. These
badges led to a nickname for the profession that remained in use forever after:
coppers. Even as late as the 1890s, communication between headquarters and
the individual precincts was accomplished by telegraph, and policemen walking
their beats received orders or instructions via messenger.[5]

The ensuing decades brought improvements in investigative techniques and crime prevention measures. The Detective Bureau was formally created in 1882, and in 1906, Police Commissioner William McAdoo sent Det. Sgt. Joseph Faurot to London to learn firsthand about the science of fingerprinting, which had been in use there for years. When Faurot returned and conveyed his new knowledge to his fellow detectives, the NYPD adopted fingerprint cards as an identification tool and solved its first murder case using fingerprint evidence two years later. In 1895, the bicycle squad was formed. Consisting of almost thirty men on high speed bicycles, they made more than 1,300 arrests in their first year and improved patrol service. In June 1911, Police Commissioner Waldo created the motorcycle squad to deal with the growing problem of speeding motorists. Its members wrote out more than 3,000 summonses before it passed its twelve-month mark.[6]

Progress aside, negative public image became a problem during the department's earliest years. In 1853, the state legislature, concerned by how Mayor Fernando Wood was running the city as an autonomous, personal fiefdom, passed an act ordering the formation of a Metropolitan Police Department, which would replace the current Municipal Police Force. Gov. Horatio Seymour established a new police board. Wood, however, resented the removal of control over the police department from the city and refused to either recognize the new system or disband the existing one. The matter was turned over to the courts and things remained at an impasse until 1857, when the Supreme Court ruled that the act creating the new force was constitutional, something Wood had challenged. Even then the mayor did not disband the Municipal force as ordered. Instead, he used it as his personal enforcement unit and repelled its intended replacements.

When Daniel Conover, whom Gov. John A. King had appointed as the new state commissioner, arrived in the city to take a post that Wood had already handed to a crony, the mayor employed his cops as bouncers to throw Conover out of the building. Capt. George Walling of the Metropolitan camp went to arrest Wood at City Hall but was swarmed by a gang of Municipals who ejected him. In response, fifty uniformed Metropolitan cops marched from their headquarters on White Street to take the mayor into custody, only to be intercepted on the front steps of City Hall by a Municipal unit. A half-hour brawl followed, and the Metropolitans were violently repelled. It wasn't until the Seventh Regiment of the National Guard under Gen. Charles Sandford surrounded the building that Mayor Wood submitted to arrest.

But until the Court of Appeals affirmed the Supreme Court decision in the fall, compelling Wood to finally disband the Municipals, there were two opposing police forces in the city, and the result was chaos. If a policeman from one side made an arrest, an opposing officer would interfere and set the prisoner free. The two sides were even known to swarm into one another's jails and break criminals out of their cells. New Yorkers lived in fear for months, relying on their own resources for protection. The police force now had an indelible image as political, not public, servants, whose first duty was not to the law, but to their masters in office.[7]

Department image was further degraded when, during the Draft Riots of 1863, police officers took their clubs to unruly crowds in the absence of the state militia, which was aiding Union soldiers. In January 1874, a protest conducted by unemployed citizens in Tompkins Square Park was dispersed with equal severity. Use of the police to combat public demonstrations generated resentment, and as the years passed, accusations of police brutality piled up. Some complaints were justified—there were zealous and sadistic cops who beat suspects, drunks, or anyone who challenged their authority. Their actions subjected their more moderate colleagues to excessive criticism and scrutiny whenever a policeman used force to bring a person or situation under control.

Corruption was also deeply ingrained in the department. It rose to shocking levels during the 1880s and maintained the momentum for decades. Inspector Thomas Byrnes, who published *Professional Criminals of America* in 1886 and compiled a book of mug shots that became known as the "rogues' gallery," appeared to take a strong stand against crime. He was credited with the implementation of the "third degree" interrogation method and instituted the "Mulberry Street Morning Parade," in which recent arrestees were presented to his detectives so their faces could be memorized and possibly linked to later crimes. But he also banked a personal fortune totaling hundreds of thousands of dollars, although his salary never exceeded $5,000 annually. He professed to have the proper lawman's disdain for professional crooks, but he came to an arrangement with many of them that allowed them to steal, run con games, and solicit for sex in defined territories on the condition that they kicked back a portion of their profits. Byrnes also did not bother to investigate robberies unless a substantial reward was offered for the return of the missing merchandise.[8] He was compelled to resign in 1895 during a purging of the force conducted by Theodore Roosevelt, then president of the New York City Police Commission.

Police venality was a problem that no one knew how to handle except by calling a series of committees (the Lexow Committee in 1894 and the Mazet Committee in 1899) that conducted public interviews, made inquiries, and in the end accomplished nothing save the dismissal of a few sacrificial lambs in the department. In the case of the Lexow hearings, which went on for ten months and cost the state more than $185,000, thirty-one police officers were indicted and fired. Six went to trial, and of that six, two were acquitted and a third went free after his jury deadlocked. The remaining two were convicted, but the Court of Appeals reviewed their cases, set the verdicts aside and ordered new trials. The Lexow prosecutors must have bemoaned their wasted efforts when eighteen of the thirty-one dismissed officers were reinstated at the direction of the courts, and one, Inspector William W. McLaughlin, received an estimated $25,000 from the city to compensate him for lost wages and attorney fees. The Mazet Committee five years later sat for nine months, cost the state $46,066, and accomplished nothing beyond the suspension of two grafting policemen. No prosecutions arose from its findings.[9]

The Lexow hearings did cost Tammany the municipal elections of 1894 and result in reform Mayor William Strong's assuming office. Strong, who would serve as New York's last mayor before the city consolidated in 1898, hired the charismatic and capable Theodore Roosevelt as president of the Board of Police Commissioners. Roosevelt introduced long-overdue reforms in the police department, such as forcing prospective recruits to pass written and physical tests, ordering all officers to report for target practice (therefore laying the foundation for one of the country's first police academies), and getting rid of veteran grafters like Thomas Byrnes. He also patrolled the city himself in the late hours, on the alert for policemen not at their posts. But when he began enforcing the excise laws a little too stringently, his popularity plummeted among the citizenry and he left office in April 1897 to become Assistant Secretary of the Navy under President William McKinley.[10]

In 1930, Capt. Cornelius Willemse addressed the police susceptibility to grafting and corrupt behavior in his memoir *Behind the Green Lights*. He pointed out that in 1901, the salary scale for an officer ranged from $800 to $1,400 a year. The starting wage of $800 (about $66 per month) was nearly impossible for a man, especially one with a family, to live on.[11] They were also expected to pay for their own bedding, uniforms, and equipment, pay dues to the policeman's association, and contribute during charity drives to enhance the department's public image. "Every one of the men started his police career under heavy debt," Willemse complained. ". . . Many a man I have worked with has taken a dollar that went against his principles and his conscience, but there was sore need of the extra money at home."[12]

He admitted to accepting money himself, although supposedly not from crooks: "If I found an open door on post, or picked up a man for safe keeping while helplessly drunk, found a lost child or warned a man of a violation before taking action, and they felt like slipping me a few bucks, I took it and my conscience didn't bother me, nor does it now. Of course there are cops who have never taken a dollar, at least I have heard about them, but I never saw one."[13]

Whenever pressed during official inquiries to reveal the source of their bulging bank accounts, the policemen were inventive about explaining away their windfalls. Thomas Byrnes credited Wall Street. Capt. Alexander "Clubber" Williams told the Lexow Committee that he made his pile "speculating in town lots in Tokyo, Japan." Others cited rich, deceased relatives, making the listeners wonder whether New York's wealthiest families all had a cop or two in their fold.

Even those who did not include greed among their personal vices grafted because career ambition could be expensive in the NYPD. During the earliest days of the force, policemen were appointed by aldermen and assistant aldermen. In 1853, a Board of Police Commissioners was formed that consisted of the mayor, the city recorder, and the city judge, but all that really changed was who bribe money was paid to. Aspiring policeman presented $40 to the captain of the precinct where he wanted to be employed and $150 to $200 to obtain the appointment to the force. Captains shelled out a minimum of $200 for their position.[14] The prices, but not the system, had changed by the 1880s. Unless they were lucky enough to be appointed via the Civil Service Board, applicants obtained their positions by paying $300 to $500 to one of the police commissioners. Men who sought a promotion to sergeant paid an average of $4,000, and a captaincy could set a prospect back $12,000.[15] When men started their police service on poor wages and bore heavy financial obligations, and advancement was fueled by bribes instead of merit alone, the system practically mandated corruption.

The desirability of certain precincts was based on graft potential. Sixth Avenue just northeast of Greenwich Village[16] was packed with brothels and gambling resorts of a significantly better quality than the rickety dives that relieved workmen and merchant seamen of their pay in the Bowery and along the waterfront. The cops assigned to the Twenty-ninth Precinct, which held sway over this fat territory, prospered thanks to the handsome kickbacks from vicemongers who included wealthy businessmen and entertainment world celebrities among their regular customers. The region had its share of dives, cribs, and cellar clubs, but the champagne bars, five-star brothels, and six-figure card games attracted an elite clientele and elevated the standards for vice in the city. Capt. Alexander Williams, when transferred from the humbler Oak Street station district to West Thirtieth Street, declared, "I've been living on chuck steak for a long time, and now I'm going to get a little of the tenderloin." The district was thenceforth known as the Tenderloin, and a transfer there was akin to winning the lottery as far as increased fortunes went.[17]

An article published in *Outlook* magazine in October 1912 listed the fixed rates that the city's gamblers paid to the police for immunity. To open a house with faro and roulette games available, the required "toll" was $500, with $300 a month afterward. Depending on the size of the proceeds, the cops raked in $50 to $250 a month from crap game operators, while those running a poker club forked over anywhere from $50 to $100.[18]

"It is but a fiction," writer William Brown Meloney cautioned, "that the police are public servants. They are public masters. They are a law onto themselves."

Those who believed that James McAuliffe had been murdered by his police custodians in 1902 tended to agree. Frequent reference was also made to the Dillon case, another murder scandal. In June 1909, patrolman James Dillon stormed into the store of Isaac Probber, a shopkeeper on his beat. He was roaring drunk and livid because eggs that he'd obtained from Probber had been bad, or so he claimed. When the terrified delicatessen owner and his wife told their twelve-year-old son to telephone for help, Dillon shot and killed the boy. The rogue cop, with help from a fellow officer who arrived in response to the

Probbers' call, slit his coat with a knife to back up his claim that he'd shot young Probber in self defense. The earliest witnesses to reach the scene, however, had noticed no slashes on Dillon's coat, and when the case came to trial, the prosecutor convinced the jury that the garment had been stealthily cut somewhere between the murder scene and the station house. Even then, Dillon was only convicted of manslaughter and sentenced to seven years at Sing Sing.[19]

By the summer of 1912, the people of New York were willing to believe the worst when it came to their police department. It was a hostile outlook that would have disastrous consequences for one officer in particular.

CHAPTER FOURTEEN

CHARLEY BECKER

When Charles Becker joined the New York Police Department in 1893, he was a bit of an anomaly, being of German descent and Republican in his political leanings at a time when the typical policeman was an Irish-American Democrat. Physically, he suited the role, standing six foot two and composed of more than 200 pounds of pure muscle. "Charley," as his friends called him, was a handsome man, with strong features and a charming dimple that appeared when he smiled. Less endearing was his tendency to apply the law of the nightstick a little too often, even at a time when the public was pushing hard for tougher methods of crime prevention. Becker was also ambitious, and except in rare circumstances, a New York City police officer seeking advancement needed more cash than his pay scale provided. Therefore, he grafted, became wealthy, and, in the eyes of reformers and the general public, a despicable figure.

Born in July 1870 on a farm outside Callicoon Center, a tiny community nestled at the foot of the Catskill Mountains in Sullivan County, New York, Charles Becker seemed predestined for a laborer's life. His German-born father, Conrad, worked hard to make the family farm productive, and it was expected that his six sons would see to its ongoing operation. But after the patriarch died in 1877, the young Becker men began leaving the area one by one. In 1890, at the age of twenty, Charles arrived in New York City in the wake of his brother John, who had moved there two years previously and joined the NYPD.[1]

He secured a position as a clerk in a Chatham Square furniture store but left months later to take other, equally menial jobs—baker's assistant, salesman.

When his size and fighting ability got him hired as a bouncer in a German beer garden off the Bowery, he was on his way to becoming a policeman like brother John.[2]

Bartenders and saloon owners carried more clout than their job descriptions would imply; the more shrewd and gregarious of them were unofficial mayors in their neighborhoods. Monk Eastman's old employer Silver Dollar Smith used to boast that he ran the Essex Market Court from behind the bar of his saloon across the street. Many of them, like Big Tim Sullivan, actually held political office. Guarding the door to one of these watering holes, as Becker did, put aspirants to public office or the police force in the ideal position to be noticed by the men capable of making their goal happen.

When it came to joining the New York City Police Department in 1890, who you knew was a big factor in a successful application. Technically, prospective recruits could apply via the Civil Service Board, a respectable and upright committee that based its choices on rigorous points of merit, but that route met with less success than directly approaching one of the four police commissioners, who were part of the same political establishment that Tammany flourished in, and therefore open to taking bribes in exchange for smoothing an otherwise unsuitable applicant's way through the process. It all made for a police force that was well-connected politically, but whose loyalties did not totally lie with the cause of law and order. An editorial published in the December 15, 1893, edition of the *Times* gave a dire synopsis of the problem:

> The Police Department has been, ever since it was organized, one of the most powerful, persistent, and inveterate obstacles to the good government of New York. Considering the relations of the department to "politics," and politics to crime, this is not at all a matter for wonder.[3]

An NYPD historian admitted, "It is safe to say that nearly every appointment is made through personal or political influence." In a weak attempt to defend this arrangement, he explained, "Those who cavil at this should remember that this almost invariably secures for the department men who have lived long enough in the city to know it, for politicians and friends of police commissioners are not disposed to interest themselves in strangers."[4] Charley Becker, who hadn't been resident in New York City for three full years before making his application, invalidated the historian's argument. Money factored more heavily than length of residency, something that would surely have been impressed on him by John Becker.

In the fall of 1893, when Becker willingly parted with $300 to secure an appointment to the force, the four police commissioners were John McClave, of whom the *Times* once wrote, "If anybody can give any intelligible reason why he should continue to be a Police Commissioner, the production of the reason would be novel and interesting"; James T. Martin and John Sheehan, both Tammany district leaders; and a man named MacLean, who was more conscious of his civic duty but powerless to exercise it when his three colleagues kept him caged by three-to-one votes for politically favored applicants.

Of the four, it was almost certainly McClave who was Charley Becker's entrée into the NYPD.[5] The two men had some common ground: both were Republicans in a Tammany-dominated political climate. The fact that Becker was willing to pay $300 for a job he could have tried to come by honestly also suggested to the decision makers that he would not be inclined to protest against or jeopardize a system that involved the buying and selling of favors and services. He was accepted in November 1893, began training in December, and was in uniform two months later.

During his training period, Becker learned the basics of criminal law, the sanitary code, and department rules and regulations, and absorbed the textbook version of how a police officer was supposed to conduct himself and deal with criminals. Outside the proverbial classroom, veteran policemen like Inspector Alexander Williams, who became a personal friend, showed him how things really worked. Williams, who'd been nicknamed Clubber because of his deadly skill with a nightstick, was so famous locally that those passing him in the street would often stop and stare after him in awe. He had been born in Nova Scotia, Canada, in 1839 and joined the department in 1866 after abandoning his old trade as a ship carpenter.[6] On the surface, his crime-busting activities, measured by arrest levels and celebratory press coverage, were spectacular. His more talked-about feats included the recovery of $7,000 in diamonds and jewelry from two Swedes who'd stolen the items in South America and fled to New York, and the raiding and closure of the cutthroat Florence Saloon at Broadway and Houston Street and Milligan's Hell at 155 Broome, a dive "considered so dangerous . . . that policemen . . . were loathe to enter the place."[7] Such accomplishments bestowed on him a mystique that obscured some less palatable truths. For the most part, he merely clubbed aggressive barflies and unconnected crooks into submission and took bribes from the more successful lawbreakers who wanted him to look the other way while stolen finery was bundled through their back doors, their girls accosted men on the streets, and their saloons served liquor all night.

The only thing that Williams was truly honest about was how corrupt he was. When the Lexow hearings in 1894 had grafting cops become perfect angels on the witness stand, Clubber was the picture of defiance. He admitted to Counsel John Goff that he'd been charged with beating more people than any other man on the force, and when asked whether any other officer had been accused of as much corruption, he replied calmly, "If so, I have not heard of it."[8]

William S. "Big Bill" Devery was another NYPD legend who, while openly corrupt (he conducted public meetings with vicemongers and crooks from a favorite post at the corner of Ninth Avenue and Twenty-eighth Street), survived all attempts on the part of reformers to unseat him. He was charged several times over the years with bribery, extortion, blackmail, and related crimes, but suffered no serious consequences. Part of it was his personal charm. He was touchingly down to earth when dealing with people, and even detractors like Lincoln Steffens admitted to leaving his presence with a smile. In the summer of 1894, months after Becker joined the force, it looked as if his activities had finally become his undoing. The police board put Devery on trial at headquarters for extortion; he'd been raking in such a blatant amount of graft in the Eleventh Precinct that action was demanded. He did not attend the proceedings, claiming illness, and the board voted to dismiss him. Devery took his opponents to court and won—in June 1895, the Supreme Court ordered his reinstatement, claiming that his constitutional rights had been violated when he was tried in absentia.[9] He even became the first chief of police of consolidated New York during Mayor Van Wyck's administration, proving to junior officers like Charles Becker that friends in high office were of the utmost importance.

Becker must have learned the unwritten rules quickly, for his earliest posts were good ones. Instead of being consigned to dirt-road beats at the city's outskirts, he was posted to the Second Precinct, where his duties involved patrolling and safeguarding the waterfront. In early 1895, he had performed well enough to be transferred to the Tenderloin. For Becker, it came at an auspicious time. That February, he had married a young woman named Mary Mahoney. She caught a severe cold on her wedding night, resulting in damage to her lungs, and was diagnosed with tuberculosis more than a week later. Becker now had medical bills to pay, and concern over his wife's health would have quashed any guilt he may have felt at taking graft money. Despite bed rest and treatment at a Catskills resort run by an eminent specialist, Mary Becker died on October 15, a bride of only ten months.[10]

In the Tenderloin, Becker took cash from prostitutes, gamblers, and other vice operators. He became a close friend and student of Clubber Williams. He raked in both graft money and press mentions, not all of them positive.

In August 1895, a saloonkeeper named Augustus Elder appeared in court after an officer named McConnell accused him of being open on a Sunday. Becker, who surely had been solicited for aid by Elder's political patrons, rebutted his brother officer's testimony by claiming that he had found the premises locked and deserted during his own rounds. The judge, Recorder John Goff, did not believe him, and Elder was sentenced to thirty days in jail. Despite having perjured himself, no action was taken against Becker.[11]

Stephen Crane, whose Civil War novel *The Red Badge of Courage* made him a literary sensation when it was published in 1895, had a run-in with Charley Becker in Satan's Circus one night in September 1896, setting off a chain of events that soured Crane's relations with the NYPD and ultimately drove him from the city. The writer was at the Broadway Garden, a raucous establishment at the corner of Broadway and West Thirty-first favored by the demimonde and those accused of being on the fringes of it, such as chorus girls, actors, and young couples whose behavior would have made them unwelcome in more respectable surroundings. He was conducting research for a series of articles about colorful Tenderloin characters that he intended to write for the *New York Journal*. Crane left the hall at close to 2 a.m. in the company of three girls he had met inside. He escorted one to a streetcar stop, and during the few moments that the other two were left unattended, Charles Becker, who had been watching the quartet with suspicion, moved in and arrested them for solicitation.

Arresting unescorted women was a form of extortion commonly practiced, especially in the Tenderloin. The girls, who were not always prostitutes, would be taken into custody and locked up at the nearest station. Bail money was raised via pimps, madams, or, in the case of the wrongly accused, families. The original charge would be dropped in exchange for an understood forfeiture of the bail money, which would then be split between the cop who made the arrest, his precinct captain, and the bondsman.

Crane hurried back and protested that the girls had been doing nothing wrong, and when Becker refused to relent, saved one of them by insisting that she was his wife. But the other, a red-headed prostitute named Dora Clark, aka Dora Wilkins (real name Ruby Young), was marched off to the Nineteenth Precinct station house. Crane, his sense of justice violated, went to the station himself and declared his intention to testify on Miss Clark's behalf in the morning.

True to his word, the writer showed up at Jefferson Market Police Court just before noon, ready to do his duty and prevent another person from being victimized by a police system that he constantly criticized as being too harsh and venal. Becker gave his evidence first. Clark, through angry sobs, told Magistrate Cornell that a month before, a plainclothes cop named Rosenberg, who was Jewish and swarthy, had approached her on the street and she had scorned him, mistaking him for a black man. He arrested her, and each time she set foot in the Tenderloin district, she had been locked up.[12]

Becker denied the conspiracy theory, and the magistrate himself was inclined to disbelieve a woman who admitted to frequenting the Tenderloin in the predawn hours. Crane jumped in with a rescue. He told his side of the story, and Cornell, impressed by the young man's earnestness as much as his celebrity, ordered Dora released from custody.

If Becker actually didn't despise Dora Clark for insulting a fellow officer, he had ample reason to be gunning for her after making him look bad. Weeks later, he ran across her at three in the morning while walking his beat, seized her, and began to beat her. Passers-by intervened, but the punishment was completed by another streetwalker, Chicago May, who was a close personal friend of Becker.[13]

Dora fought back. Three weeks later she marched into the police headquarters on Mulberry Street and pressed charges against Becker and another officer, both of whom she accused of harassing her. Becker prepared for trial, which always took place before one of the four police commissioners, by hiring a shrewd attorney named Louis Grant. When the proceedings began on October

15, every cop from the Nineteenth Precinct who was not on duty at the time showed up to support Becker, a sight that must have chilled the blood of Dora Clark and Stephen Crane, who had agreed to testify for her once again.

Attorney Grant thoroughly mauled Clark and Crane on the stand. Tenderloin denizens who had good reason to desire Becker's goodwill swore that they had seen Dora soliciting men on a regular basis. Crane cringed when Grant told the court that opium paraphernalia had been found during a police search of his apartment. The novelist explained that away by saying that he'd picked it up as a curio during research for one of his newspaper articles, but when Grant confronted him with the fact that he'd rented rooms in a house occupied by prostitutes and lived for weeks with drama critic Amy Leslie, a woman not his wife, Crane's reputation as a gallant hero was severely tarnished.[14]

Becker was acquitted. Dora Clark continued to be a hunted woman, risking arrest each time she entered the Tenderloin, and Crane found New York City so uncongenial that he left to report on the growing insurgency in Cuba. On one occasion when he did return, a patrolman recognized him in a theater lobby and tried to arrest him. The novelist's death in 1900 was the only event that ended the police department's vendetta against him.[15]

Less than a week after the Dora Clark arrest, Becker made the papers again. He and another policeman named Carey were chatting in front of the Marlborough Hotel when they saw three men exit furtively from Richard Katz's cigar store at 1335 Broadway. As the two officers later explained to their superiors, Becker chased them along Thirty-fifth Street while Carey tried to head them off at Thirty-seventh Street and Seventh Avenue. When Becker turned the corner of Broadway and Thirty-fifth and saw that the fugitives were outdistancing him, he drew his revolver from his pocket, fired twice, and shouted for them to halt. They kept going. Becker fired again, and one man crashed so heavily into a pedestrian that both nearly fell to the sidewalk. Becker charged up, struck the suspected thief in the head, and told the pedestrian, "Hold onto him. I'll be back directly."

The other two escapees were headed in the path of Officer Carey. One escaped by slowing his gait once he was out of Becker's sight and walking so nonchalantly that Carey assumed him to be a nocturnal stroller. The other man kept going. Carey, seeing him cross Seventh Avenue and head for Eighth Avenue, pulled his revolver and shouted, "Stop where you are or I'll shoot!" When the fugitive swore at him and yelled, "Shoot!" Carey tried to put a bullet in his leg but ended up killing the man instead.

The press initially praised the actions of the two officers, pointing out that the alleged burglars had been given repeated chances to stop and that deadly force was a necessary evil when so many city criminals carried guns and knives. Police Commissioner Grant formally commended Becker. The glory was tarnished when it came to light that the dead man was not a burglar but a plumber's assistant who had accidentally walked into the line of Carey's fire.

Luckily for Becker and Carey, the tragedy was accepted by the authorities as an accident, and no action was taken against them.[16]

Becker had had some run-ins with the public that could have been his undoing. In February 1897, he arrested a woman for soliciting after she approached him to ask directions to the subway. This time no payoff was forthcoming, for she turned out to be the wife of a New Jersey textile manufacturer and had to be persuaded to refrain from suing the department for false arrest.[17] Later that spring, a teenage boy accused the large policeman of pummeling him in the lobby of a movie house. There were inquiries made and mild censures handed out, but Becker had too many friends in high places for such incidents to be a threat to his career.

In the summer of 1898, he was applauded in the papers for saving a man from drowning in the Hudson River. The NYPD awarded him the department's medal for heroism. The man, an unemployed clerk, later proclaimed that the entire affair had been a stunt, that Becker had offered him $15 to jump in the water and allow himself to be rescued. He complained that he never got the expected payoff. A clamor followed that took a while to subside, even after the man retracted his story.[18]

With his career in the NYPD on the upswing, Charley Becker married for the second time, in April 1898. His wife was a Canadian girl, Letitia Stensen, with whom he had a son, Howard Paul, in December 1899. This marriage lasted longer but was also fated to end. In March 1905, Letitia sued Becker for divorce, claiming that he had been unfaithful to her for years, and specifically complaining about his liaison with another woman at the Eagle Hotel on Cooper Square. She went to Reno, Nevada, with their son and in a bizarre turn of events, married Becker's older brother Paul.[19]

For Charles Becker, it was third-time lucky in the marriage game. Helen Lynch, the daughter of a saloonkeeper, worked at Public School 41 on Greenwich Avenue as a teacher when she and Becker met. The big, handsome policeman had originally been interested in her sister Alice, but Helen's sweet countenance and gentle manner shifted his affections completely. They went out for lunch, took long, leisurely carriage rides together, and became engaged within a few months. They married when the divorce from Letitia came through, and by all accounts were a happy, devoted couple. When Helen took a job teaching at P.S. 90 on West 148th Street, with a class whose pupils were learning disabled, her husband assisted her by correcting papers and writing out report cards. Helen, it seemed, brought out a softer and affectionate side of a man who had gotten ahead in life only by subduing his conscience and his finer nature.

The marriage to Helen coincided with an improvement in his career prospects, which had been declining at that point. Becker risked, and incurred, severe consequences when he stood with the rank and file against the big brass during the 1902 "Revolt of the Cops." For years, policemen had suffered under a Draconian two platoon arrangement, which required men to be available for active and then reserve duty up to twenty hours a day. Those in favor of the three platoon system, which would have limited the hours of duty to eight at a time, campaigned aggressively for it, and Becker was one of three leaders.[20] He was still a mere patrolman in 1902, but he met with Police Commissioner John Partridge without flinching and pleaded the three-platoon cause.[21] His stance cost him dearly. He was denied a promotion to sergeant in 1905 and transferred from precinct to precinct with dizzying regularity, which was a favorite punishment for troublemakers.

Things began to improve in 1906, when Deputy Police Commissioner Rhinelander Waldo assigned Becker and two other officers to investigate Inspector Max Schmittberger, who was the current police overlord of the Tenderloin. Waldo had chosen his sleuths carefully, as Becker had a negative personal history with the inspector. In 1901, he had been transferred to Schmittberger's Upper West Side precinct, but the two men were hostile to each other because Becker was a friend of Clubber Williams, and Schmittberger had offered testimony adverse to Williams during the Lexow hearings. Motivated by spite, Becker began enforcing the law more diligently than he had since his police career began. He collared saloonkeepers for selling liquor after hours, openly implying that Schmittberger was either corrupt or too incompetent to control crime in his precinct. When the irate inspector engineered his transfer, Becker fought back by filing complaints against his former superior. The matter was quietly settled when higher-ups stepped in, but Becker and Schmittberger remained bitter enemies.[22]

Waldo, who surely knew about the bad blood between them, wanted the investigation to be vigorously conducted, and an avowed enemy could be counted on to be as thorough as he was partial. Becker and his co-detectives conducted a series of sensational raids that exposed the Tenderloin's festering vice and corruption to public scrutiny, and Schmittberger was transferred out to Staten Island with the threat of charges and a departmental trial hanging over his head. Becker's promotion to sergeant in 1907 was without question a reward for his work in exposing his old nemesis. Schmittberger had been a safe and ideal target. Although exposing a brother officer ordinarily would have been frowned upon, too many cops bitterly remembered the inspector's testimony before the Lexow Committee, which had exposed the system of police-protected vice to a furious public.

Once the Schmittberger triumph was over, Sergeant Becker lapsed into four years of mundane police work: routine cleanups, desk duty, and a spell with the traffic squad. Then, in 1911, he was promoted to lieutenant, and soon afterward Waldo, now police commissioner, named him to head one of the newly minted strong-arm squads.

These elite enforcement units were the brainchild of Mayor William J. Gaynor, a former Brooklyn Supreme Court judge. Although Tammany had supported him in the mayoral election (its leaders evaluated voter sentiment and concluded that the machine's best option for survival was to back an upright candidate or risk losing City Hall altogether), Gaynor demonstrated his scorn for the whole mutual-favor system by kicking Tammany partisans off the municipal payroll, eliminating superfluous, absentee positions, and making it risky to pillage the city coffers. His popularity insulated him from any reprisal they might have considered.[23]

Gaynor was in his early sixties when he assumed office but as lively and spirited as a man half his age. He worked hard and lived austerely, walking several miles to and from his office each day. Personality-wise he was unpredictable, being sweet-tempered one minute and pugnacious the next, but the fairness he displayed in his dealings with people compensated for the odd burst of temper.[24] He believed in the sanctity of personal liberty; one newsman wrote after his death that he "really believed in the Bill of Rights." A regular target of his judicial wrath had been the police. From the bench, he had excoriated many cops whom he suspected of overstepping their authority and handed down decision after decision undoing wrongs such as false arrests and search warrants obtained on improper evidence. As mayor, he used his position to put an end to arbitrary arrests of the type that Becker had once excelled at, as well as stop the department from breaking up strikes and meetings held by anarchists and socialists. He marched into magistrates' courts without warning to search for evidence of violations of due process, and woe to the parties involved when he found anything incriminating.[25]

Gaynor also tackled saloon graft. To prevent police officers from taking bribes from bars that violated the Sunday closing law, he made them report violations directly to the district attorney's office instead of to their captains. Uniformed patrolmen were forbidden to enter saloons and communicate with the owners, hampering the old system of walking into a place the moment an excise breach was observed and demanding a few dollars to ignore it. Plainclothes detectives could enter places with rear entries but could not make arrests, removing a threat that had often been wielded over a bartender's head if money were not forthcoming. As a result, graft via the liquor interests weakened, but gambling and commercial sex remained, so Gaynor rearranged the way the police were permitted to deal with them.[26]

The mayor rightly suspected that gambling, prostitution, and after-hours drinking flourished because the responsibility for controlling them rested at precinct level, and securing protection was as easy as visiting the local station house and making arrangements with the party in charge. Gaynor therefore placed the responsibility for vice prevention at Headquarters, thereby destroying the old system of locally purchased immunity, and orchestrated the formation of special squads that would attend to the business of investigating suspicious places and raiding them. These units reported directly to the commissioner, Rhinelander Waldo, who despite the difference in their ages, was an intimate of Gaynor.

Waldo, unlike the men who served under him, had been born with the mixed advantage of wealth and good social position. His name was in the *Manhattan Register* and his mother was, as one writer put it, "one of THE Rhinelanders." He was in his mid-thirties and had a military background, having graduated from West Point and served with the U.S. Army in the Philippines. He also ran the New York Fire Department for years and, as deputy police commissioner, had supervised Becker's exposure of Schmittberger. In May 1911, he was appointed commissioner. Waldo was an intellectual who thought that the regimented and (supposedly) incorruptible British police service should be used as the model for a new NYPD, and had big plans for reforming and improving the force. But despite his avowed dedication to creating a clean and honest police force, Waldo had a personal staff that was far from above reproach. His deputy commissioner, George Dougherty, was an ex-Pinkerton and a grafter. His secretary, former *New York World* reporter Winfield Sheehan, was the liaison between corrupt politicians and the police, and a personal friend of Big Tim Sullivan. Since Waldo was essentially honest, the most plausible explanation for his office's employment of men like Dougherty and Sheehan was that he mistakenly believed that serious corruption in the department existed only among the rank and file, and investigated no higher.[27]

Following Gaynor's edict, Waldo put together first a vice squad, then, in June 1911, a secret squad that was tasked with infiltrating the underworld.[28] Two strong-arm squads, one led by Daniel "Honest Dan" Costigan and the other by Dominick Riley, were ordered to suppress gambling. The following July, Waldo created a third team whose main purpose was to fight the gangs. Called the "special squad," it consisted of around twenty husky policemen who could tackle the hoodlums on equal terms. Charles Becker was taken from the Madison Street precinct and given command of this squad soon after its formation.

His earliest assignment as squad leader was to take down the deadly Car Barn Gang, which terrorized the area between Ninetieth and 100th streets, and Third Avenue and the East River. They were pathologically vicious and not afraid of the police—they even displayed a sign in their clubhouse window that warned cops to keep out of their territory. To show that they meant business, half a dozen patrolmen who ventured across approved borders were stabbed, beaten, or shot.[29]

Becker and his men broke into their headquarters and rounded its primary members up in two raids—during the first assault, Becker barely escaped being scalded by a pot of hot water. The Car Barners fought like wildcats but were clubbed into submission. They were targeted by the police until their leaders, Bill Lingley and Freddie Muehfeldt, were sent to the electric chair for murdering a Bronx liquor dealer, thereby ending their gory days.[30]

Becker's squad went on to tackle the Gophers in Hell's Kitchen and a black gang from north Harlem.[31] In early 1912, they were tasked with breaking up an escalating war between Zelig's old nemeses, Chick Tricker and Jack Sirocco, and Chinatown gangster Jimmy Kelly.

At one time Tricker and Sirocco ran a hangout, known locally as "the Fleabag" in Park Row, near Chatham Square. When the police closed the place down, they suspected that Kelly was behind the raid. Kelly, so the rumor went, was a little too friendly with the cops and was suspected of being a stool pigeon. During Sirocco's annual ball on February 9, 1912, plans were made to launch a retaliatory assault on Kelly's saloon on East Fourteenth Street. When word of the intended attack reached headquarters, Becker and his men maintained a vigil at Kelly's all Friday night and most of Saturday morning. Before noon, they went to Little Rock's Poolroom at 396 Broome Street, which had served as the Sirocco-Tricker headquarters ever since the Fleabag was closed up. A search of the place revealed a small cache of weapons that was quickly confiscated.

A continued police presence near Kelly's saloon prevented Tricker and Sirocco from attacking it, so the duo aimed higher and went after their enemy directly. On the morning of Tuesday, February 13, Kelly was walking along the Bowery with Louis Poggi, the slayer of Kid Twist, when shots were fired at them from a dark hallway. Neither was hit. Another attempt was made to kill them later the same day, as they strolled along Baxter Street, near Franklin. Once again neither man suffered injury, and Poggi[32] managed to squeeze off three return shots, one of which struck a laborer and inflicted a nonfatal wound. He and another man were arrested, while Kelly fled in terror to the Elizabeth Street police station and begged for protection.

The police moved in on Sirocco first. He was arrested for selling tickets to his ball without a license but was quickly bailed out. At 2:30 p.m. on the afternoon of February 14, Becker and two of his officers returned to Little Rock's Poolroom. The dozen or so men and boys who were hanging around playing billiards and pool recognized them and stiffened.

"Put on your coats," one of the officers ordered. Everyone obeyed. One coat was left hanging after all in the place had dressed, something that the policemen, who must have been looking for one party in particular, took exception to. "Whose coat is this?" another officer demanded. He addressed the question to a young man named Michael Cassella, who shook his head and muttered, "I don't know whose coat it is."

The policeman grabbed a heavy cue from one of the tables. "Whose coat is this?" he repeated. When Cassella shook his head again, the officer struck him across the back with such force that the cue snapped in two. When the youth collapsed, groaning and pleading, the still-irate cop whirled on another man, Joseph Menella, and repeated his question.

"Honest, I don't know," Menella pleaded, terrified. His failure to give a satisfactory response earned him a broken arm. Other men in the poolroom were roughed up by Becker and his men, although not as severely as Cassella and Menella had been.[33] Such severe treatment of those found in known gang hangouts met with popular approval—the *Times* had even run a feature piece in its August 13, 1911, edition titled, "The Strong Arm Squad a Terror to the Gangs."

Although Becker's squad was primarily an anti-gang unit, it may have provided occasional backup when Costigan or Riley performed raids. Bald Jack Rose would later claim that he met Charles Becker in August 1911, when a club he partially owned was raided. The next day, he recalled, he drew Becker aside at Exeter Market Court and offered to become an informer if Becker would throw out two unexecuted warrants against the club. The policeman agreed and arranged for the current case to be thrown out in exchange for $200. Jack Rose proved to be a useful connection when, in October 1911, Becker's squad expanded its duties to include cracking down on gambling.[34] Over the ensuing months, the three squads made close to 200 raids and 900 arrests. Rose went on to become a collector for Becker's gambling graft as well as a stool pigeon, an arrangement that the police lieutenant would one day severely regret.[35]

Although the headquarters-based squads were widely hailed as an improvement over the easily manipulated precinct-level control of vice and gambling, their effectiveness hinged solely on the appointment of incorruptible men to lead them. Honest Dan Costigan was an ideal example of the type required. William McAdoo described him as "one of those rare men who are naturally, aggressively, and absolutely honest." Becker, whose enthusiastic exposure of Schmittberger gave the illusion of his being a dedicated crimebuster with no use for either graft money or those who took it, was not. From the moment his squad was tasked with controlling gamblers as well as gangsters, he was in a position to use his authority to make money, and he acted on it.

Becker could not offer ironclad protection to paying establishments because he was not a semi-autonomous entity like the precinct captains had once been. He took orders from the mayor and the police commissioner, but he could postpone raids, provide advance warnings, and arrange for evidence to be lost before the cases came to court. He had plenty of customers for what safety he was able to sell, however. Between October 1911 and July 1912, he banked an average of $10,000 a month in fifteen separate accounts, some his own, others held jointly with Helen, and some under a false name. In the spring of 1912, the Beckers paid $9,000 cash for a mock-Tudor house in Williamsburg.

In early 1912, Becker hired his own press agent, Charles Plitt, to keep his name in the papers.[36] His friends included several reporters, such as Deacon Terry of the *American,* Fred Hawley of the *Sun,* and ex-gunfighter Bat Masterson of the scandal sheet *Morning Telegraph.* He rode around in a chauffeured car owned by Col. Henry Sternberger, a National Guard commander who had taken a liking to him. His showboating behavior made him enemies in the NYPD, and even his own attorney, John Hart, would later admit, "Becker knows he is very unpopular in the police department."

There are signs that Becker suffered spells of uneasiness about his dual position as gangbuster and grafter. In addition to alienating other squad leaders like Costigan and Riley, who saw their chances at a captaincy become more remote each time Becker's name appeared in print, he had made powerful enemies among the gamblers, many of whom were well-connected politically. Sam Paul, whose clientele included rich and influential New Yorkers, had been outraged when Becker's squad raided his elite Lincoln Hotel on Columbus Circle in February 1911, throwing his customers into a panic and locking up his best girls. In late November, a reporter friend warned him that his enemies were out to get him, and feeling that he had made his pile, he tried to get Waldo to transfer him without success. Then, in March 1912, Waldo began getting letters that revealed the locations of several gambling houses that had yet to be closed down. A "Henry Williams," who was really Bridgey Webber, pointed an accusatory finger not only at Herman Rosenthal but also the strong-arm squads, which were derided as corrupt. Becker was specifically named. Waldo dealt with the letters by passing them on to Winfield Sheehan, who shrugged and gave them to Becker. Becker sent them back to Waldo with the polite suggestion that he was not one to conduct an investigation on himself. Again, he requested a transfer, but Waldo, dazzled by the news coverage and arrests that he had racked up, turned him down once more. He was trapped.

By 1912, Lt. Charles Becker had become a victim of his own greed and celebrity. He had risen to such a high point that a fall could only be fatal.

CHAPTER FIFTEEN

GOODBYE, HERMAN

It has never been properly determined how Lt. Charles Becker and Herman Rosenthal met. In two separate statements, the gambler told conflicting stories: by one account, he spoke to Becker after a Second Avenue raid the latter had overseen in the fall of 1911, and according to the other, they met at the Elks Club Ball the following Thanksgiving.[1] Rosenthal probably did cross paths with Becker during the course of the raid, but with all the commotion and activity, it's not likely they had any real chance to talk. But Rosenthal would surely have heard that the squad leader sold protection to gaming house owners, and since defying the police had only resulted in his places being dismantled and his income lost, he contrived to buy a powerful friend on the force. He needed one if his West Forty-fifth Street place was to reopen without incident.

Why Becker would agree to go into partnership with any gambler, let alone Herman Rosenthal, can only be speculated. Perhaps, as author Mike Dash postulates in his superb work *Satan's Circus,* Becker knew that his tenure as head of the special squad could come to an end at any time; all it would take was a strong enough conspiracy on the part of his enemies to expose him. Becoming a silent partner in a resort that promised to do well once the proper protection was in place was one way of continuing to line his wallet with the lucre that was poured into Satan's Circus on a nightly basis.

Becker would always deny that he and Rosenthal had any business arrangement. "I have never been connected with him in any way, either in business or friendship. He tried hard to make it seem that I was by inviting me to dinner in public places, but I always declined."[2] This denial was believable, as Rosenthal was infamous for contriving to meet important figures and then exaggerating his connection to them. Years before, he had tried to pass off process server Emil Klinge as his "good friend from the district attorney's office." But there were too many signs that Becker and Rosenthal did have an association.

On July 13, the first of two explosive affidavits were published in the *World*. In it, Rosenthal charged that an unnamed police lieutenant had been a partner in his house. Public consternation had no time to subside before the *World* published, in its Sunday, July 14, edition, a second affidavit that was more precise as to who, what, when, where, and why:

> The first time I met Charles Becker, now a Lieutenant of Police in New York City, and who was holding the same office at the time of our first meeting, was at a ball given by the Order of Elks in Forty-third Street, near Sixth Avenue, and we had a very good evening, drank very freely, and we became very good friends. Our next meeting was by appointment on New Year's Eve, 1912, at the Elks Club. Dinner was served for ten in our party, including Lieutenant Becker, Mrs. Becker and Mrs. Rosenthal, Mr. George Levy and daughter, Mr. Samuel Lewis, Mr. Louis Hyman.
>
> We all drank a lot of champagne that night, and later in the morning we were all pretty well under the weather. He put his arms around me and kissed me. He said, "Anything in the world for you, Herman. I'll get up at three o'clock in the morning to do you a favor. You can have anything I've got." And then he called over his three men, James White, Charles Foy, and Charles Steinhart [sic], and he introduced me to the three of them, saying, "This is my best pal and do anything he wants you to do." We went along and we met pretty often. Sometimes we would meet at the Lafayette Turkish Bath. Other times we would meet at the Elks Club, and many nights we would take an automobile ride, and he told me then that he wished he could put in six months of this, he would be a rich man. He was getting hold of a lot of money. I told him then, "Don't you think you are taking a chance by me being seen with you so often?" And he told me I don't have to fear. "But when that 'guy' down at headquarters [Waldo] puts it up to be about meeting you, I'll simply tell him that I am meeting you for a purpose—to get information from you."
>
> He came to my house very often during the months of January and February and he used to tell me a lot of things, about how much money he was making, and that he was making it awful fast. So I told him the latter part of February, "I want to borrow $1,500 from you." He said, "You're on, on condition that you give me 20 percent of your place when you are open."
>
> So I told him that was satisfactory to me, so he said, "Well, you go down to my lawyer in a week or so and he will give you what you want and you sign a chattel mortgage on your household furniture," and he said for me to bring my wife down with me for her to sign. I pleaded with him I wouldn't do that.

"'I don't want her to feel as though you didn't trust me with $1,500 without signing over my home," I said. He said, "All right." So I went down to see a lawyer he named in the St. Paul Building, and he says, "Are you Mr. Rosenthal?" I said, "Yes. I suppose you know what I am down here for." He said, "Yes, but how do I know that you are Mr. Rosenthal?" I said, "Why, call Charlie up." So he called up 3100 Spring and he asked a man to connect him to C. O. Squad and this conversation followed: He said, "Charlie, that party is down here." And the lawyer said, "Yes, he has a brown hat and brown tie." He said, "All right," and with that he rung off. Now the lawyer told me, "You have to sign this note and these papers." I did as he told me, signing the note for $1,500 to the order of J. Donohue. I also signed some other papers. And I got the $1,500, and the lawyer said, "It will cost you Fifty Dollars now." I said, "For what?" He said, "For drawing up the papers." So I asked him then, "Will I tell Charlie about it?" So he said, "I would rather not, if I were you." Well, I said, "All right, I'll come and see you sometime." Well, I went along for a few weeks when finally Lieutenant Becker met me by appointment and told me what a hard job he has got in stalling Waldo. That Waldo wanted him to "get" me. "I have told Waldo that I have got my men trying to get evidence, and by so doing, I kept stalling him." I met him three nights after that again. He told me that I must give him a raid. He said, "You can fix it up any way you like. Get an old roulette wheel and I'll make a bluff and smash the windows. That will satisfy Waldo, I suppose." I told him then that I would not stand for it. That if he wanted to raid me he would have to get the evidence. That I would not stand for a "frame-up." "Well," he said, "I'll do the best I can to stall him."

Two nights afterward he called me on the wire at my home and he told me to go and see a certain party at half past ten in Pabst's. When I reached Pabst's there was nobody there to meet me. Then I suspected that something was wrong, so when I came back to my home, I found the windows broken, the door smashed, and the patrol wagon waiting outside. I wanted to go in, when policeman James White told me to get away, not to come. "It's all right. Everything's all right. It's Charlie making the raid, and it's all right."

So I stood across the street and waited until everything was over and went into my house, when my wife told me that Charlie said he had to make this raid to save himself. That it's all right, not to worry, "And tell Herman to go down to the St. Paul Building tomorrow and get the papers from the lawyer. You tell him I am standing the expenses of this raid, $1,500. You tell Herman he and I are even, and I'll see him tomorrow."

They arrested James Fleming and Herbert Hull and charged them with being common gamblers. The next day in Court Charlie told me to waive examination, that he wanted to make the raid look natural and that he would turn it out in the grand jury room. I said, "Can I trust you?" He said, "Why, it's all right. You can." So I had the case adjourned until the next day to think the matter over. So I waived examination the next day. I met Lieutenant Becker three or four nights later and hired a taxicab from Frawley's on Forty-fifth Street and Sixth Avenue and met him by appointment at Forty-sixth Street and Sixth Avenue. He jumped into the taxi with me. We rode down-town very slowly, talking over different things and we finally had an argu-ment. When we left we were on very bad terms.

The last word I said to him that night [was] "You know your promise." "Well," he said, "we'll see." About a week later the grand jury handed in an indictment against James Fleming and Herbert Hull. I called Mr. Becker on the phone that afternoon and I asked him what he meant by not living up to his promise. He told me, "Aw, you talk too much. I don't want to talk to you at all." I said, "You had better reconsider. You know what you are doing." "Aw," he said, "you can go to hell."

I have never spoken to him since, but I tried to right this wrong and sent some people to Commissioner Waldo to explain things to him without any satisfaction. I went to District Attorney Charles Whitman and I laid the mat-ter before him. He told me it wasn't enough evidence for him to indict Becker. But he said, "I'll investigate this matter thoroughly."

I have repeatedly sent persons to Becker to ask him to take the policeman out of my house and he told them to tell me that as long as he was in the police department he would see that the copper was not taken out. And he did also say that I would be driven from New York. I believe that the reason Lieutenant Becker wants to drive me out of New York is because I have not hesitated to tell anybody the truth regarding my own experiences with Lieu-tenant Becker as representing the police.

HERMAN ROSENTHAL

Sworn to before me this 13th day of July, 1912

G. C. Fiegel

Notary Public, New York County, New York

This second, more damaging affidavit, contained some oddities that were obscured by the sheer sensation of the allegations. The kissing scene at the New Year's Eve Ball, if it occurred, would have been witnessed by others in a position to censure Becker for such behavior, such as Deputy Commissioner Dougherty, who, while guilty of grafting himself, would have frowned at such open fraternizing with a known enemy of the department. Rosenthal also said that Becker had called over three of his men—Steinert, Foy, and White—and "introduced" them to him. Introduced was an strange word to use in Foy's case, as Herman frequently boasted that he knew the policeman and had even secured his appointment to the strong-arm squad. Mrs. Foy was a popular hair-dresser who included Lillian Rosenthal in her client list, so the cop and the gambler surely knew each other. Jack Rose would later state that Foy and another squad member, Michaelson, would collect evidence on poolrooms after

Rosenthal identified their locations, indicating that Herman slyly used the cops to pummel his competitors out of business.[3]

What Rosenthal did not state in the affidavit was that Bald Jack Rose was installed as Becker's agent in the resort, to make sure that the lieutenant was not cheated out of his percentage. Anyone who had had business dealings with Herman would have applauded such a precaution as a wise one. But Rose and Rosenthal were professional rivals whose antipathy for one another escalated under the arrangement, and although Rose escaped mention in the affidavit— Herman knew that the district attorney and the press would have taken little interest in a war of wills between gamblers—he had good reason to fear that his name would eventually be drawn into any hysteria that Rosenthal stirred up. Hence the visit to Zelig in April, after the raid in which Lillian Rosenthal's nephew had been arrested. Rose had known from Herman's reaction to that event that a firestorm was in the works, and he didn't want to take any chances. But Zelig had refused, and Rosenthal lived to tell his tale.

In the interviews that attended the publication of the affidavits, Rosenthal described himself to reporters as a victim of the "worst police persecution in history." "Lieutenant Becker—he of the strong-arm squad who is getting so much fame by his raids—has boasted that he will keep a policeman in my house day and night as long as he is in the police department," the gambler seethed, omitting the fact that his original complaint in Police Court had been against Inspector Hayes and Captain Day. His face dripped with sweat caused both by the heat and his own indignation. "I won't stand it. There are no policemen in other houses that I know of. My lawyer tells me that they have no right in mine. District Attorney Whitman has advised me to throw them out. The mayor, I know, is opposed to such persecution. He was elected on the principle that a man's home is his castle. So out they'll go."

Lillian Rosenthal, a big, blowsy woman, joined her husband in complaining. "It is very annoying, as I do want my home to myself and don't like having strange men around. There they sit and read newspapers or books all day long and all night, too. They smoke cigars and leave the butts around. It is very annoying. They're better now, but we would like to lock them out, only we're afraid they'd break the door down."

Rosenthal took reporters on a tour of his house, concentrating on the living quarters to emphasize his insistence that the address was a private house. "You see, gentleman, mine is a plain, ordinary dwelling house, the same as any other. Is it right, I ask, that I should be persecuted this way, with a policeman for breakfast, lunch, and dinner? No, sir. He shall go out."[4]

Becker's response to Herman's public disclosures appeared to indicate that he would seek redress via the courts. On Saturday night, before the second affidavit hit print, the policeman and his attorney, John W. Hart, a former assistant D.A., came to the offices of the *World*. They met with Isaac White of the paper's legal bureau and asked for the document. "My client intends to secure a warrant for Rosenthal's arrest for criminal libel," Hart explained. White assured both men that he would release the original affidavit to them after publication. Later on the afternoon of the fourteenth, Becker announced via the press that he intended to sue his accuser.

There were other affected parties, however, who could not have resorted to the courts. Rosenthal's widely circulated complaints about his ill-treatment at Becker's hands were taking a private vendetta out of tightly circumscribed boundaries and threatening the livelihoods of New York City's other gamblers. His descriptions of his arrangement with Becker could cast the glare of publicity over the entire System, which relied on police-criminal collusion to keep operating, to keep the money flowing. A grand jury hearing could potentially come out of it, and many gamblers sweated to think that they could be called to testify. A dangerous upheaval was in the works, and more than one System member was nervous as to where it could all end up. Leo Katcher of the *Evening Post* later claimed that Tammany ward boss Tom Foley, alarmed by Rosenthal's rants, went to Arnold Rothstein. "Get that stupid son of a bitch out of town," Foley urged.[5]

Rothstein, another Sullivan protégé, was born in New York City in 1882, the son of a respected Jewish businessman, Abraham Rothstein, and his wife Esther. While his despised older brother Harry studied to become a rabbi, Arnold perverted a natural fascination with mathematics into a passion for gambling, loansharking, and related pursuits. By 1909, he had moved to the Tenderloin, where he established a popular casino and became an important liaison between the politicians and the gamblers. Rothstein, because of his high standing in the sporting community and his representation of powerful interests, was deemed the ideal party to deliver a "lay off" message that Rosenthal would take seriously.

The two gamblers had a conference at Rothstein's brownstone on West Forty-sixth Street. Authorized by Foley, Arnold offered Rosenthal $500 to leave the city. Herman refused, forcing the annoyed emissary to report failure.[6] Having aggrieved the political powers as well as his competitors, Rosenthal was now in a high-stakes game for his life.

The affidavits and the maelstrom of public outrage that attended their publication finally made District Attorney Whitman give Rosenthal the careful attention the gambler had begged for.

Charles Seymour Whitman had succeeded William Travers Jerome as district attorney in 1910. He was the son of a Connecticut pastor, a Republican, and supporter of former reform Mayor Low. After working first as a teacher at a boys academy and spending a few unremarkable years in private law practice, Whitman discovered his political niche as a crusader for reform. He became a magistrate under the Low administration, and when the Tammany Democrats experienced a factional dispute that temporarily weakened their collective power, Whitman swooped in and got himself elected chairman of the New York

Board of Magistrates. Straightaway he tackled the bail bonds racket and the saloons that stayed open late. His handling of the latter graft source made him a favorite of the press. After the clock struck the hour that legally required the dives to close, Whitman would patrol the streets and respond to violators by raiding the places himself after calling a beat cop for assistance. He became known as the "raiding judge," a moniker that had immense political value when the public became sick of Tammany abuses. When Whitman was elected district attorney in 1910, it was by a majority of 30,000 votes, a rare victory in New York for a Republican.[7] He was a sincere reformer, but he was also ambitious, and if Rosenthal's allegations led to an incisive investigation of police corruption, Whitman's political career would benefit, especially if successful prosecutions resulted.

On Sunday afternoon, he had Rosenthal brought to his office and heard him out, which as district attorney he was obligated to do anyway. During the meeting, which lasted barely half an hour, Whitman determined that as incendiary as the affidavits were, no possible prosecution could result without corroborative evidence. He sent the gambler away and might not have given the matter any more consideration had Herbert Bayard Swope not promptly stepped in.

The *World* reporter and the district attorney had long enjoyed a mutually beneficial association. Swope had given favorable publicity to Whitman's endeavors since the latter's "raiding judge" days, and Whitman had reciprocated by providing exclusive and savory news items. Worried that his scoop would fizzle and die without an encouraging statement from the D.A.'s office, Swope followed Whitman up to Newport, where he'd gone to escape the city heat, and badgered him into issuing a brief statement:

> I have no sympathy for Rosenthal the gambler, but I have a real use for Rosenthal who, abused by the police, proposes to aid decency and lawfulness by revealing conditions that are startling   . This man will have the chance to tell his story to the grand jury."[8]

The *World* city editor replied by telegram: WHAT YOU SENT SAVED THE STORY. Encouraged to the point of being relentless, Swope persuaded Whitman to come back to the city and personally oversee an investigation. He probably reassured the D.A. that Herman would round up enough witnesses to support his claims. When Whitman returned on July 15 and went to his office at the Criminal Courts Building, he found Rosenthal loitering there, agitated and anxious. The suffocating heat was not solely responsible for the sweat that made his pudgy face glisten. After meeting Whitman for the first time, Rosenthal became frightened, likely because of the cool reception. He went back to Rothstein and said he'd changed his mind and intended to get out of town. Because the affidavits had been published and the damage done, Rothstein refused, telling him, "You're not worth five hundred to anyone any more." Now in panic mode, Rosenthal sputtered, "Then you can go to hell." He went to the Criminal Courts Building and waited for Whitman.[9]

The gambler begged him to press charges against Becker, but the district attorney repeated that he could take no action because Rosenthal as a sole witness was not enough for a grand jury hearing: at least one other witness was needed to corroborate him. This reply elevated Rosenthal's fear, for he had brazenly canvassed the Lower East Side gambling fraternity for corroborative support, even beseeching Jack Rose, Sam Paul, and Bridgey Webber to back him up. They not only refused him but displayed poisonous levels of hostility toward Herman, who, they felt, was a speeding train aimed straight at their livelihoods. On Sunday July 14, the Sam Paul Association had its annual outing in Northport, taking a pleasure boat called the *Sea Gate* to reach the destination. Jack Rose, Bridgey Webber, Harry Vallon, and Sam Schepps were on the vessel along with a score of other anxious and disgruntled gamblers who muttered that if Rosenthal "did not stop his talk, someone would get him, and get him for keeps."

In a statement published by the *World,* Whitman said, "I have seen and am seeing to it that he [Rosenthal] is given the fullest chance to make good his charges, not because I am eager to see any scandal uncovered in the police department, but because his accusations are so serious as to call forth the utmost efforts of my office to determine their weight. . . ." Likely remembering Rosenthal's reputation as a complaining windbag, he added, "It must be borne in mind in these times of excitement which invariably follow alleged exposures that mere charges do not constitute proof. In fact, they do not supply sufficient basis to warrant grand jury action unless something more than words are brought out to show the probability of a crime."[10]

Commissioner Waldo told reporters that no charges had been filed yet in the police department, and none would be unless the district attorney investigated what was essentially a criminal accusation and initiated corresponding proceedings.[11]

Becker was relieved, Herman went into spasms of terror. After the D.A.'s statement hit print, he tracked down Whitman one more time and expressed a fear that he would be killed for his disclosures. He vowed that he could get corroboration if he had more time, and Whitman finally agreed to receive him at his home at 7 a.m. the next day. Rosenthal promised to secure witnesses who would support his allegations, and a nervous stir went through the gambling community. Who would Herman attempt to make into an unwilling co-conspirator in his squeal?

♔ ♔ ♔

Although it was well past midnight, people were still out when Rosenthal walked through the doors of the Hotel Metropole. The build-up of heat over the day had left the brick and stone buildings uncomfortably warm, so those who found sleep impossible sought refuge in the all-night restaurants, cafes, and clubs, where iced drinks and electric fans offered a small measure of relief.

The Café Metropole was one such oasis. It opened off the lobby of the hotel, a six-story building on the north side of Forty-third Street, near the corner of Broadway. The Metropole was owned by a pair of brothers named Jim and George Considine, in partnership with Big Tim Sullivan. Although its bright lights and all-night liquor license made it a favorite stopover for theater people, gamblers, and gangsters, it had fallen on hard times. The regulars and even passers-by could see its appearance becoming more and more shabby, and later in July it would go bankrupt. But that night, the crowded café gave it an illusion of prosperity. Two brightly lit entrances— one that led into the hotel and the other directly into the café—were wide open, making the laughter of the diners and the rollicking music pounded out by the piano player clearly audible to those passing by.[12]

Some café patrons would remember that a sudden silence fell over the dining area when Rosenthal entered. He did not appear to notice; he merely took a table, where he was joined by some East Side hangers-on named Christian "Boob" Walker, John J. Hickey, Fat Moe Brown, and Butch Kitte. Thomas Smith, head waiter at the Metropole, served him a Horse's Neck, a cocktail consisting of ginger ale, bourbon, and bitters, garnished with a lemon peel. Rosenthal declined to order food, although he did ask for a cigar, which he puffed on while chatting with his tablemates. Those at adjacent tables thought that he seemed excited, animated, but not distressed. He was mopping his round face with a handkerchief, but in this heat, so was everyone else. The only breeze in the room came from the two large rotating electric fans positioned near the front door. Even the small, red-shaded candles on each table gave off the illusion of contributing to the overall sultriness.

At around 1:30 a.m. Bridgey Webber entered the café dining room. He approached Rosenthal's table and said in a friendly voice, "Hello Herman."

"Hello, Bridgey," Rosenthal replied. Someone who saw Webber stop by the table recalled later that Herman had commented afterward, "You see, Bridgey's all right. I'll get my money."[13]

Onlookers familiar with the bitter personal relations between Webber and Rosenthal also wondered why Herman was so chummy with Boob Walker. Walker also happened to be Bridgey's man of all mayhem—bouncer, lookout, and strong arm. He continued to chat with Rosenthal while Webber exited the dining room.

Not long after Bridgey left the Metropole, the taxicabs that usually parked at the curb facing the hotel were ordered to move along by soft-voiced, hard-eyed types who exuded menace from every pore. The cabbies didn't want to lose their fares but they valued their safety more, so they reluctantly obeyed. One taxi driver named Thomas Ryan drove away as ordered, but parked his cab around the block and cautiously returned, sensing that something unforgettable was about to happen.

Pedestrians received equally brusque treatment. Waiter Louis Krause, who was on his way to see about a job at the Geneva Club, stopped near the hotel to mop the sweat from his flushed face. Max Kahn, an East Side pickpocket, approached and told him to keep moving. Krause, annoyed, asked Kahn if he thought he owned the sidewalk. When the burly pickpocket glowered, the waiter hurried across Forty-third Street, but stopped there. Like Ryan, he had a feeling that the street was being converted into a stage for a drama yet to unfold.[14]

Across the street, at the Elks Club, a British desk clerk named Thomas Coupe was writing a letter to his family. An Austrian immigrant named Giovanni Stanich stood in the shadow of the Hotel Cadillac, talking to a prostitute, and an unemployed singer named Charles Gallagher was approaching the Metropole, hoping to be hired as an entertainer for the café. Absorbed in their own thoughts and undertakings, none of them had an inkling of what they were about to witness.

In the meantime, Webber had gone to Forty-second Street and Sixth Avenue, where he had poker rooms above the United Cigar Store. He ascended the stairs, strode through the stuffy, dimly lit rooms, and approached a group of men who sat drinking and smoking at a rear table. "Herman's at the Metropole," he reported. Soon after they exited in response, he retraced his steps to the hotel to complete his role in the night's pre-planned event.

A gray 1909 Packard turned onto Forty-third Street from Sixth Avenue, made a U-turn, and paused about a hundred feet from the Metropole. While the driver remained at the wheel, men who had been in Webber's poker rooms minutes earlier got out and headed slowly, deliberately across the street.

Inside, Rosenthal noted the time and figured that the morning papers would now be out. He left his table, found a newsboy near the hotel's main entrance, and bought several copies of the *World* and the other publications. He went back into the café, waving one of the still-warm papers at the gamblers seated at the next table. "How's that for a headline?" he beamed. They said nothing, just got up and prepared to leave. Boob Walker and his other table companions were already on their way out, but Rosenthal just resumed his seat and began to read, too absorbed in his celebrity to find any of the goings-on strange. He was still perusing the pages when a short, well-dressed man approached him. "Can you come outside a minute, Herman?" he asked. "I got somebody out here wants to see you."

Rosenthal responded with a curious eagerness. He got up, left a dollar to cover his eighty-cent tab, and gathered his precious newspapers. Clutching them under one arm and holding a cigar in the other hand, he headed for the front door. Witnesses later claimed that another man came out onto the sidewalk just before Rosenthal did, touched the brim of his hat, and then hurried away.

Then it happened.

CHAPTER SIXTEEN

"I Accuse the Police"

S econds after Rosenthal stepped out of the restaurant at around 1:57 a.m., Smith, the waiter, heard gunfire. John Westland, another waiter, would later recall seeing a man run along the hallway entrance of the hotel just before Rosenthal came outside, although he did not get a good enough look at him to make an identification. It was probably the same individual who touched his hat as the signal for an execution to commence.

Policeman William J. File, a former sparring partner of heavyweight champion Gentleman Jim Corbett, was off-duty and relaxing with friends at the rear of the hotel dining room.[1] When he heard the shots, he drew his gun, ran for the front door, and narrowly missed stumbling over Rosenthal, who was lying on his back on the sidewalk. File saw the gray touring car that was parked directly across the street, facing east toward Sixth Avenue, and watched several young men run away from the supine Rosenthal and either pile into the vehicle's tonneau or take up positions on the running boards. The car roared off, with File powerless to stop it because pedestrians were running amok, frightened by the gunfire and the sight of the body. As the car sped past the Elks Club near Forty-third and Sixth Avenue, Charles Gallagher and Thomas Coupe both observed the license plate.

After determining that Rosenthal was beyond aid, File jumped into a taxi idling in front of the Hotel Cadillac, at the corner of Broadway. He was joined by Lt. Edward Frye, another policeman who came running in response to the gunfire. They ordered the driver to follow the gray touring car. The man obeyed, but first he had to crank up the cab and make a U-turn, which cost valuable minutes. Two more officers named Brady and Lynch held onlookers back from the crime scene until reserves from the West Forty-seventh Street station could arrive to take control.[2] In the meantime, they questioned those who had been in the street when the murder took place. The earliest official police report, based on these interviews, put the number of participants in the Rosenthal hit at eight. Other witnesses who later gave statements to the district attorney's office thought there were six or seven men in the gray car that sped away.[3] One thing that everyone agreed on was that the killers were short, clean-shaven and dark-complected, and wearing dark clothes and soft hats pulled low over their foreheads.[4]

Butch Kitte, who had been at Rosenthal's table only minutes before and was now on the sidewalk with Boob Walker, looked at the body and then ran, never to publicly discuss what he'd seen.[5] His actions contrasted with those of almost everyone else who had been alerted to Rosenthal's murder; so many curious spectators poured into the street in front of the Metropole that Officer Brady had to call for reinforcements. Forty policemen responded by cab, but even they were barely sufficient to contain the crowd, which was later estimated to be between 3,000 and 5,000 people. Among the bevy of reporters who arrived was Alexander Woollcott, currently covering the police beat for the *Times* but later becoming its theater critic, and Edward Dean Sullivan, who would soon move to Chicago and become celebrated for his books about the Windy City's bootleg mobs.

Very few expressed shock or horror at the crime. On the contrary, curiosity and black humor prevailed. One gambler leaned toward the bloody corpse and chirped, "Hello Herman!" Seconds later, he concluded with, "Goodbye, Herman!" provoking laughter from the spirited congregation.

One party who did not laugh was Jacob Reich, alias Jack Sullivan. A one-time bodyguard to William Randolph Hearst, he and Rosenthal had been friends for years—Herman had been best man at his wedding. When the murder happened, Sullivan had been drinking a soda at a fountain beside the George M. Cohan Theatre on Forty-second Street near Broadway. Upon hearing the shots, he joined the general rush toward the Metropole, taking care first to conceal his diamond stickpin because of the pickpockets that would surely work the crowd. Taking advantage of the fact that he ran a newspaper distribution service (he relished his nickname, King of the Newsboys), Sullivan shouted, "Press! Press!" and succeeded in bluffing his way to his murdered friend's side. Leaning over the body, he blurted, "Who did it, Herman?" ("But he was dead already," he later reminisced sadly.) Then he hurried to the nearest telephone to call the story in to the *American.* After providing the news to the person who answered, he headed for Bridgey Webber's place, rightly suspecting who one of the chief instigators in the crime was.

Although the touring car had disappeared from sight even before the cab was hailed, Frye and File made a valiant effort to pick up its trail. As the taxi passed the Elks Club, Thomas Coupe ran into the street and shouted. "New York 41313"—the plate number of the fugitive vehicle—after them, but they either didn't hear or were too intent on pursuit to take notice. At Forty-third and Madison the policemen, having lost sight of their quarry, queried a milk wagon driver, who told them that he had seen the gray car go north on Madison.[6]

They went north and drove as far as Central Park, where they were forced to concede defeat and return to the Metropole. They found the street in front of the hotel, which had been quiet only minutes before, swarming with people. Rosenthal's body had been shrouded by the newspapers that fell from his dying grip, but a waiter, feeling that more dignity was in order, had fetched a table-cloth from the dining room and draped it over the corpse. An ambulance arrived from nearby Flower Hospital, bearing a doctor who pronounced the gambler dead. He certainly was: blood flowed heavily from gaping head wounds. When the shots were fired, one missed Rosenthal and hit the hotel doorframe. The second struck him in the face, passing through his cheek and jaw and breaking his teeth. A third entered his head just above the hairline.[7]

The killing surprised no one. In fact, it had been anticipated for days. According to the *New York Herald,* an anonymous caller contacted one of the newspaper offices twenty minutes before the shooting and asked, "Has Rosenthal been killed yet?"[8] No one except Jack Sullivan seemed especially upset either. His status as a murder victim aside, the police department could rejoice that his never-ending string of accusations were finally brought to an end, and gamblers whose livelihoods could have been threatened by any further front-page revelations could finally relax. Or it initially seemed.

The mortal remains of Herman Rosenthal were conveyed via patrol wagon to the Sixteenth Precinct station house on West Forty-seventh Street at close to 3 a.m. Two officers carried the tarpaulin-covered stretcher from the vehicle to a dimly lit back room, then made their report to the lieutenant in charge. The gambler's bloodied clothes had been searched and yielded pitiful results— $85.87 in cash, two Yale keys, one pair of glasses in their case, two metal cuff buttons, two metal collar buttons, and three handkerchiefs.

John Reisler, a barber and fight manager, who had been dining at the Metropole with his wife when the murder took place, knew the Rosenthals well, and went to break the devastating news to Lillian. Mrs. Reisler barely had time to speak before the new widow burst into tears.

"He's been shot! He's dead! I know it! I know it!" she screamed. "I warned him to stay home tonight. I pleaded with him not to keep that engagement. It was that man he went to see —"

She swayed a bit and then fainted. The Reislers assisted her onto a sofa and hovered protectively nearby as she shouted at the reporters who were gathering at the Rosenthal home. "I know what you are going to ask me. I blame the police and nobody else." She added that Rosenthal had gone to the Metropole in response to a telephoned summons, although she denied knowing the caller's identity. She finally composed herself enough to throw a long coat over her nightgown and hurry to the Metropole, but Rosenthal's body had long since been removed.[9] Traces of the tragedy were still evident, mainly in the form of feverishly excited newsboys who waved papers and screamed, "All about the big murder! Extra! Rosenthal shot dead in the street!"

Lillian's statement about Herman's intention to meet someone at the Metropole added to the general speculation as to exactly what he was doing there at that time of night, when the café patrons included gamblers who had muttered threats against his life during the Sam Paul Association outing. No one understood how Rosenthal could venture, alone, into their midst only hours before his scheduled appointment with Whitman, acting as if he had never been in any danger. It was too brazen, even for him. For some unknown reason he had lost the fear that drove him to haunt the sidewalk outside the Criminal Courts Building, anxiously awaiting Whitman's return from Newport. One rumor, to which Herman's friends would later give credence, was that he had decided that he could not go through with the rest of his squeal, possibly because of the D.A.'s lukewarm attitude and his failure to get corroborative support. He had, they hinted, persuaded someone—probably Big Tim—to give him a big enough payoff to get out of town. His comment "I'll soon get my money," together with the relaxed manner in which he had gone outside to his death, suggested that he had indeed changed his mind in exchange for cash and would be on his way out of New York by the time 7 a.m. rolled around.

Reporters arrived at the West Forty-seventh Street station house in time to witness the puzzling spectacle of Charles Gallagher, the singer, being rushed into the building by an annoyed police escort. Gallagher, who had observed a slew of incorrect license plate numbers for the getaway car being supplied to the police by witnesses, had told Patrolman Thomas Brady that the right number was New York 41313. Strangely, Brady responded by grabbing him, hissing, "You're wanted as a material witness" and summoning a second cop who hauled him to the station house. Gallagher gave his story to a sergeant there, but when he protested some questions he thought were inane, the sergeant lost his temper and ordered the singer locked in a cell.

Herbert Bayard Swope was among the pack of newsmen who watched this and other baffling, chaotic incidents taking place in the station with a growing concern. Clearly, no serious effort was being made to get to the bottom of the Rosenthal murder. Bad license plate numbers were still being bandied about, and the brusque treatment Gallagher had received convinced Swope that finding a solution to the crime would never be a police priority, given the trouble that Herman had caused the department for years. To get the investigation on the right track and ensure that the story he had crafted so carefully did not go cold along with Rosenthal's corpse, Swope located the nearest telephone and placed a call to Charles Whitman's apartment on East Twenty-sixth Street.

Whitman answered the phone, but at that hour, he was not inclined to abandon his quiet bed for the madcap goings-on at the station house. Undeterred, Swope took a cab to the D.A.'s home and brought him down personally. Whitman's annoyance at the early morning summons manifested itself in the abrupt, critical manner in which he took charge of the proceedings. After finding a vacant office and sitting down, he took a call from William Day, the precinct captain, who had been informed of the killing and wondered whether his presence could not wait until morning. The district attorney coldly told him that he had to come down immediately. Inspector Edward Hughes, Day's supervisor, was given an equally terse summons. When Whitman learned about Charles Gallagher's ordeal, he ordered the man's release. Only after repeated apologies did Gallagher calm down enough to give his information to the first sympathetic listener of the night. The district attorney, noting that the license number New York 41313 was the same one that Thomas Coupe had reported, concluded that he had a winner and ordered the police to locate the owner of the automobile to which that plate had been assigned.[10]

Noting that no police officer had gotten the number right, Whitman could not resist a hostile comment. "It seems mighty strange to me," he said to the press, "that these cops missed what rank amateurs had no trouble seeing." The implication was clear: the district attorney did not believe that the police had made any serious effort to solve the crime, and had he not arrived at the station that night, the investigation would have fizzled within a few days.

They certainly stepped up their efforts after Whitman commandeered the station. Using the license number, the car was traced to one Louis Fass, alias Libby. Libby, who hung out at the Café Boulevard at Second Avenue and Tenth Street, was American-born and, like a surprising number of the key players in the Rosenthal tragedy, came from a pious, respectable family. As a young man he joined the navy, and upon his discharge, went to work for a man named Schuss as a delivery driver. After leaving that job, he took a job as a coach driver at a stand in front of the Café Boulevard, which became his home away from home. It was there that Libby met Frances, an attractive dark-haired prostitute, who moved in with him and supported them both while he learned how to drive a car. After successfully completing his training, he drove for the New York Taxi Company and an individual named Hymie who owned an automobile that he offered for rental by the hour. Libby and a friend, William Shapiro, finally bought their own car together. Since Shapiro was not a citizen, the large gray four-cylinder Packard, which had formerly been owned by onetime heavyweight champion John L. Sullivan, was purchased in Libby's name. The price was $900. They paid $200 on the spot and $100 a month afterward until the entire amount was paid.

Their enterprise was a success. Calling themselves the Boulevard Taxi Company, they rented the Packard out at $50 an hour. Abe Shoenfeld wrote, "[They] made plenty of money at the Boulevard, since they carried gamblers, gunmen, crooks, and macks, and most of the jobs being robbery jobs. . . . They took all kinds of chances."[11] Zelig's friends had rented the car the day he was shot outside the Criminal Courts Building, intending to take him home, but Torti's bullet had cut those plans short.

The now-notorious Packard was found in a garage at 75 Washington Square South.[12] When Acting Captain Gloster spotted it, he asked a mechanic when it had come in for the night. The man replied that it was brought in at midnight after being driven to Coney Island and back. Gloster touched the hood and found it still warm. The garage doors were therefore secured and the police searched for Libby and Shapiro. In the meantime, other mechanics admitted to Gloster that Libby had returned the car shortly after 2:15 a.m.[13]

Libby was in bed when officers arrived at his Stuyvesant Place boarding house, but dressed quickly and was taken to the Sixteenth Precinct station house, where Second Deputy Commissioner George S. Dougherty and Inspector Hughes questioned him. Libby said that he was only aware of the car's whereabouts until ten o'clock Monday night, after which time his partner William Shapiro drove it for night owl passengers. He admitted much later that Shapiro woke him up about an hour before the police arrived and told him that the car had been involved in a shooting episode.[14] He seemed so rattled that Libby agreed to get out of bed and take the car back to the garage for him. When Shapiro was picked up afterward, he predictably refused to talk.

William Shapiro was born in Odessa, Russia, and came to the United States with his parents when he was barely eight years old. His parents and four sisters—Tillie, Rosie, Fannie, and Bertha—were respectable, but his brother, Harry, was a heavy cocaine user who sold the drug from his usual hangout at the corner of Rivington and Eldridge streets.[15] William left home at fourteen and never returned, to the dismay of his mother, who would frequently walk the dangerous night streets looking for him. Like Libby, he "copped a battleship" (hooked up with a prostitute) whose earnings tided him over during lean times. He found employment as a coach driver and, when automobiles became more common, a chauffeur. The latter undertaking was a challenge because he could neither read nor write. One pimp friend taught him how to drive, and another spent hours showing him how to write his name, finally enabling him to get a license. He secured a job at the Union Garage on East Fifteenth Street, near University Place, and went into business with Louis Libby, whom he knew from the Café Boulevard.

Ironically, Charles Becker had actually been in the vicinity of the Hotel Metropole not long before the murder occurred. At around 1:30 a.m., when Bridgey Webber was exchanging Judas pleasantries with Rosenthal, the police lieutenant rode up Sixth Avenue in Colonel Sternberger's touring car. It had been a long and busy evening for him. At 8 p.m. he went to attorney Hart's home on West Ninth Street to discuss their next step in dealing with Rosenthal's accusations. After leaving, he continued to the automobile garage on

Fiftieth Street, where he arranged to hire Sternberger's car, and invited the garage's chauffeur and bookkeeper to join him in watching the boxing event at Madison Square Garden. Becker left at nearly midnight and strolled to the Prince George Hotel with Jack Sullivan and *American* reporter Deacon Terry, whom he ran into at the arena. When the car arrived to pick them up, Becker offered to take Terry directly to his home in Jersey City, but the reporter declined with thanks, requesting instead that he be dropped off at Thirty-third Street and Sixth Avenue, where he could catch the next train on the Hudson tube line. Becker and Sullivan then proceeded to Park Row, where the King of the Newsboys visited the *American* offices while the policeman went into the *World* building to speak with Isaac White again and wait for the paper's early edition. Having collected a copy, he rejoined Sullivan in the automobile, where both men spent the ensuing ride reading the *World,* the *American,* and the *Morning Telegraph,* which Sullivan had picked up. Whitman's cautious, noncommittal statements about Rosenthal's allegations reassured the policeman. "Lieutenant Becker smiled when he read what Whitman had said," Sullivan would later testify. "He said he was very relieved."[16]

The car paused outside Webber's poker rooms long enough to discharge Jack Sullivan, who owed Sam Paul money and had made arrangements to meet him there. Then Becker was chauffeured to his home on West 165th Street, arriving a few minutes after two.[17] Helen got up when she heard him come in and made him a roast beef sandwich. At around quarter to three, the phone rang. It was Fred Hawley, police reporter for the *Sun,* calling to get Becker's response to the Rosenthal murder.

"Have you heard the news?" he blurted. When Becker replied that he hadn't, Hawley exclaimed, "Rosenthal's been killed."

"You're kidding me."

"No, Charley, I'm serious. He was shot down outside the Metropole."

"I think you've got a hangover."

"No, Charley, it's true. I'm on the story, and I'd like a statement from you."

Becker thought. "Well, I don't know what I can say. I don't know anything about the shooting. But I'm sorry he's been shot, because I wanted to show up the son of a bitch."[18]

Hawley suggested that he come down to the station immediately. After hanging up, Becker discussed his obvious dilemma with his wife. Because of his connection to the victim, it was hard to tell which course of action was the right one. If he did go downtown, it might be assumed that he had come to gloat over the murder of the man who could have ruined his police career. If he stayed home, the papers would say he showed no interest or emotion when informed of Rosenthal's death. In the end, convinced by both Fred Hawley and Helen, he went. He emerged from the subway station at Times Square at three-thirty and reached the precinct by four, just as the murder car was being driven up to the front entrance. Several policemen hurried down the steps, opened the door, and rushed Louis Libby out of the dark interior into the station. Reporters were held back, having been banished outside at Whitman's request (a decree that, naturally, did not apply to Swope), but Becker, who was dressed in civilian clothes, went inside without being challenged. He reached Captain Day's office, where Whitman, Inspector Hughes, and Dougherty were sequestered with the sweating, anxious Libby. Hughes waved Becker off before he could enter. The police lieutenant turned away, but not before he saw Whitman in Day's chair.

Becker hung around the station for around half an hour. At one point he said that he wanted to see Rosenthal's body, but the D.A. sternly ordered him to stay away from it. (Whitman would later state that he was concerned that the policeman might plant some kind of questionable evidence on it). Becker then went outside and hung out on the pavement with the exiled newsmen. "Everyone knows that I wanted Rosenthal to live," he told a reporter for the *New York American*. He reiterated that he had spent the last few days collecting information and affidavits to discredit his accuser when everything was finally laid before the grand jury.

The newsmen said that rival gamblers must have instigated the killing, while Becker wagered that it was the Spanish Louis gang. At four-thirty, Hughes came outside and took him to see the body, presumably without Whitman's knowledge. The two policemen went into the station house's yard and peered through the window of the back room where Rosenthal lay, his still face swollen and dark with clotted blood. "Whoever done him, done him good," Hughes observed. They then went back inside, where a lineup was underway. Libby, dressed in dirty overalls and a driver's cap, was standing in a line with an assortment of plainclothes officers, all of whom were clad in business attire. Thomas Coupe, who had come to the station, picked him out easily, and added that although Libby had not been alone, he had fired all the shots. The identification would be invalidated after several of Libby's fellow lodgers swore that he had been home all evening, but for a time Whitman was able to demonstrate progress to the legion of reporters camped in the street outside.

At dawn, the district attorney left the station house and gave a statement to the press before going to his office in the Criminal Courts Building and leaving Day and his men to type up reports and organize evidence.

"It would be idle for me to say that the investigation had not been greatly hampered," Whitman said, "but we will go on with it."[19]

He dismissed the theory that gamblers were behind Rosenthal's murder. When reporters pressed him for an opinion, he refused to make a direct accusation against anyone in particular, but added, "It seems curious that four policemen, who were standing within less than a hundred yards of the scene of the shooting, should all fail to give a corroborative account of it." Later, in his office, he waved the police blotter report for the murder, which included seven different versions of the murder car's license number, all of them wrong.

After Whitman left, Waldo arrived and made a statement to the press. He had learned of Rosenthal's murder at around 2:30 a.m., when someone phoned him at the Ritz-Carlton. He exclaimed "Ye Gods," then went back to bed when assistants assured him that the local precinct had things under control. It was probably the last good night's sleep he experienced for a long time.

The commissioner vowed that all of the department's resources would be committed to finding the killers. In a *World* article published that morning, it was alleged that the NYPD was in a state of mortal fear that the trail of evidence in the investigation would lead to its doorstep. Scorning the gambler theory, the paper suggested that Rosenthal's enemies on the force had arranged the shooting and expressed surprise that Becker had not been suspended from duty or even classed as a suspect.

The paper was echoing Whitman's stance. In the *World*'s July 17 edition, the D.A. charged, "I accuse the police department of New York through certain members of it with having murdered Herman Rosenthal. Either directly or indirectly it was because of them that he was slain in cold blood with never a chance for his life. . . . The public feels that the killing was a part of the work of a great and powerful secret organization which can defy the law as it pleases. The feeling is that this murder is intended to be an example of what anyone may expect who dares assail. In none of the other times when the police have been accused of doing this thing has there been such justice underlying the accusation as now."[20]

The other New York dailies were not so quick to jump on the conspiracy bandwagon. Responding to Whitman's assertion that the NYPD was behind the gambler's death, the *Sun* called the district attorney "unfortunately excitable." The *Times* adhered to the theory that Rosenthal died as the result of a gamblers' fight. "No right-minded person would have suspected either that any policeman had a direct hand in the murder or that it was instigated on behalf of any member or set of members on the force."[21] The blunt suggestion that he might be blinded by fanaticism caused Whitman to back off a bit. He did not relinquish the belief that Lieutenant Becker was behind the murder, but he kept his opinions more private until additional evidence could be brought to light.

Although they remained in custody, Libby and Shapiro, who were the closest thing that the department had to a key to the whole affair, were treated unusually well. Not only were they not roughed up as was customary, but they were permitted to lounge in the corridor outside their cells, indulging in conversation, and in the interview room they were questioned civilly. Attorney Aaron Levy, who had a Lower East Side clientele and had agreed to represent them, was surprised to see them in such good shape. Whitman's discovery of the Gallagher incident had quashed any impulse on the part of the police to beat their stories out of them, and when Levy decided that his clients would give their statements not to Hughes, but to the D.A. directly, their police interrogators acknowledged the wisdom of leaving them without marks or bruises that could not be explained to Whitman's satisfaction.[22]

The prisoners did give Inspector Hughes some fragments of information. Libby said that he knew Rosenthal slightly from the Hesper Club, and that Zelig was one of his best customers. He denied knowing anything about the murder itself. Shapiro admitted driving the car to the Metropole. But he denied recognizing the passengers, and said that when he did not drive away fast enough after Rosenthal was shot, one of them pistol-whipped him. A bruise along his hairline supported his statement.

It wasn't until late afternoon that the pair yielded a truly critical piece of information: the name of the person who had booked the car that night. It was none other than Becker's collector and Rosenthal's dedicated enemy, Bald Jack Rose. It had been hired via a call made to the Café Boulevard stand. The operator who answered recognized Bald Jack's voice. This was a breakthrough, as Rose would certainly know who the passengers were, plus he worked for Becker, so there was now a link, however tenuous, between the policeman and the Metropole slaying.

In the meantime, Becker met with reporters in his attorney's office at 60 Broadway. "I would give anything in the world if this had not happened," he said earnestly, "for it robs me of my chance to clear myself absolutely of this man's accusations. It is the worst thing that could have happened to me."

Becker admitted that he had met Rosenthal in the Elks Club, as the gambler had sworn in his affidavit. "We had been to a ball, my wife and I, and we met the Rosenthals. I couldn't shake him off. He wouldn't let me lose him."

John J. Donohue, the party named by Rosenthal as the dummy in the mortgage transaction, came forward to tell the district attorney that he didn't know Herman Rosenthal or Charles Becker, but that he had gone on record as a "dummy" in a mortgage transaction at the request of one of the lawyers at Lesinsky & Hibbard, who had paid him $10 to do so. He said that he'd been told that the man furnishing the $1,500 had some judgments against him and didn't want his name appearing in the transaction. Donohue obliged by executing the mortgage and then an assignment in blank.

Hibbard, one of the firm's partners (who, coincidentally, had been Helen Becker's lawyer for years), declined to offer any explanation, stating that he was under subpoena to appear before the grand jury, but he did say, "Lieutenant Becker did not appear in the transaction at all." Hibbard fingered Jack Rose, not Becker, as the pivotal figure in the dummy mortgage transaction. The lawyer said that Rose had come to him to arrange the lending of money to Rosenthal, and that the mortgage papers were later destroyed at Rose's request.[23]

Another breaking development in the case occurred early on the evening of the sixteenth, when Detective Shevelin arrived at headquarters with Bridgey Webber. While curious reporters, scenting a sensational new angle to the case, looked on, cop and gambler went up to Waldo's office. They soon reappeared, left the building, and came back in a taxi at close to 11 p.m. Shortly after midnight, word arrived that Shevelin had detained Webber as a "suspicious person," which was a catch-all charge to hold a suspect until more evidence of their real crime could be obtained.[24] When that evidence was not forthcoming, he was released.

Webber told a *Herald* reporter the next day that no threats of any kind had been made against Herman Rosenthal during the outing of the Sam Paul Association, but his words were greeted with skepticism, as so far more evidence was being shown of gambler than police involvement in the crime.

One individual who read with avid interest Webber's statement and all other locally available press coverage of the murder investigation was Zelig. He had spent more than a week in Hot Springs, giving himself time to recover more fully from the gunshot wound's painful effects. He returned on July 10 for a scheduled appearance before Judge Malone on the concealed weapons charge, but because Detective White was ill in hospital, the trial was postponed indefinitely and Zelig left immediately for Boston. Until he was required to appear in court, he wanted to stay out of the reach of any police officers who might view his frame-up claims against Steinert and White with enough disfavor to make more trouble for him.[25]

When he read about Rosenthal's murder, at first Zelig wondered who Jack Rose had finally gotten to do his dirty work. The gang leader had to admit that the timing of the crime had been perfect: with Herman's inflammatory accusations against Lieutenant Becker hitting print only the day before, the automatic assumption would be that he had been violently silenced to prevent further damage to the policeman's reputation and career. He frowned when he read about Libby and Shapiro's arrest, as he knew both men from the many times he had rented what was now being widely referred to as the "murder car." Their taxi company also paid him $100 per month for protection. But overall, his reaction to the entire affair was that of a semi-concerned onlooker who knew some of the participants but was otherwise uninvolved.

On July 18, however, Dopey Benny Fein, whom he had wired upon reaching Boston to disclose his location, arrived from New York with additional details about the Rosenthal hit, namely the identities of the shooters and the manner in which they had been roped into duty. After Zelig heard what he had to say, his response was first disbelief, then white hot fury.

He was not as uninvolved in the case now as he had thought.

CHAPTER SEVENTEEN

ANOTHER FRAME-UP

Fein advised his friend that Jack Rose had gotten the gang in possibly serious trouble. The day of the murder, he said, Lefty Louis, Whitey Lewis, and Gyp the Blood had been in Rockaway, acting on a tip that Dollar John Langer was there. Langer was still owed a beating or worse for engineering Zelig's frame-up, so they went to the popular summer resort area the previous week and searched for him.[1] Unable to find their quarry and with Seidenshner so ill from sunstroke that he'd required medical attention, they returned to the Lower East Side early Monday evening and passed some time at Segal's. While they were there, a call came for Rosenberg—it was Bridgey Webber, who had been looking for him and wanted him to come to the latter's poker rooms. When Webber said that it had something to do with the despised Dollar John, Louis went at once, accompanied by Seidenshner and Horowitz.

Soon after they arrived, the now infamous Packard pulled up and discharged Jack Rose, Sam Schepps, Harry Vallon, and Dago Frank Cirofici. The three gamblers had gone to an apartment at 2529 Seventh Avenue, which Dago Frank shared with a girlfriend, on the off chance that Lefty Louis would be in. He, Whitey, and Gyp had been staying there since the hunt for Langer began, so that Mrs. Horowitz and Mrs. Rosenberg would not overhear anything. When Cirofici said that Louis was downtown with the other two, the gamblers invited him to accompany them. They and Webber had a proposal to make that he could pass on to Rosenberg when he saw him.

Everyone assembled at a table at Bridgey's place, and Rose made the gunmen a proposition. He said that he could deliver Dollar John into their hands, but he wanted something in return. Reminding them that Herman Rosenthal's squeals in the *World* meant trouble for the gamblers as well as the cops, he said that he wanted his enemy beaten up. Not killed, he added quickly, so Zelig was sure to approve, especially if Langer would be handed to the Boys of the Avenue in exchange. But Herman had resisted all efforts to buy him off or appeal to his conscience, and the next step up on the persuasion scale would be to leave him in no shape to talk for a long time.

The gunmen agreed to the offer. Lefty Louis had committed murder for hire for Webber in the past, and in Zelig's absence, Bridgey's approval of the beating job carried weight. Any reserve they might have entertained about making deals with Jack Rose was dampened by the liquor and cocaine that was delivered to the table by Webber's staff during the discussion. Horowitz in particular had a fondness for "coke," and although his cohorts preferred opium when they did indulge in drugs, no one declined the gamblers' hospitality that night.

Webber went out while the others drank and smoked, coming back soon afterward to say that Herman was at the Metropole. Cirofici opted not to go, as his girlfriend was irate that he had gone downtown in the first place, and he was anxious to make up. Vallon, Schepps, Louis, Whitey, and Gyp left the poker rooms, got into the gray Packard, and motored the short distance to the hotel.

Then things went wrong. Harry Vallon had led the advance on Rosenthal when the latter emerged from the hotel interior, but instead of planting a fist in Herman's soft gut, took a gun out of his pocket and opened fire. Seidenshner, Horowitz, and Rosenberg produced revolvers and shot, too. Whitey's gun supposedly misfired, but the others accomplished their deadly work.

Zelig exploded over the dangerous situation that Rosenberg, Seidenshner, Horowitz, and possibly Zelig himself, were now in. The Packard had been traced via its license plate and Libby and Shapiro were now in custody. The day surely wasn't far off when the two chauffeurs would fear the threat of the electric chair more than the shadow of gangland retribution and identify their passengers. Although Zelig had been out of town when the murder took place, he was the gang's recognized leader and could face oppressive investigative measures from the police, who would suspect that Rosenthal had been assassinated at his command or after obtaining his approval. His name was only dimly connected with the case after the New York press published in their July 17 editions that he had rented the gray Packard occasionally in the past, but should Libby or Shapiro name the gunmen, he would no longer be enjoying such a safe distance. Zelig, who already had enough on his plate with the gun-carrying charge hovering over his head like a sword of Damocles, cursed Jack Rose violently.

He didn't believe that Rose had really intended for Herman's punishment to be confined to a beating. "It didn't make sense," Abe Meyer would recall. "The boys were all armed. After Zelig was framed, no one—*no one*—from our circle carried a gun unless it was going to be used within an hour. It was too risky. The cops were working the frame-up angle everywhere, especially if you had the kind of record those fellows did. Besides, why would you have needed a gun if you were just going to work over a tub like Herman Rosenthal?

"I don't believe for a second that the boys were heeled when they went to Bridgey's place. But when they went out to that hotel, they were [armed]. And the sorry shape they were in! I heard Gyp was so snowballed that he couldn't sit still. No, maybe before the boys got into the booze and the other junk they thought it was just going to be a muscle job, but after? Look what happened."[2]

Fein, who'd been alarmed enough to travel to Boston and inform Zelig of this chaotic development personally, said that Whitey, Gyp, and Louis had gone into hiding after the news of Libby and Shapiro's arrest broke. They had enough funds to keep them going for a while, but supposedly to forestall any anger or suspicion they might have felt at the deadly turn the evening had taken, Rose met with them the following afternoon and gave them more than $1,000. He urged them to get out of town until the excitement over the shooting died down.

At the moment, Jack Rose was nowhere to be found. Fein suggested, and Zelig hotly agreed, that until it was necessary to appear in court, the gang leader should stay out of New York. He would be supplied with money from the slush fund that the Boys of the Avenue had cultivated for emergencies like this one, and if more cash should be necessary, he could steal it himself. He could spend the temporary exile fantasizing about what he would do to Rose when they met again. The bald gambler had finally brought about Herman Rosenthal's demise by proposing a routine beating and ensuring that it would become a slaughter.

It was possible that Jack Rose's complicity in Rosenthal's death would eventually be discovered by the authorities and result in his imprisonment and even execution, but should he manage to remain a free man, Zelig vowed on that hot July afternoon that he would soon be a dead one.

Murder cases were a fixture of the New York dailies. Violent death in the city was so common that most spousal killings, card game casualties, and saloon stabbings never even made it into print. Of the handful of cases that garnered a mention, only a tiny percentage had the ensuing trials and related aftermath followed by the press and public. These tended to be dramatic spectacles involving the rich, famous, and beautiful, such as the 1904 murder of wealthy gambler Francis "Caesar" Young by his showgirl mistress Nan Patterson, or Gilded Age architect Stanford White's 1906 assassination at the hands of demented multimillionaire Harry Thaw, who accused White of "ruining" his wife, ex-Floradora chorus girl and famed beauty Evelyn Nesbit. Under normal circumstances, the shooting of a waning gambler outside a shabby hotel would not have been newsworthy. But when Swope and Whitman hinted that a highly placed police officer could have directed the murder, New Yorkers were shocked—and afraid, because the concept of a bloodthirsty cop shattered their sense of security. Suddenly, there was a mass recollection of such sinister events as the death of James McAuliffe and the shooting of the young Probber boy.

All of the papers dug through their clipping files for police abuse cases of the past year and republished their findings. The *New York Herald* of July 17 recalled that the previous September, policeman Reuben R. Huntington of the Union Market station and a confederate were indicted for robbing $300 from a Lower East Side saloon. Five other officers came forward to swear that they were with him when the crime took place, but the jury refused to believe them and voted for conviction. The paper also reminded readers that in February 1911, Officer Michael Meyers had been caught encouraging gamblers to open resorts that he would protect for a generous fee. In January 1912, Officer James Franzen from the Clymer Street station in Williamsburg was charged with extorting money from a prisoner and held for the grand jury. On April 29, John Maroney of the Leonard Street station was sentenced to six months in jail for larceny. More than two weeks before Rosenthal's murder, policemen John Hyland and Edward Farley, both from the West Seventeenth Street station, were indicted for allegedly stealing diamonds worth more than $1,600 from a diamond cutter whom they had arrested the previous February for intoxication.

With tales of thieving and murdering policemen greeting New Yorkers each time they opened a newspaper, the Rosenthal affair was a collective nightmare come to life. By keeping the public informed and reassured that justice would prevail, Swope and Whitman were building themselves a glowing future. Had Rosenthal lived, he might have been discredited and disgraced, but dead, he provided the means for the reporter and the D.A. to rise to the top of their respective professions.

Both men scorned any suggestion that Herman Rosenthal had been killed at the direction of irate gamblers. That angle would not sell newspapers, and there would be no attendant fanfare and glory if Whitman ended up prosecuting a bunch of Lower East Side lowlifes. For Swope and the D.A. to benefit, there had to be a more distinctive target. Lt. Charles Becker—head of the strong-arm squad, no stranger to underhanded and brutal behavior, accused by the victim only hours before the latter's death—was made to order as a perfect suspect.

Rhinelander Waldo worked just as hard to solve the murder, only his objective was damage control. He conferred with Mayor Gaynor on July 18. Newsmen watched from City Hall Park, looking into Gaynor's window, as the two men had an animated discussion, with Gaynor poking Waldo with his hat whenever he wanted to make a point. The message was clear: get to the bottom of the case. Not that Waldo needed much prompting. The best way to disprove the *World*'s thinly disguised suggestion that the NYPD was a stable of uniformed thieves and killers was to chase down the real culprits and bring them to justice.

Waldo was furious enough at Whitman's open accusation of police complicity in the murder to write the district attorney a letter. This message, which was also shared with reporters, did not dispute that rogue policemen were a genuine problem but added that "the good reputation of 10,400 men who are honestly doing their duty should not be besmirched by individuals who may be rascals." Taking a direct stab at Whitman, the commissioner stated, "It is unfortunate that the desire for publicity should lead anyone to unjustly attack a body of men on account of alleged wrong doings of a few."[3]

Whitman's response was to publicly upbraid Waldo for "the insulting tone of your letter." Relishing his shining role as public defender, the district attorney convened a grand jury to investigate Rosenthal's original graft allegations. Later he attended a mass meeting at Cooper Union. After he declared to his eager audience that "the murder of Rosenthal is a very challenge to our civilization," he received frenzied applause. When his statements were supported and embellished by the newspapers, Waldo's defense of the department appeared weak and obligatory in comparison, and Becker loomed large as a conniving opportunist who resorted to murder to save himself.

In his 1959 book *The Nan Patterson Case,* attorney Newman Levy deplored the damage that a scandal-mongering press did to unpopular defendants' cases during these roaring years. "The practice of 'trying a case in the newspapers' is a pernicious one and has been condemned in recent years by the bar associations and the canons of professional ethics," he wrote. "It deprives a defendant of a fair trial if statements are broadcast without benefit of oath and the acid test of cross-examination. The practice still unfortunately continues, but there was far greater abuse fifty years ago than there is today."[4]

The publicity brought the district attorney's crusade to the attention of a group of affluent and civic-minded New Yorkers, who sent a representative to Whitman with an offer to fund a private investigation independent of the NYPD. Whitman gratefully accepted their aid, sending a legion of Burns detectives on evidence-gathering missions, much to the chagrin of the police. The "Simon Pures," as rich reformers were often tagged, even paid for a large suite at the Waldorf, which Whitman used as an office and command center.

Gangsters and gamblers began to leave the city to avoid becoming unwilling witnesses for either side. There was a mass exodus to the Catskills, Hot Springs, and other destinations where summer crowds offered adequate camouflage. Rosenthal's Metropole table companions were among the first to take flight. With the police determined to prove that one of their number was not responsible for the killing, no one with the remotest connection to the tragedy or Rosenthal personally wanted to be accessible.

Escape was not an option made available to Shapiro, who remained behind bars. Inspector Hughes, determined to get his full story out of him, had him arraigned for murder on his second day in custody, which loosened his tongue a bit. He "suddenly" remembered that Harry Vallon and Sam Schepps had been in the car during the ride to the Metropole. This revelation was music to the ears of his custodians, as it provided additional proof that gamblers, not cops, were behind the murder. Hughes had Bridgey Webber brought in again for questioning, but the dapper gambler insisted that he had known Rosenthal all his life, that they were close friends, and he knew nothing about the killing. He was released because there weren't yet any grounds on which to hold him, but Hughes rightly suspected that he knew more than he was telling.

Not long after Shapiro talked, on July 18, Jack Rose strolled into police headquarters, a debonair sight in a gray suit with matching silk hat. He had been hiding in the uptown apartment of his friend Harry Pollock, either ill or simply waiting to hear what Shapiro might say—he would offer both explanations at different times. In actuality, he had consulted with James Sullivan, a Tammany-connected lawyer friend whom he'd known back in Connecticut, and been advised to turn himself in.

Sullivan's counsel, and the appearance of Aaron Levy, who also had ties to the Democratic machine, to act for Shapiro and Libby, were two of the earliest indicators of what stance Boss Charlie Murphy's branch of Tammany Hall was taking on the Rosenthal affair. Tammany would normally be inclined to stand behind the police, who collected its graft. But the district attorney was clearly intent on using the case as a political springboard, and if he could not convince a jury that Becker was guilty, there was a real danger that he might go for even bigger fish, threatening the System's higher-placed components. Their position was already tenuous with a crusading Republican in the D.A.'s office and the ferocious, honest Gaynor as mayor. Therefore, their best chance at weathering the storm was to let the buck stop with Charles Becker. Jack Rose and his co-conspirators were a means to make that happen, especially if they understood that their own survival was at stake.

Despite the manhunt that had been going on since he'd been named as the party who rented the Packard, none of the police officers who hurried throughout the building took any notice of Jack Rose as he wandered about in search of Waldo's office. Learning that the commissioner was conferring with Mayor Gaynor at City Hall, Rose left. He returned by cab half an hour later and once again walked through the stuffy corridors until he located Waldo's office. When he identified himself to the officer on duty in the outer room, the man eagerly hurried him into the presence of Deputy Commissioner Dougherty.

Rose told Dougherty that he had gone to Bridgey Webber's the night of the murder because a friend of his wanted to meet for a poker game, and he had no idea what had happened with the hired car. After leaving Webber's, he went to a café called Jack's, and it was there that he learned of Rosenthal's death. Displaying a seasoned gambler's caution, he said that he didn't *think* that Lieutenant Becker had anything to do with the affair. Dougherty told him that he was under arrest and stepped out to arrange for a message to be sent to Whitman informing him of this newest development. He was gone long enough for a disaster in timing to occur, a mishap of fortune that Jack Rose would squeeze every last ounce of drama from in a courtroom full of rapt listeners.

Moments after Dougherty left, Charles Becker entered the office. He would later say that he'd come to tell the deputy commissioner where Rose might be hiding, as he'd received word from Harry Pollock that the bald gambler had been holed up at his place. He jerked to a stunned halt in the doorway when he saw Rose sitting there, staring back at him.

"I shall never forget that face if I live to be a thousand years," Rose proclaimed dramatically weeks later. "I never had been so scared in all my life. I wanted to go to the electric chair right then—anything to get away from him and his eyes."[5] Dougherty returned just then and asked the lieutenant to step out. Becker obeyed, and if the deputy commissioner regarded the visit as an attempt to intimidate Rose, he did not make the opinion known to reporters.

"Rose's statement to me," Dougherty told the press after the gambler was escorted to the cells, "does not implicate Lieutenant Becker. I believe that Becker was entirely without knowledge that the murder was going to take place, and all I ask in this case is fair play until the facts are made known." But until then, he told Becker after calling him back into the office, the lieutenant would be relieved of his command of the strong-arm squad and assigned to desk duty at headquarters.

Told that Mayor Gaynor wanted to see him, Becker left the building, only to be greeted by a crush of eager reporters who were following up on a rumor that he'd killed himself. "Well, boys, I have committed suicide, as you can see," he said in a tone sharp with sarcasm. He went to City Hall, where Gaynor lambasted him for dining with Rosenthal at the Elks Club Ball and consorting with the likes of Bald Jack Rose. Becker defended himself by pointing out that Rosenthal had conned his way to the policeman's side at the ball, and that Rose had acted as his stool pigeon, which made regular contact necessary. When he left City Hall, the lieutenant was so frazzled from the meeting that he rounded on the reporters who trailed after him and shouted for their arrests to no one in particular.

Despite the removal of the strong-arm squad from Becker's control and the summons to the mayor's office, Waldo maintained that the policeman would not be suspended unless what he called "real evidence" was brought against him. Although Becker's association with gamblers personally displeased him, Mayor Gaynor sternly advised the commissioner, "Do not bend a single bit to clamor . . . until you obtain some evidence you have no ground for suspending and trying Lieutenant Becker." He also made a not-so-subtle dig at the district attorney when he complained about certain public officials "scheming for higher offices for which they are mentally and morally unfit." State Assemblyman John C. Fitzgerald, a crony of Big Tim's, also sprang to the policeman's defense. Fitzgerald argued that Becker had no reason to want Rosenthal dead, for the gambler's reputation was so bad and his loathing for the police so well known that only the press would give his tales any credence. Under Becker's direction, Jack Rose had gone so far as to obtain an affidavit from Dora Gilbert, Herman's ex-wife, which had been published in the *Morning Telegraph* and spelled out the maltreatment she had undergone at his hands. This suggested that the policeman had intended to fight words with words, not gunfire.[6]

Fitzgerald's statement confirmed that the Murphy and Sullivan factions of Tammany Hall were taking opposing stances on the issue of Becker. Big Tim had his own reasons for standing by the policeman (reasons that would not come to light until it was too late for both men), but his support was not the guaranteed breakwater that it used to be. Since the previous April, he'd been exhibiting symptoms of an illness that was never publicly identified, although it was privately believed to be syphilis. After Rosenthal was killed, Sullivan's condition worsened. He became manic, believed that enemies were poisoning his food, suffered from violent hallucinations, and threatened suicide. The following September, after the funeral of his wife, Big Tim suffered a complete nervous breakdown and had to be confined to a private sanitarium in Yonkers.[7]

As far as Becker was concerned, Sullivan could not have been taken out of commission at a worse time. Had he not been ravaged by illness, his support might have shielded the policeman from the investigations, trials, and execution that lay ahead. Now Charlie Murphy's agenda would prevail.

Although Big Tim could no longer be counted upon, there was at least one other party, someone without direct involvement in Rosenthal's death, whose testimony could exculpate Becker. This individual knew as early as April that Jack Rose wanted Herman Rosenthal dead and had made active attempts to secure the gambler's murder. He also had no police connections, no tangible reason to defend a cop that Whitman might have pounced upon and used to batter his story.

It's doubtful that Zelig himself fully appreciated the impact his knowledge could have on Charles Becker's future. During the days immediately after the murder, the policeman didn't appear to be in danger of arrest; Jack Rose, Harry Vallon, and Sam Schepps were the ones named by Shapiro. Zelig was more concerned with the fate of his friends, who'd been foolish enough to step into a trap that could cost them their lives.

By July 20, the four gunmen who met in Webber's place just before the errand of death began were no longer anonymous boogiemen that emerged from the murky depths of the Lower East Side's dives just long enough to slaughter Rosenthal before vanishing back into the shadows. Dougherty released the names of Lefty Louis, Whitey Lewis, Gyp the Blood, and Dago Frank to reporters, and the police began a nationwide manhunt. Their chilling, Stokeresque monikers alarmed the public and added to the horror of the entire debacle.

Rosenberg, Seidenshner, and Horowitz were known Zelig satellites, but Dougherty said that he didn't believe that the gang leader had anything to do with the murder. "I don't think Zelig himself was connected with the job. We have learned that he went out of town as soon as he was released on bail after the last shooting scrap he was in near the Criminal Courts Building, and his lawyer assures us that he will be back on Monday ready to stand trial if his case comes up."[8] The deputy commissioner's statement contradicted a rumor, published the day before, that Zelig had been seen speaking to Jack Rose at Twelfth Street and Third Avenue the night that Rosenthal was killed. The gangster's lawyer, Judge Charles F. Wahle, had protested that his client was nowhere near New York City on the night of July 15, and Dougherty, who must have been confronted with supporting evidence, concurred. But mug shots and descriptions of the four missing gangsters as well as Sam Schepps were sent to police departments all over the country. Train stations and docks were carefully watched, and undercover operatives navigated the under-worlds of most major cities, searching for a clue to their current whereabouts.

The deputy commissioner also ordered Bridgey Webber and Sam Paul to be brought in. Webber was wanted because Shapiro had picked up the killers out-side the former's poker rooms, and Paul because of the threats made against Rosenthal at the outing of the Sam Paul Association. When taken to headquar-ters and informed that he was under arrest, Bridgey was shocked. He had been so sure that he'd be let go once again that he'd asked the driver of the cab that brought him over to wait.

Although he had three gamblers along with the murder car's chauffeur in custody, furthering the reassuring (for the police) argument that Rosenthal had been the victim of vicious rivals, Dougherty had a strange conversation with the district attorney that day. It was overheard and repeated in the newspapers.

Dougherty: *Do you want me to arrest Lieutenant Becker?*

Whitman: *Not yet.*

Dougherty: *All right. I see we agree as to who is in back of this killing.*[9]

For some reason, the deputy commissioner was suddenly no longer follow-ing Waldo's example and refusing to class Becker as a legitimate suspect. A likely explanation is that Dougherty, who'd lived off the fat of New York's crim-inal enterprises for a long time himself, knew the stand that Boss Murphy's stronger Tammany contingent was going to take, and wanted it known that he was not going to pose any unnecessary obstructions.

On July 22, Becker was taken out of headquarters and assigned to the Bath-gate Avenue precinct in the Bronx, where he performed routine clerical duties. But outside his world of department routine, the net was closing in. He had been charged before Whitman's grand jury with faking the April raid at Rosen-thal's place and taking graft money. Honest Dan Costigan testified that Becker had ruined several of his planned raids, and an investigation that a relentless press conducted into the lieutenant's finances appeared to sustain the graft charge. His new three-story home in the Bronx, which sat on four big lots and even had a garage that hinted at a future automobile purchase, looked more palatial than his current salary could afford. Becker would argue that he and his wife had combined nineteen years' worth of savings to purchase it, but the excuse rang hollow when Whitman uncovered about $50,000 in bank accounts and safe-deposit boxes. Becker said that it was a sum total of Helen's savings, money borrowed from John Becker, and bequests from deceased relatives, but the explanation was received with hostile skepticism. The exposure of this money cost Becker a lot of sympathy with the public. The press made things worse by printing negative accounts of his policing career and recalling his unfortunate marital history. By the end of July the police lieutenant's public image was so heinous that a group of Bronx civic leaders protested his transfer to the Bathgate Avenue station as an insult to the borough.[10]

On Friday, July 26, Becker went to the Criminal Courts Building in response to a formal letter ordering him to appear before the grand jury that was investigating police graft. He'd asked Waldo whether or not he had to waive immunity, and when informed that indeed he did, his outlook was far from cheery. He paced outside the courtroom, waiting to be called. But when Whitman brought about an early adjournment, Becker's appearance had to be postponed until the following Tuesday.

"I am sorry that I did not have a chance to go before the grand jury," he told reporters as he left the building.[11] He emphasized that he wanted to clear himself. It's doubtful that he intended to admit to large-scale grafting, but the fact that he had agreed of his own volition to testify, without the protection of immunity, would have belied the universal portrayal of him as a uniformed crook with a wealth of sins to conceal. He disappeared into the crowd outside the courthouse, little guessing that by the time Tuesday rolled around, he would be facing a far more serious charge than grafting.

The manhunt for Harry Vallon and Sam Schepps continued. Both were believed to have fled the city. But on July 23, Vallon followed his pal Rose's lead and turned himself in at police headquarters. He admitted that he had been hiding out in the Catskills and gave such an unsatisfactory account of his movements on the night Rosenthal died that Dougherty had Vallon, along with Paul, Webber, and Sullivan, charged with conspiracy to commit murder.

The prisoners appeared before Coroner Feinberg the following day. Vallon said that he'd been drunk on the fatal night and could not remember much. Webber presented an intimidating figure to one of the witnesses, John Reisler. When Reisler, who'd sworn that he saw Webber running away from the Metropole after Herman was killed, met the gambler's chilly glare, he wilted and said he wasn't so sure after all. Whitman had him charged with perjury. Held without bail overnight, Reisler admitted that his recant had been inspired by fear and affirmed that he'd seen Webber fleeing the crime scene.[12]

Waiter Louis Krause testified that he saw Webber standing outside the Metropole until the shooting started. Then, Krause said, "I saw him running as fast as he could towards Broadway and up toward Forty-fourth Street." The Hungarian waiter then threw the proceedings into disarray when he looked in the direction of the press box, saw Jack Sullivan hanging around, and pointed him out as another man who had been outside the Metropole before the shooting. The protesting King of the Newsboys was taken into custody as a material witness. When Coroner Feinberg asked Krause how he happened to offer his

testimony to the district attorney's office, the waiter answered that his lawyer—
James Sullivan—had advised him to. The courtroom then received its second
surprise of the day—his lawyer was the same James Sullivan who represented
Jack Rose. Krause's identification of Webber threw the latter into the same dangerous situation that Rose and Vallon were now facing, and added to the list of
co-conspirators who would soon say anything to save their own skins.[13]

During the hearings before the coroner, Rose, Webber, and Vallon denied
Becker's guilt as stolidly as they did their own. Rose said that he had arranged
for the chattel mortgage, not the policeman, "because I wanted to be sure that I
wouldn't be bilked out of my money." The trio maintained that they had not
arranged for the murder of their dear friend Herman, nor had they been anywhere near the Metropole the night that he was shot. No indictments had been
handed down yet, but with all the scandal and unrest surrounding the case,
things could not be at an impasse for long.[14] Too many witnesses had linked
them to the crime, so it was only a matter of time before they took the rap themselves or shifted the burden of guilt to someone else.

The July 24 edition of the *World* contained a statement from the D.A. that
did not dismiss the obvious roles that the gamblers had played in the crime but
suggested that they were merely small cogs on a huge wheel:

> I want to get the big fish, not the small fry. I'll give them all immunity, even
> Rose, so far as I can see, if they will help me get the real culprit; if they will
> help me show how far they were aided by influences and activities outside of
> their own circles—by the police for example.[15]

The evidence that he needed to net the "real culprit" soon came. Warned by
the district attorney's men that he could be made a scapegoat, William Shapiro
finally broke. He said that on the night of the murder he had picked up Rose and
Schepps and drove them to Webber's. He waited outside the poker rooms for
just under half an hour and then saw Rose emerge with three other men:
Schepps, Vallon, and a third party whom he said that he could not make out. He
saw Rose whisper in this man's ear, pat him on the back, and say, "Now make
good," or something similar. He started for the Metropole with his passengers.
When someone spotted Jack Rose in the shadows on the north side of Forty-
third and pointed him out, another passenger hissed for silence. Obeying
instructions, Shapiro stopped on the south side of the street, about a hundred
feet east of the hotel entrance. Vallon, Schepps, and the third man stepped out
of the automobile, Vallon warning him not to move away. Tired from the late
hour and the heat, Shapiro said that he was dozing when he heard the first shot.
"I had thought this was going to be a beating-up party," he blurted, "but I realized it had turned to murder."[16]

He started the car and the gunmen piled in, one ordering him to "beat it."
When he didn't move fast enough, he was struck on the head with a pistol,

nearly causing him to lose control of the car. Shapiro said that he turned up Madison Avenue as ordered but drove at a speed of thirty-five miles per hour and kept his lights on, hoping that he would be picked up by a policeman.

When the gamblers and their legal counsel read Shapiro's story, they held a private, agitated conference. On the surface, it looked like they were all headed for guilty verdicts and the electric chair. But Whitman's comment in the *World*—about being more interested in big fish than small fry—gave them hope that they could escape punishment if they offered the district attorney a tempting enough incentive to abandon his prosecution of them.

♛ ♛ ♛

On July 25, another major arrest in the Rosenthal murder case took place. Dago Frank Cirofici was located in a flat at 523 W. 134th Street by a four-man detective squad. One of his captors, a man named Upton, spoke fluent Italian and had served under the legendary Lt. Joseph Petrosino for years. Cirofici was with his girlfriend Rose Harris, alias Regina Gordon, and another man named Fat Abie Lewis. All three had been smoking opium at the time the police arrived and were too dazed from the drug to answer coherently when Dougherty tried to question them. When he recovered enough for a series of interviews to be conducted in the Tombs, Frank admitted to knowing Gyp the Blood quite well but denied any association with Lefty Louis or Whitey Lewis. Dougherty triumphantly showed him a group photo that had been taken at Coney Island only six days before the murder. It showed Cirofici, Horowitz, Seidenshner, Rosenberg, Italian gangster Kid the Second, and three women posed for a cheery souvenir portrait. The prisoner looked at it, blanched, and refused to make further comment.[17]

By Sunday July 28, Rose, Webber, and Vallon, who were in adjoining cells, had repeatedly discussed their predicament together and with their lawyers. Webber allegedly moaned, "Why, they're trying to send me to the chair. Look here, just how bad do they want Becker? What'll they do for me if I give him to them?" When Rose expressed similar sentiments, Jack Sullivan, disgusted, snapped, "You bald-headed ———, are you going to frame up on somebody? Doing your old game again?" Rose retorted, "That is the only way we can get out of this—I would frame Waldo, the mayor, or Becker to get us out of here."[18]

That night Rose, Webber, and Vallon were brought to the hotel suite that Whitman used as his personal headquarters and began to talk. Suddenly a Whitman aide told the reporters hovering outside that all three gamblers would be sleeping there under guard overnight. The next morning, the deal that would send Charles Becker to Sing Sing's death house was done. In exchange for incriminating Becker, they would all be given immunity under the condition that not one of them had fired a bullet into Rosenthal's body.[19]

On the morning of July 29, Charles and Helen Becker rose early. He went to their new Bronx property, put the number sign up on the house, then proceeded to the Bathgate Avenue station to begin his shift, never suspecting that he was enjoying his last day of liberty.

By noon, the grand jury was almost done for the day. They had been listening to one witness after another testify on the subject of Charles Becker's raiding practices and police corruption in general, and after an early lunch, went home. But that afternoon, Rose, Webber, and Vallon were brought from their cells to Whitman's office and interrogated yet again, probably so that the district attorney could be sure of what each one intended to say on the witness stand. They repeated the previous night's statements: that Rosenthal had been shot down by a gang they hired because Becker wanted it done and had threatened them with arrest or worse if they did not comply. After supper Whitman emerged and told reporters that Sam Paul had been released, and Rose, Webber, and Vallon were going before the grand jury.

It took a while to summon the minimum sixteen men needed for an indictment, but by 7 p.m. it was done and the gamblers told their stories. Jack Rose was the star witness. While the jurors sat transfixed, he testified that about six weeks previously, Becker had ordered him to have Rosenthal killed because of the trouble Herman was making for the policeman, assuring him that no man who pulled the job off would have anything to fear from the police. Terrified over what the seemingly omnipotent squad leader could do to him if he refused, Rose arranged for the killers—Lefty Louis, Whitey Lewis, Gyp the Blood, and Dago Frank—to assemble at Webber's that fateful night and then head out to the Metropole to complete their bloody assignment. He said that after Rosenthal was dead, he called Becker to inform him. When he expressed fear, Becker sneered, "Oh, don't worry. I'll protect you. There won't be much fuss over this. . . . What do you think I am in this department? I can do as I damn well please!"[20]

Webber and Vallon corroborated parts of Rose's story. Webber said he provided the $1,000 to hire the gunmen, and that they received the money after Rosenthal was dead. Vallon said he was a merely go-between, carrying messages from Rose. They all agreed that they had been too afraid to defy Becker, who'd threatened them with phony gun-carrying charges if they did not comply. By 8 p.m. the jury had heard enough, and an indictment was handed down ordering Becker's immediate arrest.

When the gamblers expressed terror that Becker would be joining them at the Tombs, Whitman said they could spend one more night in his office, with four New York County detectives watching them. Three more detectives took the next train to the Bronx and arrested Becker as he was busy cleaning a typewriter at the station. After asking for, and receiving, permission to telephone for a replacement and change from his uniform into a tan suit, Becker and his escorts reached the Criminal Courts Building after 10 p.m. All evening the skies had been dark with assembled storm clouds, and by the time they arrived, the rain was coming down in torrents, soaking the four men. They hurried into the silent building and headed for the one court that was still in session at this hour.

With attorney John Hart at his side, Becker listened as the indictment was read to him. Hart entered a plea of not guilty and asked for a chance to confer with his client before the latter was escorted off to the Tombs. Although unable to grant the request, the judge assured him that the two would be allowed to meet later that night. Also present were James Sullivan, Rose's lawyer, and the famed attorney Max Steuer, who had agreed the day before to represent Webber and Vallon. "They looked seriously pleased with themselves," the *Herald* reporter wrote the next day.[21]

Bailiff Joseph Flaherty, an ex-cop who had formerly served under Becker, took him into custody and led him along the Bridge of Sighs, the famed and dreaded walkway leading from the Criminal Courts Building to the Tombs. He was locked up in Cell 112, which would be his home during the interval between his arrest and conviction.

Lieutenant Becker would never walk free again.

CHAPTER EIGHTEEN

"I Don't Believe that Becker Knew Anything About It"

H elen Becker was out shopping when her husband was arrested and had no idea what had happened until she came home and received the sobering news from the superintendent of the apartment building where the couple lived. "A little later some lawyers came, and a friend of my husband, a newspaperman, who brought Charley's revolver and his keys. . . . I could not believe that Charley was in any serious difficulty," she would recall.[1] The newspaperman's wife spent the night with her, and the following morning she was escorted to the Tombs.

A mob of curiosity seekers was milling outside the jail, hoping to catch a glimpse of the imprisoned cop. The reporter friend, who was accompanying Helen, said that such crowds were typical, but the reassurance was unnecessary. Helen Becker was resolved not to become hysterical or cry at any point during the ordeal, however much she might feel like it in the coming months. "It does no good and it distresses people," she said. Throughout his imprisonment at the Tombs, she visited Becker for two hours each day between Monday and Saturday, and on Sundays she brought food. She probably did not trouble him with details about the negative attention his notoriety was bestowing on her. Crank letters were arriving in droves, some asking for money, others offering testimony in support of her husband in exchange for financial aid. A weak-minded youth even showed up at her door.[2]

Despite the stress and worry, Helen worked tirelessly for her husband. She carried messages from Becker to his lawyers, went fearlessly into dodgy areas of the city in search of defense witnesses, and pored over legal documents late at night. Even after discovering that she was pregnant, she merely took a leave of absence from teaching and dedicated herself full time to the cause. Her selfless devotion aroused universal admiration and sympathy, especially after her pregnancy was revealed. The policeman's enemies must have winced at how morally unassailable she was, as a jury would wonder how villainous Becker could really be if he enjoyed a loving marriage with such a woman.

In the Tombs, Becker's chief complaint was the lack of exercise available to him. He was released from his cell twice daily and compensated for the hours of physical inactivity by running up and down the stairs for half an hour. The rest of his time was spent discussing the case with his legal advisers, reading the papers, and meeting with family members and friendly reporters like Fred Hawley. He expressed confidence that his ordeal would be short-lived.

The NYPD did not share his optimism. When Becker was arrested, a general anxiety tore through the department. The New York police were losing control of the Rosenthal murder investigation. Action was being taken under Whitman's direction, without senior officials being informed beforehand. Dougherty knew nothing about Becker's indictment until Swope told him. Waldo was enjoying a snack at his club when he received the devastating news and was visibly deflated afterward.

If Herbert Bayard Swope was indirectly responsible for Rosenthal's murder by giving him a public outlet for his dangerous accusations, Max Steuer was the one who turned Webber and Vallon from defensive defendants to contrite, eager witnesses for the state. Even Whitman conceded that without Steuer, Webber and Vallon might not have jumped on the bandwagon, and Rose's unsupported version of events would not have stood up in court.

Max Steuer's 1940 obituary in the *Times* called him "the greatest criminal lawyer of his time." Born in Austria and brought to the Lower East Side before he was ten years old, he had a sharp, calculating brain that made him ill-suited to menial jobs in garment factories and pushcart markets. A writer for the *New Yorker* said that he was born to be a lawyer the way Mozart was born to music. Like Rosenthal and Rothstein, Steuer got his break via Big Tim Sullivan, who gave him a patronage job at the post office. He put himself through Columbia University Law School and rose to the top of his profession by battling ethnic prejudices as cagily as he faced his courtroom opponents. His benefactor Sullivan was one of his clients, and earlier in 1912 he had won an acquittal for the owners of the Triangle Shirtwaist Factory, who had imposed such dangerous working conditions on their employees that 145 of them died during a March 1911 fire.[3]

By the summer of 1912, Max Steuer was in the enviable position of being able to choose his cases, and his decision to represent Webber and Vallon came as a surprise, since he'd been heard to say that he wanted nothing to do with defending any of the principals in the Rosenthal murder. But, according to the *World,* he "yielded to the persuasion of some friends who said they would not feel that the interests of a man whose name has not been mentioned in the matter would be safe unless a lawyer of Steuer's ability was there to look after him. So Steuer, out of motives of friendship, consented."[4]

The man in question was Big Tim. Although Steuer took a $10,000 cash retainer from Webber's blonde wife, Pearl, just before noon on the day of Becker's indictment, he had been to Whitman's office many times throughout the week, working out the now infamous agreement by which the three gamblers would incriminate Becker. In exchange, the D.A. agreed that Big Tim's name would not be connected with the case at any point during the trial. The acceptance of the retainer, which took place on the steps of the Criminal Courts Building in full view of gawking journalists, was merely a theatrical formality.

Rose, Webber, and Vallon never returned to the Tombs. They continued to express fears for their safety since Becker was now imprisoned there, so Whitman amiably orchestrated their transfer to the less gloomy West Side prison on Fifty-third Street. There the three-star witnesses enjoyed privileges that made their situation more like a hotel stay than an incarceration. They were permitted visits from not only their families and legal advisers, but also their friends, tailors, and launderers, and had their meals catered by Delmonico's. At the end of the second week, Webber's wife threw a "jolly" party. Some reporters (obviously not Swope) began referring to the jail as "Whitman's Ritz."

Becker, lodged in the harsher Tombs, needed an able criminal lawyer more than he did an expensive catered meal or visit from his tailor. One of the earliest possibilities suggested to him was former District Attorney William Travers Jerome. Jerome would have been a formidable opponent for Whitman in the courtroom battle that loomed ahead. But the only condition under which he would agree to accept the case would be if Becker made a clean breast of his past grafting. The policeman refused, as he feared that should the extent of his grafting become known, the jury would believe him capable of anything, even murder, to keep the cash coming in. Famed attorney Martin Littleton was another option, but he had been Schmittberger's lawyer and crossed swords with Becker during the police trials of 1906. In the end, John McIntyre, who had been Helen Becker's choice because of his past success in defending hot-potato cases, came aboard. At fifty-seven years old, he was a Tammany-connected lawyer with solid experience in capital cases. He'd once defended a Fenian terrorist tried in London for plotting to blow up the Houses of Parliament and kill Queen Victoria, and won an acquittal. McIntyre's fee came to $13,000, some of which Tammany supposedly paid on the condition that Big Tim and other sachems were not mentioned. Becker's accounts dwindled rapidly afterward, however, which implies that Helen paid most of it herself. Working alongside of McIntyre at the defense table were John Hart and two younger attorneys, Lloyd Paul Stryker and Paul Whiteside, both formerly of the D.A.'s office.[5]

While Becker's counsel worked on his defense, justice of a darker nature was being administered. On July 30, James Verrella, proprietor of the Dante Café, was shot down in a third floor room of the resort. Dago Frank had been a known patron of the place, and Verrella was rumored to be the one who had tipped the police off as to the fugitive's location.

At 1:30 a.m. Verrella and his clerk, John Pizza, were playing cards while on the floor below, a party was in full swing. Four men, two of whom were Italians, approached the entrance to the café and nodded to manager James J. Cain, an ex-cop who had once arrested Enrico Caruso. After he admitted them, they took a table in the dining room and ordered four glasses of beer. The two Italians then went upstairs to the third floor while their companions continued to drink. When they located Verrella and his clerk, they drew guns.

"You will squeal, you ———!" one shouted. Then both fired. Verrella lunged forward to tackle them, but the bullets sent him crashing to the floor. John Pizza, terrified, dodged past them and ran for the stairs. They shot at him, too, hitting him in the left knee and ankle.

At the sound of gunfire the café patrons ran for the door. In the confusion, the assassins' two companions made their escape. The police later captured the Italian gunmen, who were identified as William Lorenzo and Albert Contento, both close friends of Frank Cirofici.[6] No other connection was officially made, but the general suspicion was that Verrella had died after betraying Dago Frank to the police.

The search continued for Whitey Lewis, Lefty Louis, and Gyp the Blood. There were sightings reported all over New York State and even beyond: Toady Lefkin, who once worked for Herman Rosenthal as a doorman, said on July 20, "Whitey Lewis and Lefty Louis left for Chicago on Wednesday and are now working in a poolroom in that city, one as a lookout and the other as a capper in a fixed-wheel game."[7]

Not quite, but they might have been better off if they had. On August 1, Whitey Lewis was tracked down and captured by detectives as he was boarding a train in Fleischmanns, Delaware County. Lewis submitted to arrest without a fuss. He had just bought a ticket to New York and would insist that he had been intending to return to the city to give himself up like most wanted parties in the Rosenthal murder investigation were doing.

Despite being handcuffed to a detective, the light-haired gangster seemed to enjoy the ride to the metropolis. The reporters who occupied adjacent seats on the train were favorably impressed by his friendly demeanor and the fashionable figure he cut in his striped blue suit, blue shirt and automobile cap, and tan socks and shoes. A gold pin shaped like a hand clasping two tiny diamonds glittered on his tie. The *New York Times* reporter found him in a particularly talkative mood at three o'clock in the morning, when almost everyone else in the compartment was asleep.

"I know you," Lewis said to the newsman after staring at him for several minutes. "I've seen you several times lately. You've been spotting me, haven't you?" He was sure that the man was a Burns detective. After the *Times* man assured him that he was only a harmless scribe, the gangster dropped the subject and continued to chat. He said that he knew nothing about Rosenthal's murder and that "Jack Rose and some of the others were trying to throw the blame on me for what they had done."

When the conductor came around, the reporter reached for his wallet to pay for his fare. Lewis stopped him. "Take this," he said, holding out the ticket he had bought at Fleischmanns. "The state's paying my fare. You might as well ride on this." His police escort told him to put it back in his pocket. He obeyed with a sigh. "That's right. I might need it for evidence."

He described how "find Whitey Lewis" had been the favorite sport of amateur detectives in the resort towns he had stayed in, and to amuse and thrill himself he had joined the game and offered theories and tips side by side with unsuspecting would-be Sherlocks. He talked about a close call he had at Fleischmanns when his regular barber was so busy that the town constable came in to assist with shaving customers. Lewis had a prominent forehead scar and was worried that the policeman might spot it and guess who he was, so he opted to wait until the barber had time for him.

"Jack Rose may say I did it [murdered Rosenthal], but what does his word go for?" he pointed out. "He thinks that by lying about me and other innocent men he can save himself. I know Jack Rose. He's the kind of a man that would squeal on his own mother if it would save his own skin."[8]

After being interrogated at headquarters, Lewis joined Dago Frank in the Tombs, where the only visitors they were permitted to see were family members and their lawyers, Louis Spiegel and Cesare Barra. When Whitman looked at the newspapers and saw photos of Dougherty's men escorting the gangster to headquarters, he griped that the police must have known where Seidenshner was all along. As for Rosenberg and Horowitz, the district attorney said that Becker probably had them hidden in a safe spot, where they would be morphed into defense witnesses. His detractors scented sour grapes, since it was the NYPD and not his private Burns detective force that had found Cirofici and Seidenshner.[9]

Whitman caustically stated, "I cannot escape the conclusion that some members of the police department have known, if they do not know now, the whereabouts of these murderers." If so, the NYPD expended a lot of time and manpower as well as financial resources making it look as if they didn't know.

There was a mad competition between the police and the Burns men to find the remaining gunmen. It was hoped that Zelig, whose role in the murder plot was still unclear, would be found at the same time that the fugitives were arrested. Although Rose did not actually incriminate the gangster boss, the overall assumption was that he must have had more to do with the crime than any of the state witnesses were willing to let on. The *Times* declared, "It was intimated that the men who were accused of killing Rosenthal had been picked for the work by Zelig himself."[10]

The result was a slapstick series of wild goose chases and misidentifications. When someone claimed to have spotted Lefty Louis in Tannersville, a hamlet in Greene County, Inspector Hughes went up there personally and set up a temporary command center. Nothing came of it, but sheriffs and deputy sheriffs from Sullivan, Ulster, and Greene counties combed their districts side by side with representatives of the New York police. Reports of sightings came in from Boston, Rochester, Harlem in New York City, Greeley, Pennsylvania, Duluth, Minnesota (which Gyp and Lefty had supposedly reached by ship before diving into the concealing darkness of the local underworld), Colorado, and even Montreal, Canada. Female detectives were detailed to follow Lillian Rosenberg and Lillie Horowitz, but the girls, mindful of being watched, gave their pursuers the slip.

When not reading about the latest Gyp or Lefty sighting in remote parts of the nation, New Yorkers were treated to sordid excerpts from Jack Rose's testimony before the grand jury. These statements were supposed to be confidential, but when challenged, Whitman retorted that there was nothing illegal about a D.A. releasing reports of grand jury testimony. It was, however, illegal for anyone who'd testified to correct misquotes in the press. When Whitman issued a press release advising that Lt. Daniel Costigan had accused Becker of obstructing his raids and Waldo of being permissive where vice was concerned, Costigan tried to set the record straight and was reprimanded. Because his own witnesses were notorious lawbreakers and self-confessed accomplices to murder, Whitman resolved to make Becker look so heinous that even the testimony of criminals against him would be believed.

On August 15, the *World* published Jack Rose's confession, which he'd given to Whitman on the August 6. It was a thirty-eight-page document that gave the reading public its first unfettered account of how Charles Becker had allegedly arranged for Rosenthal's murder. It rambled in parts, the grammar was poor, and punctuation and capitalization were sporadic, but these literary blemishes gave the story an aura of raw, uncalculated honesty.

Rose described how he had met Becker and become his collector. Their agreement was that he would get 25 percent of what he collected. Bridgey Webber, whose standing in the gambling community was higher, helped him out whenever anyone balked at paying their tariff. He estimated that most resorts kicked back $300 a month.

He also detailed how Becker and Rosenthal met and became "fast friends." Herman even secured the appointment of two officers, Foy and Michaelson, to the lieutenant's squad and used these men as attack dogs against "a few people in the gambling business he had an old score to settle with." When Rosenthal approached Becker about taking an interest in his new place, the policeman agreed to let him have $1,500 on a chattel mortgage. "Becker told Rosenthal he wanted Rosenthal to take care of me, and he declared me in for 25 percent, which I agreed to split with Becker," Rose added.

Then things began to go wrong. Waldo was after Becker to raid Herman's place, and all efforts to stall him were finally exhausted. The lieutenant performed the raid and canceled the chattel mortgage as compensation, but Rosenthal would not be mollified and made threats to tell all he knew.

It was around this time, Rose said, that a dangerous rumor accusing him of instigating Zelig's frame-up on the concealed weapons charge began making the rounds. Frightened, he said he turned to Becker for advice. The policeman urged him to tell the gang leader and his followers that Rosenthal was the one stirring up trouble, and that if he were not killed, Zelig's would be the first in a series of frame-ups that would make the Lower East Side an unsafe place to be a gangster.

Rose used florid language to depict Becker as a power-drunk cop who was swelled with bloodlust and his own importance: "I said, 'Do you mean you want Zelig's friends to go after him and threaten him, that if he don't stop going after you they will beat him up?' 'Why no,' he said, 'not beat up. I want him murdered, shot, his throat cut, any way that will take him off the earth.' He went further. He said that if anybody will murder Rosenthal. nothing can happen to them. He would take care of that."

Rose denied having met Zelig before and didn't know how to arrange a hit, so he went to Webber and Vallon for assistance. They put him in touch with Whitey Lewis and Lefty Louis. To square himself with Zelig, Rose put up some bail money, but the gang boss refused to have anything to do with the murder plot. Things dragged along until Torti shot Zelig, at which point, Rose said, Becker renewed his demands. The policeman suggested that the attack on the gang leader was a perfect cover for their plans—when Rosenthal was killed, the event could be passed off as another phase in a Lower East Side underworld war.

A few days before the actual murder occurred, there was an abortive effort to kill Rosenthal at the Garden Restaurant. Webber went to where Rose was hanging around with Harry Vallon in Still's Restaurant and said that three men wanted to see him at the Lafayette Baths, one of their regular hangouts. The trio (presumably Whitey, Lefty, and Gyp) got into a taxi with Rose and Vallon and rode around until Rosenthal was located. They all hovered outside the Garden Restaurant and waited for their target to emerge, until they spotted a man whom they were sure was a Burns detective, at which point they retreated.

When Rose met Becker the next day at the Union Square Hotel and reported failure, the cop became furious and demanded that the job be done soon, for Rosenthal's chatter was beginning to attract the attention of the district attorney. He told Rose to get an affidavit from Dora Gilbert to use as ammunition should the fat gambler live long enough to make it to court, and also demanded that Rose see all of the gamblers for whom subpoenas had been issued, to insure that they did not incriminate Becker. After the affidavit was obtained and the gamblers had given their promise to stay silent, Rose telephoned the policeman, who said that if Rosenthal could "be croaked before the night was over, how lovely everything would be." He stressed again that no one who knocked off Rosenthal would have anything to fear from the police.

On the night of the murder, Rose met Jack Sullivan at the Sam Paul Association clubhouse and dropped him off at Madison Square Garden before going on to Dora Gilbert's house to pick up the affidavit. After taking it to the *Morning*

Telegraph office, he returned to Mrs. Gilbert's to collect Vallon, Schepps, and others in their party. Their car blew a tire near Fourteenth Street, so Schepps telephoned for a new one, which turned out to be the gray car driven by William Shapiro. They started uptown and stopped at the Seventh Avenue house where Gyp, Lefty, Whitey, and Frank were known to be staying. He said that Frank, the only one home, came down and joined them on a ride to Webber's, where they found the other gunmen. When someone came in and said that Herman was at the Metropole, everyone left except Rose, who made Schepps stay with him. When word arrived that Rosenthal was dead, Rose telephoned Becker, who said that a reporter had already given him the news, that no one was to worry. He came downtown and met Rose at Webber's place, his mood sinisterly jovial.

The policeman said that he had driven by the Metropole earlier that evening, intending to shoot Rosenthal himself if he saw him. When Rose asked if he'd seen the body, Becker replied, "Yes, I saw the squealing ———, and I would have liked to have taken my knife out and cut a piece of his tongue off as and hang it on the Times Building as a warning to possible future squealers."

Rose met Webber at Fiftieth Street and Eighth Avenue later that day and received the $1,000 payoff for the gunmen. He gave them the money and warned them to lay low until the storm died down. He then went to Harry Pollock's, so distressed by the entire affair that he collapsed and was put to bed. He said that he kept in touch with Becker by telephone and through messages carried by Schepps. On the morning of Wednesday, July 17, Becker sent him a message advising him to give himself up, as the police wanted to interview him about the contents of Dora Gilbert's affidavit. Rose did not comply, and later that evening John Hart and a notary came to see him at Becker's request. They wanted, and got, a statement from him that explained the $1,500 chattel mortgage transaction in a way that did not implicate Becker. The bald gambler said that he was so "sick in mind and body" that he fell for their reassurances that everything would be all right.

When Rose read A. J. Levy's statement to the press the next day, which connected him to the murder car, he concluded that he was on his way to becoming a scapegoat and decided to give himself up. Although Becker sent him a message in the Tombs via Charles Plitt, his press agent, assuring him that all would be well and advising him to retain a certain lawyer as his counsel, Rose no longer had faith in the policeman's intention to protect him. He yielded to James Sullivan's advice and confessed.[11]

Jack Rose's confession was greeted with horror by the public and Becker's defense team, who despaired of ever assembling an impartial jury. But as damaging as the story was, New York state law dictated that to secure a conviction, it would have to be corroborated by a witness who had not been an accomplice to the crime. Sam Schepps was outfitted for the role right away.

Rose's attorney, James Sullivan, had known that a corroborator would be needed and had advised Schepps to leave town and disassociate himself from

Rose, Webber, and Vallon. The "Murder Paymaster," as he came to be known after Rose had fingered him as the one who'd given the gunmen the $1,000 pay-off (the bald gambler soon amended his story to say that it was he who'd handed over the money), was caught in Hot Springs, Arkansas, on August 10 by the local postmaster, who was also a deputy U.S. marshal. When Schepps was searched after his arrest, a letter from Rose was found on him.

"Dear Sam," the note began, "I don't know what you have heard or read, but it has got down to the stage where the electric chair stares us in the face." He detailed the agreement of immunity that Whitman had extended to him, Webber, and Vallon, and added that it would apply equally to Schepps. He finished with, "My advice to you is to let me send a representative of the district attorney to bring you here. This would prevent the police from getting you and putting you through a third degree."

Possibly suspecting a trap, Schepps sent a guarded reply, which was intercepted and read. He wanted Rose to spell out exactly what was expected of him: "To prove my loyalty to you, I must be a 'squealer.' Still I am willing even at that cost on these conditions: that you will only expect me to tell the truth and nothing but the truth, or else write word for word what you expect of me. . . . May God help us."[12]

Schepps's attorney, Bernard Sandler, wired and advised him to talk to no one until he was brought to New York City and saw the district attorney, "with whom satisfactory arrangements have been made on your behalf." While waiting for men to arrive from the D.A.'s office, he was detained at the Marquette Hotel instead of the city jail. Schepps told Acting Mayor Pettit that he would not talk until he'd read Rose's confession, and that "it is up to me to make the best bargain I can."[13] On August 15, he boarded a train with Assistant District Attorney Rubin and two detectives, gleeful at how he had eluded the New York police. Whitman came aboard when the train stopped in Albany and spent the rest of the ride questioning Schepps about his knowledge of Becker's connection to Rosenthal's murder. At Grand Central Station a party of detectives was waiting to take him into custody, but Whitman overrode their authority and took his new witness to the Criminal Courts Building personally.

Afterward, Schepps joined the others at the West Side Prison. He received a weekly "salary" from Whitman and was allowed to send out to a Fifth Avenue store for luxury clothes and furniture and bedding, a generous concession that aroused envy in the others. Webber complained, "It's not fair. How come you get the special privileges?"

"That's because you aren't the corroborator," Schepps explained happily. "I got pulled in last and got to be the corroborator."

"I wish I'd of been pulled in last. Then I could have been the corroborator," Webber lamented.[14]

After Schepps was picked up, the potential witness who aroused the most curiosity and speculation was Zelig. He had stayed out of public view ever since the murder, and both the police and Whitman were anxious to interview him.

Since he was reported to be traveling with the still-missing Rosenberg and Horowitz, finding Zelig would be the most important break in the case since Schepps was found.

⚜ ⚜ ⚜

On Thursday, August 15, Providence, Rhode Island, resident Thomas Griffiths was on his way home from a long, sweaty yet entertaining afternoon spent watching a baseball game. He caught a streetcar home, alighting at Mathewson and Westminster streets. As he was about to descend the car's steps, Griffiths felt a tug at his pocket. Instinctively he reached around and discovered that his wallet, which contained $65, was gone.

Griffiths immediately suspected a tall young man who stood behind him, but he said nothing and merely followed the stranger off the car onto another. He waited until the man was seated, then approached and accused him of theft. Griffiths seized his arm. The man's dark eyes blazed with fury, and he raised a bulky fist as if to strike, but at that moment traffic policeman George M. Hindmarsh boarded the halted car, his attention drawn by the raised voices. When another passenger pointed out a wallet on the seat beside the accused, Griffiths readily identified it as his, and Hindmarsh took the thief into custody.

At the station, the man gave his name as James Golden, but just before his arraignment, with local attorney Thomas J. Dorney acting as his counsel, he changed his mind and said it was Edward Golden. "I guess you have it on me," he told the inspectors as he posed for a mug shot. He seemed affable enough, but refused to disclose any personal details save his name and the assertion that he had never been arrested before. As was customary, the Providence Police Department forwarded his photo and description to New York and other major American cities, in the event that Golden was more of a professional than he cared to admit and an outstanding warrant still existed on some book somewhere.

On August 19, at 4 p.m., Golden was released from the Providence County Jail, where he had been held since Friday. A local resident, Joseph Rosenberg, had furnished the $2,000 bail. The hearing was scheduled for Tuesday, August 27, in the Sixth District Court.

Less than two hours after the genial young man walked out the jail door into the brilliant August afternoon, Captain of Inspectors Albert E. Nickerson received a telephone communication from Dougherty in New York. The deputy commissioner, who had received the photograph and description sent to his office, was anxious to know whether Golden was still in custody. Nickerson, unaware of the successful bail posting, replied that as far as he knew, the arrested pickpocket was still broiling in a furnace-hot cell back in the jail.

Dougherty, becoming more excited, asked that the man be held for the New York authorities. He was vague as to the reason for the request but advised Captain Nickerson that he would be sending him a telegram with additional information. Puzzled by the conversation, the Providence officer hung up, paused, and then placed a call to the jail. The official who answered informed him that Golden had been released on bail. Nickerson received a second—and considerably bigger—surprise when the anticipated message from New York arrived, advising him that Edward Golden, clumsy and unlucky pickpocket, was none other than Big Jack Zelig. The official reason behind the detention request was the outstanding concealed weapons charge, but Zelig's position as a central figure in the Becker-Rosenthal investigation had rendered him too valuable—and dangerous—to be permitted off the radar.

Thomas Dorney denied all knowledge of his client's true identity. Feigning a state of surprise bordering on shock, he told the press, "I don't hardly believe it. The bail was secured by a man named Friedman, a court officer at the Chelsea Courthouse. He called me up on the telephone and wanted to know what to do about getting 'Golden' out, and I told him what the necessary procedure would be. The next I knew, 'Golden' was in my office."

He admitted that after bail had been posted, Zelig, alias Golden, appeared in his office and briefly discussed his case. Clinging to the last threads of denial, he exclaimed, "He went from there [Dorney's office] to the Crown Hotel, where he paid his board bill of $14.60 or thereabouts and took away his belongings. I don't believe, if he had been Zelig, he would have done that." Noticing the skeptical expressions with which the assembled reporters received his statement, he said, "I'll tell you what I'll do. I'll just call Friedman on the telephone and find out who the man is."

The lawyer duly made the call while the press men listened, pencils poised over their notebooks. Ten minutes later, after conversing with the Chelsea court officer, Dorney was obliged to admit that he had agreed to represent one of New York's most dangerous and sought-after gang leaders.[15]

Zelig returned voluntarily to New York. He sent word to Whitman through his attorney, Charles Wahle, that he was willing to go before the grand jury. The district attorney proceeded to feed his version of what the gangster's testimony would be to the papers. According to the *World*, Zelig would confirm that "he was so afraid of Becker and believed so implicitly in the lieutenant's power that he had no alternative but to hire the quartet of murderers and had then fled the city in terror of the policeman."[16]

Remembering his wounding by Charles Torti the previous June, the authorities posted extra guards in and around the Criminal Courts Building to preserve order during Zelig's appearances on August 20 and 21. While he was sitting outside the courtroom on the first day, waiting to be called, a photographer snapped the now-famous picture of him wearing a straw boater hat and smiling. The *Washington Post*, when it ran the photo, noted in the accompanying caption, "He is a splendid physical specimen, well-modeled, well-proportioned, all agile grace and muscle. His face is strong, his expression shrewd and domineering, and his mouth in repose is cruel, but he smiles readily and with agreeable effect."

Contrary to Whitman's predictions as published in the *World*, Zelig did not further the prosecution's case against Becker. Instead, he told the attentive jury about the frame-up at Segal's. He described his demand to be publicly searched and the hostile reactions of Steinert and White. He was wearing the same two-piece, light-blue flannel suit that he wore the day of his arrest, in order to participate in a demonstration that would prove the officers' guilt beyond any clear doubt.

The *Times* reporter noted, "The coat was skeleton lined, with two buttons and patch pockets with no flaps. The gun which, it was charged, was found in his pocket was produced. . . . With the grand jurors watching intently, Zelig was made to put the weapon first in one pocket and then another."

The weapon and the coat pocket were a poor fit, literally. The gun caused the coat hem to sag and created such a bulge that anyone glancing at Zelig even casually would have noticed it. George Greenberg, one of the diners at Segal's, testified that he had participated in the mass search of Zelig's person at the gangster's request and neither saw nor felt a gun. After Greenberg left the stand, the jury declared that no further witnesses were necessary and issued a perjury indictment against Steinert and White.[17]

Commissioner Waldo immediately suspended both detectives when word of the indictment reached his office. Steinert was locked up in the Tombs while White, who had been ill in a hospital at Far Rockaway for weeks, was arrested but not taken immediately to jail.

As Zelig and Charles Wahle left the jury room, the gangster paused for the crowd of reporters. He had achieved no small victory in his vendetta against the officers who had framed him, and the resulting pleasure put him in an expansive mood.

"First, I want it distinctly understood that I know nothing about the murder of Herman Rosenthal. If I was not in the predicament I am at the present time, I would make it a point to find out who did the killing and break his leg for him. Herman Rosenthal was my friend.

"I am convinced by the facts that Jack Rose framed me." This remark was calculated to throw off Dollar John—Zelig needed his money to contribute to a defense fund for Cirofici and Seidenshner, as well as Rosenberg and Horowitz should the law catch up with them.[18] "If I had been sent to prison, as it looked at one time I might be, Rose knew well that my friends would kill him." When Wahle offered a respectful admonishment, Zelig shrugged and corrected the unveiled threat with "avenge me."

"Jack Rose had me bailed out," the gang leader went on. "He and Bridgey Webber and Schepps and Vallon put up the money to get me out on $10,000 bail. Why they tried to get me out was only for one reason—Jack Rose was scared because it was rumored around that he was responsible for my arrest. He was interfering with the conduct of my case and with my counsel.

"I didn't know who was trying to get me out until I came over to the district attorney's office on July 2. I didn't care who got me out. I was only too glad to get out of the Tombs.

"I left the Criminal Courts Building with Schepps in a taxicab and I went out of town alone, for my case had been set down before Judge Malone before July tenth, and I returned to the city that morning. Because of the illness of [Detective White] my trial was postponed indefinitely and I went out of town again. I did not return until Tuesday. Much has been published about my traveling in the company of the fugitives, but there is not a word of truth in that."

"Did you know them]the gunmen]?" the reporter from the *World* asked.

"I knew them by sight, and I think they are decent chaps compared with this man Rose." Once more the venom crept into Zelig's chatty tones. "He would hang his own brother to clear his own skirts. I know he framed me, and I don't believe that Becker knew anything about [it]. I am under no obligations to any of them."[19]

From the courthouse, Zelig proceeded to Wahle's office, where Henrietta and a lady reporter, Evelyn Campbell, were waiting. Campbell, who'd been expecting a scarred, gruff, Eastmanesque figure in a slouch cap and battle-ragged suit, was surprised and not a little intrigued by the tall, elegant figure who cordially greeted her before settling beside his wife. Her story appeared in the *New York Herald* the next day:

"Best Husband that Ever Lived" Says Gunman's Wife

"I want my boy to grow up like District Attorney Whitman, honest and upright, that's my idea of a man."

"Big Jack" Zelig was speaking, and I, who had seen him only a few minutes before alternately flippant and savage as the questions of a circle of newspaper men amused or angered him, sat amazed at the tenderness of his voice, at the tenderness of fatherhood that shone in his voice.

"Big Jack" Zelig's has been a name most frequently mentioned in the city's criminal annals. Gun man, gang leader, cleverest pickpocket in the city—that is his reputation. Few know the other side of his life, know that up in the pretty Harlem apartment a sweet-faced woman calls him "the best husband that ever lived" and that a curly-headed lad of nine counts the days that "Dad" is home as red-letter ones.

Name Not Zelig at Home.

In the Harlem apartment the name on the door is not Zelig. As widely separated as the poles on the earth is the life the big chap lives at home and among his pals.

He and his pretty wife sat yesterday at 220 Broadway, in the offices of Judge Charles Wahle, Zelig's attorney, and told me of their boy, Harry, and their plans for his future.

"He is only nine years old and he is in the fifth grade at school," the brown-eyed, girlish mother spoke with a wealth of pride in her voice. Then she turned shyly to her husband. "He looks just like his father," she said, "and I guess he gets his brains from him. You know, his father's awfully bright."

Her husband shifted his six feet of splendid physique in an embarrassed fashion and laughed tenderly.

"He isn't any more like me than he is like you," he told his wife, and then his fatherly pride got the upper hand.

"But he is just a little bit of all right, that boy," he said, "and the only fear I have is that some day he is going to find out about me."

He looked at me with the contemptuous little smile that comes to his lips when he is asked concerning the doings or motives of New York's finest.

"A boy that ever got started wrong in this town never had another chance with the police," he said emphatically. "They either used him or jobbed him. But I think when Mr. Whitman gets through things will be pretty nearly cleared out and a fellow will have a chance."

"Are you training your boy in any special way so that he may not also go wrong?" I asked.

"Am I?" The words came like an explosion, so emphatic were they. "Indeed I am. There is only one thing to do, you know?"

"Yes?" I queried.

"Keep him busy and interested," he returned. Then he laid down some rules for the upbringing of boys which came from long and careful study of his problem, and which incidentally might well be posted up on the wall of every father's room:

Make an athlete of your boy

Keep him off the streets

Never let him play marbles for keeps.

Keep him away from the small dice and poolrooms

Make a companion and chum of him

"One of the worst things a small boy can do is play marbles for keeps," Big Jack reiterated. "I know, for that is the thing that started me wrong. It gives a boy his very first taste of gambling and gives him an idea of getting something without working for it, which is a mighty bad thing to get a taste for. You see, there were so many of us and my parents were so busy that they couldn't keep me from the street the way we can keep Harry.

"Harry and I are great chums," he went on, warming to his subject as he thought of the little lad waiting for him at home. "I take him with me to the ball games and I have a punching bag fixed up for him at home. We box with each other. I take him swimming and to Coney Island. I tell you, we have great old times, that boy and I."

"Big Jack" Zelig is as pretty a problem in psychology as any enthusiast would wish to study. From his reputation I expected to see a cross between Captain Kidd and Deadwood Dick.

What I really saw was a smiling young chap with an impression of immense reserve strength behind his lithe, erect figure. One would think him the ordinary, careless, good natured fellow holding down a good job and enjoying life to the utmost, were it not for the eternal watchfulness that is in his gaze.

"When this is all over, I shall be so happy," sighed his wife, whose personality is as retiring and mouselike as her husband's is assertive. "I can't understand all this. I don't believe one word they say about him. He is the best husband in the world. When this trouble came up, I thought I would go out of my mind but things look so much brighter now. I believe that he will be proved innocent of this charge that the police have framed up against him. Then he has promised me that he will quit all the foolishness and we will start all over again."

"Have you any profession or business at which you could earn a good living?" I asked her husband.

"I have," he returned in the deliberate, emphatic manner in which he answers questions which he deems important.

"May I ask what that is."

"I am a diamond expert."

There was an instant's silence, and then we all burst into laughter at the unconscious humor of the answer, for "Big Jack" Zelig has been credited with expertness in not only valuing but in removing precious stones. He was not at all disturbed, joining good humoredly in the laugh against himself, but persisted in his answer.

"I really mean it," he said. "I can make my living honestly, and I mean to."

"Will you tell me some of the things you like to do best?" I hastened to ask.

The answer came promptly. "To swim and read."

"And your favorite authors?"

He did not hesitate. "Shakespeare, Victor Hugo, and Eugene Sue. I like Les Miserables best of all," he went on. "Isn't that part fine where he goes up that wall?"

Another reporter to whom Zelig granted a brief interview was O. O. McIntyre, who would achieve newspaper celebrity during the 1920s and 30s with his widely read column "New York Day By Day." McIntyre was also favorably impressed. "He did not conform to the beetle-browed scar-faced type of the headlines," the columnist would recall in 1928. "He seemed more [like] an overexuberant boy having a lot of fun out of life. In a small town he would have been classed as a 'barbershop sport.'"

Zelig chose his words carefully when he spoke to Campbell and McIntyre. He had failed to fortify Whitman's case as anticipated and would have been mindful of a recently published statement by Becker's lawyer: "As soon as someone gives an indication that he will testify for the defendant, he is brought to the grand jury room and grilled by the district attorney." This tactic was condemned as an attempt "to menace and intimidate prospective witnesses."[20]

Zelig's complimentary words about Charles Whitman in the Campbell interview were duly noted by his followers. "He came to Segal's wearing a new coat," Abe Meyer remembered, "and someone said, 'Who got you that, Zel? Your wife or the D.A.? Both of them are in love with you.' Even he thought that was funny. He was full of shit with those comments in the papers, but if the D.A. didn't think that he was harmless, he'd have ended up [jailed as a material witness] like the others."

He gave no outward indication of it during those last days of August, but Zelig had decided to testify for the defense. To preserve his liberty, he would conceal his real intention until the last possible moment.

Although not naturally inclined to support a policeman, he was raging at the chaos his world had been thrown into since Jack Rose had approached him in April. He'd been arrested on a trumped-up charge, forced into semi-exile to avoid additional consequences, had his name connected to a murder job he had turned down months before, and had two friends hiding for their lives while two others—one of whom had not even been there when Rosenthal was shot—were languishing in the Tombs. Worse still, he could do nothing to extricate them from their dilemma. He did, however, possess knowledge that could liberate Becker from the Tombs and send Jack Rose back there in his place.

Asked whether Zelig would have been even faintly troubled by "squealing" on Rose, Abe Meyer replied, "Not a chance. Zelig followed his own rules."

He was correct. Zelig Lefkowitz had always scorned tradition in favor of his own personal belief system when deciding a course of action. He squeezed protection money out of quivering shopkeepers and small-time gamblers, but quietly provided drug trade investigators like Florence Clark with valuable tips. He had no compunction about killing, but the thought of anyone, even a cop like Becker, being railroaded into the electric chair for a crime they did not commit bothered him enough to want to take action.

That type of aggressive independence had its dangers. The stronger Tammany faction led by Boss Murphy had already decided that Lieutenant Becker would take the fall for Herman Rosenthal's murder to prevent the district attorney from endangering the System's higher-placed components.[21] If Zelig's testimony brought about the policeman's release, Rose, Webber and Vallon might bargain for their lives by presenting the ambitious D.A. with another, more tantalizing target. No one wanted to be the new carrot on the stick, and those who were faced with that dangerous possibility would use any means, even murder, to prevent it.

CHAPTER NINETEEN

SILENCED

On August 20, Charles Becker was rearraigned under a blanket indictment that also charged William Shapiro, Frank Cirofici, Jacob Seidenshner, Louis Rosenberg, Harry Horowitz, and Jacob Reich, alias Jack Sullivan, with murder. Up until that point, Sullivan had merely been held as a material witness. It was viewed as an intimidation tactic, as he refused to play ball with Whitman, and Becker's lawyers speculated that it was meant to keep him out of the defense camp until after the trial. The district attorney also persuaded the grand jury to indict all four gunmen, although only Frank and Whitey were currently in custody.[1]

Whitman tried to hasten the arrest of the missing gunmen by offering a reward. "I am now in a position," he said, "to offer a reward of $5,000 for the apprehension of Louis Rosenzweig [sic], alias Lefty Louie, and Harry Horowitz, alias Gyp the Blood, or of $2,500 for the apprehension of either one." He added that this incentive was not available to anyone associated with the NYPD, as both killers would have been in custody by now if the police were doing their job properly.

The long-delayed inquest into Rosenthal's death was also held just before the mass arraignment. Assistant District Attorney Rubin, who had escorted Sam Schepps back from Hot Springs, addressed the coroner's jury. The foreman, incidentally, was none other than theater kingpin Daniel Frohman, who would go on to be a managing partner in Famous Players Film Company.

Rubin explained that since the grand jury had already issued indictments in connection with the killing, their only task was to determine the actual cause of death. The jurors listened to the testimony of Dr. Otto Schultz, policeman File, the restaurant employees, and others, and then promptly found that Herman Rosenthal had been murdered by "a person or persons unknown to the jury." Louis Libby was released from custody when Rubin made the official request.

Reporters flocked to Waldo's office and asked him for his feedback on the indictment. Becker had been one of his most trusted and valued officers, and the commissioner's response was not a restrained one: "Just tell Charles Whitman for me that he can't get to be governor by lying."[2]

♔ ♔ ♔

Under regular circumstances, Becker would have gone on trial late that fall in New York's Court of General Sessions. But during the third week of August, Whitman went to see Gov. John Dix and persuaded him to transfer all cases arising from the Rosenthal murder to the state Supreme Court of New York County. It placed Becker under the jurisdiction of Justice John Goff.

A self-educated lawyer with a raging temper, Goff had been chief counsel for the Lexow Committee, and on the strength of that accomplishment, been elected a judge of the Court of General Sessions. He had faced Becker at least once before, in 1895, when, as recorder, he discounted Becker's testimony defending saloonkeeper Augustus Elder. During his younger days he was a vigilant member of the Clan Na Gael, an Irish revolutionary group whose purpose was to free Ireland from British rule by whatever means necessary. With his snow-white hair and beard, cool blue eyes, and stately bearing, he resembled the popular idea of a saint. In his case, appearances were savagely misleading—any defendant or lawyer who provoked his wrath was practically guaranteed an unhappy trial outcome.

Attorney Newman Levy appeared before Goff many times and recounted his observations in his memoirs:

> He used to speak in a low voice, but he could make himself heard when he wanted to. When he charged a jury in a criminal case, it sounded something like this: "Whst, whst, whst, GUILTY! . . . Whst, whst, whst, GUILTY! . . . Whst, whst, whst, GUILTY! . . ." It did not matter if the jurors understood anything else he said; that one word uttered with the explosive force of a rifle shot was burned indelibly in their minds.[3]

Goff hated to preside over long or slow-moving cases, and would either snap at the attorneys and witnesses to hurry along or hold night sessions to cut down the number of days a trial would be in session. He had little patience with those who found such marathon sessions exhausting and was universally despised. When the judge seemed to be approaching the constitutional retirement age of seventy, he showed no inclination to do so, and the New York bar, desperate to get rid of him, sent a committee of attorneys to Ireland to determine how old he really was. To their despair, the parish church in which he had been baptized had burned down and its records lost. Goff therefore stayed on as a judge until he decided on his own to retire.

His penchant for sadism aside, Goff was the worst possible choice for Becker's case. He was a dedicated cop-hater. He also had friendly connections to the district attorney's office, having worked with Frank Moss, one of Whitman's assistant D.A.s, at the Lexow hearings. His personal association with Whitman was amiable enough for the two to meet at his upstate farm to discuss another grand jury investigation into police corruption that the D.A. wanted him to preside over. At the same time, Whitman later admitted, they took the opportunity to "iron out a few kinks in the Becker case."[4]

Whitman didn't have to try too hard to persuade Goff to launch an inquiry into the allegation that the gunmen currently in custody had letters from Becker on them when arrested. A committee run by a Republican alderman named Henry Curran initiated yet another police corruption investigation, with the D.A.'s approval. Five inquiries began running almost simultaneously—Whitman's, Goff's, Curran's, Mayor Gaynor's, and that of committee of citizens who met on August 12 and voted to fund a private inquiry. Their discoveries would keep the furor over police misconduct at fever level and ensure that the topic stayed on the front pages during the interval between Becker's indictment and his trial.

Soon after Goff's appointment, both Whitman and McIntyre appeared before him to present a string of opposing motions. The district attorney wanted Becker to be tried first, and separately from the others under the same indictment. McIntyre protested, saying that Cirofici and Seidenshner had already denied that the policeman had anything to do with Rosenthal's murder, and if they should be tried first, their testimony would be valuable defense evidence when Becker's turn came. Goff listened, then proceeded to grant all of Whitman's motions while denying McIntyre's.

Whitman asked that Becker's trial date be set for September 12. This allowed for next to no time to prepare for a good defense. McIntyre argued that Becker could not get a fair hearing so soon after the murder, but Goff tossed his petition. In desperation, McIntyre obtained a hearing before another Supreme Court judge, George Bischoff, and secured a postponement, but the additional time granted was barely a month—the trial was scheduled for October 7. Bischoff also granted a defense request that a commission be sent to Hot Springs to determine what Schepps might have said about the case during his talkative, pre-agreement phase. When Frank Moss complained that, as a courtesy to Goff, both motions should have been transferred before him, Bischoff issued a sharp rebuff: "It is not a matter of courtesy to another justice which is in question. It is a matter of justice to an accused man being tried on a charge for which the penalty is death."[5]

Dire as things were looking, Becker was apparently offered a potential escape during the last week of August. Rose's attorney, Sullivan, met with reporters at Shanley's restaurant and passed out a letter that he sent to the policeman's legal team. In it, he urged Becker to reveal all he knew about corruption in the NYPD's higher echelon and save himself "from a disaster that seems inevitable." He stated his certainty that Whitman would be inclined to be merciful if such an important public service were performed. When the newsmen asked Becker for a response, the policeman snapped, "Tell them I'm no Schmittberger."[6] On August 23, Deacon Terry supposedly carried a message direct from Whitman to Becker. It offered immunity in exchange for his assistance in snagging Dougherty, Winfield Sheehan, and other higher placed grafters in the department. Jack Sullivan, who was present, later swore in an affidavit that Becker heard his reporter friend out, then retorted, "I would not give that rat anything."

One can only speculate as to why James Sullivan, who was supporting the Murphy faction's course of action, would have sent Becker a letter encouraging him to sell out his grafting superiors, which was exactly the outcome that Murphy wanted to avoid. Although it's likely that Whitman would have agreed to the deal, Sullivan's gesture was probably an attempt to gauge the likelihood that Becker would talk. The policeman's hostile response reassured Tammany while simultaneously driving another nail into his coffin.

♔ ♔ ♔

On the night of September 14, Louis Rosenberg and Harry Horowitz were finally captured in a three-room flat on Ridgewood Avenue in the Glendale section of Queens, where they had been hiding with their wives and a pickpocket friend named Kramer. When a police squad led personally by Dougherty broke into the flat, everyone was just sitting down to dinner. While the women burst into tears and clutched their husbands, Gyp cried, "Drop the guns! We're not going to start anything." Rosenberg and Horowitz insisted on changing into suits before leaving, and a cop loaned Gyp his hat because he refused to go hatless.[7]

The arrests came about after Mrs. Rosenberg and Mrs. Horowitz had been under police surveillance for several days. The two women, who were surely aware of this possibility, kept eluding their pursuers by taking the subway or trolley car to a designated rendezvous, where they would be met by an automobile that sped away. Finally, one of the women was overheard saying that the two men were not too bothered by their confinement, as movies being shown in an open-air theater could be seen from their rear window. This was not the greatest clue, as there were thousands of open-air picture shows in the city during the summer months, but when another conversation was overheard, this one stating that there was a laundry in the building where they were hiding, a successful process of elimination began. When Lillian Rosenberg was seen leaving one of the possible locations, the police moved in.

Neighbors told the police that the two couples and Kramer, who also used the alias Max Kahn,[8] had occupied the apartment since August 15, and were frequently seen perched on the rear fire escape, watching the films. A Mrs. Schwartz encountered Rosenberg in the hall one day and asked him why he seemed to have so much time on his hands during the day. "Why, I work on a newspaper at nights," he said with a straight face.[9]

At headquarters, both men responded courteously to all questions Dougherty put to them and even agreed to pose for a photo with their captors. They said that they knew nothing about Rosenthal's murder. Rosenberg and Horowitz were arraigned before Goff on September 18 and entered a plea of not guilty through their counsel, H. S. Kringle, whose partner, Charles Wahle, represented Zelig. Goff ordered them remanded to the Tombs, and both young men were led across the Bridge of Sighs. Their wives were held in the House of Detention as material witnesses.

Their arrests caused Zelig's mood to plummet. "For around a week after Gyp and Louis were taken in," Abe Meyer said, "Zelig was like a different person. He came around to Segal's and the other places we'd go to, but he would not talk unless you said something to him, and even then you wouldn't get much of an answer. We'd go to Benny Fein if we needed to be told what to do. But once Zelig snapped out of it, he told us himself that he was going to get his lawyer to talk to Becker's lawyer. He couldn't save the boys, but he could make sure that Jack Rose didn't walk away from this."

Zelig was correct about not being able to save them. A story had been making the rounds that the shooting of Rosenthal had been an accident, that the real intention had been to merely kidnap him and "persuade" him to cease his squealing. According to the *Times,* which noted the rumor, "One of the four men in the gray murder car automobile was drunk and . . . he fired at Rosenthal, killing the gambler before his companions could stop him." Even if it were true, the original murder indictment would still hold, as the law made the commission of a homicide in the course of the commission of a felony murder in the first degree. Whatever the original plan Rosenberg, Seidenshner, and Horowitz had bought into, Rosenthal had ended up dead, and there was no hope of a lesser charge. Dago Frank stood a chance of going free because he had not even participated in the attack, provided the witnesses that were called to establish the fact were believed.

According to Meyer, Zelig did not shout his intention to testify from the rooftops. "He only talked to us.[10] But . . ." He paused, then finally said, "But somehow the wrong people found out."

⚜ ⚜ ⚜

Zelig received a subpoena to testify for the defense at the end of September. While waiting for it to be served, he and Dopey Benny Fein canvassed business owners and even gamblers in their territory, asking for contributions to the gun-men's defense fund. He attempted to secure bail for Lillian Rosenberg and Lil-lie Horowitz, but even as late as October, had not found anyone willing to bond them out. He wrote encouraging, optimistic letters to the boys in the Tombs and received equally cheery replies care of Segal's.

On October 4, he attended a ball at the Stuyvesant Casino held by Eddie Yaller and Harry Coster, a pair of Lower East Side boys. Zelig and his entourage were seated at a table, drinking one round of wine after another. Suddenly a local character named Red Phil Davidson approached.

Davidson was tall and stocky, weighing about 185 pounds. He had thinning sandy hair that accounted for his nickname and wore a permanently bewildered expression. Although he had been a waiter in Jack Sirocco's place at one time, his primary line of work was pimping. He had an equally appalling sideline as a "horse poisoner" who went into action when businesses that relied on horse-power did not yield to extortionists. Zelig regarded him with contempt and rebuffed him when he attempted to take a seat at their table. Davidson paused, then took another shot at fitting in by offering to buy more wine. When the gang leader told him to get lost, the chunky panderer pulled $18 out of his pocket and handed it over, insisting that he would buy the next few rounds. Not considering Davidson to be worth a scene, Zelig laid the cash on the table, and more wine was purchased.[11]

The next day, Davidson came to Segal's looking for Zelig. Abe Meyer hap-pened to be there at the time.

"It was a crazy scene. Phil was at the table, whining about the money he'd spent buying the drinks at the Casino. Zelig said something about never asking him to do it in the first place and told him to get lost. Phil said something else, I wasn't near enough to hear it clearly, but suddenly Zelig got out of his chair and knocked him one right in the eye, so I guess Phil insulted him somehow. It was only one punch—the sniveling bastard ran away before anything else could be done to him."

By 7:30 p.m., Zelig was still at 76 Second Avenue, playing cards. Davidson returned, said in a low voice that he was completely broke, and asked for $3 to tide him over. Zelig only had a five-dollar bill in his pocket, along with some change, so he asked the waiter to break the bill. After Davidson apologized for the previous scene, the gang leader reluctantly shook hands with him. The sandy-haired pimp left the café but was later seen hovering around the corner of Sixth Street and Second Avenue, not too far from Segal's.

At 8 p.m., the card game having concluded, Zelig and a hook-nosed, diminu-tive follower named Willie went to a barbershop across the street at 93 Second Avenue, where the gang leader had a shave. Then, he and Willie emerged into the damp fall night and boarded a Second Avenue streetcar.[12]

♔ ♔ ♔

Six-year-old John Christie was one New Yorker for whom the world was still an innocent, safe place. Although he was a voracious reader, winning prizes at school for reciting challenging texts aloud, whenever the morning paper arrived at the Christie household he bypassed the scolding, rallying headlines in favor of the comics. His fondness for the outrageous exploits of the *Katzenjammer Kids* and *Happy Hooligan* impeded his discovery of grafting cops, dollars for votes, vice commissions, and the bloody aftermath of one gang fight after another. His mother was none too pleased with the slang and saucy tricks he learned from Hans and Fritz,[13] but that was usually solved by a trip to his room.

John, for whom events like the Becker trial were just another component of boring grownup chatter, had spent most of the evening of October 5 at his aunt's place and was glad to board the Second Avenue Streetcar for the homeward journey shortly after 8:15 p.m. Visiting, he concluded as he sat beside his mother in the open car, was a boring chore, like church on Sundays, and not half as much fun as watching Second Avenue go slowly past on this dark evening. The air was heavy and chilly from a recent rainfall, but John barely noticed the discomfort as he peered into the brightly lit cafes, cigar stores, and other buildings. Once in a while he saw someone he knew, a discovery that he relished.

He noticed a tall, well-dressed man board the car near Second Avenue and Fifth Street. Observing the small boy's curious stare, the man smiled quickly before taking a seat a few rows ahead and lighting a cigarette. "There was something about his eyes," John would remember almost ninety years later. "I could tell that this was a guy who liked kids."[14]

Another man got on at the same stop, sliding into the seat behind the tall gentleman and exchanging a few words with him, but the youngster was less intrigued. John gazed at the elegant stranger's broad back for a few more seconds, then looked out into the street again.

The car maintained a steady pace until Thirteenth Street, when it began to slow. That was when John Christie noticed something else, a prelude to a gruesome spectacle that never lost its impact on him over the decades. A stocky specimen in a dark coat was making his way along the trolley car's running board, gripping the railing as he headed gingerly from the rear of the car to the front. John caught a hurried glimpse of his profile and saw the man had a black eye and bloody nose. The streetcar conductor, Patrick Bradley, noticed the man and his injuries seconds before and asked, "What's the matter?" The sandy-haired character muttered something about having been in a fight.

The man continued along the running board until he was almost beside the seat of the stranger whose eyes had captured the boy's attention. Suddenly he leaned inward, extending an arm that gripped a handgun.

Mrs. Christie, observing the same scene, screamed just as the weapon discharged a bullet into the tall man's skull. John did not yell or even avert his eyes. He watched, childish naiveté shielding him from the terror the adult occupants of the streetcar were experiencing, as the stranger with the dancing eyes cried out once and raised a large hand to the wound. John saw blood course thickly between the brawny fingers before the man slumped forward, his forehead striking the back of the seat in front of him.[15]

The gunman jumped off the running board into the street, but John Christie did not witness his departure. The boy's mother had grabbed his hand seconds after the shot was fired and exited the streetcar at lightning speed despite her long skirts and the effort of dragging a bewildered six-year-old. She made her way to a cigar store, pleaded to use the telephone, and placed a frantic call to her husband. She was refusing to get on another streetcar without an escort, and presently John's father came to collect them.

"From start to finish, I was never a bit scared," Christie recalled in 2003. "Because I'd never seen anything like it and probably didn't think it was even real. My family lived in a clean neighborhood, where you never saw guns or fighting, and I was too young to read the papers and know that there were parts of the Lower East Side where you saw this sort of thing every time you looked out your window."

Zelig might have protested the man's inertia had he not lost consciousness the moment the bullet embedded in his brain. When he collapsed, the gunman jumped from his perch on the side of the car and ran. So did Willie, who was never questioned in connection with the shooting.[16]

Officer Paul Schmidt was nearby, having been detailed to escort the parade of the Benjamin Schweitzer Association, a political organization. When he heard the shot and saw the assassin run, the policeman drew his own gun and pursued him, ordering the escapee to stop or be shot down. The chase ended in front of 329 E. Fourteenth Street, where the man surrendered. As they were walking back to Second Avenue together, Schmidt asked, "Did you shoot anyone?" The prisoner, a wild-looking individual with one black eye and a gaping cut over the other, answered, "Yes, I gave it to someone who deserved it long ago."

Officer Robert Locke of the East Fifth Street station had come running from his post on Thirteenth Street when he heard gunfire and boarded the streetcar, which resounded with the excited voices of those who had not fled. He found Zelig slumped in his seat, chin buried in his chest and blood flowing in thick rivulets from the head wound onto his starched white collar. Locke peered around at his still face, noted that the gangster was still breathing, and ordered an ambulance from Bellevue Hospital. When it arrived, a Dr. Forbes assisted in removing the injured man from the streetcar onto a stretcher. Zelig, however, was fading fast, and before the speeding ambulance could reach Bellevue, he was dead.[17]

The disheveled gunman was none other than Red Phil Davidson. Claiming to be a retired fruit dealer, he initially tried to justify the murder by saying that Zelig, whom he admitted knowing casually, had lured him into a tenement hallway on Broome Street, near Eldridge, earlier that afternoon. Once the coast was clear, he said, the gangster beat him senseless with a blackjack. Davidson fell to the ground, coming to his senses soon afterward only to find Zelig gone, along with the $400 he claimed to have been carrying in his pocket. He admitted to purchasing a revolver and going out with the express intention of murdering his attacker.

None of it made sense. Davidson had shot down a man with vengeful and dangerous friends in full view of dozens of witnesses. He appeared to be neither suicidal nor insane, and underworld informers opined that he did not have the ferocity or ambition to kill a man of Zelig's caliber without more powerful persuasion than revenge for robbery.

News of the shooting reached Whitman at ten o'clock that night, when he was returning home from an evening spent dining at the Waldorf with his wife. He threw up his hands and exclaimed, "My God, what next? What next? I don't know what to do." He headed for police headquarters, where Zelig's slayer was being held in the records room in anticipation of his arrival.

Schmidt had taken Davidson immediately to headquarters after arresting him. (Schmidt was later rewarded for the capture by a promotion to detective first grade, which included a salary increase of $850 per year.) Capt. Joseph Faurot was only minutes into the interrogation before word arrived that Whitman wanted to be present during the questioning. Faurot sent Davidson to a cell to await the district attorney's arrival. Whitman ended up staying until two o'clock in the morning and refused to make any kind of statement to the press after emerging from the building.

Davidson, who had the air of a man about to suffer an irreversible mental breakdown, babbled to the newsmen who came. Showing no restraint or discretion, he seemed desperate to talk, to justify his action.

"I killed Zelig because he robbed me of my money. I gave him a chance to give it back to me, but he only laughed at me. With that money, all I had in the world, gone, there was nothing for me to do but kill the man who ruined me."

Changing his story somewhat, he said that the previous night he had gone to the ball at the Stuyvesant. Zelig and his crew apparently saw Davidson's "roll" when the latter took it out several times over the course of the evening to pay for drinks. "They did put drugs in my drinks, however, and I almost became unconscious several times," he said. "I finally went home with some friends and thought everything was all right."

Davidson said that he'd left his house the following morning to go to Brownsville, where he had a fruit stand. He said he had $400 in his pocket. "Before going to Brooklyn, I had to see a man in a house at Eldridge and Broome streets. I stepped into the doorway of this house, and suddenly Zelig, who had been following me, although I did not know it, jumped on me from behind. He hit me over the head with a blackjack and punched me in the eye. He then said that I should give him the money I had or he would kill me."

Davidson himself further muddled the investigation when he changed key details of his story. The next day he wailed that Zelig, after beating him, "took away $18, all the money I was carrying and all the money I had in the world."

When reminded that he'd initially claimed a loss of $400, the red-haired murderer paled and sputtered, "Did I? Did I? Why, I don't remember it. I was drunk last night anyway and don't remember what I said."

Philip Davidson's buxom wife, Dora, confirmed that Davidson had attended a ball on October 4 and returned home in a frightening state of intoxication and mental confusion. She was alarmed because in all their years of marriage she had never before seen him in such terrible shape. On the morning of the murder, he left the house at 8 a.m. That was the last she saw of him until word of his arrest reached her.

While Davidson talked, morgue attendants were itemizing Zelig's personal property as follows: two one-dollar bills; four pennies; a fountain pen; a penknife; a ring; two cuff buttons; two bath tickets; a nail cutter; an advertising contract with the "Boulevard Chauffeurs"; a slip of paper with the notation "Harry Korper, night telephone boy, Elks Club" on one side and "Kempliman, who was a guest at the Elks Club" on the other; a card with "Libby Horowitz—aqueduct—Mac No. 10 West 118th Street" scribbled on the back; and yet another slip of paper with "Eagle Store—116th Street. Doggy Kaiser, Jack Gromley, Brut Blinkey" jotted on it; and business cards from attorney Louis Fridiger and a Lieutenant Adams of Greenville, Illinois.

There were also four bloodied letters, all from his friends in the Tombs. Their contents surprised those who assumed that the average Lower East Side gunman choked on words exceeding two syllables or were callously devoid of feeling.

Whitey Lewis wrote:

Friend Jack: I read that letter you sent to Louie, and you can't imagine how I felt when I read it, for I know that everything you write comes from the depths of your heart.

Well, Jack, I want you to stop worrying about us, as we have everything that we wish for, and we are having the best of times up here. We are only up here on a very short vacation to have a good rest and fatten us up. So if we hear that you are taking things to heart we will be very angry at you. So cheer up and be good. That is all we ask of you.

Well, Jack, I wish you would thank Hannah for the kindness she has shown us by sending us the big bundles, for we know what a job she must have had to pack four big bundles for us four big brutes.

Well, Jack, I am getting fatter every day, and gaining weight at the rate of five pounds a week. I am having a lot of fun with Frank, telling him a lot of funny jokes, as he is the only one I can easily see. For the rest, I wish I had them near me, so I could joke with them and cheer them up. The only time I can see them is when the lawyer calls on them, and that is when I get them laughing.

I wish you could go to Mr. Hanley and try to get Louie down to me and get him doubled up with me, as you know how dear Louie is to me. Well Jack, I haven't got any more to write, so I close this letter with best regards to Joey and to your wife.

From your friend,

Whitey

P.S. Frank, Louie, and Gyp send regards to you, to Joey, and to your wife. Good-bye and good luck to you.

The sentimentality and sincerity in Louis Rosenberg's note to his friend was even more striking.

Dear Pal,

I received your letter and I was certainly glad to hear from you, and you certainly know how I more than appreciate what you are doing for me. Zel, old man, I ain't worrying a bit: I eat good and sleep good, and also having a little fun up here and will certainly be ready for that big Christmas dinner.

Zel, you tell me you are going to stick to me and to the boys to the end. I know that, Zel, as I know what you are made of, having full confidence in you old boy, that you will stick to the end. I know that, Zel, as I know what you are made of, and Zel, to tell you the truth, I have got it better than a lot of them bum millionaires have got it outside, and was up last night until 3:00 a.m. eating lamb chops, but who, do you think, was in our party? But George Richman, that famous jeweler from Second Avenue.

He came up here to identify Fosbrey, and as he failed to identify him, he changed his mind and thought he would keep me company for a while, and I can assure you he is SAFE. My father and his lawyer called me down to the counsel room yesterday and I had a cheerful chat with him. And after I got through with him he said he was convinced that I had nothing to do with this case, and he went away feeling much better. Now, old pal, let me know how you are and how things are on the outside. I also tell the boys to write to you. I will now close, trusting this will find you in the best of health, as I am at present; also hoping this will cheer you up as your letter cheered me up.

I remain your sincere friend and pal,

Louie

P.S. Give my best regards to your wife, Jack Wolf [sic], and my friend.

Gyp's message was comparatively brief but just as intent on allaying his friend's worries.

Dear Friend Zel: a few lines letting you know that I am feeling fine, and in good health. Also Louie and Whitey and Frank. I hope you and your wife are the same. Well, old boy, things look fine. They could not look better. I read your letter and Louie and I were tickled to death to read it. We have a hell of a time here all by ourselves; do nothing but fool and kick one another.

Gee, did you see that piece about Louie in today's Journal? We laughed ourselves sick over it. You remember that fellow who said he was stuck up last week on Second Avenue? Well he is up here with us and we kid the life out of him. Well, Zel, take care of yourself and I know you are the one who can do that. So I'll close, with regards and best wishes to yourself and wife.

Harry

Regards and best wishes from W. and F. Answer as soon as possible if you have time.

Cirofici wrote:

My dear friend Jack,

I read your letter, and Jack, it made me feel kind of bad to think that you are taking it so hard on our account, but I know what a true pal you are, so I know what [sic] about how you feel. I know the night I heard Gyp and Lefty were arrested, I cried like a little baby. I had the blues for a week. Before that—the day you turned your pockets inside out, was enough for me.

Do you remember it? Dear pal, I have more faith in you than in any living man in this whole country. I tell you the truth right from my heart. I don't know you long, Jack, and I think if it weren't for you, I don't know what would happen to me. Being a Dago, of course, you don't know what I know. But time will tell, old pal. Even at that, I was always ready to take anything they handed me and say nothing.

Dear Jack, I ought not to be writing to you my hard luck story. Don't mind it. I am as happy as a lord otherwise. Well, old boy, don't worry, we will have a grand time up at mother's house as soon as we all get out.

Let us hope they rush things along. The sooner the better. Be cheerful, Jack. There is not a bit of worrying with the four of us. If I have so much faith in you, I am sure the rest of the boys have the same. I have thought many a time how you and your good little wife, God bless her, worked making up food for us. Tell her I prayed today that I can meet her and shake her hand, with ever so much thanks for her great kindness. I think I write you a nice long letter, and hope to get one in return. I would have written long ago, but I did not know your address. Hoping this will find you and your wife happy, and with my best wishes, I remain your true friend,

Room 328 Frank Cirofici

P.S. Regards to you and Jack Wolf [sic]. Better days coming dear. Good night.

Zelig wrote a reply to Horowitz's letter but never had the chance to mail it before being assassinated. It read as follows:

Dear Pal Gyp,

Yours received and it was more than pleasant to hear from you. I want you and the boys to keep writing to me as it cheers me up and you can imagine how I feel when I hear from you boys.

Gyp, keep cheered up and keep cheering one another up. Your innocence will be proved and what a grand time we will have on that day. Gyp, you tell Frank to take that Dago idea out of his mind and he will listen to you, as you know one another better than I do. Somebody had told him that I don't give a damn for him because he is a Dago.

Well old pal I hope to hear from you often.

It seems to be the hardest thing in the world to get your wife out. No one wants to go on the bonds. But cheer up, old boy, everything will turn out the best in the end.

Jack

Frank and Sarah Lefkowitz arrived later in the evening with their daughter, Anna. Frank, struggling to maintain his composure, told the morgue attendants that his son had been born in New York twenty-five (sic) years previously and was a diamond cutter by profession. Sarah wearily told reporters that her son had not heeded her warning to avoid bad company, but she refused to believe that he was as bad as the police had made him out to be.

"Zelig told me when he was arrested by Lieutenant Becker's detectives [sic] that the charge was a false one, and I believe it was," she said. "I do not believe that my son ever shot anyone, and I am certain he never carried a revolver. This is a sad ending for the boy, and I feel it deeply."[18]

She showed just how deeply the murder had affected her when a frantic and tearful Henrietta arrived. Anna, Sarah, and Henrietta broke down completely, each woman's grief inciting fresh hysterics in the others. Whatever Zelig had been to his enemies, the police, and the public at large, he had also been a loving husband, son, and brother. Several minutes passed before the widow was composed enough to sign the burial permit. Then she and the Lefkowitzes withdrew to grieve in private.

♔ ♔ ♔

The Rosenthal gunmen in the Tombs wept bitterly upon learning of Zelig's murder and spoke candidly to reporters. Rosenberg shredded Davidson's public stance as a harried and finally crazed robbery victim. "I have known him four years, and I tell you he is a bad one. He is the lowest kind of a man. He was in the white slave game in Boston before he came here, and he has always been in it here. He didn't have the brains or the nerve to pull this thing himself. Another head put him up to kill Jack. He must have been hard forced or he would never have done it."

They also offered an explanation for the "easy life" letters they had written. Dago Frank said, "When I write to my family . . . I tell them I'm getting fat and having the time of my life. I make them think that the Tombs is a jolly place."

Gyp agreed. "Yes, we all do. Go to my wife and see the last letter I wrote her. I told her that they let me go to the theaters. Lord, the only thing I see like a show is a few mice occasionally." When asked if Zelig had feared such an end, he replied emphatically, "Positively not! Zelig had no idea of it. He felt bad only because of us and because we did not write. He was the best friend I ever had."

"The best pal any man ever had," Whitey Lewis interjected. "This man Davidson is the lowest kind of a bum. He's been a dead one all his life. He says Zelig stole $500 [sic] from him. He never had $5 at any one time in his life."

When asked why Davidson would have committed the murder, Rosenberg replied, "It wasn't his own head that did it. He didn't have the nerve to do it alone. Why, he's just a messenger boy all his life, just a lobbygow, and a cheap one at that. Zelig didn't have to hold him up and rob him of $500 or of $18. That is just a lie. Zelig would never have any dealings with a man of that fellow's class, except maybe to give him a dollar for a meal or something like that. Davidson was forced on it by someone else. You can bet on that."

They all took turns disparaging Davidson's courage and moral character, dismissing him as a white slaver, petty thief, and coward. A reporter, snatching on the white-slave comment, asked whether Zelig might have clashed with his killer over a woman.

"I should say not," snapped Rosenberg. "Zelig was a married man. He had a wife whom he loved dearly, and a little boy nine years old. He was never mixed up in affairs of that kind."

Charles Wahle stated, "The story that Zelig blackjacked this man is nonsense. I know that Zelig never carried a weapon of any kind, for fear of the police. He did not dare to even carry a cane." He added that Zelig had been carrying $500 when he left Segal's, money that was now missing. Wahle would not reveal the name of the man who had given it to his deceased client, but it was believed to have been a contribution toward the mounting cost of the gunmen's defense.

It's impossible to say what became of this sum. Perhaps the roll of bills fell out of Zelig's pocket when his body was moved and was snatched up by another passenger or even an opportunistic police officer. It also might have been stolen by a morgue attendant. Thieves were the bane of many occupations.

♔ ♔ ♔

After arrival at the Tombs, Phil Davidson was assigned cell No. 136. His pre-trial accommodations were on the same tier as those of Charles Becker, who was in cell 112. He had not been in the prison for more than an hour before an attempt was made on his life. A fifteen-pound iron bucket was hurled over the railing of the cell tier above his own, narrowly missing his head. It was purely by chance that he glanced up and dodged it. He did not completely escape injury—the bucket rim grazed his leg above the ankle, leaving a horrible black bruise.

"That's the man I think did it," he told reporters afterward, pointing at a form on the upper tier, who disappeared into a cell as soon as heads turned in his direction. The only known figure in the Rosenthal drama who was lodged on that tier was William Shapiro, but the jail authorities noted that Shapiro had no history of violence, and Davidson, after viewing him, said he was not the attempted assassin.[19]

Reynolds Fosbrey, who had escaped from the Tombs almost a month before and earned the much-bestowed sobriquet of "the most desperate criminal in New York" during his brief spell of freedom, hung to the bars of his cell and swung about, monkey style, as Davidson talked to the reporters. He punctuated the red-haired killer's statements with unnerving, cackling chuckles. Other prisoners stood at their doors and glared, silently conveying the message that Red Phil, far from being a jail hero for killing New York's reigning gang boss, was the subject of universal contempt in the prison. Only a few low-level thieves and degenerates showed any friendly feelings, by trying to catch Davidson's eye during the press conference and gesturing for him to keep his mouth shut.

"Shut up, you big boob!" the man in the neighboring cell finally shouted. "Wait till you get a lawyer," another called. "Don't you know better than to talk to those fellows? You'll be talking your life away!"

Their words had a temporary effect on Davidson, who said uncertainly, "Perhaps I am talking too much." But the reticence was only temporary, and he repeated his story about killing Zelig after being robbed and brutalized. He said that he had gone to his friend, Sandler, and asked for $10 so he could buy a gun to kill his former attacker. He went to Jersey City and purchased the weapon from a pawn shop because the Sullivan Law made obtaining a weapon more difficult in New York.

"What do you think I'm going to get for this?" he asked his interviewers anxiously. "Ten or fifteen years?"

"Probably that much, maybe more," was the reply. Davidson winced.

"That is pretty hard, it seems to me, for killing a man nearly everyone wanted killed," he complained.

When Davidson's story about the gun purchase was investigated, it was revealed that the weapon had once been the firearm of a Brooklyn police officer. Dougherty had Officer Christopher F. Maher of the Fifth Avenue station in Brooklyn, who said he had lost the gun over a year earlier, brought into his office and asked him, "Do you know Lieutenant Becker? And do you know former Detectives Steinert and White?"[20] Maher replied that he knew all three but had never worked under or with any of them. He repeated the circumstances under which he had originally lost his gun and supplied satisfactory answers to other questions.

After the interview, Dougherty met with reporters, and declined to state positively that Davidson had been motivated by any factors other than revenge. As to the sandy-haired assassin's statement that an officer at police headquarters had congratulated him for doing "a good piece of work" in killing Zelig, senior officials explained that if such a comment was made at all, it was likely motivated by the belief that the death of any gang chief was a good thing from a police perspective.

"Davidson was a failure in everything he tried," Dougherty said. "The gangsters despised him, and his ambition to become a member of Zelig's gang only made them despise him the more. When I asked him how he got up the nerve to kill Zelig, he replied that he had been beaten so much that at last his red hair got hold of him and he struck."[21]

On October 9, Phil Davidson appeared in the Coroner's Court and sobbed and trembled through the entire proceedings. "If I'd been a gang man I would have had a dozen lawyers here to look after me," he whimpered to his guards, Det. Paul Schmidt and Lieutenant Flannelly. No attorney had come forward to represent him, but Assistant District Attorney John McKim Minton assured Coroner Holtzhauer that he would see to it that Davidson's legal rights were not infringed upon.

Davidson was presentable enough, save the strong discoloration that still surrounded his left eye, but he seemed listless, even stupid, except when a fresh wave of hysterics hit. When Patrick Bradley, conductor of the streetcar, took the stand and identified him, he cringed and shrank against Lieutenant Flannelly. He muttered to himself when Paul Schmidt followed Bradley to the stand.

"As I was leading him [Davidson] back to Second Avenue, I asked him, 'Did you shoot anyone?' and he said, 'Yes, I gave it to one who deserved it a long time ago.'"

When Minton stated that he had no further evidence to submit, Coroner Holtzhauer directed the jury to return a verdict of homicide. This was done, and Davidson was held without bail for the grand jury, which returned an indictment of murder in the first degree.

On November 6, the self-confessed killer appeared before Judge Goff and was sentenced to a minimum of twenty years at Sing Sing. Davidson, who was dressed in a blue serge suit, white shirt and collar, and blue hat, maintained his composure until Sheriff Harburger led him out of the courtroom. Then he dropped to the floor, grabbed the sheriff around the legs, and begged that he not be taken back to the Tombs, where the four gunmen might kill him.[22] His fears weren't groundless. When he was being taken across the Bridge of Sighs for a recent appearance, he and his guards met Lefty, Whitey, Gyp, and Dago Frank coming in the opposite direction, having just been to court. They broke free from their escorts, piled on Davidson, and pummeled him with their manacled fists before being hauled off. When he departed for Sing Sing soon afterward, it must have come as a perverse relief.

In her book *Against the Evidence,* which was for years the definitive account of the Becker-Rosenthal case, Andy Logan said that Davidson was released after twelve years, which suggests that he was back on the street no earlier than 1924. Abe Meyer, however, claimed to have seen him on Second Avenue a lot earlier than that:[23]

> "It was the same year Prohibition came in. I'm sure of it, because my brother and I were on our way to see a bootlegger that was recommended to us. We'd never been to one before. We were only a couple of blocks from where Segal's used to be, when who do I see but Phil Davidson! Dressed really well, too, much better than he did in the old days. I remembered what he did, though, and my blood started boiling.
>
> "So I shouted, 'Phil!' He turned to me and I looked at what he was wearing and I said, 'I didn't know Sing Sing paid so good.' He says, 'Who the hell are you?' And I said, 'Oh, I don't think you want to know me, pal—Zelig was my friend.'
>
> "That was all that sorry bastard needed to hear. He takes off like a jackrabbit. I tell you, he was a coward. There was no way that he shot Zelig on his own steam. In fact, I'm telling you that he didn't.
>
> "Zelig wasn't shot because he beat Davidson up. He never did—he only punched him in the eye the one time. That was it. But there were politicians who didn't want anything to be said that would get Becker off, because they were worried that they'd be next if it didn't all end with him. They put Phil up to it by offering him a lot of money. I'll tell you what else I heard. Phil didn't have the nerve to do it at first. So they had him beaten up just before he finally did it. That's why he looked so bad in the news photos, if you've seen them. Zelig never did all that to him, but it made damn good cover afterward."

According to Joseph Lefkowitz, Meyer refused to name the politicians in question, as some parties were still alive at the time. But he could only have been referring to the Tammany Hall faction that did not want Whitman's inquisition to extend past Becker. These men would have had the resources to persuade the weak-minded Davidson, who was suffering severe money difficulties, to put his life on hold for years in exchange for financial security upon his release from prison.

Even Lefty Louis Rosenberg had said, "Davidson was forced on it by someone else. You can bet on that."

Allowing some pride to enter his voice, Meyer concluded, "Zelig would never have backed down just because they told him to. He wasn't afraid of people like that. The only way they could have stopped him was to have him killed. And they did."

♔ ♔ ♔

Gangsters were murdered in New York almost every day without public observation or editorial comment, but Zelig's demise was greeted with the fanfare normally reserved for slain royalty or assassinated political figures. Mere minutes after word of the killing reached the editorial staff at the *Evening Telegram,* an "extra" edition ran off the presses and hit newsstands throughout the city. In less than half an hour, thousands of still-warm copies were sold.

If anyone questioned the degree of awe and uneasy reverence with which the Lower East Side had regarded the slain gang leader, their doubts were laid to rest the day he was. Abe Shoenfeld witnessed the funeral procession and noted in a subsequent report to his employers, "The streets all around Broome Street were jammed. A choir consisting of twelve singers conducted by Cantor Goldberg of Newark, New Jersey, sang their Jewish hymns as the procession proceeded down Delancey Street to the bridge. There was an unbroken line of people covering the sidewalk watching the funeral. Only the funeral of Rabbi Joseph surpassed this—the funeral of Jack Zelig."

His supporters hired a fleet of cars to carry his remains to Washington Cemetery in Brooklyn, where he was laid to rest near the grave of well-known Yiddish playwright Jacob Gordin. As the coffin was being solemnly removed from 286 Broome Street, a group of Talmud Torah children followed it, chanting psalms. The *Varheyt* noted that 10,000 people gathered in the streets to watch the magnificent procession, and another 3,000 followed the coffin all the way to the cemetery, where Cantor Goldberg of the Shaare Shamayim synagogue and his choir sang the El maleh rahamim prayer. Rabbi Adolf Spiegel of the Shaare Zedek Synagogue delivered the eulogy.

Gangland was represented, too. Dopey Benny Fein, Sam Paul, Jimmy Kelly, Dinny Zweifach, Johnny Spanish, and their followers were in attendance. So were a disturbing number of Sirocco gangsters. A Captain Ryan and twenty other officers detailed to monitor the funeral procession kept an eye on them, but no violence broke out that day.

Some of the Jewish papers condemned the pomp and religious ceremony. "Imagine," scolded the *Forverts,* "if a greenhorn fresh from Ellis Island came upon this impressive funeral. He would have surely assumed that it was for a man of great distinction in Israel, perhaps a luminary in the Torah, and if not a respected figure in the community then at least a great philanthropist. So it would be in the old home. How astonished the greenhorn would be to hear that the parade to the cemetery was for a leader of robbers, murderers, and cadets whose greatest virtue was his iniquity."[24]

The *Varheyt* complained, "Imagine if all this had happened in a Jewish ghetto in the old home, with the values of the old home, with its moral consciousness and sense of duty, imagine the sort of funeral such as Zelig would have had and where he would have been buried." The *Forverts* answered that last rhetorical question: " . . . thoroughly vile criminals, murderers, and cadets received a donkey's burial, a grave beyond the cemetery fence."

"Weep not for the dead," counseled the *Tageblat,* "best weep for those who followed behind the coffin. . . . And weep, too, for those who send Talmud Torah pupils to recite Psalms, mocking the Jewish religion and Jewish honor. We should weep that there are such Talmud Torahs that sent children to say "and righteousness shall go before him" for Big Jack Zelig. Cry out, too, for the chaos and the licentiousness that reigns among us that such an episode could happen."

However much the religious community condemned him, Zelig's friends and followers were devoted to his memory. "He did so much for us," Abe Meyer confirms. "Any one of us was in trouble, he was there. You look at the tough guys today, they're worse than Jack Rose when it comes to selling each other out for favors. There's no honor among the gangs now. Say what you want about Jack Zelig, but he was going to do the right thing. And he was killed because of it."

CHAPTER TWENTY

SACRIFICED

W hen jury selection for the Becker trial began at 1 p.m. on October 7, the courtroom was packed with the 250 members of the jury panel. Police officers monitored the entrance, keeping out all but talesmen, reporters, or people that Whitman's staff vouched for. One of the latter was actress Frances Graham, who, with her daughter Estelle, lived in the same building where Dago Frank was picked up. Remarkably, Judge Goff himself was initially prevented from entering his own courtroom by a zealous young officer who did not recognize him. A detective on the district attorney's staff had to come to the rescue.[1]

McIntyre initially requested a week's delay, because co-counsel John Hart had fallen ill. He explained to the judge that it was Hart who had investigated the talesmen, as Whitman had also done, and without his partner, McIntyre was at a disadvantage. Goff refused, making it clear that he and Whitman wanted the trial to progress as speedily as possible. He kept urging Becker's lawyers to hurry in their examinations of potential jurors, but at the end of the day, only one man had been chosn to sit in the jury box. This poor record led Goff to snap that delays in jury selection were becoming a public scandal, and that if a completed jury were not obtained by 5 p.m. that day, he would inaugurate night sessions of the trial.

McIntyre gave a hint of the epic courtroom battle to come when he protested against the manner, as the *New York Times* phrased it, "Mr. Whitman had clutched Big Jack Zelig to him as a witness when Zelig was no longer of this earth."[2]

"He knew that Zelig was not his witness, and he had no intention of calling him," the Irish attorney shouted. "He knew that he was our witness, whom we intended to summon." When he went on to proclaim that a fair trial for Lieutenant Becker looked impossible, Goff admonished him. It wasn't until he was threatened with ejection from the court that McIntyre contained himself.

Becker took an active interest in the examination of each talesman, conferring with his lawyers as each one was presented for examination, and it was on the policeman's recommendation that McIntyre used many of his preemptory challenges. He was firm in what type of juror he wanted—married men, large, and blue-eyed.[3] Married men would be more considerate about the fate of a defendant with a pregnant wife, tall men would not be intimidated by Becker's own powerful physique, and blue-eyed men were, according to the policeman and his counsel, more intelligent.

As he was escorted back to the Tombs after that first day, Becker asked some newsmen how they predicted the trial would go. When they replied that they anticipated a hung jury, the policeman expressed consternation.

"What?" he exclaimed. "Do you mean to tell me I shan't be acquitted? Why, this is worse than Russia if they convict me on such testimony."

Two-thirds of the talesmen were disqualified when they admitted to having made up their minds already, and at the end of two days, only eight jurors were in the box. A hundred more prospective jurors had to be assembled, and the jury was not complete until early on the fourth day of the trial.

Goff was antagonized by how long it took, and in an effort to get the trial over with as quickly as possible, ordered that the proceedings go into night sessions, which exhausted everyone but him. He showed hostility to the defense, interrupting their questioning of a witness with demands to hurry along.

Despite the fact that both were Irishmen who had supported independence movements, Goff and McIntyre clashed violently throughout the trial. At one point the judge shouted to the attorney that if he persisted in objecting to Goff's ruling, he'd be arrested and removed from the court.

After Becker entered his formal plea of not guilty, Whitman rose and made his opening statement. Helen Becker took a chair in a location directly opposite the jury and sat quietly during the district attorney's speech, her eyes traveling anxiously over the jurymen's faces. Goff seemed perturbed by this—when Whitman concluded, the judge ordered Mrs. Becker to move to a seat not visible to the jury. He seemed determined to rob the lieutenant of any possible advantage.[4]

After describing the general circumstances of the murder outside the Metropole, Whitman called a series of witnesses who'd been on the scene that July night. Detective File and Officer Brady recalled the shots and discovery of Rosenthal's body. Medical experts detailed the victim's injuries. Metropole waiter Jacob Hecht and Louis Krause recounted what they had seen. Hecht told the jury that he'd seen one man approach Rosenthal with pistol raised while three others lingered behind.

Krause said he saw three gunmen, as well as a man who seemed to signal to them just before the victim stepped outside. He described how he'd seen Bridgey Webber fleeing the scene. Then he dropped a bombshell. The waiter told the spellbound spectators that Jack Sullivan had rolled Rosenthal's bleeding corpse over and faced one of the gunmen with a derisive laugh. McIntyre challenged his about-face, saying that Krause had told the coroner he hadn't been sure who had killed Herman Rosenthal, but now he was naming names. McIntyre succeeded in arousing a similar level of skepticism in the spectators when he got Krause to admit that his lawyer was none other than Jack Rose's own attorney, James Sullivan.[5]

McIntyre did the best he could to discredit Whitman's witnesses. When one Metropole hanger-on admitted to near-sightedness but identified one of the shooters, the attorney asked about the truth of the rumor that he'd been paid $2,500 for his story. Goff lunged to the district attorney's rescue, disallowing the question and ordering it stricken from the record.

Two of Whitman's witnesses were shackled as they entered the courtroom. Jake Luban and his brother Morris were forgers and thieves awaiting trial in New Jersey on criminal charges. Morris swore under oath that he had been outside the Metropole on the night of the murder and that he could identify three of the killers. He also said that he had been in the Lafayette Baths weeks before the killing and saw Rose and Becker there together. The policeman, he claimed, said, "If that bastard Rosenthal ain't croaked, I'll croak him myself."

McIntyre downplayed the potential weight of Luban's testimony, which was the first instance the jury heard of Becker being involved in a murder conspiracy. He undermined the thief's credibility by asking whether or not it was true that Luban had originally offered to testify for Becker, sending four letters to the effect that he was willing to exchange supportive testimony for release from custody. In these letters, Luban had claimed that he heard Rose, not Becker, wish that Herman would be "croaked."

Luban admitted that he was hoping "for some favors from the State of New York" in exchange for his role as a prosecution witness. McIntyre caught him in another lie when he said that he had been near the Metropole on the morning of July 16 because he and a girl had scheduled a rendezvous at the hotel after seeing a show at Hammerstein's Theater. Becker's lawyer triumphantly offered evidence that the theater had not even been open that night. Even Luban's own family was disgusted by his lying, and soon after he testified, one of his brothers revoked a $3,000 bond that he had posted on Morris's behalf. "I'm sure he was nowhere near the bath at the time he described!" Alex Luban snapped.[6]

Whitman attempted to patch the damage the next day by calling his star witness, Bald Jack Rose.

Additional spectators crammed themselves into Goff's stuffy courtroom the day that Rose took the stand. Despite the heat generated by densely packed bodies in a room whose windows had been closed, Rose looked cool and collected in his dark blue suit. He gave his testimony in a bland monotone, but with the story he had to tell, no one noticed its robotic delivery.

Answering the questions put to him, he talked about his former position as graft collector for Lieutenant Becker and described his own "friendly enemy" relations with Herman Rosenthal, whom he had known for more than twenty years. After Becker and Rosenthal fell out over the April raid, Rose stated, the policeman came to him and began dropping hints that he wanted his former partner dead. Finally, Becker made the demand in no uncertain terms and warned that failure to comply would be a one-way ticket to jail on a trumped-up charge. Rose—reluctantly, he claimed—went to see Lefty Louis and Whitey Lewis. He told the gunmen what the policeman wanted done, and they answered that they were ready to go ahead with it if Zelig approved.[7]

He said that Becker had sent him to the Tombs to solicit Zelig's assistance. Becker, strangely, plotted a capital crime but had no objection to Rose bringing Harry Vallon and Bridgey Webber in on it. The impression the gambler tried to make was that Becker was too psychotic with his own self-importance to worry about normal precautions. When Zelig refused, the policeman seethed, "Well, let him rot in the Tombs then."

Rose claimed that he tried to dissuade Becker from going through with the murder plot, stressing that Herman wasn't worth the risk. But Becker became threatening as well as insistent, and Rose agreed to go see the gunmen again.[8] He recounted the Garden Restaurant stakeout and how it had been called off because a Burns detective was thought to be nearby.

Rose then painted a scenario that placed Becker, Rose, Vallon, and Webber together for the purposes of jointly planning Herman's demise. He said that sometime in June or early July, the lieutenant had been ordered to raid a crap game on West 124th Street in Harlem. He asked Rose and Webber to meet him, and Vallon showed up as well. Schepps came with Webber but loitered a short distance away, where he could see the four men in conference but could not hear what was being said.

During this "Harlem Conference," as the event universally would be called, Becker ranted about Rosenthal's attempts to reach Whitman and ordered Webber to take charge of the task of silencing Herman forever. When Webber hedged, the policeman assured him that nothing would happen to anyone who had a hand in Rosenthal's demise—he would see to that personally. Webber finally agreed to use his influence to galvanize Zelig's boys into action, and Becker seemed relieved. "With Bridgey on the job, I think we will get quick results," Rose recalled saying.

A second conference took place at the Murray Hill Baths, near Webber's clubhouse, soon after the murder. A smiling Becker commended all concerned for "a job well done." He gloated over the memory of seeing his victim's damaged corpse in the station house back room and told Rose to see to it that the gunmen laid low until investigators and the public lost interest.[9]

Jack Rose's testimony enthralled everyone—even Goff leaned over from the bench to catch every word. McIntyre objected continually, especially when Rose's testimony placed inflammatory words in Becker's mouth ("I don't want him beat up; I could do that myself. . . . Cut his throat, dynamite him, anything. . . . Walk up and shoot him right in front of a policeman if you like.") but Goff overruled him each time.[10] On the other hand, when Whitman's team made repeated references to Becker as a "grafter," it was allowed, even though the allegations were based on evidence not admissible in court.

McIntyre's cross-examination lasted for six hours. He hammered at the witness and made every effort to disparage his character, but Whitman thwarted him with a stream of objections that Goff upheld. Several spectators remarked on the judge's protective and friendly stance toward the star witness—when McIntyre shot questions at him that intended to make him look like a crook, Goff urged him to plead the Fifth Amendment. The judge even prevented the defense from introducing into evidence Rose's earlier witness statements, which conflicted with his current version of events, protecting Rose further and barring McIntyre from questioning him about the discrepancies.

When it came to malicious behavior, Goff outdid himself when McIntyre began faltering four hours into his questioning of Jack Rose. The defense attorney expressed his fear of imminent collapse, having been on his feet for hours. Goff insisted that he proceed, and McIntyre attempted to do so, but his stamina lowered by the minute and his requests for an adjournment were repeatedly refused. At 8:45 p.m., the lawyer finally reeled and clutched the edge of his desk. When he gasped that he could not carry on, Goff declared the cross-examination closed and excused the witness.[11]

At some point Goff must have realized that his callous treatment of the defense's objections might, just might, form the basis for a future appeal. He told McIntyre that he might recall two previous witnesses and ask them some questions that had been overruled. When the attorney declined, saying that it was a case of too little too late, Goff requested that the district attorney pose the questions in his stead!

Bridgey Webber took the stand on October 14. He corroborated most of Rose's testimony and added "facts" of his own that were frankly unbelievable, namely that he and his fellow witnesses had read none of the press coverage of the case. He was followed by Harry Vallon, who, like Rose and Webber, could not recall exactly when the Harlem Conference had taken place but added an additional, seemingly obscure detail: while Becker and the gamblers had stood around talking, the cop spotted "a little colored boy" on the other side of the street and called him over.[12]

Then it was Schepps's turn. While Rose had been colorless personally but had a riveting story to tell, Schepps was an arrogant smart aleck whose tale was merely supportive instead of enlightening. He was smartly dressed, and his bow tie, spectacles, and intelligent expression made him look more like a clerk or banker than a man who lived by his wits. He dodged McIntyre's attempts to smash his position as a blameless third-party corroborator, saying that murder was never discussed openly in front of him, and that Rose, Webber, and Vallon often whispered to each other when he was around. McIntyre was additionally hindered by Goff's ruling that Schepps's earlier statements, which contradicted his current testimony, were inadmissible. For example, he said on the stand that he barely knew Becker, while weeks previously he'd told Whitman that not only had he known the policeman for years, he'd even visited him at home. When McIntyre demanded to know what "harmless" conversation he could possibly have had with Zelig's gunmen when he was driving about the city with them, he gave a flippant reply about having discussed the lovely weather. Asked whether he was suspicious when Webber arrived at the poker rooms and announced "Herman's at the Metropole," Schepps smirked, "No, why should I be suspicious?" "You're treating this matter as a joke," McIntyre hissed.[13]

Concerned that Schepps's flippancy might undermine instead of solidify his case, Whitman's team gave him some "heavy kicks," as one journalist termed it, during the recess. He was better behaved when he returned to the stand in the afternoon and supported Rose and Webber's version of events almost to the letter.

McIntyre planned to open his case by calling William Travers Jerome and Police Commissioner Waldo. Rose had said that he took a call from Becker after the murder and was given advice to "lay low" for a few days, but unbeknownst to him, Jerome had been in the room when Becker placed the call and had heard no such suggestion. Waldo was prepared to swear that he, not Becker, had ordered the police guard placed in Rosenthal's house, an admission that would have damaged the prosecution's claim that Becker had harassed his former partner before having him killed. Goff disallowed their evidence. *Sun* reporter Fred Hawley testified that he had been with Becker constantly from 3:30 a.m. until 7:30 a.m. on the day of the murder, with the exception of a five-minute interval. His testimony was intended to disprove the gamblers' statement that Becker had met them at the Murray Hill Baths during that time frame. Hawley added that he did not advise the district attorney's office of his intended evidence beforehand because too many defense witnesses had been threatened with indictments. His statement enraged Whitman, who termed it "insulting" and demanded to be sworn in. Getting Moss to question him, the D.A. testified that Becker had been at the precinct house at 3:30 a.m. but left after 4:00, which would have given him ample time to visit the baths.

Jack Sullivan was the defense's star witness. He testified that while in the West Side Jail with Rose, Webber, and Vallon, he heard them actively conspire to frame Becker in order to save themselves.[14]

"Krause said that you leaned over the body of Rosenthal and smiled?" McIntyre queried, knowing that this ghoulish image would have remained in the minds of the jurymen. Sullivan answered, "He had to say that to have me framed. Mr. Whitman knows that . . . I didn't get there until ten minutes after the shooting." Webber, he said, offered to give him $1,000 up front, then invest $25,000 in a hotel and give him half the profits if he would back up the gamblers' stories in court. The King of the Newsboys was a volatile, expressive witness who took pride in his refusal to participate in the frame-up while oozing with contempt for those who did.

William Shapiro had been subpoenaed to testify for the defense and name the passengers he had taken to the Metropole on the murder night, which, according to an earlier deposition, had included Rose and Schepps. Just before his scheduled appearance, Whitman requested and received an adjournment. When the proceedings resumed, it was learned that the district attorney had persuaded Goff to reconvene the grand jury investigation into police corruption, and Shapiro was a scheduled witness. Whitman recommended immunity in exchange for his cooperation, a concession that transformed him from a defense witness into a witness for the state. Not surprisingly, Shapiro retracted his earlier testimony, and said Schepps had not been in the murder car that night.[15]

Becker's remaining defense witnesses were policemen and neighbors who testified to his good character. But their statements could not undo the damage caused by the gamblers' inflammatory testimony, or prove without a doubt that the Harlem Conference and the Murray Hill Baths meeting, which were key components in the case against the policeman, had not occurred.

At 10 a.m. on October 23, McIntyre delivered his summation to the jury. He scored some good points by discrediting Morris Luban as a perjurer whose testimony had been motivated solely by personal gain, and pointing out that the whole murder plot as told by Rose and his accomplices was too staggered and haphazard for a man of Becker's obvious intelligence to have guided. "His accusers are vile creatures, not lovers of the flag or the institutions under which we live," he warned the jurors.[16]

Frank Moss summed up for the prosecution. He contended that Becker was so drunk with power that he had no qualms about openly threatening Rosenthal's life and planning his murder. "In a matter of life and death, what was Rosenthal? Just a gambler. You see that Becker was the center, and step by step this plan unfolds, and it does not help the defendant that his hands did not extend from the auto, touch the gunmen, or pull a trigger. He worked on Rose, Webber, and Vallon." Concluding, he said, "Although Lefty, Gyp, Whitey, and Dago Frank are the murderers who fired the actual shots, although Rose, Webber, and Vallon are participants in murder, the man who is responsible is the man who urged the murder—the man who prostituted himself as a policeman is the man to be tried first, and not the gunmen."[17]

The following morning, Goff delivered his charge to the jury. His three-hour analysis of the case tipped the scale irrevocably in the prosecution's favor. He spoke of the meeting at the Murray Hill Baths and the Harlem Conference as if they were established facts and repeated Luban's testimony as if he were accepting it as truth. He ruled that no testimony had proved that Schepps was an accomplice, as the defense contended. He quoted regularly from Rose's testimony, suggesting to the jurors its reliability. Becker remarked glumly afterward that the charge was basically a direction to the jury to find him guilty.

The jury retired shortly before 4:30 p.m., and Becker and his supporters awaited the verdict in the sheriff's office. John Becker and old Clubber Williams remained close to him, while Helen was comforted by her brother, John Lynch. Hours passed, which raised the defense camp's hopes, as it typically took longer to bring in not-guilty verdicts.

At five minutes to midnight, word arrived that the jury had reached a verdict. Becker was returned to the courtroom, but Helen reached it too late and found it full. Unable to obtain admission, she learned from a reporter who raced past her once the doors opened that her husband had just been found guilty.

♔ ♔ ♔

Charles Whitman became an instant celebrity after the verdict. Telegrams of congratulations poured in from all over the nation. On New Year's Eve he was guest of honor at a dinner party held at the Astor Hotel. Many influential Republicans saw him as gubernatorial material. When he actually admitted to reporters that he would like to be governor one day, committees were formed and funds raised to back that venture. At a fundraising dinner held at the Café Boulevard, where Libby and Shapiro once had their taxi stand, Whitman told a cheering assembly that he would test the political waters by running for mayor first. He did run for that office the following September, but New York was a traditionally Democratic stronghold, and past Republican mayors had been elected on a fusion slate, whereby two or more political parties agreed to support a common candidate. He lost the fusion vote to Alderman John Purroy Mitchel but was confirmed as the fusion candidate for another term as district attorney.[18]

On October 30, Judge Goff sentenced Becker to die in Sing Sing's electric chair sometime during the week of Monday, December 9, 1912. The policeman flinched slightly and caught his breath, but otherwise he remained stoic. All around him, the courtroom was dead silent. The circus was over, and now a man's life could be measured in months, maybe even less.

Becker maintained control as he was handcuffed to the sheriff and led away. He was returned to the Tombs, but only for one night—the following morning, he was taken by train to Sing Sing prison. His brother John and other family members joined the crowd of supporters who saw him off at the Forty-second Street Station. Helen was permitted to accompany him, but they could have no private conversation, because the smoking car that they rode in was packed with reporters and officials.

When the Becker party disembarked from the train at Ossining, they walked the rest of the short distance to the prison. They attracted a crowd and constituted a small procession by the time they met Warden James Clancy and his staff at the gate. Half an hour after Becker was installed in a death-house cell, Helen was permitted to see him. He was too distraught to talk to her, so she left, but returned the next day for what would be the first of many visits.

Condemned prisoners were sequestered in a new block that had its own cells, kitchen, hospital, and even power source. They exercised for half an hour each day and had more access to newspapers and writing materials than the general population enjoyed. Like most death-house inmates, Becker could have visitors no more than twice a week and was restricted in how many letters he could send or receive. He bore these restrictive conditions well and even did what he could to entertain and counsel the other prisoners.

Becker had to find new legal representation for his appeal. John McIntyre had stepped down, and John Hart was now practicing law in California. His defense had cost an estimated $20,000, forcing Helen to re-mortgage the Olinville Avenue house to fund an appeal. Finally a well-known personal injury lawyer named Joseph Shay agreed to represent Becker. Shay had little experience with criminal cases, but the policeman was in no position financially to be picky.[19]

Helen maintained a brave face despite the tragedies that continued to mount in her life. She was alone in the large Bronx house, and unnerved by the dark and quiet, she bought a guard dog that had to be shot after it bit the milkman. A maid committed suicide, and soon after, a pet canary that Helen had bought for company died, too. A weaker soul would have wilted, but Helen could not afford to collapse. She had to be strong for Becker, as well as the baby that she was carrying.

On February 1, 1913, she gave birth, via caesarean section, to a baby girl who died hours later. At first there was universal sympathy for her, but then the public learned that complications had arisen at the end of the pregnancy, and faced with the choice of saving herself or the baby, Helen had chosen the former option. "I thought of the position my husband was in, there in prison under sentence of death, and I knew that my life would be more help to him than the baby's," she explained. "So I decided that if there had to be a choice, my life would be saved." Suddenly she was a betrayal of motherhood and was even likened to Lady Macbeth. When Becker learned of his daughter's death, he wept for the first time since he'd been arrested.

⚜ ⚜ ⚜

The four gunmen were tried three weeks after Becker was convicted. On November 3, Charles Wahle, who was now representing them, said that they would each receive a separate trial, with Whitey Lewis going first. Less than a week later, he informed Whitman that his clients had changed their minds and elected to be tried as a group. Jury selection began on November 8, and proceedings were soon under way, with Goff presiding.

The quartet held a mini press conference when one of the evening papers published the suggestion that one of them intended to confess and plead to murder in the second degree. Dago Frank said, "Now, all this 'pleading' business is bunk, pure and simple." Rosenberg added, "Why should we confess? We have nothing to confess to. We will beat this case."

"How will you deny the story of William Shapiro?" one newsman asked. Rosenberg answered, "We will take care of him, all right." When laughter rippled throughout the room, he hastened to add, "No, we won't do what you are thinking of."[20]

The trial began on November 12 and lasted a week. Most witnesses who testified that first day were familiar faces from the Becker trial: the policemen who reached the murder scene first, Louis Krause, Metropole waiter Jacob Hecht, and of course Jack Rose. There was one new face, however—William Shapiro.

Shapiro, who was still technically under indictment for murder, had not testified at Becker's proceedings, but he told his story now, freely admitting that if Zelig were still alive, he might not have been so cooperative. Whitman, who conducted the direct examination of his star witness personally, had Shapiro approach the defense table and identify all four gunmen before resuming his story. He said that when the car reached the Metropole, he heard Cirofici say, "Everything is all right. There are no cops around. Becker said so." He identified Gyp the Blood as the one who hit him with the gun afterward and yelled at him to drive off.

"You said you didn't identify these men before? Why?" Whitman prompted. The chauffeur answered quickly, "I was afraid I would be killed."[21]

When Charles Wahle made his opening statement, he was sure to use his clients' legal names in referring to them, aware that their dodgy nicknames reflected unfavorably on them. He said that it was Webber, Vallon, and a mysterious character named Itzky, who actually committed the murder while his clients watched, stunned.

Harry Horowitz was the first defendant to take the stand. He said that he, Lefty, and Whitey had been sitting in Segal's on July 15 when a call came for Rosenberg, summoning them to Webber's place. When they arrived, Dago Frank, Jack Rose, Schepps, Vallon, and Itzky were already there.

At that point, his story veered from what Benny Fein had told Zelig. For obvious reasons, Horowitz did not want to admit that he and his friends had agreed to beat up Herman Rosenthal. He said instead that Rose wanted them to meet Steinert and White and hear for themselves that Rose had had nothing to do with Zelig's arrest. Webber told the quartet to order whatever they wanted to drink, and everyone else went outside. Itzky returned after several minutes and told them that both cops were at the Metropole, waiting for them. He swerved back to the truth when he said that Cirofici went home while he, Lefty, and Whitey joined the mass exodus to the Metropole.

"Webber and Vallon walked in front, and Schepps and Rose walked behind. [Itzky] was on one side. They got near the Metropole when all of a sudden I heard shots and saw Webber and Vallon and the stranger firing from revolvers." Thinking that they were the intended victims, Horowitz, Rosenberg, and Seidenshner fled to the subway station at Times Square, where they took a train to the Seventh Avenue hideout. He concluded his testimony by denying that there had ever been an attempt made on Rosenthal's life at the Garden Restaurant, or that they had ever agreed to harm the pudgy gambler.

Moss conducted a rough cross-examination, but the witness kept his cool, answering questions about their post-murder travel itinerary. When Gyp said of Dago Frank, "He wasn't even at the shooting, and still they arrested him," Moss dove in and demanded to know why Horowitz, Rosenberg, and Seidenshner had not come to Cirofici's aid with this information when they learned of his arrest. Gyp's reply was reasonable enough: if someone who had not even been there was seized as a suspect, what chance did anyone who *had* been present when the killing took place, however unwittingly, have?

His three co-defendants took the stand after him and corroborated his story. The four gunmen actually made better witnesses than any of the others called by Wahle, some of whom just muddied the case further. On November 15, the defense rested, then the prosecution took over. They must have presented their case much more convincingly, because it only took one ballot and twenty-five minutes for the jurors to return a verdict of guilty. The prisoners looked stunned but maintained their composure until they were taken back to the Tombs. Then Whitey Lewis complained, "When we heard Goff [make his charge to the jury], we knew it was all off. . . . He ordered our conviction, and the jury obeyed orders. The jury would have convicted a priest after listening to that charge."

Wahle and his partner Kringle appealed the verdict but to no avail, and the four-man execution was set for sunrise after April 13, 1914. Only Dago Frank faced the inevitable with a keen sense of injustice. The others knew they were guilty, but it was a shared culpability that only they would be executed for.

After the November 1912 conviction, Rosenberg insisted to both Deacon Terry and Emil Klinge that Harry Vallon had fired the first shot at Rosenthal. He admitted that he and Gyp had also discharged their guns but added that the waiting period at Webber's had been passed by taking drugs. It was at Webber's that they were given guns, he said. Gyp told Jack Sullivan the same story when both men were confined in the Tombs. The assertion that Vallon was one of the murderers was supported by none other than Bridgey Webber, who seemed remorseful after the slew of death sentences were pronounced. He told his attorney, Harford T. Marshall, that Vallon had been the one to start shooting. Years later, a restaurant manager told a police official that he'd heard the same story from Webber.

The Jewish gunmen had their spiritual needs ministered to by Rabbi Jacob Goldstein, the Jewish chaplain, and Rabbi Mayer Kopfstein from the Bronx. Cirofici was counseled by Father Cashin, the Catholic chaplain, after the Italian gangster returned to the Catholic faith. The night before the executions, all four were surprisingly calm, breaking down only when meeting with their loved ones for the last time.

Cirofici's mother and sister Mary came to the prison and pleaded with him to make a confession. He just shook his head. "It's no use," he said. "It wouldn't be believed anyway." But Mary Cirofici, according to the priest, Father Cashin, persuaded him to talk. He blurted in one breath, "I didn't do the shooting. The men who fired the shots were Gyp, Louie, and Vallon. Whitey missed fire."

The warden was called into the office as a witness. After listening, he hurried off to get paper in order to take down the statement. Cirofici told those present, "I had nothing to do with the shooting, and as far as I know, Becker had nothing to do with this case. It was the result of a gamblers' fight which had been going on for fifteen years."

When asked if he knew anything about a plan to kill Rosenthal, he admitted that at Webber's place he'd had an inkling that something was in the works but didn't know what it was. He repeated that he was never at the scene of the shooting itself—he'd given an excuse to the gang before they left for the Metropole and went uptown.

Alone with Father Cashin, he admitted to the priest that he feared the consequences of any confession he might make. Reprisals followed swiftly and savagely in the world he had lived in for so long. He cited the murder of Herman Rosenthal as the typical fate of squealers, adding that he feared his family's house would be bombed and his siblings would be unable to keep their jobs if he opened a can of worms. In short, he was resigned to dying.

He was the first to be executed, as Sing Sing physicians, after assessing the four prisoners, decided that he would not be able to bear the strain of waiting while the others went before him. At shortly after 5:30 a.m., he said goodbye to his three friends, left his cell, and, supported by Father Cashin, entered the death chamber. He was strapped into the electric chair, and while mumbling "God have mercy" over and over, executioner Edwin R. Davis threw the switch, sending 1,920 volts into his body. Whitey Lewis was the next to go, then Gyp the Blood, and finally Louis Rosenberg, who actually pushed his escorts away, walked to the chair himself, and sat down with a bored expression. By 6:17 a.m., all were dead.

♔ ♔ ♔

The gamblers were released the day after the gunmen were declared guilty. Sam Schepps announced that he was leaving New York. Webber joined his wife in time to board a ship to Havana. Rose was in buoyant spirits now that Zelig was dead. While more than 1,500 people watched, he, Vallon, and Webber climbed into a large touring car that waited for them outside the prison. "I will be at the office of my lawyer, to meet any gangsters who might care to see me," he shouted out the window before the vehicle departed.

Joseph Shay soon resigned, finding criminal law too demanding. He was replaced by Martin Manton, an attorney of no small ability, whose services were paid for when Helen signed the house over to him. Manton's law partner was another shrewd lawyer, Bourke Cockran, a Tammany man who had been Grand Sachem from 1905 until 1909, when he and Boss Charlie Murphy clashed.

Becker's new legal team went straight to work. In the meantime, a group of his supporters went to Albany in January 1913 and met with Gov. William Sulzer, who had been a protégé of Big Tim Sullivan. Sulzer examined the affidavits and documents that pointed at the policeman's innocence and counseled the delegates to wait for the Court of Appeals verdict. He later said that if a second trial were refused, he'd have stepped in. "I intended to commute Becker's sentence and then to pardon him. I was convinced of Becker's innocence without considering the affidavits submitted." He never had the chance, unfortunately for Becker. The following summer, he fell out with Boss Murphy and was subsequently impeached and removed from office, to be replaced by a deputy who was more tractable where Murphy was concerned.

Whitman went to work locating new witnesses. He found them in the form of people who came forward to say that they had been bribed, in some cases with amounts as high as $10,000, to testify for the defense. One man said that John Becker tried to coerce him into committing perjury.

At the beginning of September 1913, Big Tim Sullivan died. His mind had disintegrated to the point that he had been institutionalized. He made repeated escape attempts, during which he slipped away from his guards, made for the railway yards, and hid himself on a freight train bound for New York City. He invariably headed for his old haunts, such as the Occidental Hotel, so locating him was an easy matter. His final escape occurred on August 31, when he waited until his guards had fallen asleep over a late-night card game, and then ran off. For more than two weeks, speculation abounded as to his whereabouts, as he was in none of the usual hideouts. Sullivan finally turned up in a Bronx morgue, identified by a policeman whose duty it was to try and put a name to unclaimed bodies. The former senator had been struck by a train and killed. It was a risk he ran each time he tried to ride the rails into the city in the past, but the grisly death of another figure in the Becker-Rosenthal case fueled the expected rumor that he had been murdered to prevent him from telling anything he knew. After his body was restored to his family, more than 25,000 New Yorkers who wanted to celebrate his life as well as ponder over his sobering death attended his magnificent funeral.[22]

‎ ‎ ‎ ‎ ‎ ‎ ‎ ☙ ☙ ☙

Three months after receiving the evidence that Becker's defense team had assembled, the Court of Appeals overturned the policeman's conviction by a six-to-one vote. In their decision, which was handed down on February 24, 1914, the appellate judges excoriated Whitman for whipping the public into a frenzy via inflammatory press releases. He had, they added, made prejudicial comments to the jury, referring to Becker as a cool and grafting police officer. Special venom was reserved for Goff's conduct: he'd shown marked bias in favor of the prosecution, was openly antagonistic to the defense, and made a charge to the jury that practically mandated a guilty verdict.

The court touched on several key points that justified their decision. Whitman, they said, acted beyond the boundaries of legal propriety when he arranged the release of the Luban brothers from prison so that they could testify. Sam Schepps was also, in their opinion, an accomplice, not a corroborator. They questioned whether Becker had real motive to order Rosenthal murdered in the first place, as the deceased gambler was such a troublemaker and a windbag that it was debatable whether any of his "disclosures" could have harmed the lieutenant. The judges also doubted whether the Harlem conference had ever occurred in the first place.

Judge Nathan Miller wrote, "I emphatically deny that we are obliged to sign the defendant's death warrant simply because the jury has believed an improbable tale told by four vile criminals to shift the death penalty from themselves to another."

The overturned conviction necessitated Becker's transfer from Sing Sing to the Tombs pending his anticipated retrial. He and Helen, whose tired faces were now illuminated with a glow of hope, rode into the city together.

The second trial opened on May 14, 1914, and was presided over by Judge Samuel Seabury who, like Goff, was known to be tough on police corruption. Manton did an admirable job, catching Jack Rose on the numerous discrepancies between his earliest depositions and the evidence he offered at the Becker trial. However, public feeling was still against Becker—when Manton questioned Rose as to his conscience throughout the whole murder plot, Rose's response that his conscience had been under Becker's control drew applause of support.

Manton questioned Bridgey Webber and Harry Vallon (Sam Schepps, for obvious reasons, was not called as a witness at the second trial) about the alleged Harlem Conference, confronting them with the fact that at the time it supposedly took place, the site had been a gigantic pit—excavations had been under way. Bridgey collected his wits after a brief recess and said that the conspirators had been standing on untouched ground along the edge of the thirty-foot hole. Harry Vallon said the same and went into a little more detail about the young black stool pigeon who had been hovering in the background while Rosenthal's intended destroyers talked.

His reason for touching on the black youth a second time became abundantly clear on the last day of prosecution testimony. That figment materialized as a live witness, young James Marshall, a tap dancer who had a sideline in feeding the strong-arm squads tips about Harlem gambling houses. Unlike Schepps, he had no known ties to any of the plotters except in his capacity as a stool pigeon for Becker. He had frequently infiltrated black-owned gambling operations to collect enough evidence for Becker's squad to launch raids.

Marshall's testimony itself was relatively benign—he said that on the night of June 27, he had seen Becker talking near the conference site with a man in a hat, whom he identified as Jack Rose. Being a distance away, he could not testify as any conversation that had taken place, but Marshall's very being suggested to the judge and jury that Vallon's statements about the Harlem Conference must have been true.

Manton and his team pushed forward with testimony from the fiery Jack Sullivan, who forcefully stated his belief that Becker had been framed by Rose, Webber, and Vallon.

After all testimony had been heard, there was a universal uncertainty as to which way the verdict would go. Both prosecution and defense had scored key points and suffered setbacks. Then Judge Seabury made his charge to the jury, and although he was less antagonistic to the defense than Goff had been, he had political aspirations and was acutely aware that public hostility toward Becker had not lessened by much. He validated the prosecution's argument with each point he made, prompting one of Becker's defense team to cry out, "I object to the whole charge on the grounds that it is an animated argument for the prosecution."

The jury deliberated for an hour and a half, then returned a verdict of guilty. Lieutenant Becker was on his way back to Sing Sing and death row.

♧ ♧ ♧

Life at the prison was bearable only because its current warden, Thomas Mott Osborne, was a dedicated reformer. That and the fact that he did not owe his position to patronage made him a unique figure. He was not a pushover but did make a sincere effort to better the lot of Sing Sing's prisoners, even those on death row. One of his more innovative measures was to facilitate the creation of the Mutual Welfare League, or MFL for short, which inmates could join if their good behavior levels warranted it. Osborne was a staunch opponent of the death penalty and insisted that he would be present during no executions. Although his initial impression of Charles Becker was not a favorable one, the warden gradually developed an admiration for the former policeman's manly demeanor and obvious intelligence. He became convinced that Becker was innocent: "If such a man had set his mind on murder, he would have made a better job of it."

Becker received spiritual counseling in the form of Father William Cashin, Catholic chaplain at Sing Sing, and Father James Curry, a priest from New York who made frequent visits. He wrote to Helen, who responded with lengthy letters that radiated encouragement and good cheer. She had been forced to vacate the Olinville Avenue house when Martin Manton put it up for rent to recoup his legal fees, and now lived in a University Avenue apartment with her twin brother, whom gossips initially mistook as a new boyfriend. Her hopes were pinned on an appeal.

♔ ♔ ♔

Whitman's two victories over Charles Becker bore the desired fruit. He became the Republican nominee for governor and was elected by a 145,000-vote majority. Once installed in Albany, though, his performance was unremarkable and notably absent-minded. His thoughts were not on his current governorship but on the White House. However, he was definitely in an interesting position—he had put Charles Becker on death row after two volatile trials, and now he was the final authority when it came to rescuing the policeman from the electric chair.

In the meantime, Becker's defense team was busy lodging a second appeal. In February 1915, they received welcome news. James Marshall, the young black man whose testimony had given the gamblers' story more believability, was now living in Philadelphia and had admitted to his wife that he had perjured himself during the Becker trial. When the couple fell out as a consequence of him hitting her during an argument, Mrs. Marshall told the police officer who took her statement about the perjury admission. She was overheard by a pair of newsmen, who visited Marshall in his cell and got even more details. According to the ex-stool pigeon, Whitman had paid him to tell the story that had sealed Becker's fate. The thrilled reporters filed their stories.

Manton learned about the new development when the editor of the *Philadelphia Evening Ledger* sent him a telegram requesting comment on the breaking story. In response, the attorney sent one of his assistants, John Johnson, on the next train to Philadelphia. Sitting in the *Ledger*'s offices with reporters and a commissioner of oaths present, Marshall said that an assistant D.A. named Frederick Groehl had offered payments totaling $355 in exchange for his incriminating testimony. The tap dancer admitted that he had been an occasional stool pigeon for Becker, and only agreed to testify after being promised money and threatened with prosecution for some minor perjuries he had committed in the form of false affidavits pertaining to his stool-pigeon activities. He recalled Becker speaking to a man outside a Harlem gaming place but didn't know who he was, although he had dutifully said under oath that it had been Jack Rose.

It didn't take long for the district attorney's office back in New York to learn about Marshall's recantation. Assistant D.A. Groehl showed up at the East Seventy-sixth Street apartment of the tap dancer's mother, just in time to intercept a call from Marshall, who was back in town. Groehl informed him that an indictment for perjury was now a dangerous possibility, unless he showed up at the apartment, and fast. The frightened young man retracted his Philadelphia statement later that day, insisting that he was drunk when he told his story to the *Ledger* reporters. He added that John Johnson tried to offer him a $2,500 bribe. He also accused Johnson of dictating his retraction and "fooling" him into signing it.

Martin Manton was crestfallen by the turn of events but pushed forward anyway with the appeal. He devoted some pages of his argument to a supposed partiality that Judge Seabury had shown to the prosecution, but it had little impact because Seabury's statements and conduct had been nowhere near as outrageous as Goff's. Although he and the current incumbents in the district attorney's office tried to win their cases before the Court of Appeals by dissecting the opposing side's weakness, their efforts were in vain, as the court declared itself concerned only with whether there had been any procedural irregularities during the trial. Examining the record, they found none and ruled that there was no legal basis on which an appeal could be granted. The original guilty verdict was affirmed, and Becker's execution was scheduled for July 12.

Bridgey Webber stated the obvious when reporters tracked him down at his New Jersey home and asked him for a comment: "Governor Whitman certainly can't pardon the man he prosecuted."[23]

♛ ♛ ♛

Martin Manton was joined during the final weeks of the fight for Becker's life by his law partner, Bourke Cockran. Cockran, a shrewd and experienced attorney of whom Winston Churchill once said, "I have never seen his like or in some respects his equal," applied to the U.S. Supreme Court for a writ of error, charging that Whitman's offer of immunity to the self-admitted criminals had been unconstitutional. If granted, it would have meant a retrial, but the application was denied, and Whitman, to no one's surprise, rejected an appeal for clemency. Cockran did succeed in getting the execution date delayed until late July and then organized a petition asking Whitman to let the Board of Pardons decide Becker's fate. The governor rejected that proposal as well as one made by Manton that requested that a special panel of Court of Appeals judges be formed to reconsider the case evidence.

Cockran's last attempt to ward off the inevitable took place on July 23, when he brought a motion for a new trial before the Supreme Court of New York County. There was also an order to show cause (requiring the D.A.'s office to give reason as to why a third trial should not be granted). New evidence presented by Cockran included Becker's own handwritten deposition detailing his version of the entire affair and an affidavit from Harry Applebaum, Big Tim's former secretary. The latter was especially sensational—Applebaum confirmed his late boss's involvement with Rosenthal and implied that Jack Rose had been the real driving force behind the gambler's murder.

Applebaum's affidavit, which was published in full in the newspapers on July 22, was one of the documents submitted to Justice John Ford as part of the motion for a new trial. Ford denied it, but strictly on legal grounds.

The information it contained may not have fulfilled the legal requirements to overturn or in any way affect Becker's death sentence, but in every other respect it threw a harsh and unsettling new light on the events that led to Rosenthal's murder.

According to Applebaum, Rosenthal approached his longtime benefactor in early 1912 and requested a loan. The secretary advised Sullivan not to do it, as Rosenthal's track record with money management suggested that he would just lose it and then beg for more. Sullivan agreed, but Rosenthal was persistent, even going up to Albany in an effort to corner Big Tim and plead his case. Finally, the anxious gambler encountered Sullivan, whose resolve melted. As he gave Rosenthal $2,000 in cash he pleaded that Applebaum not be told, as the secretary had advised against it.

Discretion had never been Herman Rosenthal's strong suit. He confronted Applebaum and, after trumpeting the fact that he'd gotten the money, demanded to know why the secretary had counseled Sullivan against helping him.

"When I saw Tim a short time afterward," Applebaum's affidavit stated, "I said to him, 'Well, boss, I see you have fallen for the works.' He said, 'What's that?' I said, 'You let Rosenthal touch you.' He said, 'Who told you?' I said, 'Herman did.'"

Sullivan, sheepish at his own weakness where Herman was concerned, protested, "How could I refuse him?" Applebaum shrugged and warned him that the gambler would be back for more, and soon. He was right. Days later, Rosenthal sought Sullivan out again and complained that his other "bankroll men" had let him down, and although he now had his new gambling house set up, he needed more funds to get the operation off the ground. Sullivan yielded and gave him two notes worth $2,500 each. This, stated Applebaum, was the extent to which Big Tim had any interest in Rosenthal's place.

When the gambling house was raided and Rosenthal began shouting his accusations against the police in any public forum that would accommodate him, Sullivan came to Applebaum in a state of agitation. He had slowly been deteriorating mentally; when the secretary met him in Paris in May during a European sojourn, the former was struck by the change in his boss. Sullivan claimed that people were warning him that Rosenthal was going around town telling everyone that Big Tim was supporting his vendetta against the police. Sullivan asked Applebaum to bring Lieutenant Becker to him so that he could disclaim any association with or ability to control Rosenthal's antics, but the secretary convinced him that none of his friends would believe Herman, a known blowhard, and the best thing to do was not acknowledge the rumors in any way.

Sullivan took the advice for a time. Then the morning papers published a statement, attributed to Becker, that he had seen one of the $2,500 notes that

Big Tim had given Rosenthal, and that Tim was interested financially in Herman's gambling house. That, along with the Rosenthal affidavit that appeared in the *World*, convinced Sullivan that he had to see Becker. That Sunday, July 14, he ordered Applebaum to bring Becker to his house at 3 p.m. that day.

Applebaum only knew how to contact Becker through his collector, Jack Rose. He went downtown looking for the bald gambler and learned that he was at the Sam Paul Association outing. When the excursion returned, the secretary rode to Fourteenth Street and saw Rose talking with Webber and Vallon. He called Rose aside and explained his mission. The gambler obliged by going to a phone, calling Becker, and securing an immediate audience at the policeman's home.

Applebaum told Becker about Sullivan's agitated mental state, as well as the senator's concern that Becker's statement about the $2,500 note would cement the rumor that he was Rosenthal's partner in the gambling operation. The policeman denied making that statement, and although tired, agreed to meet Sullivan in person that day and assure him that his reputation was not being dragged into the depths that Rosenthal currently wallowed in.

Rose, who rode with Becker in Applebaum's car on the way to Big Tim's, was overheard grumbling that "someone ought to croak Rosenthal." The policeman's response was, "No, they hadn't. He wants to be left alone. No friend of mine must harm a hair on his head, for if they do, it will be blamed on me, and I can beat this thing all right."

Politician and police officer had an animated and frank conversation in the former's office. Sullivan repeated that he was not backing Rosenthal in any way. Becker assured him that he believed him but that other people were less convinced because Herman was going around town, showing off Sullivan's notes and claiming a business relationship with the senator. Becker yielded to Sullivan's plea that his name not be mentioned further in connection with Rosenthal's antics.

Before Becker left, Sullivan called Applebaum over and stressed that the secretary had to see Rosenthal that night and use all his powers of persuasion to get the man to lay off. If Herman were convinced that his public wailing would cause Sullivan to cut him off entirely, it might shock him into compliance. After taking Becker home, Applebaum drove with Jack Rose to Fourteenth Street, called Rosenthal, and arranged to meet him at Forty-seventh Street and Sixth Avenue.

Herman listened to what Applebaum had to say and finally promised to do as Tim asked—not persist in locating witnesses to corroborate his published affidavit. When the secretary, understandably wary, asked for reassurance that the gambler's word was good, Rosenthal stressed that Sullivan was his best friend as well as longtime benefactor, and the only man for whom he would lay off. Relieved, Applebaum reported the results of the conversation to both Sullivan and Becker.

The Sunday night conference between Big Tim Sullivan and Charles Becker, had it been made public knowledge at either of the policeman's trials, would have impressed both juries that Becker was strongly opposed to having Rosenthal taken out of the picture. He was keenly aware that beating, kidnapping, or killing the gambler would have made matters worse for him, and time proved his fears in that respect to be real. Had he known what the gamblers planned to do, he would have tried to prevent it.[24] Sullivan reassured Becker that Rosenthal was going to be paid $5,000, which had all the calming qualities of five million to the broke and desperate gambler.

According to Applebaum, Rosenthal had been in his apartment for part of that hot Sunday afternoon on July 15, speaking to fellow gamblers on the telephone and reassuring them that he was not going to go through with the planned exposé. As a safety precaution, Applebaum slipped money to Lillian Rosenthal and secured her promise that she would prevent her husband from making any more public charges.

It looked as if Rosenthal was indeed going to lay off. His close friend of twenty years, Benjamin Kaufman, was with him when the call came from Applebaum, and was still at the residence when Herman returned. "Ben, it's all off," he said. "Big Tim sent word for me to quit." He added that he expected to get $15,000. He and his wife made plans to board the *Chicago Limited* and leave to live off the money that his wailing had earned him

Satisfied that the crisis had been averted, Applebaum went to Scranton, Pennsylvania, and Big Tim hurried to the bedside of his dangerously ill wife in the Catskills. Neither one had any inkling that the nightmare was just beginning.

Rosenthal went to Whitman's office on Monday morning and remained there until eleven. Afterward he and Emil Klinge went to breakfast at Childs' Restaurant on Broadway. Feeling expansive over a good meal, the gambler told Klinge that he had refused $2,500 from Jack Rose to go west for a year. After breakfast he and Klinge returned to Whitman's office, but only remained for half an hour. He had a lot of packing to do. He didn't want to completely sour his association with Whitman, in the event that Sullivan failed to come through with the money.

Curious as to how things were progressing, Kaufman rang the Rosenthal residence early Monday evening and was told by Lillian that Herman had gone to a place called Oppenheimer's to play poker. More than an hour later, he saw Rosenthal at Broadway and Forty-fifth, talking to Chick Beebe and others. When he spied Kaufman, Rosenthal approached and confided, "I'll be out late tonight. Be at my house at two in the morning. I must be at the Metropole to get the money." Rosenthal added that he intended to go away for only a month, until the furor died down, then slip back into New York and resume business.

Becker's statement also touched on Sullivan's role in the Rosenthal tragedy. He recalled that in January 1912, Sullivan had summoned him and explained that he wanted Rosenthal's gambling houses in the Tenderloin to run unmolested. Becker responded that orders for raids were issued from Commissioner

Waldo's office, and that if Waldo saw fit to leave Herman in peace, then he himself would have no reason to do otherwise. Becker admitted to feelings of awe where Sullivan was concerned—Big Tim was a local legend, and his influence in the police department was believed to be enormous. For that reason alone, Becker readily agreed when Sullivan requested that his name be kept out of the Rosenthal affair.

Becker stated that the night before Rosenthal was killed, Applebaum, accompanied by Jack Rose, sought him out and rode with him by automobile to Big Tim's private office on Sixtieth Street. Sullivan seemed agitated by Rosenthal's public squeals and insisted that it could not be allowed to continue, that, in Becker's words, "Rosenthal has gone so far now, he can't be stopped. He must be got away." The police officer said that he told Sullivan that Rosenthal's disappearance would be the worst possible outcome, as everyone would accuse Sullivan or Becker of being behind it. The only way to do damage control at that point was to face Rosenthal and disprove his statements.

Becker said that he had promised Sullivan that he would never mention his connection to the case, and kept that promise until now. As far as he was concerned, Sullivan's death absolved him of that vow, and he wanted these previously withheld facts to be made known before a final decision was made to let him die.

Justice John Ford of the state Supreme Court mulled over the documents that Cockran submitted for more than a week. To give time for him to render a decision, the execution date was postponed to July 30. On July 28, Ford denied the motion. He explained that the Applebaum affidavit and Becker's statement were not new evidence in the technical sense. They could have been presented at either of the previous trials because the fact they contained were known at the time. Delayed submission of old evidence did not constitute grounds for reopening the case.

Assistant Warden Charles Johnson relayed the devastating news with commendable sympathy, even reaching through the bars to grasp the condemned prisoner's hand. Although he seemed "dazed," as Johnson would recall, he still squeezed the offered hand and replied, "Well, I'll die like a man anyhow."

Helen Becker refused to give up. Governor Whitman was her last hope, despite the fact that he had sent her husband to death row in the first place. She telephoned Martin Manton, who arranged for her to see Whitman in Albany. Accompanied by John Johnson, she left New York City via train early on the morning of July 29 and reached the governor's mansion before noon, only to be told that Whitman had gone to Peekskill to review a contingent of the National Guard. Calls were made, and it was arranged for Mrs. Becker to meet Whitman at Poughkeepsie. She and Johnson hurriedly boarded another train and reached their destination at close to 6 p.m.

While Helen waited in a hotel parlor, Johnson presented his arguments before the governor, who heard him out, then denied the application. Helen finally got her long-desired audience before him as evening fell, but it was a devastating experience. She found Whitman so drunk that he had to be supported by aides during their interview. She begged and pleaded for twenty-five minutes, at one point dropping to her knees. Whitman replied that there was nothing he could do, and Helen departed. She was beside herself emotionally but commanded enough spirit to tell the press about the state Whitman had been in. A reporter who obtained access to the governor immediately afterward found him slumped over the side of a chair, hopelessly drunk.

♛ ♛ ♛

Invitations to the execution had gone out in the middle of July. Reporters were included, but ironically Swope was unable to attend, as he was recuperating from a severe bout of rheumatic fever. Another *World* man was sent in his place. Because of the massive amounts of press coverage that was anticipated, linemen spent days installing additional telegraph wires and a shack adjacent to the execution house was set up to accommodate Morse code operators.

On the last morning of his life, Becker was roused early and his prison uniform exchanged for black cotton "execution garb" that contained no metal traces such as buttons. One guard shaved the hair away from a spot of Becker's temple in preparation for the electrode, while another slit his trousers to the knee to make his calf accessible for another electrode. This sobering business concluded, Becker wrote letters to relatives and a final statement to the press. His brothers John and Jackson came to visit him, struggling to present a strong, comforting front.

Helen arrived soon after 11 p.m., exhausted and sick at heart from her failed effort to save her husband. She and Becker spent an hour and a half together in the warden's office under the sympathetic eye of guards who had come to admire and respect the condemned man. Helen left at 1:30 a.m., and Becker was returned to his cell, where he received a final visit from Warden Osborne an hour later. Osborne left at 5 a.m., leaving Deputy Warden Johnson to officiate at the grim proceedings. The warden was vehemently opposed to the death penalty and refused to be present during executions.

At 4 a.m., Father Cashin heard Becker's final confession, which the policeman concluded with, "I am sacrificed for my friends."

At 5:42 a.m., the door leading into the execution chamber swung open. Witnesses watched as Becker, accompanied by guards, went to the chair and sat down, his face an inscrutable mask. Before the leather strap was secured across his mouth, Becker said, "Into Thy hands, Lord, I commend my spirit."

Bells rang to signal the commencement. The executioner threw the switch. There was a droning sound as the current hummed to life, and Becker's massive body lurched against the straps. His head shook violently. He was the largest prisoner ever to be executed at Sing Sing, and for that reason, miscalculations had been made regarding the required current strength. His body temperature-was now 140 degrees Fahrenheit, and flames even shot from the temple electrode, but Becker remained alive—the prison doctor found that his heartbeat was strong. Nine minutes and three separate shocks were required to bring the gruesome affair to a close. Doctors who performed the autopsy found a photo of Helen pinned to the dead man's undershirt, facing his heart.

Arnold Rothstein and some friends were sitting in Jack's Café, down the street from the Metropole, when Becker took his seat in the electric chair. As the time of execution drew nearer, Rothstein took his watch out of his waistcoat, set in on the table, and watched until the hands read 5:45 a.m. Then he snapped it shut, repocketed it, and said, "Well, that's it." With that, he and his associates rose from the table, left the café, and emerged into another New York dawn.[25]

♣ ♣ ♣

Becker's body was delivered to Helen's home at 2291 University Avenue shortly before 4 p.m. and laid out in the parlor. The next day, a Sunday, saw a stream of messenger boys bearing flowers, as well as Becker's relatives and closest friends. Old Clubber Williams paid his respects, and his wreath was given a place of honor at the foot of the coffin.

Helen's gentle nature was leavened by a hatred of Governor Whitman, as evidenced by a silver plate that she commissioned a local engraver to make for her husband's coffin. It read:

CHARLES BECKER

MURDERED JULY 30, 1915

BY GOVERNOR WHITMAN

Whitman's response was to dispatch three policemen to the apartment, where they informed Mrs. Becker that the inscription could form the basis for a criminal libel suit. They confiscated it and took it to headquarters to preserve it as evidence in case Whitman decided to sue. The governor wisely chose not to press the matter, and the offending plate was replaced by an aluminum one that merely gave the deceased's name and date of death.

The day of Becker's interment was hot and muggy, and thousands packed the area outside the University Avenue residence. It was a noisy, disorderly crowd as women fainted and children exposed to the heat by thoughtless parents cried in distress. Getting the coffin to the waiting hearse was an ordeal. When the crowd was cleared sufficiently for the procession to the church to commence, there was a mad stampede for the church as citizens, reporters, and motion-picture operators charged along the sidewalks and across private property in a wild dash to get to the location.

At the Church of St. Nicholas of Tolentine, more than 1,400 people crammed into a building meant to hold half that number. Father George Dermody, who had known the Beckers for years, conducted the requiem mass. There was no sermon or eulogy. Then the coffin was borne to Woodlawn Cemetery, where unruly crowds once again predominated. There was a delay at the cemetery gates when an attendant refused to allow admission until inflammatory messages such as "SACRIFICED FOR POLITICS" were removed from the floral tributes. Once this was done, Becker was laid to rest beside the tiny grave of his infant daughter.

♔ ♔ ♔

Finally, it was over—or so it seemed. In his last letter to Governor Whitman, Becker warned, "You have proved yourself able to destroy my life. But mark well, Sir, these words of mine. When your power passes, the truth about Rosenthal's murder will become known. Not all the judges in this State, nor in this country, can destroy permanently the character of an innocent man."

Time has proven Charles Becker right.

EPILOGUE

I t's tempting to speculate how much longer Jack Zelig would have lasted in the Manhattan gang universe had he not been killed when he was. While not as financially brilliant and business savvy as Arnold Rothstein or even Dopey Benny Fein, he was several notches above the typical 1912 gangster, who was in most cases a hired goon for the gamblers and the politicians. He was intelligent, articulate, and inspired just the right levels of fear and reverence among his men and the business operators who paid him well to keep them safe from him as well as shakedown artists. Big Jack backed down from no one and persisted in doing what he thought was right no matter what risk was entailed. In the Lower East Side of 1912, he was practically an anomaly.

But times change, and as the years went by, gangland mutated into an urban ecosystem that was not welcoming to Zelig's type. His inability, or more accurately, refusal to take anything into account except his own belief system when making business decisions would have been practically fatal after 1920, when Prohibition spawned bootleg empires and turned gangsters into CEOs. In Chicago, Irish-American gang lord Dean O'Banion let personal differences get between him and the Johnny Torrio-Al Capone Syndicate, breaking an inter-gang peace treaty that had made everyone profit from the liquor gold rush. O'Banion was killed for his abrasive independence, and Zelig would probably have met a similar fate sooner or later. Unlike his friend and adviser Benny Fein, he didn't know how to keep his personal feelings in check, a required skill for surviving in the bootleg jungle.

His death may even have launched the gangster film genre. Legendary director D. W. Griffith's seventeen-minute Biograph Company film, *The Musketeers of*

Pig Alley, released in the United States in November 1912, was popularly believed to have been inspired by the Becker-Rosenthal affair. Production began, however, soon after Zelig died, raising the possibility that his murder was the catalyst for Griffith's decision to do a gangster film. The director filmed on location in the Lower East Side and used actual gangsters, such as Kid Broome and Harlem Tom Evans. According to the *Biograph Bulletin* of October 31, 1912: "This picture production, which does not run very strong as to plot, is simply intended to show vividly the doings of the gangster type of people."

O. O. McIntyre, one of Zelig's many reluctant admirers, noted in a November 1932 edition of his "New York Day By Day" column, "[Edward G. Robinson] has made the gangster glamorous, but at the same time, stressed his evil finish. That is acting. In Manhattan thickets and underbrush I have met 'Eat Em Up' Jack McManus, Monk Eastman, Big Jack Zelig, Kid Twist, and others. None was glamorous. . . . Even so, the old-time sluggers were Sir Galahads compared to the machine-gun sniping rats of today."

Seen from that perspective, Zelig represents an era in American gangster history when strength and fearlessness counted for as much as the ability to make crime pay. If Shoenfeld's opinion was accurate, Big Jack Zelig was "one of the nerviest, strongest, and best men" of a long-vanished breed.

♔ ♔ ♔

Henrietta Zelig was desperate for money after her husband died, as he had left no will and a negligible estate. On January 6, 1913, a dance was given at Arlington Hall for her benefit. She sat in the box with Jack Wolff, middle-aged proprietor of a Second Avenue thieves hangout. Wolff had the distinction of being the first Jewish graft collector for the police on the Lower East Side and had even appeared before the Lexow Committee. He had been a close friend and somewhat of a father figure to Zelig and contributed substantially toward the defense of the four gunmen. He watched while Henrietta accepted cash donations. All attendees received a button of the now-famous photo of Zelig smiling on the day he testified against Steinert and White.

The affair, however, was a calamity. Humpty Jackson showed up with a few friends, got drunk on champagne, and began raising a racket at his table. Dopey Benny Fein alternated between offering moral support to the widow and quelling such disruptions. Police officers who patrolled the event noticed that most of the attendees were lower level pimps, prostitutes, pipe fiends, and thieves. None of the gangster elite except Fein and Jackson were in attendance.

Abe Shoenfeld approached a prostitute named Kitty, whom he knew by sight, and asked her, "Where are all the girls from Fourteenth Street?"

"Oh, I don't think they'll come up," she replied. "I asked them to, and they said, 'Who is Mrs. Zelig? Let her go out and sell it the same as we do.'"

Abe Shoenfeld wrote, "Indeed, it was a sad affair to behold, and let us wind up the story before we shed tears. Amen. . . . There were never and will never be any tougher than Jack Zelig was."[1]

After all her expenses were paid, the ball netted Mrs. Zelig less than $50. Needing funds, she appeared before Judge Ely in Boston Municipal Court on February 27, 1913, to recover money from Henry K. Friedman. Friedman, a well-known professional bondsman, had been arrested the previous week on Henrietta's complaint that he was withholding $600 from her. Dressed in black and her face concealed by a heavy veil, she sat silently at the back of the court-room until her attorney, John Feeney, called her to the stand.[2]

When Feeney questioned her about the murder of her husband, she broke down and took several minutes to recover her composure. Finally she said that after Zelig was arrested in Rhode Island, she telephoned Friedman for assis-tance, met him in a South End hotel, and gave him $900, with the understand-ing that he would keep $100 for his "professional services," $200 would go to the man who stood bail, and the remaining $600 would be returned to her. In November 1912, Henrietta returned to Boston to collect the money, as Zelig's case had been disposed of. Friedman met her and told her that he didn't have it. She pressed her case, and finally Friedman gave her $50 and assured her that he would pay back the balance within a month. When no more money was forthcoming, she made one final, aggressive appeal to the bondsman, whose response, she told the court, was to call her a crook and blackmailer and to sue him if she wanted to recover her money.

Attorney James, counsel for Friedman, questioned Henrietta about her life with her notorious husband. Glaring daggers at him, she said that she had married Zelig in Canada in October 1902 and refused to be more precise as to location.

"Did your husband not go by another name?" James prodded.

"No, his name was Jack Zelig, and my name is Henrietta Zelig."

James surveyed the courtroom and announced, "I am prepared to prove that no such person as Jack Zelig existed at all. I am also prepared to prove that Jack Zelig was the pickpocket's alias." Turning back to the teary-eyed, angry woman on the stand, he asked, "What was your maiden name, Mrs. Zelig?"

"Objection!" Feeney shouted from his table. Judge Ely sustained him.

Friedman, when he took the stand, admitted that although he took Henri-etta's money, he did not end up arranging the bail, saying that a man named Rosenberg did. He also mumbled that he had no property in his own name. Feeney jumped in for the kill.

"What did you want to go surety for if you didn't own property?"

Friedman looked at the floor and refused to answer.

Judge Ely, after hearing all of the evidence, ruled in Henrietta's favor. Not only did Friedman have to pay her back, he was also sentenced to fifteen months in the House of Correction for fraudulent business practices.

"When Kid Twist died, his wife inherited property—houses—quite a for-tune of money which he had made," Shoenfeld observed. "Jack Sirocco is worth a barrel of money, although in recent months he has had some real estate rever-sals. Chick Trigger [sic] owns a saloon and is also worth some money." Zelig never possessed a similar degree of wealth to pass on to his wife, but Henrietta did not seem to resent him for the poverty his death plunged her into. In con-trast, she cherished and guarded Zelig's memory. According to Joseph Lefkowitz, she was offered certain incentives by the district attorney's office to swear that she had also been present when Rose and Vallon visited her husband in the Tombs and heard the gamblers say that they were emissaries of Becker. She rejected the offer angrily.

On May 18, 1913, she, Benny Fein, and Jack Wolff started a subscription list to raise funds for an elegant tombstone, which they hoped to place on his grave on the first anniversary of Zelig's death. They raised more than $500, and the stone that they erected still marks his resting place in Washington Cemetery.

The Hebrew part of its inscription, translated into English, reads as follows:

HERE IS BURIED *(abbreviated with two letters)*
ZELIG ZVI SON OF REB EPHRAIM
DECEASED 24TH TISHREI 5773
MAY HIS SOUL BE BOUND IN THE ETERNAL LIFE *(abbreviation of five letters)*

Beneath the Jewish notation was Henrietta's own expression of remem-brance and affection:

IN MEMORY OF MY BELOVED HUSBAND
SELIG HARRY LEFKOWITZ
BORN MAY 13, 1888
DIED OCTOBER 5, 1912
MAY HIS SOUL REST IN PEACE

It is not known what became of Henrietta Zelig and her son Harry after-ward. She did not maintain contact with the Lefkowitz family, another faint suggestion that young Harry might not have been Zelig's son after all. Henrietta may have married again, or perhaps she elected to raise Harry alone, with help from her family. No one knows for sure.

♛ ♛ ♛

Lillian Rosenberg, now known to the press and public as "Lefty Louie's Lily," wrote a serial version of her life with her "boy husband" that she sold to the *Washington Post*. She also testified for the prosecution at Becker's second trial, saying that on the afternoon of the murder, her husband and Dago Frank came into the flat with a package of money. The four gunmen went into an adjacent room, and when they emerged, Whitey had some bills clutched in his hands.

Martin Manton, after examining her testimony at the gunmen's November 1912 trial, asked her, "Do you remember this question and your answer? 'While you were your apartment, in your presence, did you hear Jack Rose say anything to your husband or to any other man about the killing of Herman Rosenthal?' Answer: 'No.'"

"Well, I lied to save my husband at the time," she replied. When pressed, she admitted that she had conferred with Assistant District Attorney Groehl three days previously. Like Henrietta Zelig, she had been left in difficult financial circumstances after losing her husband, and she appears to have chosen cooperation with the D.A.'s office as the best chance she had for survival. There's no reason to doubt that she received some type of compensation for supporting Whitman's case, and evidence suggests that she tried to bring other potential witnesses into the prosecution's fold.

Jack Wolff was subpoenaed by the district attorney's office on May 16, the day after she testified. When he arrived, he was taken aback to see Lillian Rosenberg sitting in Groehl's office. When Groehl asked Wolff what he knew about the Becker case, he replied, "I know nothing."

Lillian broke in. "Go on, Mr. Wolff, and help us; you know what we want."

Wolff took the wind out of her sails by feigning an aggressive ignorance. "I don't know anything, and furthermore, I never saw you in my life. I don't know who you are."

"Oh, yes you do," she replied. "Go on now, help us; be a good fellow."

Wolff spun on his heel and left. He was later given a subpoena to appear before the grand jury on May 18. He was questioned there and turned loose after he made it plain that he knew nothing of any value. Shoenfeld wrote, "This is to show what straight and forward men can be found in Mr. Whitman's office. They would frame up a man without consideration for anything."[3]

Shoenfeld noted that after her husband's execution, Lillian was seen in the company of one Johnny Burt, who had police records in New York and Chicago as a strong-arm and pickpocket. Burt had an exclusive franchise from a major New York drug pushing combination to sell cocaine in Philadelphia and the surrounding area. Shoenfeld wrote that Lillian "hasn't been seen on the East Side for some time now and evidently must be with him [Burt] now in Philadelphia." Her day in the sun over, Lillian Rosenberg disappeared into obscurity.

👑 👑 👑

The first woman to be widowed by the entire tragedy, Lillian Rosenthal, was forced to accept charity from her husband's one-time colleagues. She saved enough to invest in a movie house, and when that lost money, she put the rest of her funds in a dressmaking business that did no better. When she tried to organize a campaign of exposure against the System, her patrons stopped supporting her. She died in September 1928 in New York City's French Hospital, a cynical and defeated version of her former self.

♧ ♧ ♧

Helen Becker struggled with a staggering debt for years after the execution. Legal fees had consumed the money Becker had hoarded and also left her owing several thousand dollars. She managed to pay it all back out of her teacher's salary and make the odd additional expenditure on a fruitless campaign to clear her husband's name.

Helen never remarried, choosing instead to channel her energy into her pupils. She became an assistant principal of an elementary school and finally retired sometime during the 1940s. She died in 1962, her love for Charles Becker never having faltered.

♧ ♧ ♧

One of Jack Rose's post-trial ventures was the Humanology Film Producing Company, of which he was president. In January 1915, it released through the United Film Service a five-reel underworld drama titled *Are They Born Or Are They Made?* Rose advertised the film as being autobiographical. When funds ran out, he abandoned movie making and stepped into a new role as a preacher. He appeared before church congregations, YMCA groups, and other assemblies and lectured about his life in the underworld and the evils he had witnessed. When that occupation stopped paying well, he became a caterer. He even created the Jack Rose cocktail, a forgettable mixture of applejack, grenadine, and lemon juice.

Jack Rose died on October 4, 1947, of an "internal disorder" at Roosevelt Hospital in New York City. He was seventy-two years old. His two sons, one of whom lived in California, the other in New England, were remembered by author Harry Golden as "pillars of their society and deeply religious men. . . . Their communities [respected] them for their industry, their decency, and philanthropy. The notoriety they had to overcome would have confounded all experts on youth problems."[4]

Rose's co-conspirators led tamer, less public lives. The four gamblers fell out over money soon after their November 1912 release from jail. Webber and Vallon clashed when Vallon refused to return the $1,000 Webber had given him to go toward the bond for Zelig's July 2, 1912, release. Webber also broke with Schepps, so by 1913 no one was speaking to anyone else.

Webber left New York and went to Passiac, New Jersey where he worked at his brother-in-law's box-making factory. Sam Schepps went into the antique furniture-selling business and died in 1936. Harry Vallon, to whom Whitman's immunity agreement should never have applied, dropped out of the picture entirely.[5]

In 1927, Henry Klein, a former reporter who had been a deputy commissioner of accounts under Mayor John F. Hylan, published *Sacrificed*, a 400-plus-page book that argued for Becker's innocence. In 1936, he contacted District Attorney William Dodge and demanded the rearrest of Jack Rose and Harry Vallon for the Rosenthal murder. On September 9, Dodge informed Klein that he would not do so unless Klein could furnish new evidence justifying such action.

"It is my recollection," said Dodge, "that the matters you refer to were thoroughly investigated by District Attorney Charles S. Whitman at the time of the prosecution of Becker and his co-defendants. . . . If, however, you have any evidence, or any knowledge of any evidence, in addition to that which was passed upon at the time of the conviction of Becker and the other defendants, or was not at the time called to the attention of Governor Whitman, I shall be very glad to give it such attention as is proper."[6]

Klein wasn't able to do that, but he did get some satisfaction in 1951, when he blasted away at Herbert Bayard Swope in the letters column of the *Times*.[7] He chose his target well, as most authorities on the Becker-Rosenthal affair agree that had it not been for Swope, the entire debacle never would have occurred.

♛ ♛ ♛

In 1920, Swope was promoted from city editor to executive editor of the *World*. By the late twenties, he had become such a newsworld icon that he resigned from his paper in favor of serving as a consultant to an assortment of large American corporations. He hobnobbed and liaised with presidents and the leading political figures of the day and was on a first name basis with Winston Churchill, Franklin Roosevelt, and Humphrey Bogart, to list a few. When he died in 1958, the Columbia School of Journalism named a room after him.[8]

♛ ♛ ♛

Jacob Reich, alias Jack Sullivan, died on December 24, 1938, at the Home for Incurables in the Bronx. He was sixty-one years old and had been battling severe illness for eighteen months. The murder indictment had hung over his head until August 20, 1936, when his attorney, Klein, moved for a dismissal before Supreme Court Justice Lloyd Church. When Church obliged, Reich felt vindicated at last.

♛ ♛ ♛

Charles Seymour Whitman never realized his dream of becoming president. He served two terms as governor of New York State, but it was an administration that was remarkable only in its ordinariness. His political ineffectiveness came to the fore after the fanfare from the Becker conviction and execution abated. He lost the 1916 Republican presidential nomination to Charles Evans Hughes. When he faced ex-Becker trial judge Samuel Seabury in the gubernatorial race, one of Whitman's staunchest opponents was Thomas Mott Osborne, who had resigned as warden of Sing Sing in order to campaign against a man he despised. Whitman managed to win a second term, but the press was hugely uncomplimentary and voiced the opinion that his political success was attributable only to the Rosenthal case and not to his own ability. He showed up at public events in a severe state of intoxication, which his enemies suggested was his way of dealing with his guilty conscience in connection with the Becker execution. He tried for the presidency again in 1922 but lost the Republican nomination to Herbert Hoover. Soon afterward, he sought reelection as district attorney but was soundly defeated. He went into private practice and died in 1947 at the age of seventy-eight.

♔ ♔ ♔

In March 1922, Chick Tricker packed up and moved to California to be an adviser to those who wanted to create movies about the old-style New York low life. In a 1915 newspaper interview, he foresaw Prohibition, and he retired from the saloon business with a fortune. He emerged from retirement only when someone who either knew him or had heard of him spread his name around the Los Angeles film lots and he received a tempting offer. "I don't need the kale [money]," Tricker told a reporter in February. "But when I go, my wife and baby can use some more, maybe, so I might as well work. I am only thirty-nine now and have no idea of quitting the game [dying], but you never know what is going to happen." He was quick to add that the money alone was not his sole reason for going into the movies. "I am going to show them how to do it the way it ought to be done. There is too much make-up and not enough reality. I want to show them the Bowery and the East Side the way it used to be."

Jack Sirocco, his longtime partner, chose to stay in Manhattan, running one fleabag dive after another. He died in 1954, a lucky survivor of New York's era of big gang wars.

♔ ♔ ♔

Dopey Benny Fein, who took command of the Zelig gang when his friend and chieftain died, went into a grieving fury that propelled him to strike out at prosecution witnesses in the Becker case. In January 1913, he sent death threats to Jake and Morris Luban, resulting in an arrest that only made him angrier. A seventeen-year-old Fein adherent known as Little Yiddle stabbed Bridgey Webber in the back. While this rampage went on, anyone with something to worry about ran for cover.

Even those who desecrated Zelig's memory were fair game. In April 1913, one of Abe Shoenfeld's investigators was standing in front of the Essex Market Court, talking to associates. Suddenly Benny Fein stormed through the crowd of more than a hundred milling about on the sidewalk and grabbed hold of a thug known as Little Butch, who was a henchman of an enemy labor goon named Pinchy Paul. Before anyone could stop him, Fein punched Butch in the face several times. The attack shocked onlookers. Dopey Benny was enraged because Little Butch had gloated over Zelig's death and hinted that he could do the same job on Fein if given the chance.

Shoenfeld's investigator, who must have been burly or brave, locked his arms around the raging Fein and pulled him off his victim. The gangster broke free and ran up Second Avenue, shouting that he was going to get a gun and settle the matter once and for all. Strangely, Pinchy Paul was in the crowd, but made no attempt to intervene. Butch was hidden away in Alderman Max Levine's office minutes before Fein, true to his word, came back with a gun, but when he failed to find his target, he went away, grumbling.⁹

At first Fein had to deal with another contender for the vacant leadership spot: Joe "the Greaser" Rosenzweig, a veteran labor warrior who had also been a favored Zelig lieutenant. Rosenzweig was ambitious but he was also a realist: Fein commanded more jobs and more money in the labor racketeering field, which meant more support from the rank and file. The Greaser soon conceded defeat and merged his resources with those of "the Dope."

By 1913, most of the Lower East Side gangs who specialized in labor slugging had been eliminated or assimilated in favor of the Fein-Rosenzweig conglomerate. But there were others, namely splinter groups led by Philip "Pinchy" Paul, Billy Lustig, and Abraham Roth, alias Little Rothie, who united to tackle the two giants. They were holdouts from a cooperative system that Fein had developed to ensure that everyone would profit from the vast riches that labor unrest offered the underworld.

He laid out the city in "districts" similar to the police precinct system and formed combinations with the Hudson Dusters gang on the Lower West Side and the Car Barn Gang and the Gas House Gang further uptown. Whenever Fein received a contract to demolish a shop or beat up workers outside his territory, which was from Fourteenth Street to the Battery, east of Broadway, he turned the job over to the reigning gang, who showed the same courtesy when they were hired to do something in his territory.

He also assisted in organizing a "General Sessions Court" and a "Special Sessions Court" to discipline workers. One handled minor offenses such as working overtime and accepting freelance jobs, and the other major offenses, such as being a scab. In a room adjoining the "courts" was an arsenal containing revolvers, blackjacks, ammunition, and sawed-off lead pipe, so that punishment could be meted out immediately after sentencing. Those found guilty could have their thumbs broken to prevent their working in the needle trade, or their ears and faces slashed to publicly mark them as disobedient. The courts were operated by a mixture of gangsters and union officials calling themselves the Cloakmakers Club.

Fein's activities drew the ire of the reform element and the police, who acted accordingly. On January 22, 1913, he assaulted some strikebreakers, was arrested, and spent thirty days in the workhouse. Upon his release in late February, Fein succeeded in evading further arrest, which may have inspired a plot to take him out of commission.

Police Sgt. Patrick Sheridan claimed that the owner of a Turkish bath on Forsyth Street called in a complaint on August 19 about Dopey Benny hanging around his place. (The owner later denied it.) The sergeant went to the address, saw Fein lounging on the stoop, and ordered him to move along. According to Sheridan, Fein became so incensed that he grabbed the officer's nightstick and assaulted him with it.

Abe Shoenfeld had a different tale to report to his superiors. "The sergeant . . . saw Dopey Benny sitting on the stoop and beckoned to him to come over to him. . . . When [Fein] did so, the officer struck him a terrible blow under his right eye without warning or cause and almost threw him down senseless." Shoenfeld allowed that Fein did punch Sheridan in retaliation, but the officer's reaction was not in proportion. "The sergeant then pulled out his night stick and struck the Dope across the head with it. After doing this, the officer then called for assistance."

Two more cops arrived and joined Sheridan in hauling the prisoner as far as the National Hotel at the corner of Grand and the Bowery. There Fein put up a struggle, and his three escorts, reinforced by two others, threw him through the hotel's storm door. Then they drew blackjacks and gave him the beating of his life. By the time it was over, his eyes were black, his scalp had a wound that would require six stitches to close, two front teeth were knocked out, and his nose was fractured. The fact that an ambulance was waiting upon their arrival at the station, and had been for a while, led to whispers that the beating had been premeditated. Although Sheridan did not have a scratch on him, Fein was charged with felonious assault on an officer doing his duty.

Soon after being released on $5,000 bail to await the action of the grand jury, Benny and an entourage of ten thugs went to Philadelphia. He was still sore from his injuries, but he had a strikebreaking job to do. On September 12, his guerillas and some tough scabs got into a brawl that a police officer tried to break up. Fein shot at him and inflicted a minor wound, resulting in the gang boss's arrest. As soon as he was allowed to post bail Benny left the city, returning to New York in time to appear in court. With Zelig's former attorney Charles Wahle representing him, he pleaded not guilty to assaulting Sergeant Sheridan and was granted bail in the amount of $2,500.

Aware that he would need money to finance his courtroom battle with the police, Fein organized a ball, which was scheduled to begin on October 31 at the Progress Assembly Rooms at 28-30 Avenue A. He and a henchman, Jimmy

Britt, went around to various storekeepers, demanding that they take out advertisements in the ball journal. According to Abe Shoenfeld, the endeavor was unsuccessful, as the storekeepers pleaded that the Kehillah would not let them advertise. The police covered the event when October 31 rolled around and kept out more than fifty well-known thieves, including Fein himself. Shoenfeld wrote somewhat smugly, "Imagine everyone dancing and enjoying themselves, and he [Fein] left out in the cold, not even allowed to get a glance into the place. He tried to reach everyone and anyone. By his absence from the box office, he lost five to six hundred dollars . . . although he claims to have lost over $1,000."

Police surveillance on Fein had increased over the past month, thanks to a devastating gun battle that took place on Grand Street between Chrystie and Forsyth. On September 23, Pinchy Paul and Little Rothie had spotted Jack Wolff, Little Yiddle and a third hoodlum named Hymie Rubbernose, all of whom carried guns for Benny, and rushed toward them with pistols drawn. Wolff and the Fein men ran with Pinchy Paul firing at their fleeing backs. None of the gangsters were wounded, but some bystanders were. Fein took no part in it, but his men did, and that was enough for the police.

Another gang fight took place two months later. A striking union hired Fein to protect their picketers while the management secured the services of Jack Sirocco and Chick Tricker to break the strike. One of Fein's most valued men, Maxie Greenwald, had been shot and killed earlier in the month during a clash with Sirocco gunmen, so Benny was dying to get even. On November 28, 1913, the two factions collided on the picket line. One Sirocco man was killed. Another, Charles Piazza, broke the traditional code of silence and named the shooter, but he later recanted when brought face to face with the killer. Jack Sirocco struck back on December 12, sending a crew out to ambush Dopey Benny during the Madison Square Garden bicycle races. During the gunfire exchange that ensued, Sirocco man Anthony "Tony the Cheese" Scantuli was shot in the left hip. Both factions tangled again later that night in front of the London Theatre in the Bowery near Canal Street, but no one was seriously injured.

Neither side was willing to concede defeat. On the afternoon of January 9, 1914, Fein called a meeting of his gang in a Forsyth Street saloon. He told them that he'd bought a spy in the Chick Tricker ranks and had been informed that the Siroccos were throwing a party at the Arlington Dance Hall that night. With Irving Wexler, alias Waxey Gordon, who would become a prominent gangster in his own right, taking charge of the logistics, Benny and his boys went to the party site and huddled in various doorways across the street. When Charles Piazza, the squealer, arrived, the Fein brigade opened fire. No gangster was hurt in the fusillade, but Frederick Strauss, an elderly bystander, was struck by a stray bullet and killed.

Public outcry was immediate. The police grilled the dance hall's doorman, Edward Morris, until he broke down and blurted that the shooters had been Dopey Benny, Waxey Gordon, "Little Abie" Beckerman and Rubin Kaplan.

They were all arrested and charged with murder but released three days later due to lack of evidence.

Fein had more problems in the forecast, however. On January 21, a jury convicted him of second-degree assault in connection with the alleged attack on Sergeant Sheridan. The trial had been conducted under strict security conditions. The names of the jurors were kept secret, a police officer was assigned to escort each man when court was not in session, and admittance to the courtroom was denied to all who were suspected of being Fein gunmen. When he heard about the guilty verdict, Abe Shoenfeld wrote, "This is a good thing for the Dope. . . . We can safely say that we are saving his life, or else he would have been killed in the course of time, or he might have reached the electric chair." Benny's distraught father, Jacob, stormed down Second Avenue after the verdict was read, stopping at gangster hangouts and calling everyone thieves and bloodsuckers.

On January 24, Judge Malone sentenced the gang leader to five years in Sing Sing. Fein could barely conceal his shock.

"So confident was I of acquittal," he said later, "that I patiently awaited trial." He pointed out that had he considered himself guilty, he could have fled jurisdiction at any time during the seven months he was free on bail. After he was taken to the Tombs prison to await transportation to Sing Sing, a four-page letter he had written was handed to Clerk Gallagher, who made its contents public:

> Last July, it was an open rumor in police circles . . . that I was to be "framed up" before long. For that reason I took particular care not to have disputes of any kind, even at times when it seemed as though they were trying to lead me into a trap. Since my release from Sing Sing [in 1912] I have tried my best to be a good boy and avoid trouble, but the police would not have it that way. I am not without heart. I am human, although the police think otherwise. They gave me a handle to my name. It helped to allay suspicion in the minds of the Public as to the capabilities of the Police Department.

Benny's loyal followers showed their support by hosting a benefit boxing match on April 1, 1914, at the Olympic Athletic Club. The $1,500 the event took in was used to finance an appeal of his conviction. On April 7, Jacob Fein ran another benefit at Kessler's Theatre with assistance from Jack Wolff. The theater presented a melodrama called God, Man, and the Devil, and all the unions in the Hebrew Trades were forced to buy tickets. It had also been arranged that Mr. Fein would receive $25 from the Neckwear Union for every week that his son remained in jail. Abe Shoenfeld commented dryly, "For Mr. Fein's sake, I hope his son goes completely crazy and never comes out."

Fein did come out, not long after those very words were written. On May 29, 1914, the Appellate Division reversed the conviction and ordered a new trial, stating that the testimony did not justify conviction for felonious assault. The judges agreed that Fein did strike Sheridan, but that the policeman was not hurt severely enough to warrant the gangster being charged with assault to such a severe degree. Fein was released on bail while his case was being appealed, and subsequently exonerated.

The first thing he did, after reuniting with his father and his fiancée Gertrude Lorber, was hurry to Brooklyn, where he had a new and urgent contract to smash up another clothing factory. After leading his goon squad to the site, Benny stood across the street, lit up a cigarette, and waited for the fun to start. Minutes later, a terrible din arose, and people began jumping out of the windows and climbing, screaming, onto the fire escape. He stood there, smoking calmly as terrorized factory workers ran past him, hurried along by revolver shots. When it was over, he went to a corner drugstore and phoned his employer with a report. The man was effusive with both praise and money.

Fein's liberty temporarily came to an end on September 18, when Lt. Daniel Costigan arrested him for extortion. A newspaper editor had complained to the police that a friend, East Side butcher Benjamin Solomonowitz, was being shaken down. Fein had done some work for the Butcher's Union, which Solomonowitz represented, and he was claiming that $300 was still owed to him. Accompanied by a henchman named Willie Siegel, he went to see Solomonowitz at the union headquarters on Clinton Street on September 18, unaware that two of Costigan's men and a stenographer were in another room, listening in. Most of the conversation was in Yiddish, which none of the eavesdroppers could understand, but Solomonowitz managed to get Fein to confirm in English that major bodily harm would be forthcoming if the money wasn't. The union official pretended to relent and promise to pay the $300 on an installment plan, beginning with a down payment of $50—which was in marked bills. The moment Fein and Siegel took the cash, the police officers surged into the room and took them into custody after a struggle.[10]

His bail was initially set at $7,500 but later raised to $10,000, which he could not immediately raise. He turned to the labor officials who had relied on his services in the past and demanded their assistance in securing his freedom. No one responded with aid, as this time around the evidence against the gangster was too damning, and he was considered a flight risk. Fein took their silence as betrayal and retaliated by cutting a deal with District Attorney Charles Perkins and making a full confession of his labor strong-arm work.

Fein's action drew mixed reactions from gangland. A labor slugger identified only as "Manny from Forsyth and Grand Streets" told one of Shoenfeld's men, "They [the unions] all got big bellies, and we are going to cut them open for them." Little Abie Beckerman, one of Fein's closest friends, used maudlin sentiment to show what the unions had "forced" men like him to do: "I've got a poor old mother who always said to me, 'Be what you want to be . . . but don't go out and beat poor Jews like we are.' We are all Jewish boys, and what we did, we did for the unions. We hadn't any sense. We never knew anything. They showed us how to make easy money, but it is the toughest money in the world.

When the rag pickers' strike was on, we went out and slugged poor old Jews who wore long beards, men no longer young and were Jews like ourselves. We had no right to do it. See what we are up against now?"[11]

Fein spent four days before the February 1915 grand jury. He volunteered that he had kept a diary over the years detailing the jobs he had pulled and for whom. Since grand jury proceedings were secret, Benny sent for reporters on May 19. He wanted to make it clear to his gangster associates that he was only blowing the whistle on those who abandoned him, and not his old friends.

Sitting in his Tombs cell, he told the assembled press, "They tried to frame me up on the extortion charge on which they had me arrested. They knew I knew too much, and they thought they had better put me out of the way. So with treacherous methods they lured me into a case where it appeared that I was trying to extort money from one of them, and then they called in the police and district attorney."

Mass indictments resulted from Fein's revelations, and Benny himself was released on $5,000 bail at the end of May. In December, he was arrested for beating up a strikebreaker and, on January 1, 1916, was sentenced to two months in jail for assault. He may have talked, but he had not reformed.

Ironically, Benny became the victim of a squealer himself soon after his release. In May 1914, Joe "the Greaser" Rosenzweig had an underling named Benny Schneider kill Pinchy Paul so the Greaser could take over the strong-arm work for the furriers' union. Schneider was arrested for murder and squealed on his boss, who offered to name those involved in the Frederick Strauss murder in exchange for leniency. He named the four who originally had been arrested, plus seven other gunmen who had been in the battle. Fein and the others were arrested but acquitted at their trial.

Disgusted with Rosenzweig's betrayal, Benny temporarily quit the slugging business and used his savings to become a garment manufacturer. On June 18, 1917, he married Gertrude Lorber, who gave birth to their first child, daughter Jean, on November 11, 1918. Two more children would follow, both sons: Morton on October 8, 1924, and Paul on July 26, 1929. A caring father, Benny did everything he could to shield them from his notoriety. "His kids were kept in the dark [about his livelihood]," Paul Fein's son Geoff remembers.

Some accounts of Fein's career state that he entered the narcotics business during the 1920s, but if so, he was never arrested on related charges. It would only have been a temporary undertaking, as by 1930, he was back in the thick of labor racketeering.

In July 1931, he appeared in court for the first time in years. He and cohorts Sam Hirsch and Sam Ruben were arraigned at Essex Market Court on felonious assault charges after they threw acid on businessman Mortimer Kahn. Kahn, who had been sitting in front of his neckwear shop to catch a stray breeze at the time, required emergency treatment at Gouverneur Hospital to deal with the burns. His attackers evaded punishment, and Fein spent the rest of the Thirties throwing terror into New York's garment district. It was estimated that between 1938 and 1941, his gang took in $250,000 by looting the lofts and garages of the district and selling the stolen clothes.

In October 1941, detectives arrested Fein in a raid ordered by District Attorney Thomas E. Dewey. Also taken into custody were mobsters Abraham "Nigger Abe" Cohen and John Ferraro, as well as two Dallas businessmen, Herman Fogel and Samuel Klein., who had purchased a recently stolen garment shipment valued at thousands of dollars.

Knowing that Morton and Paul Fein were old enough to understand any sensational press that was sure to erupt, Benny ordered his wife to send the boys to an upstate boarding school so they could be insulated against the trial coverage and the talk on the street. He was determined that the old adage about the sins of the father not be applied to his sons.

A jury convicted Fein and Cohen after a brief trial, and on February 24, 1942, General Sessions Judge Owen Bohan sentenced Benny to a state prison term of ten to twenty years. As a four-time offender, the fifty-five-year-old gangster should have gotten a mandatory life term, but Judge Bohan decided that one of his prior convictions was a misdemeanor and not a felony, sparing him the more devastating punishment. Fein and Cohen went to jail, but for far less time than anticipated. In 1944, they were freed on appeal and retried. This time both were acquitted.

It's doubtful that Benny Fein mellowed with age, but he did stay out of further legal trouble until his death from cancer on July 23, 1962. He was buried in a New York cemetery just a short distance from the city whose labor history he had shaped, for better or worse.

Former police Capt. Cornelius Willemse wrote of Fein in 1931, "He was New York's first real racketeer, and he made it pay." It could have been his epitaph.

᭜ ᭜ ᭜

On December 26, 1920, Jack Zelig's old mentor Monk Eastman, long the overlord of Lower East Side mayhem, met an end that he could have predicted for himself. He likely never guessed that it would strike so late in his life.

After Zelig had rejected his offer of a partnership, therefore denying him access to the fear factor that could have wooed customers away from their existing suppliers, Eastman worked with Jonesy the Wop and probably others also in an opium sales ring. He was busted for selling in 1912 and served an eight-month sentence on Blackwell's Island. While there, he granted an interview to a lady newspaper reporter and told her that he wanted nothing more than to kick the opium habit that was driving him to commit criminal acts in order to support it.

Upon his discharge, he moved upstate. He was arrested in Buffalo in February 1914 for robbery but was discharged. Eastman packed up and transferred his operations to Albany, where he escaped detection until May 1915, when police departments between Albany and New York City were requested to keep an eye out for a seven-passenger sedan containing men who were suspected of stealing a thousand dollars' worth of silver and jewelry. The car was spotted on May 17 at one of the entrances to New York City. One officer stopped the driver on the pretext of scolding him about a speeding issue, while others, guns drawn, moved in and surrounded the vehicle and its passengers, one of which was Monk Eastman. Eastman smiled wanly when he was recognized but became philosophical when a search of the car revealed the stolen merchandise. "Well, you have the silver," he said. "So go as far as you can, but don't expect any help from me."[12]

A judge sent him to Clinton Prison for two years and eleven months. He was released after two years and returned to New York City, where he was arrested yet again, this time for fighting. Although discharged, this last arrest inspired Eastman to do something no one could have anticipated. He walked into a Yonkers recruitment office and joined the army. Despite his age, his enlistment was successful and he was sent overseas with the 106th Infantry, 27th Division.

Eastman's military career was exemplary. He served with valor and was decorated for heroism. Once, when wounded by shrapnel and disoriented from a gas attack, he was sent to a field hospital. The moment he collected his wits, Eastman slipped out, salvaged a uniform from a dump, and rejoined his company at the front. Deeds like this won praise even from those who would have declared him fit only for the electric chair during his pre-military days. When the war was over, his supervising officers petitioned Gov. Al Smith to restore Eastman's citizenship, which he had lost as a convict. This was done in May 1919, and Monk returned to Albany a decorated war hero.

It didn't take long for the glow of heroism to subside, and for Monk Eastman to face the cold, hard reality that he was nearing fifty and an ex-convict with no real record of honest employment. He went back to the only life he knew, and it caught up with him on December 26, 1920.

Shortly before 5 a.m., two patrolmen came across a body lying in front of the subway entrance on the south side of Fourteenth Street. Five bullets had hit their mark, all clearly issued from a .32-caliber pistol later discovered on the steps of the B.R.T. subway entrance at Union Square.

The policemen, who noted the man to be in his early fifties, thought they were able to detect a faint heartbeat, so a hurried call was placed to St. Vincent's Hospital. When doctors there pronounced him dead, the body was removed to the morgue and searched. A label on the inside coat pocket was marked "E. Eastman. Oct. 22, 1919. No. 17434 W.B." Henry Witty of Witty Brothers Tailors confirmed over the telephone that he had made that suit for Monk Eastman, whose tailoring requirements he had supplied for many years.

The only witnesses were cab drivers standing in a small group a block away at Broadway and Fourteenth Street. Upon hearing five shots, they paused and waited until the noise stopped. Then they ran to the subway entrance and found the dying man lying on the pavement. They had barely completed their examination when the two officers arrived. At the same time, the subway ticket agent, who had also heard the shots, joined them, finding the discarded weapon on the step.

Robbery had clearly not been the motive for the aging gangster's murder. In addition to two pairs of glasses, a watch and chain, and punch of keys, his pockets contained $140 in cash. Charley Jones, who had been one of Eastman's most aggressive head-breakers many years before but now lived in quiet obscurity as an automobile sales agent, told the press that as far as he knew, Eastman had not made any attempts to continue his criminal career after Gov. Al Smith had restored his citizenship. As far as Jones knew, his former boss had opened a pet store somewhere on Broadway.

Although he shot down the idea that Monk Eastman had been trying to make a comeback in the territory where he had once been king, Jones did allow that "young squirt gunmen" might have spotted the former gangster monarch in the area on an unrelated errand and, trying to make a name for themselves, gleefully shot down a legend in cold blood.

"Monk hadn't a real personal enemy that I knew of," said Jones. "He was never a thief and he was always a big money kid. A thousand dollars was his minimum for any sort of job. Most of his acquaintance with the police was due to the troubles of others that he took up because he was the leader of the gang. If he was over in Manhattan after all this time on any business, you can bet it was big business and no piker affair."

On January 4, Eastman's killer finally turned himself in. Jerry W. Bohan, a Prohibition agent, had been tried for murder before. In 1911, he stood trial for the shooting death of Joseph Faulkner, alias Joe the Bear, but a Brooklyn jury acquitted him. His record also included four arrests for disorderly conduct, three of which resulted in fines. During the war, he got a job along the Brooklyn waterfront representing the stevedores' union, which at the time was in a battle of wills (among other things) with its employers. Monk Eastman was also involved in that struggle, but as an agent of the employers. "It was thus," wrote the *New York Times,* "that the two met and became friendly enemies."

After turning himself in to the Brooklyn police, Bohan explained that the killing had been spontaneous, unpremeditated, and within the legal realm of self defense. He said that eight months previously, he and Eastman had met at the Spatz Café on Havermeyer Street in Brooklyn. The former gang boss "got mussy," a condition hurried on by liquor, drew a pistol, and threatened to shoot him. When Bohan dared him to follow through, Eastman backed off, pocketed the weapon, and apologized.

On Christmas night, Bohan continued, he, Eastman and a group of friends went to the Blue Bird Café and spent hours drinking and carousing. At about 4 a.m., a dispute arose over how the staff were to be tipped. Eastman wanted to give something to everyone working that night; others thought that the piano player, who had stayed overtime to entertain their party, deserved most of the money. Bohan objected to one waiter in particular, John J. Bradley, getting anything, as the man had not even served them and it was well known that Bradley had gotten his job via Eastman's friendship with one of the café owners. In the end, only the waiter who had handled their table was rewarded, a fact that apparently did not sit well with Monk.

The Blue Bird, a basement cabaret, was two doors west of the station entrance where Eastman's body was found. It was owned by former prizefighter Willie Lewis and a small group of others, with Lewis himself being shot and seriously wounded on the premises more than a year earlier.

Bohan was leaving the Blue Bird alone when, he said, Eastman grabbed him from behind and accused him of having been a "rat" ever since he got his Prohibition agent job. Bohan saw the gangster reach into his right coat pocket (which was later found to be empty of even a penknife) and reacted by pulling his gun and emptying it into his attacker. When Eastman dropped, Bohan threw away the weapon, jumped onto the running board of a cab heading north on Fourth Avenue, and made his escape.

Rumors abounded that the fatal brawl had been caused by a disagreement over the split of drug or liquor money. Special Deputy Police Commissioner Simon said he had it on good authority that Eastman had been actively involved in the drug trade and had no fewer than twenty agents in his employ.

On January 5, state Rep. Lester B. Volk of Brooklyn used the Eastman murder as the basis for the introduction of a resolution in the House authorizing a thorough investigation of Prohibition and its feeble enforcement. He detailed Jerry Bohan's appointment as a dry agent despite Bohan's criminal record and insisted that strong improvements in the enforcement corps hiring practices were needed.

Bohan stood trial, was found guilty, and on January 2, 1922, arrived at Sing Sing after Judge Crane sentenced him to three to ten years for manslaughter. On June 23, his minimum term reduced thanks to good behavior, he was ordered paroled. He returned to the work he knew best—stevedore—and when last heard of, was living in Brooklyn in a comfortable house with his wife, Margaret, and their children.

👑 👑 👑

Monk Eastman's death before the first year of Prohibition had ended was eerily symbolic. The oldtime criminal that he embodied had long since become a city myth, gone except for a few grizzled survivors and the odd bullet-pocked building that hadn't been repaired in twenty years. Now the gangsters and racketeers lived in penthouse suites paid for by bootleg riches, rode around in chauffeured limousines, and used a Thompson submachine gun when they deigned to do their own killing. It was a new era that Zelig, as well as Eastman, did not live to see, which was just as well. There would have been no place for them.

NOTES

Foreword II

1. Arthur A. Goren, *Saints and Sinners*, p. 14

2. Ibid., p. 13

3. Ibid., p. 16

4. Henry J. Stern, 1945: *Looking at Local Politics, World History and Popular Culture*, June 1, 2005. Available online at http://www.nycivic.org /articles/050601.html

5. 2006 interview with Richard Shoenfeld, who recalled his uncle's diligent investigation of pro-Nazi activities during World War II-era New York

6. Herbert Bayard Swope was then editor of the *New York World* and responsible for Herman Rosenthal's headline accusations against Lt. Charles Becker

7. Although the term "racket" is commonly used to mean a criminal money-making scheme (e.g., extortion), in Zelig's time it was slang for an underworld soiree held in a prominent gangster's honor

8. Robert Rockaway, *But He Was Good To His Mother*, p. 111

Introduction

1. "B. C.," a "special contributor" who supplied a chapter on New York City vice for Ernest Bell's 1910 exposé *War on the White Slave Trade*, noted that most pimps, or "cadets," got six months

2. Zweifach was dead and Kelly semiretired by 1912, but the example they set continued

Chapter One / From Eastern Europe to the East Side

1. Irving Howe, *World of Our Fathers*, p. 42

2. Jenny Lind and Lola Montez were among the notables who performed

there. See the comprehensive Web site at www.castlegarden.org

3. No relation to the 1912 murder victim

4. Herman Rosenthal, "The Martyrdom of the Russian Jew," *Outlook*, Jan. 21, 1911; 97; 3, p. 109

5. Shlomo Lambroza and John Doyle Klier, *Pogroms: Anti-Jewish Violence in Modern Russian History*, p. 212

6. A territory that Catherine the Great set aside in 1791 to segregate the Russian Jews. Although 90 percent of the Jewish population resided there, it consisted of only 4 percent of Imperial Russia's territory

7. Ephraim's parents came originally from Galicia, an Austrian-controlled section of Poland. They left in 1864, when the Austrian government suspended all civil liberties and declared a state of siege, alarmed by the revolts cropping up in nearby Russian Poland. They foresaw better opportunities in Russia, which in 1864 was ruled by the humane Tsar Alexander II

8. Irving Howe, *World of Our Fathers*, p. 7

9. Ibid.

10. Lawrence J. Epstein, *At the Edge of a Dream: the Story of Jewish Immigrants on New York's Lower East Side 1880-1920*, p. 9

11. Howe, p. 5

12. *Washington Post*, Feb. 2, 1882

13. *New York Times*, Feb. 2, 1882

14. Howe, p. 28. Howe estimated that there were four primary escape routes and outlined them, but acknowledged that paths of migration were seldom direct. Ukrainian Jews, for instance, might embark from Odessa and travel the Black and Mediterranean seas to the Atlantic. Or they could cross the Romanian border. The primary ports of

embarkation were Hamburg, Bremen, Rotterdam, Amsterdam, and Antwerp

15. "Alien Nation," *The Guardian* (UK), May 10, 2004

16. Interview with Joseph Lefkowitz

17. Howe, p. 41

18. Ibid., p. 67

19. Joyce Mendelsohn, *The Lower East Side Remembered & Revisited,* p. 9

20. Ibid., p. 12

21. Jacob Riis, *How the Other Half Lives,* p. 8

22. Ibid., p. 20

23. *New York Times,* March 3, 1896

24. Mendelsohn, p. 12

25. Although today a poolroom is an alternate term for a billiard parlor, during the late 1800s and early 1900s, it was a location where one bet on race results

26. *New York Times,* May 5, 1891

27. Howe, p. 98

28. Ibid., p. 76

29. Albert Fried, *The Rise and Fall of the Jewish Gangster in America,* pp. 9-10

30. George Kibbe Turner, "Tammany's Control of New York by Professional Criminals," *McClure's Magazine*; June 1909; Vol XXXIII, No. 2, p. 117

31. Mike Dash, *Satan's Circus,* p. 38

32. *New York Times,* March 9, 1900. See also Andy Logan, *Against the Evidence,* pp. 59-60

33. Turner, p. 118

34. Luc Sante, *Low Life,* p. 252

35. Richard J. Tofel, *Vanishing Point,* p. 34

36. *New York Times,* Oct. 7, 1871

37. Tofel, p. 38

38. *New York Times,* May 13, 1888

39. Ibid.

40. Ibid.

41. Ibid.

42. E-mail exchange with Rabbi Meyer Schiller

Chapter Two / Butch's Apprentice

1. The 1900 U.S. Census gives his name as Harris, which may have been how the census taker interpreted *Hersh,* which was how his family addressed him. His first criminal alias was Harry Smith. He also went by the name Harry Morris

2. Interview with Joseph Lefkowitz

3. The New York City Directory for 1890 lists the Zweifachs living at 70 Norfolk, and Max Zweifach later stated that they resided there until 1893, when they moved to 171 Delancey

4. Milton Reigenstein, Ph.D., "Pictures of the Ghetto," *New York Times,* Nov. 14, 1897

5. Ibid.

6. *New York Times,* Dec. 28, 1892

7. *New York Times,* July 24, 1897

8. Interview with Joseph Lefkowitz

9. Howard Markel, *Quarantine,* p. 31

10. Ibid., p. 32

11. Ibid.

12. *New York Times,* Aug. 25, 1902

13. The other directors were listed as David Blankenstein, 261 Division Street; Max Mayper, 90 East Broadway; Nochman Reichman, 105 First Avenue; Abraham Peskowitz, 170 Monroe Street; Mortiz Grozinsky, 1 Pike Street; Louis Rorkowitz, 130 Attorney Street; Harris Platkin, 122 Forsyth Street, and E. Loudon, 206 Clinton Street

14. Luc Sante, *Low Life,* p. 10

15. Ibid., p. 12

16. Timothy Guilfoyle, *A Pickpocket's Tale,* pp. 60-62

17. Ibid., p. 24

18. Alfred Henry Lewis, *The Apaches of New York,* pp. 209-210. See also Herbert Asbury, *The Gangs of New York,* p. 226

19. *New York Times,* July 1, 1904

20. For years Eastman kept a pet store on Broome Street, where Zelig probably saw him on a regular basis, and was a dedicated pigeon fancier

21. Cornelius Willemse, *Behind the Green Lights,* p. 288

22. Adolph Zweifach's tailoring business

seemed to undergo one trouble after another. In July 1908, a mysterious fire at 133-35 Greene Street destroyed the premises, and he filed for bankruptcy in November of the same year

23. Zweifach's death certificate states that he was born in Austria and brought to the United States at the age of two

24. Possibly an Americanization of his surname. The phonetic similarity between "Zweifach" and "Slyfox" is remarkable

25. Not to be confused with Whitey Lewis (Jacob Seidenshner) who occasionally used Jacob Goldberg as an alias

26. Jacob Goldberg would later say that Zelig called himself Harry Smith during this period. Although he rightly suspected that it wasn't his friend's real name, Goldberg never asked questions

27. Interview with Karen Lefkowitz

28. Probably to escape the jurisdiction of the Society for the Prevention of Cruelty to Children, which stepped in automatically when the offender was under sixteen and made regular and intrusive home visits

29. Although Jacob Goldberg escaped imprisonment on that charge, weeks later he was arrested again for picking pockets and rejoined Harry at the House of Refuge

30. House of Refuge official record for Harry Smith, Inmate 28461

31. Ibid.

Chapter Three / Monk Eastman Junior

1. *New York Times,* Aug. 18, 1903

2. *New York Times,* Aug. 19, 1903

3. Monk Eastman, Ritchie Fitzpatrick, Paul Kelly, and other gang leaders had all been born in New York

4. *Washington Post,* June 21, 1914

5. Referred to in some texts as "Rosetta Peers"

6. Hot-corn girls sold buckets of steaming ears of corn and occasionally prostituted themselves

7. Luc Sante, *Low Life,* p. 199

8. State Republicans who were convinced that the police force had become irreparably corrupt under Mayor Fernando Wood, proposed legislation that would disband the Municipal Police Force, in which Wood's supporters had a controlling interest, and replace it with a state-run Metropolitan Police Department. Wood refused to disband the Municipal force, and the two rival police forces spent more time fighting each other than combating the gangs. This went on for most of 1857, until the courts ordered the Municipals to disband that July

9. Sante, pp. 206-207

10. Ibid., p. 215. Herbert Asbury, *The Gangs of New York,* p. 307 claims that at the height of his power, Zelig quoted a similar price list to clients who sought mutilation or murder for hire. Abe Meyer, who worked for Zelig, denied to Joseph Lefkowitz that there was any such list

11. Patrick Downey, *Gangster City,* p. 4

12. George Kibbe Turner, "Tammany's Control of New York by Professional Criminals," *McClure's Magazine;* June 1909; Vol XXXIII, No. 2. See also *New York Times,* Dec. 7, 1901

13. Asbury, p. 235

14. Downey, p. 115

15. Asbury, pp. 238-239

16. Ibid., p. 239

17. The family is noted as living at 311 E. Seventy-fifth Street in the U.S. census of 1880

18. Edward and Margaret told the enumerator for the 1900 census that of two children born to them, neither survived

19. Alfred Henry Lewis, *The Apaches of New York,* p. 211, mentions a weakness for pigeons. Asbury p. 255 states that he had an equally strong affinity for cats. On April 7, 1929, a patrolman from the Fifth Street station arrested two boys for breaking into a jewelry store and stealing pens. When the boys explained that they intended to sell the pens so they could buy pigeons and a coop, the

Times noted that the officer thought immediately of "Monk Eastman and Dopey Benny Fein, other East Side boys who began as pigeon fanciers."

20. Interview with Joseph Lefkowitz
21. Downey, p. 3
22. Ibid., p. 4
23. *New York Times,* Dec. 23, 1899
24. *New York Times,* Dec. 5, 1894
25. One of many hangouts the Eastman gang used over the years
26. Asbury, p. 255
27. *New York Times,* April 15, 1901
28. *New York Times* Sept. 30, 1902
29. *New York Times,* Oct. 5, 1902
30. Ibid.
31. Downey, p. 9
32. *New York Times,* July 6, 1903
33. See Downey, pp. 3-17, for an excellent examination of the New Jersey incident and Eastman's subsequent decline
34. *New York Times,* Aug. 1, 1903
35. Downey, p. 7. See also *New York Times,* Sept. 17, 1903
36. *New York Times,* Sept. 2, 1904. See also Downey, p. 10
37. Interview with Joseph Lefkowitz
38. Downey, p. 11
39. Lewis, p. 23. See also Downey p. 12
40. *New York Times,* May 27, 1905
41. *New York Times,* Nov. 23, 1905
42. *New York Times,* May 17, 1905

6. Two burnings were reported in the *New York Times* on Feb. 3, 1891, and Nov. 30, 1894
7. Herbert Asbury, *The Gangs of New York,* p. 267, and Patrick Downey, *Gangster City,* p. 49
8. *New York Times,* Nov. 2, 1904
9. *New York Times,* March 1, 1905
10. *New York Times,* June 9, 1912
11. *New York Times,* March 17, 1905
12. Alfred Henry Lewis, *The Apaches of New York,* p. 123, See also George Kibbe Turner, "Tammany's Control of New York by Professional Criminals," *McClure's Magazine*; June 1909; Vol. XXXIII, No. 2, which refers to Zweifach having a sideline in celery tonic production
13. In 1897 the pair murdered one William Guldensuppe in Queens. Mrs. Nack turned state's evidence and obtained a prison term, while Thorn was electrocuted in 1898
14. *The People vs. William Albert,* June 1905. Indictment No. 5185
15. Ibid.
16. Interview with Joseph Lefkowitz. See also *New York Herald,* Aug. 23, 1912
17. Asbury, pp. 305-306
18. Interview with Joseph Lefkowitz
19. Denis Brian, *Sing Sing: the Inside Story of a Notorious Prison,* p. 43
20. Ibid., p. 61
21. *New York Times,* Dec. 21, 1906

Chapter Four / Twist on the Rise

1. A repeater was someone who voted more than once, using fictitious names and sometimes disguises each time
2. Samuel Pristrich death certificate
3. Both the Zweifach and Pristrich death certificates listed the same home address; interview with Joseph Lefkowitz
4. Abe Shoenfeld, Story #107, Oct. 8, 1912, part of the Magnes Papers Collection
5. As noted on both the 1880 and 1900 New York Census reports

Chapter Five / Death on the Boardwalk

1. Alfred Lewis alludes to this incident in *The Apaches of New York* (1912) but did not name Greenwich personally, and stated that Cyclone Louie (Samuel Pristrich) was the killer
2. *New York Times,* June 3, 1907
3. Lewis claims in *The Apaches of New York* that Cyclone Louie actually shot the Bottler (Greenwich) while Zweifach and Stahl (who is referred to as "Kid Dahl" in the book) were noisily creating alibis elsewhere. Initial reports of Greenwich's shooting indicate that witnesses saw Stahl, not Pristrich, running away from the

scene of the murder. Lewis's version was probably shaped by the fact that at the time of the book's publication, Harris Stahl was still alive and active

4. *New York Times,* June 2, 1907

5. Lt. Larry Sullivan, who knew her, described her in later years as having "the morals of a nymphomaniac in solitary for ten years."

6. *New York Times,* May 15, 1908

7. Zweifach's death certificate indicates only a head wound. Pristrich's, on the other hand, makes reference to bodily as well as head injuries

8. Ibid.

9. *New York Times,* May 19, 1908

10. *New York Times,* May 21, 1908

11. Twenty years later Scudder presided over the joint murder trial of Ruth Snyder and Judd Gray, who had killed Snyder's husband for his insurance money. Both were found guilty and electrocuted

12. *New York Times,* Oct. 8, 1908

13. *New York Times,* Sept. 21, 1908

14. Abe Shoenfeld, undated report

15. Confidential report submitted by Abe Shoenfeld, Oct. 8, 1912, Magnes Papers Collection

16. Interview with Joseph Lefkowitz

17. *New York Times,* Nov. 21, 1908

18. Alfred Henry Lewis, *The Apaches of New York,* pp. 220-221

19. Interview with Joseph Lefkowitz

Chapter Six / Back from the Dead

1. *New York Times,* Oct. 6, 1912

2. Interview with Dick Shoenfeld, nephew of Abe Shoenfeld

3. Interview with Joseph Lefkowitz

4. Or so Tricker always claimed. Interview with Joseph Lefkowitz, who heard the story from a former Tricker associate

5. *New York Times,* Oct. 6, 1912

6. Interview with Joseph Lefkowitz

7. Interview with Joseph Lefkowitz

8. Interview with Joseph Lefkowitz

9. Sonia Cuneo, MD, confirms that strychnine, a vaso-restrictant, was used as a "reanimator" in the pre-adrenaline days

10. Joseph Lefkowitz never heard of surgery taking place, but most head injury-related deaths are brought on by severe brain swelling, and opening the skull to relieve pressure is and was a common emergency treatment

11. http://www.ahs.uwaterloo.ca/~cahr/headfall.html

12. Ibid.

13. *New York Times,* Aug. 24, 1909

14. *New York Times,* Nov. 16, 1909

15. Although Zelig and Henrietta also rented a flat at 286 Broome, the Harlem address was their principal residence

16. *Middletown (NY) Times-Press,* Oct. 7, 1912

Chapter Seven / New King on the Block

1. Herbert Asbury, *The Gangs of New York,* p. 294

2. Ibid.

3. Abe Shoenfeld, report #66, submitted September 1912, part of the Magnes Papers Collection

4. Ricey, whose nickname was Dippy, was a questionable backup, as he showed more talent for harming himself than others. Three years previously he shot himself on Water Street, but survived. A year later he attempted suicide in a Chinatown resort, and in 1909 he fired a bullet into his head at the Bridge Café at Delancey Street and the Bowery. A month after the altercation with Zelig, Ricey called his girlfriend from a telephone in a Chatham Club back room, and discharged a bullet into his right ear while arguing with her. When surgeons at the Hudson Street hospital told him that he would live, he groaned

5. Abe Shoenfeld, report #14, submitted September 1912, part of the Magnes Papers Collection

6. Abe Shoenfeld, report #14, submitted August 1912, part of the Magnes Papers Collection

7. Interview with Joseph Lefkowitz

8. Interview with Joseph Lefkowitz

9. Shoenfeld was referring to the Sirocco-Tricker mob, but he often used the 'Italian" designation for the Five Pointers in general

10. Nicknames did continue after Prohibition (e.g., Benjamin "Bugsy" Siegel, Abe "Kid Twist" Reles, Vincent "the Chin" Gigante), but the trend was less prevalent

11. Interestingly, the nickname was applied only by non-Jewish gangsters and police officers, such as Cornelius Willemse

12. Arthur Goren, *Saints and Sinners,* p. 14

Chapter Eight / The Boys of the Avenue

1. He told his young wife that he acquired the nickname because he favored his left hand when playing cards. The actual reason was because he had remarkable pistol aim with that hand

2. Lillian Rosenberg, "The Story of an Underworld Wife," *Washington Post,* June 21, 1914

3. Albert Fried, *The Rise and Fall of the Jewish Gangster in America,* p. 3

4. Abe Shoenfeld, Report #53, Sept. 26, 1912, Magnes Papers Collection

5. Fried, p. 6

6. Abe Shoenfeld, Report #49, Sept. 14, 1912, Magnes Papers Collection

7. Interview with Joseph Lefkowitz

8. Telephone interview with Jean Gold

9. Fried, p. 1. Also telephone interview with Dick Shoenfeld

10. Abe Shoenfeld, report #14, submitted August 1912, part of the Magnes Papers Collection

11. Arthur Goren, *Saints and Sinners,* p. 17

12. 'Sparking" was a slang term for a heavy petting session

13. Interview with Joseph Lefkowitz, whose collection includes a letter from Florence Clark

14. *Washington Post,* March 21, 1914

Chapter Nine / Terror and Guardian

1. *New York Times* of Sept. 27, 1911, mistakenly referred to them as three members of the Johnny Spanish gang

2. Abe Shoenfeld, report #66, submitted September 1912, part of the Magnes Papers Collection

3. Thanks to Jenny Floro-Khalaf, author and expert in Italian genealogy, for pinpointing the Cirofici family's date of arrival in the United States

4. Andy Logan, *Against the Evidence,* p. 74

5. Abe Shoenfeld, report #128, Oct. 21, 1912, part of the Magnes Papers Collection

6. Interview with Joseph Lefkowitz, who heard the story from Abe Meyer. According to Meyer, neither Horowitz nor Cirofici were regular members of Zelig's gang. "They were what we called 'now and then' guys, who just came around occasionally. I only met Gyp once, and never saw either of them at Second Avenue [Segal's] with the rest of us"

7. Patrick Downey, *Gangster City,* p. 54

8. *New York Times,* Dec. 3, 1911, p. 12

9. Alfred Henry Lewis, *The Apaches of New York,* p. 79

10. Downey, p. 54

11. *New York Times,* Dec. 3, 1911

12. Downey, p. 55

13. *New York Times,* Jan 2., 1912, p. 6

14. *New York Times,* Feb. 18, 1912

15. Ibid.

16. Despite this predilection for attacking Jewish tough guys, Jonesy took Monk Eastman in as a partner in an opium joint at 335 East Fourteenth Street in 1911. Joseph Lefkowitz claims that Zelig and Eastman were "estranged" by this point, although it's not known whether the partnership with Jonesy was a factor

17. Interview with Geoff Fein, Benny's grandson

18. *New York Times,* Oct. 4, 1905

19. *New York Times,* Jan. 12, 1914

20. The 1910 U.S. census confirms that Ida was a waist factory worker

21. The building was located at 23-29 Washington Place, on the northern corner of Washington Square East
22. Interview with Joseph Lefkowitz
23. *New York Times,* May 13, 1915. See also Downey pp. 64-65

Chapter Ten / Framed

1. Interview with Miriam Goldberg
2. Abe Shoenfeld, report #122, submitted Oct. 21, 1912, Magnes Collection
3. Interviews with Joseph Lefkowitz and Miriam Goldberg
4. Interview with Miriam Goldberg
5. *New York Times,* Nov. 11, 1912
6. Interviews with Joseph Lefkowitz and Miriam Goldberg
7. Abe Shoenfeld, report #180, submitted October 1912, Magnes Collection
8. Ibid.
9. Ibid.
10. Interview with Joseph Lefkowitz, who heard this version of events from former Zelig gangster Abe Meyer. Abe Shoenfeld reached a similar conclusion in a report to the Kehillah
11. Shoenfeld submitted a colorful glossary of gangland slang, and the "bridge" reference was included
12. Abe Shoenfeld, report #123, submitted Oct. 21, 1912, Magnes Collection
13. Ibid.
14. Interview with Miriam Goldberg
15. Patrick Downey, *Gangster City,* p. 56
16. Interview with Joseph Lefkowitz
17. Interview with Joseph Lefkowitz
18. Jack Poggi's brother was Louis the Lump, slayer of Kid Twist
19. Abe Shoenfeld, story #14, submitted October 1912, part of the Magnes Papers Collection. Also interview with Joseph Lefkowitz
20. *New York Times,* June 4, 1912

Chapter Eleven / Bullets and Bombs

1. Patrick Downey, *Gangster City,* p. 57
2. Interview with Joseph Lefkowitz, who has a letter that Zelig wrote to a friend, "Julie," detailing the shooting

and bragging about his defiance of the police. Thanks to Rabbi Meyer Schiller for translating

3. *New York Times,* July 11, 1911
4. Abe Shoenfeld, story #14, submitted October 1912, part of the Magnes Papers Collection. See also *New York Times,* June 4, 1912
5. *New York Times,* June 4, 1912
6. Abe Shoenfeld, story #14, submitted October 1912, part of the Magnes Papers Collection
7. Ibid.
8. *New York Times,* June 6, 1912
9. *New York Times,* June 9, 1912
10. The same Gamberdella who orchestrated the Annie Sugar robbery
11. The Sullivan Act, which was enacted on May 29, 1911, imposed heavy penalties for possessing unlicensed firearms small enough to be concealed. Ironically, it was the brainchild of Big Tim Sullivan, and one of his rare concessions toward reform. Critics charged that he had gotten the law passed so that his gangster friends could not be thwarted during robberies by citizens carrying concealed weapons. The truth was that gun murders had gone up drastically after 1910, resulting in public demands for regulation. Sullivan, conscious by necessity of the public mood, responded
12. *New York Herald,* June 6, 1912
13. *New York Times,* June 9, 1912, p. 16
14. Interview with Miriam Goldberg, who recalled the prison visit and the conversation as Jacob Goldberg relayed it
15. Interview with Miriam Goldberg
16. Interview with Miriam Goldberg
17. Abe Shoenfeld, story #125, confidential report submitted Oct. 21, 1912, Magnes Papers Collection
18. Interview with Miriam Goldberg
19. Henry Klein, *Sacrificed,* p. 425

Chapter Twelve / Hello, Herman

1. *New York Morning Telegraph,* July 16, 1912

2. Vina Delmar, *The Becker Scandal—A Time Remembered*, p. 42

3. http://BigTimSullivan.blogspot.com

4. Mike Dash, *Satan's Circus*, p. 92

5. On June 15, 1904, the *General Slocum*, a steamer carrying 1,300 Lower East Side residents, caught fire while en route to a picnic site at Long Island Sound, and 1,021 passengers, mostly children, perished. It was New York's deadliest tragedy before Sept. 11, 2001

6. *New York Times*, Dec. 26, 1905

7. Delmar, p. 45

8. *New York Times*, Aug. 16, 1903, p. 3

9. *New York Times*, Feb. 4, 1909

10. Feb. 16, 1909, Court of Appeals Calendar—Supreme Court Trial Term II, Case No. 3899—*Kohler v. Rosenthal*

11. Andy Logan, *Against the Evidence*, p. 63

12. Patrick Downey, *Gangster City*, p. 53

13. Andy Logan, *Against the Evidence*, p. 64

14. Dash, p. 145

15. Henry Klein, *Sacrificed*, p. 9

16. Dash, p. 152

Chapter Thirteen / "Our Police Disease"

1. *New York Times*, Feb. 21, 1902

2. *New York Times*, March 11, 1902

3. *New York Sun*, March 8, 1902

4. George L. Lankevich, *American Metropolis: A History of New York City*, p. 84

5. Mike Dash, *Satan's Circus*, p. 46

6. These landmarks and statistics are itemized on the New York Police Museum's Web site

7. Luc Sante, *Low Life*, p. 238

8. Timothy J. Guilfoyle, *A Pickpocket's Tale*, p. 248. Dash p. 50 puts Byrnes's financial worth at $600,000 at the time of his retirement, other sources (*New York Times*, Dec. 30, 1894) put the amount at $300,000. Byrnes credited his wealth with successful speculations on Wall Street

9. William Brown Meloney, "Our Police Disease," *Outlook*, Oct. 5, 1912, p. 260

10. An excellent examination of Roosevelt's life, including timeline, photos, and even film clips, can be found at the Theodore Roosevelt Association at www.theodoreroosevelt.org

11. Sante p. 238 points out that the earliest police officers were paid $500 a year; their 1901 counterparts received only $300 more

12. Cornelius Willemse, *Behind the Green Lights*, p. 60

13. Dash, p. 55

14. Sante, p. 238

15. Dash, p. 49. See also *New York Times* Dec. 15, 1894

16. According to the *New York Herald* of Oct. 9, 1898, the Tenderloin of Clubber Williams's day lay between Fourth and Seventh avenues and along Broadway between Fourteenth and Forty-second streets. By 1898, it had expanded as far up as Sixty-fifth Street, and its east-west boundaries were Second and Tenth avenues

17. Sante, p. 17. See also the *New York Times* of May 13, 1906, which quoted Williams as saying, "It's been chuck steak for me; it'll be tenderloin now." During his testimony before the Lexow Committee (1894), the veteran cop denied that he'd applied the nickname to the district, only saying that he "got a better living" once he was transferred there. See Dash p. 377

18. William Brown Meloney, "Our Police Disease," *Outlook*, Oct. 5, 1912, p. 260

19. Ibid., p. 263

Chapter Fourteen / Charley Becker

1. Mike Dash, *Satan's Circus*, pp. 21-23

2. Ibid., p. 30. See also Logan p. 105

3. *New York Times*, Dec. 15, 1893

4. Andy Logan, *Against the Evidence*, p. 106

5. Dash, p. 371

6. Augustine E. Costello, *Our Police Protectors*, Chapter XVI, Part III (online version)

7. Ibid.

8. Logan, pp. 106-207

9. *New York Times*, June 21, 1919

10. Dash, p. 71. See also the New York dailies of July 30, 1915, in which Becker, in his final letter to now-Gov. Charles Whitman, detailed his marital history. There had been rumors that he'd somehow incurred the death of his first wife, and he wanted to dispel them before dying

11. *New York Times,* Aug. 17, 1895. See also Dash, p. 59

12. *New York Times,* Sept. 17, 1896

13. According to Nuala O'Faolain, biographer of "Chicago May" Churchill-Sharpe, Becker had once hidden May when she was "in trouble," and she in turn gave him a ring that she'd stolen after observing him admiring it. She claimed that her connection with the policeman was via a friend who "was crazy about Becker," but their mutual support suggests that their relationship wasn't quite so superficial. See Nuala O'Faolain, *The Story of Chicago May,* p. 68

14. Stanley Wertheim, *A Stephen Crane Encyclopaedia,* p. 194

15. Logan, p. 111

16. *New York Times* and *New York World* Sept. 21, 1896, describe the officers' version of the shooting. See also Logan p. 111 and Dash p. 60

17. *New York World,* July 17, 1912. See also Dash p. 59 and Logan p. 111

18. Logan, p. 112

19. Logan, p. 98. See also Dash pp. 111-112

20. Becker's exact motive for ringleading the revolt is unclear. Perhaps the punishing hours that police officers worked in 1902 had been wreaking havoc on his home life. Marriages and personal lives were luxuries that few policemen could enjoy without hindrance

21. *New York Times,* Aug. 21, 1902. See also Dash p. 104

22. Dash, p. 108. See also *New York Times,* June 30, 1901

23. Dash, p. 115

24. Some temper on Gaynor's part was especially forgivable after August 1910, when he became the first (and as of 2008, only) New York City mayor to suffer an assassination attempt. A bullet was lodged in his throat and deemed by his physicians to be too risky to remove. Gaynor was left with a raspy voice, frequent coughing spells, and elevated irascibility

25. Dash, p. 117. See also Logan pp. 88-89 and *New York Times* April 30, 1910, June 22, 1911, and July 1, 1911

26. Dash, p. 118

27. Ibid., p. 122. See also Logan p. 23

28. *New York Times,* June 8, 1911. See also Klein p. 346, Dash p. 124, and Logan p. 116

29. Herbert Asbury, *The Gangs of New York,* p. 335

30. Dash, p. 124, see also Asbury pp. 334-335

31. Ibid., p. 124

32. It's surprising that the Sirocco-Tricker gunmen would shoot at Poggi, who had always been affiliated with the Five Pointers. Perhaps they did not recognize him as Kelly's companion that night, or he may also have been at odds with Tricker and Sirocco by 1912. Kelly was also responsible for Poggi's being arrested on a concealed weapons charge, so why they were together that night remains a mystery

33. *New York Times,* Feb. 15, 1912, p. 1

34. Henry Klein, *Sacrificed,* p. 346. In his final letter to Governor Whitman, Becker stated, "As the work for which my squad was organized [gang-busting] became less onerous, Commissioner Waldo began to assign me to the duty of raiding different gambling houses. I was never given general authority to deal with gambling."

35. Klein, p. 59

36. Logan, p. 116

Chapter Fifteen / Goodbye, Herman

1. *New York World,* July 14, 1912

2. New York *Times,* July 13, 1912

3. *New York World,* Aug. 15, 1912 for mention of Rosenthal getting Foy and

one other officer, Michaelson, to Becker's squad. See *New York Times* Oct. 23, 1912, for the connection between the wives of Foy and Rosenthal

4. *New York Times,* July 13, 1912

5. David Pietrusza, *Rothstein,* p. 74

6. Mike Dash, *Satan's Circus,* p. 155. See also Pietrusza, pp. 74-75

7. Andy Logan, *Against the Evidence,* p. 31. See also Dash p. 169

8. Dash, p. 169

9. David Pietrusza, *Rothstein,* p. 74

10. *New York World,* July 15, 1912. Note the contrast between this statement and the one that Swope sent to his editors from Newport. Dash p. 169 suggests, probably accurately, that Swope wrote the 'Newport dispatch" himself

11. *New York Herald,* July 16, 1912

12. Logan, p. 5

13. Ibid., p. 12

14. Ibid., p. 13

Chapter Sixteen / "I Accuse the Police"

1. Andy Logan, *Against the Evidence,* p. 6

2. Henry Klein, *Sacrificed,* p. 7 See also Logan pp. 18-19

3. *New York Times,* July 16, 1912

4. Logan, p. 18

5. Klein, p. 421

6. Logan, p. 19

7. Mike Dash, *Satan's Circus,* p. 178

8. *New York Herald,* July 16, 1912

9. *New York Times,* July 17, 1912

10. Dash, p. 178. See also Logan p. 34

11. Abe Shoenfeld, report #121, submitted October 1912, part of the Magnes Papers Collection

12. According to Logan p. 32, the same garage contained an Imperial that Rosenthal used to hire, as well as a Pierce-Arrow that had recently been used in a jewellery heist

13. Dash, p. 184. See also *New York American,* July 18, 1912

14. *New York Times,* July 17, 1912

15. Magnes Papers Collection

16. Logan, p. 47

17. *New York Herald,* July 17, 1912

18. Logan, p. 29

19. *New York Times,* July 17, 1912

20. Klein, pp. 15-16

21. Ibid. p. 40

22. Dash, p. 190

23. *New York Herald,* July 18, 1912

24. *New York Times,* July 17, 1912

25. Interview with Joseph Lefkowitz. Abe Shoenfeld also confirmed in one of his reports that Zelig had been in Boston at the time of the Rosenthal hit, contrary to Klein pp. 424-425, which suggests that he was seen across the street from the Metropole when the gambler was shot

Chapter Seventeen / Another Frame-up

1. Henry Klein, *Sacrificed,* p. 326 includes a final statement from Dago Frank Cirofici confirming Fein's account

2. Interview with Joseph Lefkowitz

3. *New York Times,* July 18, 1912

4. Newman Levy, *The Nan Patterson Case,* p. 73

5. Andy Logan, *Against the Evidence,* pp. 77-78. See also Dash p. 201

6. Logan, p. 80

7. New York State Supreme Court, "In the Matter of the Application for the Appointment of a Committee of the Person and Property of Timothy D. Sullivan." Jan. 24, 1913

8. *Syracuse Herald,* July 21,1912, p. A-3

9. Mike Dash, *Satan's Circus,* p. 202. See also Logan p. 92 and *New York World,* July 21, 1912

10. Logan, pp. 98-99

11. *New York Evening Post* July 27 1912

12. Dash, p. 202. Also Klein pp. 28-30

13. Logan, p. 99

14. Ibid., p. 103

15. *New York World,* July 24, 1912

16. Klein, pp. 26-27

17. *New York Times,* July 27, 1912

18. Klein, p. 183

19. Dash, p. 213

20. Ibid., pp. 215-216

21. *New York Herald,* July 30, 1912. See also Logan p.104

Chapter Eighteen / "I Don't Believe that Becker Knew Anything About It"

1. Andy Logan, *Against the Evidence,* p. 120. The newspaperman was almost certainly Fred Hawley

2. Mrs. Charles Becker, "My Story," *McClure's Magazine,* September 1914, Vol XLIII, No. 5

3. David Von Drehle, *Triangle — the Fire that Changed America,* p. 221

4. Logan, p. 125

5. Ibid., p. 157

6. *New York Times,* July 31, 1912

7. *New York Times,* July 21, 1912

8. *New York Times,* Aug. 3, 1912

9. Logan, p. 132

10. *New York Times,* Aug. 4, 1912

11. *New York World,* Aug. 15, 1912

12. Henry Klein *Sacrificed,* p. 73

13. Ibid., p. 78

14. Mike Dash, *Satan's Circus,* p. 235

15. *Providence Journal,* Aug. 21, 1912

16. *New York World,* Aug. 20, 1912. See also Logan pp.136-137

17. *Washington Post,* Aug. 23, 1911

18. Interview with Joseph Lefkowitz

19. Klein, p. 83

20. Logan, p. 137

21. Ibid., p. 80

Chapter Nineteen / Silenced

1. *New York Herald,* Aug. 21, 1912. See also *New York Times* of the same date and Andy Logan, *Against the Evidence,* p. 139

2. Logan, p. 139

3. Newman Levy, *The Nan Patterson Case,* p. 107

4. Logan, p. 159

5. *New York Times,* Sept. 13, 1912. See also Logan p. 160 and Dash p. 242

6. Logan, p. 139

7. Henry Klein, *Sacrificed,* p. 81

8. As it turned out, Kramer was the same Max Kahn who allegedly warned the waiter Krause away from the front of the Metropole before Rosenthal was shot. Krause later identified him in court

9. *New York Times,* Sept. 15, 1912

10. Not quite. According to Miriam Goldberg, whose great-grandfather Jacob spoke with Zelig about the case in September, he was quite explicit about his intention to incriminate Jack Rose. Goldberg had not seen Zelig for years, so it's doubtful that the gangster confined his plans to close friends only

11. Abe Shoenfeld, report #14, submitted October 1912, part of the Magnes Papers Collection

12. An often-repeated fallacy about that night is that Zelig left Segal's in response to a phone call from a woman. Shoenfeld makes no mention of such a call, and according to Abe Meyer, Henrietta Zelig stopped briefly by the café earlier. She refrained from disturbing his card game, but left a message for him to come home as soon as possible. Her reason for wanting to see him is unknown

13. Created by Rudolph Dirks, the *Katzenjammer Kids* comic strip originally appeared in a *New York Journal* supplement in 1897. Still in circulation today, it is the world's longest-running comic strip

14. Phone interview with John Christie

15. Jonathan Root, *One Night in July,* p. 134 claims that Zelig collapsed onto the lap of a woman sitting beside him. John Christie insists that Zelig was the sole occupant of the bench upon which he was sitting when he was shot

16. Abe Meyer did not name Willie, but said that Zelig's companion thought the Siroccos were firing on them, and because he was unarmed, ran for his life

17. *New York Times,* Oct. 7, 1912

18. *New York Herald,* Oct. 7, 1912

19. *Washington Post,* Oct. 7, 1912

20. *New York Times,* Oct. 7, 1912

21. *New York Times,* Oct. 9, 1912

22. *New York Times,* Nov. 7, 1912

23. A check of the 1920 U.S. census shows a Philip and Dora Davidson living at 190 Second Avenue, in the same building that housed a family named Alter (which was Mrs. Davidson's maiden name). The same census, however, lists a Philip Davidson as an inmate at Sing Sing prison. It's possible that the enumerator visited the prison before Davidson's release was finalized, or he may have been getting his data from an outdated list or ledger. Probably the latter, as the enumerator who found him living on Second Avenue visited on January 14

24. Arthur A. Goren, *Saints and Sinners: the Underside of American Jewish History,* p. 19

Chapter Twenty / Sacrificed

1. *New York Times,* Oct. 8, 1912

2. Ibid.

3. Mike Dash, *Satan's Circus,* p. 250

4. Andy Logan, *Against the Evidence,* p. 179

5. *New York Times,* Oct 11, 1912

6. Henry Klein, *Sacrificed,* p. 418

7. Klein, p. 418. See also *New York Times,* Oct. 13, 1912, and *New York Herald* of the same date

8. Dash, p. 261

9. Ibid., p. 262. See also Klein p. 126

10. Dash, p. 263

11. *New York Sun,* Oct. 13, 1912

12. *New York Times,* Oct. 15, 1912

13. Dash, p. 261. See also Logan p. 197

14. *New York Times,* Oct 19, 1912

15. *New York Sun,* Oct. 23, 1912

16. Klein, p. 196

17. Ibid., p. 207

18. Logan, p. 264

19. Ibid., p. 212

20. *New York Times,* Nov. 10, 1912

21. *New York Times,* Nov. 13, 1912

22. Dash, p. 297

23. Ibid., p. 317

24. Klein, p. 418

25. David Pietrusza, *Rothstein,* p. 91

Epilogue

1. Abe Shoenfeld, Report #272, submitted Jan. 6, 1913, Magnes Papers Collection

2. *Boston Globe,* Feb. 28, 1913

3. Abe Shoenfeld, Report #871, submitted May 19, 1914, Magnes Papers Collection

4. *Chicago Tribune,* Feb. 19, 1961

5. Meyer Berger, "The Becker Case," *New York Times Magazine,* Nov. 11, 1951. See also Mike Dash, *Satan's Circus,* p. 349 and Andy Logan, *Against the Evidence,* p. 333

6. *New York Times,* Sept. 10, 1936

7. Meyer Berger, "The Becker Case." See also Logan p. 338

8. Dash, p. 341. See also Logan pp. 338-340

9. Abe Shoenfeld Report #443, submitted April 18, 1913, Magnes Papers Collection

10. Abe Shoenfeld, confidential report #871, submitted Sept. 24, 1914, Magnes Papers Collection

11. Ibid.

12. Patrick Downey, *Gangster City,* p. 14

Bibliography

Books

Anbinder, Tyler. *Five Points*. New York: The Free Press, 2001

Asbury, Herbert. *The Gangs of New York*. New York: Alfred A. Knopf, Inc, 1927

Brian, Dennis. *Sing Sing: The Inside Story of a Notorious Prison*. Amherst: Prometheus Books, 2005

Costello, Augustine E. *Our Police Protectors: History of the New York Police from the Earliest Period to the Present Time*. Privately published, 1885

Dash, Mike. *Satan's Circus: Murder, Vice, Police Corruption, and New York's Trial of the Century*. New York: Crown Publishing Group, 2007

Delmar, Vina. *The Becker Scandal: A Time Remembered*. New York: Harcourt, Brace & World, 1968

Downey, Patrick. *Gangster City: The History of the New York Underworld 1900-1935*. Fort Lee, NJ: Barricade Books, 2004

Epstein, Lawrence J. *At the Edge of a Dream: the Story of Jewish Immigrants on New York's Lower East Side 1880-1920*. Indianapolis: Jossey-Bass, 2007

Fido, Martin. *The Chronicle of Crime*. London: Carlton Books, 1993

Fried, Albert. *The Rise and Fall of the Jewish Gangster in America*. New York: Columbia University Press, 1980

Gilfoyle, Timothy J. *A Pickpocket's Tale: The Underworld of Nineteenth Century New York*. New York: W.W. Norton and Company, 2006

Hershkowitz, Leo. *Tweed's New York: Another Look*. Garden City, NY: Anchor Press, 1977

Howe, Irving and Morris Dickstein. *The World of Our Fathers*. New York: NYU Press, 2005

Klein, Henry. *Sacrificed: The Story of Police Lieutenant Charles Becker*. New York: Private Publication, 1927

Lambroza, Shlomo and John Doyle Klier. *Pogroms: Anti-Jewish Violence in Modern Russian History*. Cambridge: Cambridge University Press, 1992

Lane, Brian. *Chronicle of 20th Century Murder Volume 1: 1900-1938*. New York: Berkley Books, 1995

Lankevich, George L. *American Metropolis: A History of New York City*. New York: NYU Press, 1998

Lewis, Alfred Henry. *The Apaches of New York*. New York: M. A. Donohue & Company, 1911

Logan, Andy. *Against the Evidence: The Becker-Rosenthal Affair*. New York: The McCall Publishing Company, 1970

Markel, Howard. *Quarantine! Eastern European Jewish Immigrants and the New York City Epidemics of 1892*. Baltimore: The Johns Hopkins University Press, 1997

Mendelsohn, Joyce. *The Lower East Side Remembered and Revisited*. New York: The Lower East Side Press, 2001

O'Donnell, Edward T. *Ship Ablaze: The Tragedy of the Steamboat* General Slocum. New York: Broadway Books, 2003

O'Faolain, Nuala. *The Story of Chicago May.* New York: Riverhead Books, 2005

Pietrusza, David. *Rothstein: The Life, Times, and Murder of the Criminal Genius Who Fixed the 1919 World Series.* New York: Carroll & Graf, 2003

Riis, Jacob. *How the Other Half Lives: Studies Among the Tenements of New York.* New York: Penguin, 1997

Rockaway, Robert A. *But He Was Good To His Mother: The Lives and Crimes of Jewish Gangsters.* Jerusalem: Gefen Publishing House, 2000

Root, Jonathan. *One Night in July.* New York: Coward-McCann Inc., 1961

Sante, Luc. *Low Life: Lures and Snares of Old New York.* New York: Farrar, Straus, and Giroux, 2003

Stein, Leon. *The Triangle Fire.* New York: J. P. Lippincott, 1962

Von Drehle, David. *Triangle: The Fire That Changed America.* New York: Atlantic Monthly Press, 2003

Wertheim Stanley. *A Stephen Crane Encyclopaedia.* Westport, CT: Greenwood Press, 1997

Willemse, Cornelius. *Behind the Green Lights.* New York: Alfred A. Knopf, 1931

ARCHIVED RESOURCES

House of Refuge official record for Harry Smith, Inmate 28461. Dated 1901

Judah Leib Magnes Papers—held at the Central Archives for the History of the Jewish People in Jerusalem. Contains the Abe Shoenfeld reports

New York City Directory, 1890

New York State Censes for the years 1880-1920

NEWSPAPERS

Boston Globe

Chicago Tribune

Middletown (NY) Times-Press

New York Herald

New York Times

New York World

Providence (RI) Journal

Washington Post

MAGAZINES AND PAMPHLETS

William Brown Meloney, "Our Police Disease," *Outlook,* Oct. 5, 1912

Herman Rosenthal, "The Martyrdom of the Russian Jew," *Outlook,* Jan. 21, 1911

George Kibbe Turner, "Tammany's Control of New York by Professional Criminals," *McClure's Magazine;* June 1909; Vol. XXXIII, No. 2

INDEX